The Cambridge Companion to Tango

Tango music rapidly became a global phenomenon as early as the beginning of the twentieth century, with about 30 percent of gramophone records made between 1903 and 1910 devoted to it. Its popularity declined between the 1950s and the 1980s but has since risen to new heights. This *Companion* offers twenty chapters from varying perspectives around music, dance, poetry, and interdisciplinary studies, including numerous visual and audio illustrations in print and on the accompanying webpages. Its multidisciplinary approach demonstrates how different disciplines intersect through performative, historical, ethnographic, sociological, political, and anthropological perspectives. These thematic continuities illuminate diverse international perspectives and highlight how the art form flourished in Argentina, Uruguay, and abroad, while tracing its international and cultural impact over the last century. This book is an innovative resource for scholars and students of tango music, particularly those seeking a diverse international perspective on the subject.

KRISTIN WENDLAND is Professor of Teaching in the Department of Music at Emory University. With her research partner Kacey Link, she has coauthored and published *Tracing* Tangueros: *Argentine Tango Instrumental Music* (2016), and articles for *Chamber Music Magazine* (2018), *Naxos Musicology* (2020), and the Chicago Symphony Orchestra (2021).

KACEY LINK is an independent scholar and pianist residing in Los Angeles. With her research partner Kristin Wendland, she has coauthored and published *Tracing* Tangueros: *Argentine Tango Instrumental Music* (2016), and articles for *Chamber Music Magazine* (2018), *Naxos Musicology* (2020), and the Chicago Symphony Orchestra (2021).

Cambridge Companions to Music

Topics

The Cambridge Companion to Ballet
Edited by Marion Kant

The Cambridge Companion to Blues and Gospel Music
Edited by Allan Moore

The Cambridge Companion to Caribbean Music
Edited by Nanette De Jong

The Cambridge Companion to Choral Music
Edited by André de Quadros

The Cambridge Companion to the Concerto
Edited by Simon P. Keefe

The Cambridge Companion to Conducting
Edited by José Antonio Bowen

The Cambridge Companion to the Drum Kit
Edited by Matt Brennan, Joseph Michael Pignato and Daniel Akira Stadnicki

The Cambridge Companion to Eighteenth-Century Opera
Edited by Anthony R. DelDonna and Pierpaolo Polzonetti

The Cambridge Companion to Electronic Music, second edition
Edited by Nick Collins and Julio D'Escriván

The Cambridge Companion to the "Eroica" Symphony
Edited by Nancy November

The Cambridge Companion to Film Music
Edited by Mervyn Cooke and Fiona Ford

The Cambridge Companion to French Music
Edited by Simon Trezise

The Cambridge Companion to Grand Opera
Edited by David Charlton

The Cambridge Companion to Hip-Hop
Edited by Justin A. Williams

The Cambridge Companion to Jazz
Edited by Mervyn Cooke and David Horn

The Cambridge Companion to Jewish Music
Edited by Joshua S. Walden

The Cambridge Companion to K-Pop
Edited by Suk-Young Kim

The Cambridge Companion to Krautrock
Edited by Uwe Schütte

The Cambridge Companion to the Lied
Edited by James Parsons

The Cambridge Companion to The Magic Flute
Edited by Jessica Waldoff

Composers

Instruments

The Cambridge Companion to the Organ
Edited by Nicholas Thistlethwaite and Geoffrey Webber

The Cambridge Companion to the Piano
Edited by David Rowland

The Cambridge Companion to the Recorder
Edited by John Mansfield Thomson

The Cambridge Companion to the Saxophone
Edited by Richard Ingham

The Cambridge Companion to Singing
Edited by John Potter

The Cambridge Companion to the Violin
Edited by Robin Stowell

The Cambridge Companion to Tango

Edited by

KRISTIN WENDLAND

KACEY LINK

CAMBRIDGE
UNIVERSITY PRESS

Shaftesbury Road, Cambridge CB2 8EA, United Kingdom

One Liberty Plaza, 20th Floor, New York, NY 10006, USA

477 Williamstown Road, Port Melbourne, VIC 3207, Australia

314–321, 3rd Floor, Plot 3, Splendor Forum, Jasola District Centre,
New Delhi – 110025, India

103 Penang Road, #05–06/07, Visioncrest Commercial, Singapore 238467

Cambridge University Press is part of Cambridge University Press & Assessment,
a department of the University of Cambridge.

We share the University's mission to contribute to society through the pursuit of
education, learning and research at the highest international levels of excellence.

www.cambridge.org
Information on this title: www.cambridge.org/9781108838474

DOI: 10.1017/9781108974936

First published 2024

A catalogue record for this publication is available from the British Library.

Library of Congress Cataloging-in-Publication Data
Names: Wendland, Kristin, 1956– editor. | Link, Kacey, 1981– editor.
Title: The Cambridge companion to tango / Edited by Kristin Wendland and Kacey Link
Other titles: Companion to tango
Description: New York, NY : Cambridge University Press, 2024. | Series: CCMC Cambridge
companions to music | Includes index.
Identifiers: LCCN 2023042943 (print) | LCCN 2023042944 (ebook) | ISBN 9781108838474
(hardback) | ISBN 9781108971423 (paperback) | ISBN 9781108974936 (ebook)
Subjects: LCSH: Tango (Dance) – History. | Tango dancers. | Tango musicians. |
Performance practice (Music) | Tango (Dance) – Social aspects. | Tango (Dance) – History –
Cross-cultural studies.
Classification: LCC GV1796.T3 C27 2024 (print) | LCC GV1796.T3 (ebook) | DDC 793.3/
309–dc23/eng/20230921
LC record available at https://lccn.loc.gov/2023042943
LC ebook record available at https://lccn.loc.gov/2023042944

ISBN 978-1-108-83847-4 Hardback
ISBN 978-1-108-97142-3 Paperback

Dedicated to the memory of those lost during the COVID-19 pandemic, especially those of our international tango community, both the renowned and the unknown musicians, dancers, and poets.

Contents

Figures

Musical Examples

Notes on Contributors

PAULINA L. ALBERTO is Professor of African and African American Studies and of History at Harvard University. An Argentine-born historian of Afro-Latin America, her work explores Afro-Latin American lives, thought, and politics as they unfolded in the aftermath of slavery, particularly in Brazil and Argentina. She is the author of *Terms of Inclusion: Black Intellectuals in Twentieth-Century Brazil* (2011) and *Black Legend: The Many Lives of Raúl Grigera and the Power of Racial Storytelling in Argentina* (2022), among other books and articles.

CHRISTOPHE APPRILL is a sociologist, dancer, and independent scholar in Marseille, France. He is the author of numerous books relating to dance, gender, and society including *Slow. Désir et désillusion* (2021), *Les mondes du bal* (2018), and *L'invention politique de la danse contemporaine* (forthcoming, 2024).

YUIKO ASABA is Lecturer (equiv. Assistant Professor) in Music at SOAS University of London. She is the author of the forthcoming book, titled *Tango in Japan: Cosmopolitanism Beyond the West*, currently in production with the University of Hawai'i Press for publication in 2024. Her research examines the significant presence of Latin American music cultures in the Asia-Pacific. She has published in journals including the *Ethnomusicology Forum* and *Popular Music Studies*, with forthcoming articles appearing in the *East Asian Journal of Popular Culture*. As a tango violinist, she previously played professionally in tango orchestras in Argentina and Japan.

ORTAÇ AYDINĞLU is a musician and scholar in Turkey. He studied piano and composition at the conservatory in İstanbul and the bandoneón in Rotterdam and Buenos Aires, and he focused his PhD research on orchestration and arranging in tango. Currently he teaches at the conservatory in İstanbul, directs his band TangEsta, dances tango, and broadcasts a radio program on tango.

KATHY DAVIS is a senior research fellow in the Sociology Department at the Vrije Universiteit Amsterdam in the Netherlands. She is the author of many articles, anthologies, and books, including *Reshaping the Female Body* (1995), *Dubious Equalities and Embodied Differences* (2003), *The Making of Our Bodies, Ourselves: How Feminism Travels Across Borders* (2007), and *Dancing Tango: Passionate Encounters in a Globalizing World* (2015).

ROMINA DEZILLIO is a researcher and musicologist at the Instituto Nacional de Musicología "Carlos Vega" in Buenos Aires, Argentina, and studies Argentine professional women composers and performers in the first half of the twentieth century from a feminist approach and a critical gender perspective. Her teaching includes Argentine and Latin American Music History, considering cultural and sociological aspects. She is a PhD candidate in History and Theory of Arts at the Universidad de Buenos Aires, presently writing her dissertation titled "Primeras compositoras profesionales en Buenos Aires: historias, mundos poético-musicales y legados feministas" ("First professional women composers in Buenos Aires: herstories, poetic-musical worlds and feminist legacies").

OMAR GARCÍA BRUNELLI is a researcher and musicologist at the Instituto Nacional de Musicología "Carlos Vega" in Buenos Aires, Argentina, where he directs the research program Antología del tango rioplatense. He recently earned his PhD in History and Theory of the Arts from the Facultad de Filosofía y Letras, Universidad de Buenos Aires, with a specialty in Musicology. He is the author of *Discografía básica del tango, 1905–2010: su historia a través de las grabaciones* (2010), *La música de Astor Piazzolla* (2022); co-author with Carlos Kuri of *El Octeto Buenos Aires de Astor Piazzolla* (2022); and the editor of *Estudios sobre la obra de Astor Piazzolla* (2008), and of *El Mudo del tango. Ocho estudios sobre Carlos Gardel* (2020).

JULIÁN GRACIANO is a tango guitarist, composer, and arranger in Buenos Aires. Raised in a family of tango musicians, he has systematically worked out a pedagogical method for teaching tango based on his jazz studies. He is the author of *Roberto Grela "La guitarra del tango"* (Melos 2024), *Método de guitarra tango/Tango Guitar Method* (2016), and *El libro Real del Tango (The Real Tango Book)* Vol. 1–6 (2020). He also maintains an instructional YouTube channel for tango guitar called "Tango Licks."

MADELEINE E. HACKNEY is Associate Professor of Medicine at the Emory University School of Medicine and a Research Health Scientist with the

Atlanta VA. She holds a BFA in Dance Performance from New York University Tisch School of the Arts and a PhD in Movement Science from Washington University in St. Louis. She researches the design and effects of adapted Argentine Tango as a therapy for older people with neurodegenerative disease.

ERIC JOHNS is Archivist and Curator for the Stone Center for Latin American Studies at Tulane University. His musicological research focuses on epistemology and genre in Latin American popular musics. In particular, he is interested in the intersections of race, nation, and music, and the complex networks that bind them.

MATTHEW B. KARUSH is Professor of History at George Mason University in Fairfax, Virginia, and coeditor of the *Journal of Social History*. An expert on Argentine political and cultural history, he is the author of several books, including *Musicians in Transit: Argentina and the Globalization of Popular Music* (2017).

KACEY LINK is an independent scholar and pianist residing in Los Angeles, California. With her tango research partner Kristin Wendland, she has coauthored and published *Tracing Tangueros: Argentine Tango Instrumental Music* (2016), and articles for *Chamber Music Magazine* (2018), *Naxos Musicology* (2020), and the Chicago Symphony Orchestra (2021).

MORGAN JAMES LUKER is Associate Professor of Music at Reed College in Portland, Oregon. He is the author of *The Tango Machine: Musical Culture in the Age of Expediency* (2016) and the founding director of Tango for Musicians at Reed College. Morgan's current research examines the materiality and management of historical sound recordings in and about Argentina.

J. LUCAS MCKAY is Assistant Professor of Biomedical Informatics and Neurology at the Emory University School of Medicine. He holds ScB and ScM degrees in Electrical Engineering from Brown University, a PhD in Electrical and Computer Engineering from the Georgia Institute of Technology, and an MS in Clinical Research from Emory University. He uses technology-driven approaches to measure and understand the symptoms of neurodegenerative disease.

CAROLYN MERRITT is an anthropologist and dancer, and the author of *Tango Nuevo* (2012). She lives in Philadelphia, where she works as a writer and ethnographer, teaches yoga, and bakes desserts.

RIELLE NAVITSKI is Associate Professor in the Department of Theatre and Film Studies at the University of Georgia in Athens. She is the author of *Transatlantic Cinephilia: Film Culture between Latin America and France, 1945–1965* (2023) and *Public Spectacles of Violence: Sensational Cinema and Journalism in Early Twentieth-Century Mexico and Brazil* (2017), and co-editor of *Latinx Media: An Open-Access Textbook* (2022) and *Cosmopolitan Film Cultures in Latin America, 1896–1960* (2017).

PABLO PALOMINO is Associate Professor of Latin American and Caribbean Studies at Oxford College, Emory University. A cultural historian, born and raised in Buenos Aires and trained there and in Berkeley, California, he published *The Invention of Latin American Music: A Transnational History* (2020, translated into Spanish by Fondo de Cultura Económica in 2021).

BÁRBARA VARASSI PEGA is a faculty member at Codarts University of the Arts, Rotterdam, and Fontys University of Fine and Performing Arts, Tilburg. An Argentine pianist, arranger, composer, researcher, and educator specializing in tango music, she is the pianist of the Quinteto Astor Piazzolla and the author of *The Art of Tango* (2021).

REBECCA SIMPSON-LITKE is Associate Professor of Music Theory in the Desautels Faculty of Music at the University of Manitoba. Her research explores rhythmic interactions between music and dance, focusing on the Latin social dances that she has taught and performed in her spare time for the past twenty years. Her salsa research is published in *Music Theory Spectrum* and in a 2022 special issue of *Journal of Music Theory* devoted to dance research.

KENDRA STEPPUTAT is Associate Professor and Head of the Institute for Ethnomusicology, University of Music and Performing Arts Graz, Austria. Her research topics include choreomusical aspects of Balinese performing arts, in particular *kecak*, and *tango argentino* in a European perspective, which she captures in her book *Tango Dance and Music: A Choreomusicological Exploration of Tango* (Routledge, 2024).

IGNACIO VARCHAUSKY is a musician, producer, researcher, and educator who has been working in tango for over twenty-five years. He is the creator and artistic director of the Orquesta Escuela de Tango Emilio Balcarce; the founder of Orquesta El Arranque and the nonprofit organization TangoVia; and the author of the performance-practice books *The Bass in Tango* (2016) and *The Art of Tango* (2021). His YouTube seminar "Los Estilos Fundamentales del Tango" and personal website www.ignaciovarchausky.com are followed on social media by tango musicians, dancers, and aficionados from all over the world.

KRISTIN WENDLAND is Professor of Teaching in the Department of Music at Emory University. With her tango research partner Kacey Link, she has coauthored and published *Tracing* Tangueros: *Argentine Tango Instrumental Music* (2016), and articles for *Chamber Music Magazine* (2018), *Naxos Musicology* (2020), and the Chicago Symphony Orchestra (2021). Her book *The Power of Practice: How Music and Yoga Transformed the Life and Work of Yehudi Menuhin* (SUNY Press, 2024) examines the connections between music and yoga.

Notes on the Text

www.tangocompanion.com

As an added resource to *The Cambridge Companion to Tango*, we have created an open-access website illustrating the sights and sounds of tango with audio and video resources and relevant web links. The reader will see these resources cited in the print book with the web references in parentheses. We categorize the web materials accordingly:

- Web Audio (WA): Our own audio files streamed from the website
- Web Examples (WE): Musical examples
- Web Figures: (WF): Diagrams and charts
- Web Links (WL): Links to Spotify recordings, YouTube videos, and other internet resources. (Note: these links were accurate at the time of writing.)
- Web Photos (WP): Supplementary photos
- Web Scores (WS): Supplementary scores
- Web Video (WV): Our own video files streamed from the website

The website also contains bibliographies for each chapter of the book.

Acknowledgments

We first express deep gratitude to the authors presented in this book. Since we conveyed a hope in the conclusion of our 2016 book *Tracing Tangueros: Argentine Tango Instrumental Music* that our work would lay a strong foundation for future tango studies, we have watched the field grow with contributions from music, dance, and literary scholars. We have also become better acquainted with scholars who write about tango from humanistic disciplines beyond the performing arts. As we step back and see how our aspiration is being fulfilled by the contributors to this volume, we see how their work carries tango studies even further forward. What's more, they have enriched our understanding of tango in the contexts of their fields. Their passion and enthusiasm for the art form inspired us throughout the editing process, and as we built and strengthened this international community of tango scholars.

Next, we wish to acknowledge the hard work of the translators to bring the Spanish, French, Turkish, German, and Japanese texts and sources into English. Translators' hard work often goes unnoticed or unrecognized, but without their language expertise, we could not have shaped the English translations presented here to flow smoothly for our target reader.

We are extremely grateful to Katharina (Kate) Brett, our managing editor at Cambridge. She had the vision to expand Cambridge's titles in Latin American music, and to encourage us to propose this addition to the *Companion to Music* series. She consistently provided unfailing support throughout the entire process, and she was always available to answer questions and guide us in all of its stages from conception to fruition.

Finally we acknowledge those in our close network and safety net of family and friends for their love, support, and patience as we worked on every step of this volume: Link thanks Jake Rose, Henry and Adrian Rose, and Lexi Mosier; Wendland thanks Heidi Lee Burroughs (née Wendland), Karen Wendland Dix, Ines Freixas (her "Argentine sister"), Don Wendland, and Pat Webster. She further expresses deep gratitude to her colleagues in Emory College of Arts and Sciences, Emory

University, especially Michael Elliott for his inspirational work to promote and support the humanities in higher education as Dean of the College, and Stephen Crist, chair of the Department of Music, for his steadfast encouragement of and departmental funds for research and related travel.

Introduction: Tango Studies across Disciplinary and Geographic Boundaries

KRISTIN WENDLAND AND KACEY LINK

Tango's multicultural origins foreshadowed its current international status. It was spawned and fostered at the turn of the twentieth century from a confluence of Afro-Argentine, rural Argentine, and European cultures and traditions in the Río de la Plata region of present-day Argentina and Uruguay; traveled to France and beyond in the 19-teens; and then reached its height of fame in Argentina during its Golden Age (1930s–1955). Since the hit show *Tango Argentino* opened in Paris in 1983, the tango art form has experienced a significant revival and is presently seeing an international resurgence.

Yet, stereotypical images and sounds of tango persist in a time capsule, typically containing a white heterosexual couple dressed in formal yet risqué attire (probably accented with red) who are engaged in a flashy dance to a standard tango tune such as "El choclo." Try testing yourself with free association (this is how we open the first day of a tango class or presentation). What do you imagine when you hear the word "tango"? Do you see dancers like we just described here? Do you recall how tango is portrayed in a passionate Hollywood movie scene? Or, do you hear the tango icon Astor Piazzolla (1921–1992) mightily playing the bandoneón?

While such images of the art form are frequently perpetuated by tango shows in Argentina and abroad, they sadly project a simplified version of what tango really is – a multidimensional art form comprised of music, dance, and poetry. They overlook tango's rich and dynamic history and presence in today's modern global society. Such clichéd depictions also neglect to account for tango's impact on culture and society throughout the world, from milongas (tango dances) in Europe to concert stages in Japan, or how tango can be viewed as a case study for understanding broader humanistic concepts in the realms of politics, race, and gender.

Since the 2000s, scholars have begun to shatter such static viewpoints of the art form, and tango research has significantly increased in breadth, quantity, and quality within the last ten years. They are now publishing books and articles in English about tango from all perspectives – historical, ethnographic, sociological, political, and anthropological – and deepening

1

our understanding of the music, dance, and poetry of the art form. Some of these scholars are represented in the present volume. Paulina L. Alberto retells the story of the origins of tango to include its Afro-Argentine influences in *Black Legend: The Many Lives of Raúl Girgera and the Power of Racial Storytelling in Argentina* (2022). Julián Graciano's *Método Guitarra Tango/Tango Guitar Method* (2016) provides "how-to" instructions on tango musical techniques and performance practices and, more broadly, a window into the cultural sounds of Argentina. Matthew B. Karush's *Musicians in Transit: Argentina and the Globalization of Popular Music* (2017) examines Latin identity in transnational Argentine musicians of the twentieth century, including Piazzolla. He also looks at race in tango in his article "Blackness in Argentina: Jazz, Tango, and Race before Perón" (2012) and his book chapter "Black in Buenos Aires: The Transnational Career of Oscar Alemán" in *Rethinking Race in Modern Argentina* (2016, also a Cambridge book co-edited by Alberto). Our *Tracing* Tangueros*: Argentine Tango Instrumental Music* (2016) offers a musical analysis of tango's instrumental compositional and arranging techniques and performance practices. Morgan James Luker's *The Tango Machine: Musical Culture in the Age of Expediency* (2016) explores how Argentina uses tango as a national resource for economic, social, and cultural projects. Kathy Davis' *Dancing Tango: Passionate Encounters in a Globalizing World* (2015) studies the dance and how individuals negotiate issues relating to gender, sexuality, and global relations of power. In *Tango Nuevo* (2012), Carolyn Merritt looks at how the younger generation has transformed tango dancing in Argentina since the early 2000s. Madeleine Hackney conducts and publishes medical research on the therapeutic application of tango dance for patients with neurological diseases, most recently in "Adapted Tango Improves Mobility, Motor-Cognitive Function, and Gait but Not Cognition in Older Adults in Independent Living" (2015). Rielle Navitski writes about an iconic tango figure in "The Tango on Broadway: Carlos Gardel's International Stardom and the Transition to Sound in Argentina" (2011). Numerous scholars beyond those represented here have contributed to the tango field, like Michael O'Brien's study of tango's institutionalization in Buenos Aires in "Activism, Authority, and Aesthetics: Finding the Popular in Academies of *Música Popular*" (2015); Lloica Czackis's exploration of Yiddish influences on tango in "Tangele: The History of Yiddish Tango" (2009); and John Turci-Escobar's examination of Piazzolla's relationship with the famed Argentine writer, Jorge Luis Borges in "Rescatando al tango para nueva música: Reconsidering the 1965 Collaboration between Borges and Piazzolla" (2011).

Scholars writing in Spanish are also expanding the gamut and examining a multitude of areas of tango. Omar García Brunelli, also a contributor to this Cambridge book, has an outstanding edited volume on the music of Piazzolla (2008) as well as a book providing a comprehensive discussion of Piazzolla's recordings (2010). María Mercedes Liska has published on tango queer studies (*Argentine Queer Tango*, 2017) as well as edited volumes relating to contemporary tango (*Tango: ventanas del presente* I and II, 2012 and 2016). Sofia Cecconi writes of tango tourism (2018), youth's role in tango's rise in the 1990s (2017), as well as the musical identity of tango and its relationship to Buenos Aires (2009). Some scholars even examine sampling in electronic tango (Greco and López Cano, 2014). Diego Fischerman and Abel Gilbert also have a book dedicated to the life and music of Piazzolla (2009). Jorge Dimov and Esther Echenbaum compiled a study of the bandoneonist Leopoldo Federico (2009), while Pablo Kohan published a substantial book outlining tango orchestral practices from 1920 to 1935 (2010). Additionally, Paulina Fain has spearheaded a series to approach performance practices for individual instruments titled *Método de tango* (2010), following two previous performance practice and arranging manuals by Julián Peralta (2008) and Horacio Salgán (2001).

As many academic music programs seek to expand and diversify course offerings, tango is also spreading into curricula in colleges and universities. Aside from the firmly established undergraduate and graduate Latin American music programs at major research institutions, such as the Butler School of Music at the University of Texas at Austin and the Jacobs School of Music at Indiana University, new courses either dedicated solely to tango or incorporating tango in a broader survey of Latin American music have taken shape in North American universities. As the study of Latin American music in general gains strength in the United States, many smaller music programs are expanding their offerings in this field as they update their curriculum. In Buenos Aires, established programs for tango music studies include La Escuela de Música Popular de Avellaneda and El Conservatorio Superior de Música "Manuel de Falla." Established European programs include the Argentinian Tango studies curriculum in the World Music Department at Codarts in Rotterdam, and the Conservatoire à Rayonnement Régional du Grand Avignon (CRR du Grand Avignon) offers classes in bandoneón. Ethnomusicologists study dance-music relationships through fieldwork in milongas at the University of Music and Dramatic Arts Graz in Austria.

Educational tango programs and activities outside the academe also further advance tango knowledge. The Orquesta Escuela de Tango Emilio Balcarce in Buenos Aires facilitates the transmission of the great *maestros'* cultural legacy from the tango orchestras of the 1940s and 1950s in a two-year program instructed by actual musicians from that era who remain active, as well as important tango musicians of successive generations. "Tango para músicos" ("Tango for Musicians") offers a week-long intensive workshop to study and share knowledge on the fundamentals of tango and Argentine music, with an annual summer edition in the United States through Reed College in Portland, Oregon. Intensive tango dance workshops and festivals abound around the world, often featuring guest Argentine teachers, in such US cities as Chicago, Philadelphia, and Tucson, and European cities such as Amsterdam, Berlin, and Rome.

As demonstrated by this brief overview of recent scholarship and educational course offerings, the field of tango studies is growing tremendously; however, the publications are primarily limited to monographs or area-specific articles and edited volumes. With this collaborative and interdisciplinary volume, we hope to remedy the status quo and present an innovative tango collection that will impact the performing arts and the humanities in powerful ways. *The Cambridge Companion to Tango* offers a more "user-friendly" approach to understanding the art form as a whole. We draw together the current scholarship in an innovative volume that incorporates all the facets of tango studies, and it is geared toward undergraduate and early graduate-level students and tango enthusiasts. As the book unites twenty-two scholars and scholar-artists from a variety of disciplines under the umbrella of tango, the reader may find common points and intersections across such fields as musicology, Latin American studies, and political science. We hope the reader will ultimately broaden their knowledge of this complex art form and its relationship to culture and society.

While envisioning how to lay out this book, we asked ourselves broad research questions such as: How do diverse humanistic fields of inquiry further shape our understanding of the tango art form? Inversely, how does the tango help us further understand culture and society? How do interdisciplinary perspectives on tango influence current scholarship? How do international perspectives on and research approaches to tango differ, and why are they important? To address these questions, we solicited proposals from an array of tango scholars and scholar-artists. We sought those active in research through distinctive pathways to represent various national and international viewpoints. We asked for proposals under such broad topic titles as "Tango Antecedents," "Tango History," "Tango Poetry," "Tango and Jazz," "Tango and Film," and "Tango and Politics," and then began to map out how these chapters would flow within sections organized by the art form's three dimensions of music, dance, and poetry, and a section of interdisciplinary studies. As the reader will notice, our final product actually presents only a handful of authors, namely the scholar-artist practitioners, focused on a singular tango dimension. Most authors organically cross at least one disciplinary boundary in their chapter, thus demonstrating the essential nature of the art form itself and the enlarging field of tango studies. We hope the reader will find answers to the questions we asked ourselves as we embarked on this book project, and that this collection will raise additional questions for them to carry tango research into new directions and promote future collaborations across disciplines.

The scope of our addition to *The Cambridge Companion to Music* series presents a comprehensive view of tango studies on the global stage in twenty chapters. The chapters collectively cover tango's history, culture, and performance practices from multiple perspectives; highlight how it flourished in its native Argentina and abroad; and trace its international impact over the last century. The authors signify tango's global reach, including Argentine nationals living both in Argentina and abroad, North Americans, Europeans, and a Japanese and a Turkish national, as they represent diverse approaches to the study and practice of the art form in our globalized world.

Omar García Brunelli's Chapter 1 provides a solid historical overview of tango music, dance, and poetry. It first broadly lays out tango's African, European, Argentine, and Uruguayan origins in the Río de la Plata region of South America, then focuses on the musical changes that took place through time. In doing so, García Brunelli highlights important contributors from the *guardia vieja* (Old Guard), *guardia nueva* (New Guard), and Golden Age; discusses Piazzolla's *nuevo tango* (New Tango); and brings his overview up to today by describing active contemporary tango musicians.

We organize the other nineteen chapters into four groups: Tango Music, Tango Song, Tango Dance, and Interdisciplinary Tango Studies. Within these groups, the reader will encounter diverse approaches and methodologies to studying tango. Six chapters focus on various aspects of tango music. In Chapter 2, Ortaç Aydınoğlu explores the bandoneón as a symbol of tango, focusing on the great interpreters in Argentina and abroad. In Chapter 3, Morgan James Luker examines tango through the early recorded sound industry, using archival recordings of tango artist Ángel Villoldo (1861–1919). Ignacio Varchausky's Chapter 4 examines tango music through its standard instrumental performance practices. He draws on the orchestral styles of two Golden Age orchestras, those of Juan D'Arienzo and Aníbal Troilo, and illustrates with important archival recordings and scores from the tango repertory. In Chapter 5, scholar and guitarist Eric Johns focuses on contemporary tango guitar performance practice, highlighting two important schools of playing established by Aníbal Arias (1922–2010) and Roberto Grela (1913–1992). Our Chapter 6 moves into the post–Golden Age beginning in 1955 and compares the life and works of two great pillars: Horacio Salgán and Astor Piazzolla. As a composer/practitioner, Julián Graciano offers insights into tango as a transnational musical form by analyzing the performance element of spontaneity and improvisation in both tango and jazz in Chapter 7. As a bonus to the numerous musical examples of his own tango-jazz hybrid compositions and other living tango composers, he provides a video tutorial on how to realize a tango lead sheet.

Two chapters by Argentine scholars delve into the *tango canción*, or tango song. In Chapter 8, Romina Dezillio considers female tango singers' artistic and social contributions to the professionalization of women within the national and international tango scene. Her study of the consolidation process of the *tango cancionista* (female tango singer) during the 1930s in Argentina reveals gender-based relationships between the *tango canción* and Argentine society as she highlights the personal styles and careers of three star *cancionistas*: Rosita Quiroga (1896–1984), Azucena Maizani (1902–1970), and Libertad Lamarque (1908–2000). Pablo Palomino analyzes broader cultural themes and aesthetic currents in lyrics from tango's Golden Age. His Chapter 9 considers the historical context in which tango lyrics became a sentimental, philosophical, and aesthetic lens for several generations of listeners in Argentina and beyond through a unique mix of modernism and vernacular speech. He then examines the poetry around three central themes that emerged in the Golden Age: the urban space, the sociological and poetic issue of the relationship between *love* and *self*, and the modern experience itself.

Four chapters focus on aspects of tango dance in its social, rather than show, context. Sociologist and dance practitioner Christophe Apprill begins his Chapter 10 by providing a solid historical overview of tango dance. He then explores gender relations and roles in tango by examining tango stereotypes in relation to tango dance, while opening new perspectives on contemporary dimensions of globalized tango scenes. Sociologist and tango dancer Kathy Davis provides an ethnographic exploration of passion in tango dancers in Chapter 11, and she illustrates how such passion is embodied, attached to strongly felt emotions, and implicated in biographical transformations. She argues that tango dancing offers a perfect site for understanding the importance of passion in ordinary people's everyday lives, gender relations in late modernity, and the possibilities and pitfalls of transnational encounters in a globalizing world. In Chapter 12, Kendra Stepputat examines the choreomusical aspect of tango through an ethnographic lens in European countries. She focuses on one of the currently very popular tango social dance events in Europe called *encuentros milongueros*, paying particular attention to how these events, originally set up to mimic tango dance environments in Buenos Aires, have developed into translocal/contemporary tango music-dance practice that is particular to Europe. Anthropologist and social tango dancer Carolyn Merritt had begun to take dance lessons in leading, then the COVID-19 restrictions shut down in-person classes and milongas. In Chapter 13, Merritt reflects on her experiences and insights about how tango is politically generative, confronts the struggles many women face with tango, and pursues a more profound examination into tango's evolution and future.

The last seven chapters of this volume highlight how tango studies have advanced through interdisciplinary and multidimensional pathways to its analysis and practice. Historian Paulina L. Alberto leads this final group in Chapter 14, using original research about a multigeneration family of Black musicians to illustrate different stages of musical experimentation that fed into tango. In doing so, she sheds new light on the relationship between the Afro-Argentine musical and dance tradition of *candombes* and early tango, and she challenges the entrenched racial narrative of Afro-Argentine "disappearance" over the course of the nineteenth century. In Chapter 15, music theorist and social dancer Rebecca Simpson-Litke brings tango music and dance together through the current interdisciplinary lens of choreomusical analysis. As she explores the connection between movement and music through her transcriptions and analyses of Juan Carlos Copes's choreography of the famous "La cumparsita," she shows how music and dance reinforce or complement each other through rhythm. Historian Matthew Karush delves into tango's role in Argentina's political and social history in Chapter 16. He specifically analyzes how the art form functioned within Peronism and anti-Peronism of the mid-to-late half of the twentieth century. Film scholar Rielle Navitski applies her discipline's lens to tango and Argentine culture in Chapter 17. She provides an overview of tango's intersections with film; analyzes how tango's affective qualities and transnational wanderings have shaped a long and productive *pas de deux* with the cinema; shows the influence of each in a historical context; and raises broader questions of cultural exchange and hegemony. Ethnomusicologist Yuiko Asaba provides a solid global view of tango in Chapter 18. She examines tango's transnational dynamics with historical and ethnographic approaches and embraces themes of affect and transculturality between Japan and Argentina. Bárbara Varassi Pega's Chapter 19 represents how tango studies have become institutionalized in her case study of the Tango Department at Codarts University in the Netherlands. She focuses on the work of its founder Gustavo Beytelmann (b. 1945), and the educational exchange with scholars and practitioners in Argentina. To conclude the volume and demonstrate how widely tango reaches across disciplines, health professionals Madeleine E. Hackney and J. Lucas McKay offer a case study for how medical research projects incorporate tango therapeutically in Chapter 20. Hackney and McKay utilize tango for promoting health and preventing or changing declining conditions, and they illustrate how their current research applies "Adapted Tango" to improve motor and cognitive functions in individuals with Parkinson's and Alzheimer's diseases.

An Epilogue rounds off the book. First, we offer some final reflections to help the reader evaluate what they have learned, as we summarize various themes that run through the twenty chapters. Then, we present a list of resources to guide the reader into further tango studies. Finally, to aid the reader in keeping track of all the historical information scattered through-out these chapters, and contextually understanding the art form, we pro-vide a historical tango chronology framed in a backdrop of political, social, and cultural events in the Appendix.

Although this tango volume draws together authors from a diverse array of disciplines and geographical locations, it cannot be completely compre-hensive. We hope readers will not be offended if they note inevitable omissions in their own field of interest. Our intent with this volume is to offer the reader a compendium of diverse, multidisciplinary, and multi-national perspectives united broadly around tango. It reflects how, in addition to writing about music, dance, and poetry, tango scholars are now writing about tango from numerous viewpoints, including race, gen-der, and even medical research.

In 2009, UNESCO declared the tango as Argentina and Uruguay's "intangible cultural heritage of humanity," highlighting how the multidi-mensional art form of music, dance, and poetry has captivated the world for over a century. Tango research, too, has captivated scholars and artist-scholars. In our conclusion to *Tracing* Tangueros, we expressed hope that "our work here lays a strong foundation for further studies of tango music," and that "scholars and musicians will . . . carry and invigorate tango into the future."[1] Indeed, the authors presented in this book are already fulfill-ing our aspirations. As this volume brings them together, we trust their contributions to the field will carry tango studies even further forward. We hope this book will stimulate even more new research as readers through-out multiple disciplines ask their own significant questions.

Notes

1. Kacey Link and Kristin Wendland, *Tracing* Tangueros: *Argentine Tango Instrumental Music* (New York: Oxford University Press, 2016), 332.

1 | A Brief History of Tango

OMAR GARCÍA BRUNELLI

TRANSLATED FROM SPANISH BY LAURA AZCOAGA

The history of tango spans over a century and is the story of music, dance, and poetry. It was born as a close-embrace dance with complex figures, some charged with eroticism, and improvised performance. The music that became exclusively associated with this dance was based on the *habanera* rhythm. It incorporated elements from Africa that remain present, although at times hidden, in tango's DNA. Tango lyrics were initially influenced by Spanish theater, but they took their own developmental path to reach new heights as popular poetry by the 1940s. Originally from the Río de la Plata region in Argentina and Uruguay, tango, as a multidimensional art form, has risen to great fame and has expanded throughout the world; yet through its history, it has had pinnacles of splendor and low ebb moments. Tango has even taken root outside of its region of origin and become a local form of music in some places, such as in Paris in the 1920s. Since then, tango has come back to Argentina from these foreign places and has been filled with influences that have changed how it is played or danced. The present-day tango is not the same music, dance, and poetry from a century ago, but indeed its essence has been preserved in many guises. This brief account traces tango's musical, choreographic, and poetic changes from its origins in the nineteenth century to today.

Origins and Early Tango

Instrumental Music to the 1920s and the Guardia Vieja *(Old Guard)*

Tango, as music, originated in the late nineteenth century in the cities of Buenos Aires and Montevideo, the capitals of Argentina and Uruguay, respectively, on the banks of the Río de la Plata.[1] In the beginning, the word "tango" was associated with the music of enslaved Black people on the eastern coast of Latin America as expressed in their instruments, dances, or festivities. Later, the name was applied to an Afro-Argentine, Afro-Uruguayan way to recreate certain European musical forms introduced

10

to the New World. This musical genre of tango resulted from the blend of the *habanera* and *milonga* as well as popular and traditional melodies circulating in the Río de la Plata region.

The *habanera* as both music and dance, originated in Cuba and was derived from the European *contradance*. Although the *contradance* was born in England as the "country dance," it was later adopted by France and Spain as *contredanse* and *contra danza*, respectively.[2] From Spain, it moved to Cuba, where it mingled with Afro-Cuban music and changed its name first to *danza habanera* then simply to *habanera*. With its characteristic accompanimental rhythm of a dotted eighth note, sixteenth note, and two eighth notes, and frequent use of syncopation and triplets in the melody (Ex. 1.1),[3] the *habanera* traveled in its most popular versions together with traded goods shipped down the Atlantic coastline until it reached the Río de la Plata region. Eventually, it returned to Spain, where it was considered a new genre, as its *contradanza* origin was no longer recognized. Then, the people in Spain called this new music "American tango" when they used it in plays, especially when illustrating scenes with Black characters in the Americas. At other times, they called it "*habanera*" when they converted it into a ballroom dance of embracing partners. After settling in Spain, both "American tango" and the "*habanera*" returned to the Americas, specifically Buenos Aires, where both types met the *milonga* and the popular Afro-Cuban *habanera* brought in by sailors.

The origin of the *milonga* is uncertain, though it was already found in the outskirts of Buenos Aires by 1880, yet it clearly absorbed the rhythm of the *habanera*. The term "*milonga*" – perhaps of African roots – also designates both the music and dance art form and the venue where the dance takes place. In addition to being sung in the countryside, the *milonga*, as an art form, became very popular when sung in the theater and the circus. Toward the end of the nineteenth century, the *milonga* merged with early tango. Yet, it still lives on today as folk music in rural areas and as one of the *tres ritmos* (three rhythms) of tango (tango, *milonga*, and *vals*). Some piano scores were published using both the labels "tango"

Example 1.1 Contradance (*habanera*) of the nineteenth century.

and "*milonga*," proving the close association of the two genres. As these two genres' music began to fuse at the turn of the twentieth century, composers interspersed short popular melodies in their tangos. Simultaneously, African descendants played this ebullient music, adding traits characteristic of the Afro-Argentine culture. During Carnival, in particular, the Black population, enslaved or freed, participated in their lively activities. Although no recordings of the musical accompaniments have survived, there can be no doubt that the Afro-Argentine musical expressions were crucial in the origins of tango.[4]

By the turn of the twentieth century, tango music began to take on its own shape as an independent genre. While still called at times "*milonga*," "*habanera*," "*tango habanera*," and "*tango milonga*," it became the same identifiable music, and eventually, all these names converged into a single one: "tango." The music presented peculiarities that set it apart from the forerunners that contributed to its creation. Tango scholars have identified and defined these distinct features to typically include an initial motive that defines a distinct musical character and identity; a formal structure comprised of three sixteen-bar sections, with a contrasting third section called a trio (occasionally, these early tangos had only two sections); a four-bar phrase structure; a *habanera* melodic amphibrach rhythm (short-long-short, Ex. 1.2a); and a *habanera* accompanimental rhythm (Ex. 1.2b).

Dissemination of Early Tango Music

Early tango music, commonly called the *guardia vieja* (Old Guard) by scholars, was disseminated by piano scores and early audio recordings. Publishers printed piano sheet music in great numbers to be played in affluent homes by those who could afford a piano, which in those days were imported in large numbers. This upper-class audience also listened to tango recorded on wax cylinders and shellac. With such intense commercial and industrial activity, tango expanded to all social levels and was no longer restricted exclusively to brothels.[5]

Example 1.2 *Habanera* rhythms. a. Melodic amphibrach rhythm. b. Accompanimental rhythm.

As tango became popular, phonographic activity intensified. The existence of around 2,800 recordings reflects how the early genre took shape until 1920, a date scholars agree signals the end of the first leg of tango's history and the *guardia vieja*. Many of these early recordings have survived and been reissued, which makes it possible to listen to early tango music recorded by a variety of ensembles from this era, including brass bands, *rondallas* (typically string groups, though they later had more eclectic formations), and *orquestas típicas criollas* (creole, or local Argentine, typical orchestras).

Military-style brass bands began to make tango recordings around 1907. Some were Argentine, like the Buenos Aires Municipal Band. Others were foreign, like the Republican Guard Band from Paris, which made several recordings on order by a Buenos Aires department store, for example, in the tango "El Sargento Cabral" ("The Sergeant Cabral," WL 1.1). These brass bands performed tango arrangements originally for piano in an *habanera* rhythm with a brilliant timbre and a choppy gay air characteristic of the first tangos. The *rondallas* recordings of tango reflect a less martial style, which, while perhaps less professional, sound warmer and more amiable. These two types of ensembles stopped recording around 1913–1914 and were replaced in the public favor by quartets with bandoneón – an instrument of German origin brought to Argentina by immigrants in the late nineteenth century and adopted by tango musicians beginning around 1905.

Early Tango Ensembles

One of the great *guardia vieja* musicians, bandoneonist Vicente Greco (1888–1924), made his first recording in 1910 with his quartet of bandoneón, guitar, violin, and flute. The recording label called the ensemble an *orquesta típica criolla*, a designation that continues to denote the classical formation of a tango ensemble as an *orquesta típica*. The bandoneón was immediately a huge success, and bandoneón players became stars. Quartets performed in all tango venues and began to appear in downtown cafes. All quartets played without written scores in the same straightforward style, where the flute, violin, and bandoneón carried the melody while the guitar provided the rhythmic accompaniment. The sections of each composition were repeated with no change or embellishment. Despite the structural and stylistic monotony, the groups' sound, particularly that of the bandoneón, captivated audiences. Besides Greco's quartet, other bandoneonists formed ensembles, including Juan "Pacho"

Maglio (1881–1934, the most popular bandoneonist of the time), Arturo Bernstein (1882–1935), Eduardo Arolas (1892–1924, the most charismatic bandoneonist), and Astor Bolognini (1890–1985). Pianist Roberto Firpo (1884–1969) was the first to incorporate the piano into his orchestra in 1914.

Toward the end of the 1910s, tango ensembles changed, as flutes were left out, the piano replaced the guitar, and the string group expanded to include bass (and sometimes cello). As the ensembles consolidated their formations, the tuning differences among the three core instruments – piano, bandoneón, and strings – created a sound profile musicians call *mugre* (dirt or grit). It became a fundamental sound to the tango style, which also includes special effects such as noise, clusters, and percussive sounds, as opposed to a "pure sound" standard in European classical playing.[6] While these subtle tuning differences resulted in noise from an acoustic perspective, tango actually adopted them as an expressive technique rather than rejected them.

At the same time, some *guardia vieja* musicians became more discerning in their expressive style. In 1917, Eduardo Arolas and his ensemble produced recordings imbued with symbolic purpose, dramatism, and melancholy far from his predecessors' interpretive simplicity and lack of nuance. In these recordings, one example being "Moñito" ("Bow Tie," WL 1.2), one can sense the change in the accompaniment that would soon take place, in which musicians would leave behind the *habanera* and replace it with four equal pulses called *marcato*. Arolas exerted a great influence on tango since the prominent musicians who forged the future style either played with him or admired him. Although nicknamed "El Tigre del bandoneón" ("The Tiger of the Bandoneón"), neither he nor his colleagues had great technical facility on their instrument. Arolas was also a prolific composer; his tangos are still part of the standard tango repertory today. Other relevant composers of the time were Roberto Firpo, Juan Maglio, José Martínez (1890–1939), Enrique Delfino (1895–1967), and Juan Carlos Cobián (1896–1953).

In the late 1910s/early 1920s, some musicians with academic studies began to perform tango, attaining a correct and expressive interpretation and a precise orchestral intonation. That was the case of Orquesta Típica Select, an ensemble of two violins, bandoneón, piano, and violoncello that made fifty-two 78 rpm recordings in Camden, New Jersey, USA in 1920. Additionally, there are hints in these versions that some of the instrumental parts were notated.[7]

The Orquesta Típica Select recordings ended the first period in the history of tango,[8] even as they anticipated the way tango would be performed in the coming years. The *marcato* accompaniment – four equal beats – was standardized, as well as the instrumentation of piano, bass, bandoneón, and strings. For the first time and from present listening standards, the group's performance sounds more precise, played by trained professional musicians, for example, in "Don Esteban" (WL 1.3). Thus, 1920 is the hinge year between the two periods of the *guardia vieja* and the next, usually called the *guardia nueva* (New Guard).

Early Tango Dance

The second way one may study tango is through the dance. Some sources mentioned it near the end of the nineteenth century, and newspaper articles described it as fashionable in their Carnival chronicles in 1900. The dance's main features were the holding of the partner close in a veritable and connected embrace, the *corte* (cut), and the *quebrada* (break). The *corte* is a pause or interruption of the step associated with abrupt silences in the music, and the *quebrada* is the wiggle of the hips.[9]

Dancing with a *quebrada* and a close hold of the partner were part of several other dances, especially the *habanera*. Around 1890, this was the way of dancing both the *habanera* and the tango until eventually, the *habanera* was set aside, and this style of dance became associated exclusively with the tango. Some accounts comment on the provocative touching of the thighs and the close contact resulting from the *corte* linked to the musical pause. The *habanera* did not have such discontinuities; it lacked rhythmic or melodic interruptions caused by syncopations, off-beats, or silences. These features were particular to tango. The most remarkable aspect of the choreography is that it arose directly from the music; it is not repeated pre-established steps but different impromptu moves with the addition of *cortes* and *quebradas*. In fact, "*corte y quebrada*" became a synonym for danced tango.

Magazines and newspapers from the period confirm how by 1900 tango choreography had been accepted and settled as a popular and well-established dance. It supplanted contemporary dances such as polka and *habanera*, which gradually declined and disappeared. By 1903, tango was widely adopted during Carnival parties, and magazine and newspaper articles remark on the great variety of impromptu *cortes* and *quebradas* tried out by dancers.

As time progressed, community recreational gatherings included tango dance with music played by various early ensembles. Tango was also danced in *casitas* (little houses, but more accurately brothels rented by the night) that were tolerated by society, yet disguised. As a result of the intense instrumental and dancing activities in these *casitas*, tango came to be considered a whorehouse dance. Great pianists/composers of the time performed there, like Manuel Campoamor (1877–1941), Rosendo Mendizábal (1868–1913), and Alfredo Bevilacqua (1874–1942), while other performers and important creators of the earliest instrumental style of tango organized bands, such as Vicente Greco, Ernesto Ponzio (1885–1934), and Genaro Vázquez. The laws in downtown Buenos Aires prohibited brothels, alcohol, and dancing; therefore, tango was played and danced in the outskirts of the city, where there was a potent focus of creativity and musical tutoring. Summer restaurants and cafes patronized by families by day became dinner concerts by night; the best known was the legendary Lo de Hansen (Hansen's). And finally, tango was danced at academies, teaching venues of diverse social levels, and the *peringundines* (sordid places for dance) in the slum neighborhoods.

As tango dance reached great popularity and became commonplace in the city between 1905 and 1910, it was no longer mentioned as new or remarkable in the news. Some critical articles, however, addressed the more controversial social venues where it was both played and danced. The dance's popularity also gave rise to a simplified choreography. The most common dance style was *tango liso* (smooth tango), suitable for untrained dancers, followed by more virtuoso tango styles with complex steps and moves, and a competition style performed by trained dancers.

In 1911, tango entered the aristocratic ballrooms of Paris and became an instant success because of its exoticism and voluptuous undertones. The fad went beyond the dance and encompassed fashion and other social practices. Dance tutors, both Argentine and European, proliferated, and standard choreography, cleaned up to avoid erotic innuendos, emerged. When Buenos Aires learned of the Parisian success of tango, the reluctant elites were bewildered and debated accepting it, but by doing so, they broadened tango's popularity. Although ballrooms closed during World War I, tango came back in full force in 1919, and it has remained relatively popular in Europe, Argentina, and throughout the world up to today.

Early Tango Poetry and the Tango Canción

The third form of tango, apart from the instrumental music and the dance, is the sung version or the so-called *tango canción*.[10] The first compositions with lyrics are from the early twentieth century, and their content was influenced by the *criollo* tangos from the *zarzuela* (Spanish theatrical musical genre). In the very first recordings, several performers included tango in their repertory. The best-known female singers were Pepita Avellaneda (1874–1951), Lola Membrives (1888–1969), Flora Gobbi (1883–1952), Linda Thelma (1879–1939), and Andreé Vivianne (1863–1909); the well-known male singers included Alfredo Eusebio Gobbi (1877–1938), Mario Pardo (1887–1986), and Ángel Villoldo (1861–1919). Theatre ensembles accompanied them in ad hoc formations or, quite often, a single piano or guitar. The first lyrics were self-descriptive and cocky, in the style of *zarzuela* tangos.

The rise of Carlos Gardel (1890–1935) as a tango singer toward the end of this early period would be fundamental for the genre's future. In the early part of his professional career, Gardel dedicated himself primarily to folk repertory. Accompanied by guitar, he recorded his first tango in 1917, "Mi noche triste" ("My Sad Night," Samuel Castriota/Pascual Contursi, WL 1.4). This famous record opened new paths for tango for several reasons. First, the novel lyrics told a story about unrequited love. Second, as Gardel chose the guitar for accompaniment, which had primarily been used in folk music, the instrument became a standard fixture of tango.[11] Last, Gardel sang with a particular phrasing and rubato that echoed the accent and intonation of the language of Buenos Aires; it was a free rhythm that contrasted with the set pulse of the accompaniment. Gardel's extraordinary talent as an interpreter and the compelling appeal of the lyrics and music made that recording the starting point of the new *tango canción*, and its influence reaches to the present.

Stylistic Development of Tango: 1920–1935

While music, dance, and poetry continued to meld into the multidimensional tango genre beyond the early period of the 1910s, I mainly focus on the musical changes that took place for the remainder of this chapter. During the transitional years from the *guardia vieja* and *guardia nueva*, more than 11,000 recordings were made between 1917 and 1923, and listening to them reveals how very different instrumental tango became after 1920. The various ensembles established a standard instrumentation and polished their arrangements, even adding *variaciones* (variations) that reiterate the main melody embellished with running passagework. Yet, these new arrangements were quite simple as the musicians rehearsed and later played them either by memory or following a piano score.

Three leading figures and bandleaders emerged at this time: Osvaldo Fresedo (1897–1984), Juan Carlos Cobián (1896–1953), and Julio De Caro (1899–1980). The interpretations by the ensembles of Fresedo in 1922 and Cobián in 1923 set down an orchestral style characterized by a clear rendition of the melody with careful and precise graded dynamics. Their stylistic counterpart was expressed by Julio De Caro's *sexteto típico* (typical sextet), which established a standard formation of two violins, two bandoneones, piano, and bass. It capitalized on the experience of Cobián and Fresedo, but it also generalized the use of other tango features. De Caro translated Gardel's vocal rubato into an instrumental expression and expanded the ensemble's timbre by giving a more significant part to the bandoneones, which used their specific instrumental techniques like *rezongos* (clusters that make a grumbling sound) and *lloros* (cries, created by minor-second *appoggiaturas*) to create a rougher sound. The great interpretive diversity both Fresedo and De Caro introduced led to a change in the tango's structure, as newly composed pieces did not need three sections to achieve interpretive variety, and so the trios (the third section) were omitted.

All of these instrumental innovations defined the stylistic profile of the *guardia nueva* in the early 1920s and have nurtured tango performances to the present day. The genre consolidated anomalies that set it apart from the European musical canon – the use of unconventional instruments, vocal and instrumental melodies expressed with a particular popular rubato, and lyrics that incorporated the local *Lunfardo* (Buenos Aires slang). Fresedo and De Caro embraced progressive styles by incorporating novelties and possessing a will to polish interpretation, for example, in the Sexteto Julio De Caro's recording of "Mis lágrimas" ("My Tears," WL 1.5). Notably, Fresedo and De Caro had long careers as orchestra leaders and made hundreds of records. In contrast, other orchestras, like those of Francisco Canaro and Roberto Firpo, continued with the traditional format characterized by a steady tempo, a hammering beat effective for dancing, simple harmonies, a clearly defined melody with little rubato, and performing the standard repertory.

The lyricists (sometimes famous poets) wrote in a language that mirrored a high tension between the upper and lower classes, contrasting *Lunfardo* and street speech with classy language and favoring popular culture over canonic culture.[12] Thus, the lyrics became imbued with popular language and slang. Those written only in "correct" upper-class language were considered false and in the wrong style rather than credible tango.

Above all, the most relevant consideration in these stylistic differences between the two Guards is how tango developed. While the *guardia vieja* played tango with an original sound for its time, musicians used European instruments such as the piano, brass bands, and strings. After the emergence of the local *orquesta típica*, musicians began to develop unique interpretive devices that distinctly set the genre apart. In this way, the *guardia nueva* started from an original store of idiosyncratic instrumental forces and techniques and adapted them to tango's expressive needs, thus leaving behind the European academic standards or ignoring them.

At first, the orchestras included very few sung tangos until Francisco Canaro (1888–1964) added a singer to his orchestra in 1926. The early tango singer was called an *estribillista*, because he only sang the *estribillo* (chorus) or a fragment of the lyrics and was not a well-known soloist. Canaro even considered the singer as just a mere ornament. The sung version of tango grew with distinguished and famous soloists accompanied by small ensembles or their own orchestras. Male singers were known as *cantores* and female singers as *cancionistas*. In addition to Gardel, the best-known *cantores* were Ignacio Corsini (1891–1967), Agustín Magaldi (1898–1938), and Charlo (1906–1990); the most famous *cancionistas* were Rosita Quiroga (1896–1984), Tita Merello (1905–2002), Azucena Maizani (1902–1970), Mercedes Simone (1904–1990), Libertad Lamarque (1908–2000), and Ada Falcón (1905–2002). All these singers recorded hundreds of tangos. New songwriters and popular, acclaimed poets became tango literary figures: Celedonio Flores (1896–1947), Pascual Contursi (1888–1932), Homero Manzi (1907–1951), and Francisco García Jiménez (1898–1983), among the most celebrated.

Danced tango continued with the basic traits described earlier here, but the couples now did not look in the same direction and moved together. In this modified style, the man advanced, and the woman stepped back, so they were more or less facing each other. There were still different degrees of complexity, the simplest being a sequence of walking steps with a steady rhythm and the most complex, including a variety of figures with the legs and feet. Additionally, the man always led, cueing the woman through the energy in his chest and exerting a slight pressure with his hand on her waist or back. There are multiple examples of how tango was danced in films, which incorporated tango as a great attraction from its beginnings. Examples include *Tango!* (1933) written and directed by Luis Moglia Barth; Carlos Gardel danced in both *Cuesta abajo* (*Going Down*, 1934) directed by Louis Gasnier, and *Tango Bar* (1935) directed by John Reinhardt; *Los tres berretines* (*The Three Pastimes*, 1933) directed by Enrique Susini; *Así es el tango*

(*That's the Tango*, 1937) written and directed by Eduardo Morera; and *La vida es un Tango* (*Life Is a Tango*, 1939) written and directed by Manuel Romero.

The prosperity of tango met a serious setback with the economic crisis of 1930, caused by the New York Stock Exchange crash in October 1929. Many of the orchestras created in the peak years had to break up. Only the best-known directors continued their much-diminished activities. Unemployment and the loss of buying power significantly impacted the population's ability to purchase nonessential goods like records or entertainment. The total yearly phonographic recordings began to drop year after year until 1935, when a slow recovery started. Interestingly, 1935 is a symbolic hinge between this period and the next because of two relevant events that year: the successful launching of the new orchestra of Juan D'Arienzo (1900–1976) and Carlos Gardel's premature death. But more than just these two events, the music changed substantially before and after that year.

The Golden Age: 1935–1955

Juan D'Arienzo's orchestra appeared as something new, fresh, and light, even though some musicians considered it somewhat primitive as it contrasted the complexity of the De Caro-style sextets and Fresedo's orchestras. As D'Arienzo helped usher in the Golden Age of tango, which spanned from the 1930s to the mid-1950s, he based his straightforward interpretation on traditionalism. Although at variance with the somewhat antiquated but solid and set style of Canaro, D'Arienzo's fresh simplicity conquered not only new audiences but also dancers, giving rise to new popularity for the practice. Other directors followed this stylistic trend, and once the economic crisis subsided, the public's reaction was massive and formidable.

On the other hand, Gardel's tragic death in 1935 seemed to signal the end of the cycle of great solo singers and begin another. In this next stage, a new type of singer emerged, one whose enormous popularity became associated with the most prestigious *orquestas típicas*. These singers and orchestras included Francisco Fiorentino (1905–1955) and Alberto Marino (1923–1989) with Aníbal Troilo (1914–1975) and his orchestra, Raúl Berón (1920–1982) with the orchestra of Lucio Demare (1906–1974), Roberto Chanel (1914–1972) with Osvaldo Pugliese (1905–1995) and his orchestra, and Alberto Podestá (1924–2015) with the orchestra of Carlos Di Sarli

(1903–1960). Even as these and other singers succeeded with famous *orquestas típicas*, they continued their solo careers.

Due to the convergence of style changes, the end of the period, and the socio-economic developments, the tango recorded after 1935 sounds quite different from that of the 1920s and early 1930s. From a musical perspective, the most salient innovations are the playing in faster *tempi*, a clearer presence of the melody, and the adoption of a standard formation for the *orquesta típica* with at least three bandoneones, three violins, piano, and bass. In addition, excellent arrangers emerged, and composers created a new repertory that effectively competed with the traditional one.

D'Arienzo's enormous public success caused other musicians to form and create orchestras with the same musical drive. At first, almost all of them copied D'Arienzo's basic stylistic traits and somewhat primitive sound, including his rapid pace and simplicity. Canaro was still the main leader of the traditionalists, followed by Francisco Lomuto (1893–1950), Rodolfo Biagi (1906–1969), Alfredo De Angelis (1910–1992), and D'Arienzo himself. But gradually, musical quality gained influence over commercial success, and the more skilled musicians of the new orchestras made possible the re-emergence of the interpretive styles of the 1920s trends, now renovated and enriched. The progressives continued to follow De Caro or Fresedo. The orchestras of Pedro Laurenz (1902–1972), Troilo, Demare, Pugliese, and Alfredo Gobbi (1912–1965), in particular, adopted the instrumental and compositional techniques of De Caro's orchestra, with bandoneones taking the lead and a fluid, intense approach to melody called *fraseo* (tango phrasing). The orchestras of Di Sarli, Miguel Caló (1907–1972), Osmar Maderna (1918–1951), and Domingo Federico (1916–2000) followed Fresedo's lead by emphasizing the strings employing clear rubato and utilizing typical tango effects.

The 1940s, the peak of the Golden Age, is the richest time of tango. Even the abundant number of ensembles could hardly keep up with the demand of the multitude of dancers, who by then had adopted a standard set of basic steps. The limited length of the 78 rpm records kept the pieces about three minutes long. This short time frame for a piece demonstrated the arrangers' skill, the directors' personality, and the outstanding performers as they concentrated tango into a rich poetic, popular, and symbolic identity. At the same time, they supported a dance practiced by almost everybody with both standard and virtuoso skills.

Troilo best represents the spirit of the 1940s. While a master of his instrument, the bandoneón, Troilo also possessed a deep understanding of the orchestra as he expertly led hired professional arrangers. He was also a great composer and was gifted in identifying the best lyrics, many of which he set to music. His orchestra performed versions of the most popular tangos and with the best voices of the time. Among his more than 400 recordings, one would have difficulty finding a piece of less than outstanding quality.

Fresedo's sumptuous orchestral renditions and Di Sarli's lavish use of the violins formed a counterpoint to the De Caro-like sound cultivated by Troilo. Specifically, Di Sarli counterbalanced the minimal use of the bandoneones with his piano technique overflowing with off-beats and rhythmic surprises in the bass register. Contrastingly, Pugliese's style was more inclined to the textural and rhythmic challenges of the De Caro school.

The great orchestral leaders in the Golden Age illustrate a wide interpretive variety of tango music. They created particular traits with consistent and recognizable styles, and many had careers that, in some cases, lasted decades. It was also a period of great singers, who usually started their path to success by working with some of the foremost orchestras and eventually became soloists. More than ever before, many tango fans held up singers as idols not only because of their personal qualities but also because of the repertory that grew with excellent lyrics written by new poets like José María Contursi (1911–1972) and Manzi.

Dancing tango was a mandatory activity for the citizens of Buenos Aires. The newspapers carried, literally, hundreds of ads for dancing halls and venues, almost all with a live orchestra. The choreographic variations were coupled with one or another orchestra. Dancers who followed Pugliese were famous because of his difficult changes in rhythm, off-beats, and bandoneón rubato phrasing – all characteristics that were too challenging to follow for the average dancer.

Tango's boom lasted until 1955, at which point the military coup in Argentina affected dramatic changes in cultural policy. The public's preferences also began to change at this time, as it shifted to internationally popular hits. These two factors demonstrate a turning point for tango in 1955.

Astor Piazzolla (1921–1992) emerged as one of the most important figures at the end of the Golden Age as he shifted the trajectory of tango's musical style at the height of the period's musical development. With his innovative group Octeto Buenos Aires, Piazzolla created revolutionary works and avant-garde arrangements between 1955 and 1957. His style describes an end of an epoch in musical terms. After this, the new cultural policies and the changes in some social customs and behavior began to undermine the reign of tango in public preferences.

The Triumph of *Nuevo Tango* (New Tango): 1955–1990

President Juan Perón's fall from office in Argentina in 1955 caused profound changes in the cultural policy. As the borders opened to industrialized cultural products, mainly from the United States, people started to listen and dance to other genres, like *música tropical* (a general term for salsa, mambo, samba, etc.), jazz, and Brazilian tunes. Soon, tango was displaced as the most popular genre in Argentina as the dancing was gradually abandoned and the music scene changed. Tango became relegated to expensive venues like music clubs, where one could listen to the best musicians without the dance-hall environment.

The end of the 1950s carried on the traditions of the past, but in the 1960s, the *nuevo tango* (New Tango) created by Piazzolla steadily grew in importance. With his quintet of bandoneón, violin, electric guitar, piano, and bass, Piazzolla defined a new sound for tango, solidly rooted in features proper to the genre. Yet, he approached tango unlike the traditional style by composing pieces in new formal structures conceptually influenced by jazz and art music. His pieces usually contain a fast, rhythmic part contrasting a slow, melodic section, and they are not meant for dancing but for listening. He created a new melodic profile with rhythms taken from tango's rubato but written down in the score, and he generalized the use of an asymmetrical rhythmic grouping commonly referred to as 3-3-2 (eight eighth notes in 4/4 with stresses on the first, the fourth, and the seventh notes, Ex. 1.3).

In the 1960s, traditional tango kept losing popularity, while Argentina's national rock took over almost all the venues dedicated to younger audiences. Also, in that decade, music based on modernized folk and country music grew in popularity with the so-called *boom del folklore* (folklore boom). Piazzolla, one of the few tango success stories of the 1960s, had to settle in Europe to carry on his innovative projects. In the 1970s and 1980s, tango had fewer and fewer followers, and dancing and orchestra venues were scarce. Many musicians lost their jobs, and the younger ones cultivated careers in other forms of popular music.

Though tango found it hard to survive in Buenos Aires, it still endured in this period. Even with reduced audiences, a shrunken musical scene, and

Example 1.3 The 3-3-2 rhythm characteristic of Piazzolla's music.

the competition of other genres, some new musicians besides Piazzolla carried tango forward with excellent musical creations, including Leopoldo Federico (1927–2014), Atilio Stampone (1926–2022), Osvaldo Berlingieri (1928–2015), Ernesto Baffa (1932–2016), and Osvaldo Piro (b. 1937). Later, projects of Rodolfo Mederos (b. 1940) blended rock influences with tango; Dino Saluzzi (b. 1935) embraced a broader scope of musical fusion that characterized the times; and the trio of Néstor Marconi (b. 1942) and the orchestra of Raúl Garello (1936–2016) incorporated even more modernizing options with jazz and percussion.

The best-known singers – like Roberto Goyeneche (1926–1994), Edmundo Rivero (1911–1986), and Floreal Ruiz (1916–1978) – continued their soloist careers followed by their faithful fans. They made many albums with a new approach to tango singing that featured a greater emphasis on both the lyrics over the rhythmic beat and the interplay between free phrasing and regular accompaniment. Many singers leaned toward an off-beat expression, like those by Susana Rinaldi (b. 1935) and Juan Cedrón (b. 1939). As for the lyrics, the great pieces from the Golden Age were very much alive even as Cátulo Castillo (1906–1975), Homero Expósito (1918–1987), and several others kept writing and composing. While the new topics moved away from the standard themes of the Golden Age, they did not reach the communicative power tango had in the 1940s. The most popular new creations were by Eladia Blázquez (1931–2005) and Horacio Ferrer (1933–2014) in collaboration with Piazzolla.

There was a certain outcry for the loss of tango's traditions, which at the time seemed irreversible, and some government agencies even tried interventions. In 1980, the city government created the Orquesta de Tango de Buenos Aires, which is still active today. In 1986, the Escuela de Música Popular de Avellaneda (EMPA, School of Popular Music of Avellaneda) opened, offering a degree for tango musicians as performers, composers, and arrangers. The show *Tango Argentino*, which combined an excellent instrumental ensemble, well-known singers, and a troupe of tango dancers, marked an important turning point for the genre. The show opened with great acclaim in Paris in 1983 and then on Broadway in 1985–1986. This success brought back to life the interest in the dance all over the world, and with it, a new demand for tango musicians in Europe and the United States. Thus, musicians who had been part of the Golden Age, together with those of the new generation, found in these new institutions and shows a chance to devote themselves full time to tango.

Contemporary Tango: 1990–2020

In the 1990s, interest in Europe and tourists who wanted to see tango at its birthplace drove a renaissance of the genre. The combination of finding jobs, musical training, and a new identification with tango sparked the emergence of a new generation of musicians, both bandoneonists and other instrumentalists. One of the earliest of these new ensembles was El Arranque, which features a style characteristic of the 1960s with a modernized Troilo-like format.

Diverging from the trend to play tango with small ensemble formations (following Piazzolla's quintet paradigm with some instrumental variance) or a pop-up orchestra just for a tour or gig, some young musicians started to organize *orquestas típicas* of at least three bandoneones, three violins, piano, and bass. Orquesta Típica Fernández Branca (later Fernández Fierro, or OTFF) formed in 1999, and similar orchestras followed suit. At first, OTFF copied Pugliese's style quite accurately, but eventually, it drifted to an almost percussive tango with orchestrations based on chained riffs. They have become the most stable feature of contemporary tango in Buenos Aires, with uninterrupted performances in their own venue and a large audience of mostly young people. The group has had several offshoots, either caused by splits in the ensemble or the need to follow personal projects. Derrotas Cadenas and the Julio Coviello (b. 1983) Quartet represent the most significant, with their punk nuances due to their dry and spontaneous sound. Julián Peralta (b. 1974), the first conductor of the OTFF, subsequently created the Astillero ensemble, also Pugliese-like but with more influence from Piazzolla, and an *orquesta típica* that has recorded two anthologies of contemporary tangos with lyrics.

Tango in the new generation reflects organic rock influences since these musicians grew up with this music before moving on to tango. That influence is also perceptible in many of the new lyrics written for this contemporary version of the genre by Alfredo Rubín (b. 1961), Acho Estol (b. 1964), Alejandro Szwarcman (b. 1961), and Matías Mauricio (b. 1978). There are several singing styles: Ariel Ardit (b. 1974) follows the long-lived Gardelian tradition; others, like Omar Mollo (b. 1950) or Julieta Laso (b. 1982), prefer the vocalization derived from rock.

Present-day tango is engaged in a rather complex dialogue with its roots, ranging from outright imitation to recombining rules and conventions for novel results. Traditional styles are likely weightier than Piazzolla's *nuevo tango*, though his music permeates everything. More traditional manifestations based on Troilo and Piazzolla aesthetics, yet still in a modern language, include violinist Ramiro Gallo (b. 1966) and the ensembles of the brothers Lautaro (bandoneón, b. 1987) and Emiliano (piano, b. 1983) Greco. The dialogues between the roots of tango and other contemporary music have produced interesting results like Sonia Possetti's (b. 1973) blend of Piazzolla and Egberto Gismonti or Marcelo Nisinman's (b. 1970) versions of contemporary art music colored by Piazzollian tradition. Yet another line is the combination of electronic music with some traditional traits practiced by several ensembles, such as the remarkable Gotan Project in Paris.

In recent years, some groups have gained ground among the imitative trend by playing the original scores of diverse historical styles as art music. The formation of the Quinteto Astor Piazzolla, a Grammy winner, replicates the composer's original arrangements or exact transcriptions of his recordings. Sónico, an ensemble residing in Brussels, revives original compositions by Eduardo Rovira (1925–1980). Some versions of the traditional *orquestas típicas*, never part of the highbrow canon of tango history (like D'Arienzo's orchestra), have been rejuvenated with such refinement and instrumental delicacy that they sound like chamber music. This is the case of the Silbando orchestra in Paris, conducted by Chlöe Pfeiffer. Many orchestras have been formed in Europe, and some follow the imitation mode, like the Sexteto Canyengue (Rotterdam). Other European orchestras follow a very personal contemporary style, like Fleurs Noires, Andrea Marsili's sextet, or the quartet of French bandoneonist Louise Jallu.

Danced tango, though not on a massive scale, is profusely practiced in many venues in Buenos Aires and Argentine cities. Some new choreographies feature an alternation between the leader and follower role – something unthinkable before in such a male-chauvinist dance. Traditional hetero-norms have also been left behind with the emergence of various gender combinations for dancing partners.

The present-day tango scene in Argentina shows great flexibility and diversity. For example, the Orquesta Escuela de Tango Emilio Balcarce, created in 2000, cultivates all known orchestral styles with their original arrangements, while other ensembles and soloists of various styles work regularly. At present, about one hundred ensembles exist throughout the country, including those both well-established and others in fluid formations. All these factors reveal how the genre is going through a period of great creativity and expansion. Though not on as massive a scale as it used to be, tango shows a vitality today that promotes the emergence of great new talents and the permanence of a specialized audience.

Notes

1. For further reading on early tango, see Jorge Novati, ed. *Antología del tango rioplatense, vol 1: Desde sus orígenes hasta 1920* (1980; 4th ed., Buenos Aires: Instituto Nacional de Musicología, 2018).

2. Fred Burford, rev. Anne Daye, "Contredanse," *Grove Music Online*, ed. Deane Root, accessed April 14, 2022, https://doi.org/10.1093/gmo/9781561592630 .article.06376.

3. From Alejo Carpentier, *La música en Cuba* (México: Fondo de Cultura Económica, 1972), 142. Quoted in Novati, *Antología del tango rioplatense*, 17.

4. Omar García Brunelli, "Bases para una aproximación razonable a la cuestión del componente afro del tango," *Revista Argentina de Musicología* 18 (2018): 91–124. Editors' note: see also Alberto's Chapter 14 for more information regarding African origins of tango.

5. For more information, see Enrique Binda and Hugo Lamas, *El tango en la sociedad porteña 1880–1920* (Buenos Aires: Héctor Lorenzo Lucci Ediciones, 1998).

6. Nicolás Varchausky, "El ruido original del tango: viaje al centro de la orquesta típica," *Revista Argentina de Musicología* 15–16 (2014–2015): 181–190.

7. Enrique Binda, "La 'otra' Orquesta Típica Select," *Todotango*, accessed April 14, 2022, www.todotango.com/historias/cronica/374/La-otra-Orquesta-Tipica-Select.

8. Novati, *Antología del tango rioplatense*, 241.

9. Inés Cuello, "La coreografía del tango," in *Antología del Tango Rioplatense, Vol I (Desde sus comienzos hasta 1920)*, ed. Jorge Novati (Buenos Aires: Instituto Nacional de Musicología "Carlos Vega," 2018), 125.

10. Throughout this book, the editors chose the term *tango canción* to describe the genre of sung tango and translate it literally throughout for consistency. However, some scholars disagree with this phrase and many scholars in Argentina use the phrases *tango instrumental* and *tango cantando* (instrumental tango or sung tango).

11. Omar García Brunelli, "Gardel músico. Su proyección en la historia del tango," in *El mudo del tango. Ocho estudios sobre Carlos Gardel*, Omar García Brunelli, ed. (Buenos Aires: Instituto Nacional de Musicología, 2020), 59–76.

12. For more information, see Rosalba Campra, *Como con bronca y junando . . . : La retórica del tango* (Buenos Aires: Edicial, 1996).

Further Reading

Binda, Enrique, and Hugo Lamas. *El tango en la sociedad porteña 1880–1920*. Buenos Aires: Héctor Lorenzo Lucci Ediciones, 1998.

Cuello, Inés. "La coreografía del tango." In *Antología del tango rioplatense: Vol. 1 Desde los orígenes hasta 1920*, edited by Jorge Novati, 4th edition edited by Omar García Brunelli, 123–140. Buenos Aires: Instituto Nacional de Musicología "Carlos Vega," 2018.

García Brunelli, Omar. "Bases para una aproximación razonable a la cuestión del componente afro del tango." *Revista Argentina de Musicología*, 18 (2017): 91–124.

    ed. *El mudo del tango. Ocho estudios sobre Carlos Gardel*. Buenos Aires: Instituto Nacional de Musicología "Carlos Vega," 2020.

Kohan, Pablo et al. "Tango." In *Diccionario de la Música Española e Hispanoamericana*, edited by Emilio Casares Rodicio, Vol. 10, 143–154. Madrid: Sgae, 2002.

Novati, Jorge, ed. *Antología del tango rioplatense: Vol. 1 Desde los orígenes hasta 1920*. Buenos Aires: Instituto Nacional de Musicología "Carlos Vega," 1980. Page references in this chapter are from the 4th edition edited by Omar García Brunelli, 2018.

    "Aspectos Histórico-Musicales." In *Antología del Tango Rioplatense: Vol. 1 Desde sus comienzos hasta 1920*, edited by Jorge Novati, 4th edition edited by Omar García Brunelli, 15–76. Buenos Aires: Instituto Nacional de Musicología, 2018.

Ruiz, Irma, and Néstor Ceñal. "La estructura del tango." In *Antología del Tango Rioplatense Vol. 1: Desde sus comienzos hasta 1920*, edited by Jorge Novati, 4th edition edited by Omar García Brunelli, 77–122. Buenos Aires: Instituto Nacional de Musicología, 2018.

Vilariño, Idea. *Las letras del tango*. Buenos Aires: Schapire, 1966.

PART I

Tango Music

2 | The Bandoneón: The Magical Sound and Soul of Tango

ORTAÇ AYDINOĞLU

The bandoneón – with its distinctive and distinguished timbre – is regarded as the "sound of tango" and even the "sound of Buenos Aires." This sound automatically connects listeners to tango music and represents the emotions of *porteños* (people from Buenos Aires). Ironically, the bandoneón was invented as an easy-to-play instrument of religious music in European churches but is actually "diabolically" difficult – as described by legendary bandoneonist Astor Piazzolla (1921–1992)[1] – and was brought to life through popular music in the brothels of South America. One might say that as an instrument, the bandoneón has shared the same destiny as the tango in their similar life paths. Just as *tangueros* (tango musicians) have embraced an immigrant instrument as their own child, the city of Buenos Aires has welcomed immigrant people into a cultural melting pot to create its own art form, the tango.

The strong connection between the bandoneón and tango has been referenced in many pieces as well as influenced many tango artists over the years. To some *tangueros*, the bandoneón has become a friend – a living being with its own persona and soul. Tango poets and musicians have expressed their love and passion for this so-called friend with tangos such as "Che bandoneón" ("Hey, Bandoneón"), "Bandoneón amigo" ("Bandoneón Friend"), and "Mi fueye querido" ("My Beloved Bellows [*porteños* often refer to the bandoneón as the *fueye*]"). Others have noted its person-like qualities with the words: "Alma de bandoneón" ("Soul of Bandoneón"), "Calla bandoneón" ("Shut Up, Bandoneón"), or "Yo soy el bandoneón" ("I Am the Bandoneón"). Sometimes *tangueros* have personified the instrument, describing its "*sollozo*" (sob) or "*quejas*" (complaints), or even have described how it moans as in the tango "Mientras gime el bandoneón" ("While the bandoneón moans").

In this chapter, I describe the poignant and expatriate adventure of the bandoneón through its history and origins. Then, I examine the mechanics of this difficult instrument and its basic performance practices. Highlighting some of the most prominent performers, I end by discussing the timbre of the bandoneón and how its sound became the soul of the tango.

31

A Brief History of the Bandoneón

Origins

The bandoneón is a free-reed aerophone developed and named by German instrument maker and dealer Heinrich Band (1821–1860) in the 1850s. It belongs to the concertina family of free-reed instruments such as the harmonium, harmonica, accordion, and concertina. From the mid-1820s, European instrument makers were experimenting with developing free-reed instruments. They created those such as the free-reed (mouth) harmonica in 1828, the accordion in 1829, the unisonoric (single action, thus each button produces one pitch) "English" concertina, and the bisonoric (double action, thus each button produces two different pitches depending on the opening or closing of the bellows) German "Chemintz" concertina in 1834. In 1849, Carl Friedrich Zimmermann introduced the German "Carlsfelder" concertina, which explored alternative button layouts. Simultaneously, Band was developing his concertina, which later became known as the bandoneón.[2]

Band was a cellist, music teacher, and instrument dealer from Krefeld, Germany. His family owned a musical instrument shop that he eventually took over and expanded. During this period in Germany, free-reed instruments were enormously popular among the upper classes, and Band sold many accordions and harmonicas for leisure pastime.[3] Yet, many of these instruments were limited in pitches and range, with some having only twenty buttons (ten on each side). Like many other instrument makers, Band had innumerable ideas for improving these small squeezeboxes, including increasing the number of pitches and augmenting their range as well as refining their overall appearance. During the mid-1800s, he experimented by creating different models, varying the number of buttons, and exploring alternative keyboard layouts.

Along with his new concertina models, Band wrote method books to help amateurs learn how to play. According to musicologist Janine Krüger, Band began in 1846 with a method book for his fifty-six-note instrument and then updated this manual every few years with the latest developments.[4] Additionally, he wrote pieces for his instruments to expand the repertory to include classical, pop, folk, and general entertainment music, for example, his *Fantasie Nr. 2* (WL 2.1).

In the beginning, Band identified his instruments with the basic names of accordion, harmonica, or concertina. In 1850, he debuted his eighty-eight-tone instrument, with twenty-three buttons on the left-hand side, or bass range, and twenty-one buttons on the right-hand side, or treble range.[5] Band first called it the "bandonino." One theory is that he combined his name "Band" and the word "union" – referring to the collective of a small-scale orchestra – to create the word "bandonion." Another theory is that "union" refers to the cooperative formed to fundraise for the instrument's construction.[6] Over time, the instrument's name went through a variety of incarnations as it traveled through cultures, but it eventually settled on the Spanish "bandoneón."

Travelling from Europe to South America

Rather than producing the bandoneón himself, Band enlisted other har-monica and accordion manufacturers to make his instrument. One manu-facturer of these late-nineteenth century bandoneones was Ernest Louis Arnold (1828–1910), who sold his instruments labeled "ELA" bando-neones to Argentine importer Alberto Ohermann. Then, Ernest's son Alfred Arnold (1877–1933) took over the business and created the com-monly known "AA" bandoneón. As nearly 90 percent of the production was exported, these instruments spread throughout the Americas and specifically Argentina.[7]

The instruments travelled with European sailors, merchants, and immi-grants, who were either working or settling in the economically booming Argentina at the turn of the twentieth century. Sources differ as to who first introduced the instrument to Argentina. Héctor and Luis Bates identify Bartolo ("El Brasilero," "The Brazilian") as playing a thirty-two-tone instrument in 1870 in Argentina.[8] They also mention Don Tomás ("El Inglés," "The Englishman") as playing it in 1884.[9] At this time, nobody was aware that the Atlantic journey of this squeezebox would lead to it becom-ing the sound of this cultural melting pot's new art form, the tango. Yet later, as tango grew in popularity, instrument makers and dealers began advertising the bandoneón as "the only instrument for a perfect interpret-ation of Argentine tango."[10]

Mechanical Aspects

The bandoneón contains three main outer pieces: bellows and two button-boards, or keyboards (Figure 2.1).[11] Behind each keyboard, there is a soundboard, on which free reeds are fixed to metal plates and then plates are attached to wooden blocks (Figure 2.2). Different pitched reeds vibrate

Figure 2.1 The bandoneón.

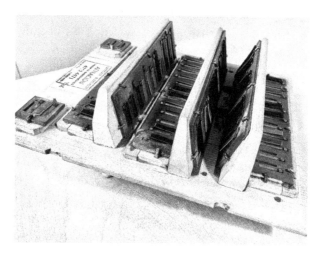

Figure 2.2 The soundboard of the bandoneón.

in the same cell depending on aspiration or expiration (the opening or closing of the bellows); thus, one button produces two different pitches.[12]

There are two individual reeds for each pitch tuned in octaves. The octave doublings add to the richness of the instrument's timbre, making it unique among the other members of the free-reed family. As Ertuğrul Sevsay notes in his orchestration book: "The very typical, melancholic sound of the bandoneón surpasses that of all the other accordion instruments and lends the Argentinian tango orchestra its special sound color."[13]

The bandoneón of today, the 142-tone "*Rheinisch*" (named after Rhine River) has thirty-eight buttons on the right/treble side and thirty-three buttons on the left/bass side. Each keyboard has a distinct pitch layout that changes depending on the opening (*abriendo*, "A") or closing (*cerrando*, "C") of the bellows. Consequently, there are four different keyboard layouts (Fig. 2.3).[14] Due to this, Piazzolla states: "it's very diabolic. The person who is interested in learning this instrument [the bandoneón] must be a little out of his mind."[15] Although the bandoneón's pitch range is almost five octaves (C_2–B_6), it does not include every chromatic note (Ex. 2.1). The bandoneón's notation, similar to the piano, utilizes the grand staff with both treble and bass clefs.

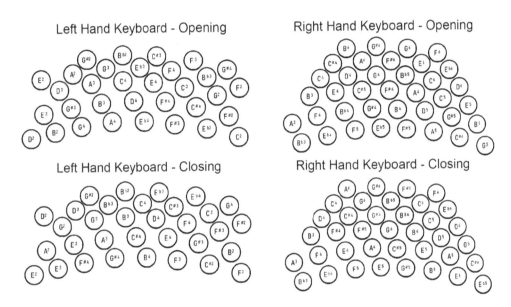

Figure 2.3 The layout of the bandoneón keyboards.

Example 2.1 Register of the bandoneón. The downbow (⊓) pitches only exist when opening the bellows. The upbow (∨) pitches only exist when closing the bellows. The single-star pitch only exists on the right side, not the left side, and the double-star pitch does not exist on the instrument.

Performance Features

Even though the instrument may be held via neck or shoulder straps when standing, performers usually play the bandoneón seated. They place the bandoneón, or *fueye*, on their thighs, and their legs follow the movement of the bellows to support the weight of the instrument. To produce tango's signature *marcato* (marked) rhythm, which literally marks the steady beat of the music, players frequently position the instrument on a single leg and support it by hitting their heel on the ground to suddenly stop the motion of the bellows. This style of executing the *marcato* accompaniment creates tango's powerful rhythmic drive. It is also possible to play the bandoneón standing up while holding the instrument on one thigh, as in the case of Piazzolla. According to bandoneonist Eva Wolff, "This position was introduced by Domingo Federico and later adopted by Astor Piazzolla as his own way of playing."[16]

The four fingers of each hand play the buttons on each side, and the right thumb controls the valve for exhaling or inhaling the air. Thus, one places thumbs outside the straps. Whether to play a passage by opening or closing the bellows is up to the performer.

Becoming "The Magical Sound and Soul of Tango"

Tango and bandoneón lived together in their bohemia.

Vicente Rossi[17]

The Bandoneón's Entrance into Tango

In the beginning, the bandoneón found hard resistances in the tango world. The art form was initially played by amateur musicians forming trios consisting of guitar/harp, violin, and flute. Moreover, many amateur musicians were not well educated and lacked the time and energy to learn such a difficult instrument as the bandoneón. Gradually, the flute began to yield its position within the tango ensemble, and the overall character of the music changed from frisky and jolly to weighty and pensive. With this transition, the bandoneón slowly seeped into the art form and undoubtedly became the progenitor of this transformation to a plaintive and sentimental tone.[18]

According to Argentine historian Luis A. Sierra, Sebastián Ramos Mejía (exact dates unknown), nicknamed "El pardo" ("The Brown"), was one of the first to introduce the bandoneón to tango.[19] He was a freed son of slaves of the Ramos Mejía family and according to some, the first master of the bandoneón.[20] During the day, he worked as a coachman on the early Buenos Aires-Belgrano tram. At night, he played tango in the clubs of Buenos Aires and later across the river in Montevideo. In 1903, he taught tango composer and bandoneonist Vicente Greco (1888–1924) to play the bandoneón. In Mejía's honor the great tango lyricist Enrique Cadícamo published his poem titled "Poema al primer bandoneonista" ("Poem to the First Bandoneonist") in 1964.[21] Other early bandoneón players in Buenos Aires and Montevideo include José Scott, Domingo Repetto, Pablo "El Negro" Romero, and Antonio Chiappe.[22]

The Bandoneón in the Hands of Tango Masters

The bandoneón continuously won new adepts by attracting many musicians with a preference for tango as the genre ascended to a popular art form in Buenos Aires. Over time, excellent players emerged who continuously increased the standard of playing, while new instrument models allowed for added possibilities. They ultimately shaped the morphology of the instrument until its final, sui generis (unique) design. From the early days of tango up to today, these masters have elevated bandoneón performance to a level of virtuosic and passionate artistic fervor. It can be said that *porteños* adopted and adapted the bandoneón.

The Guardia Vieja (Old Guard)

The bandoneón became an established tango instrument in the hands of such talented and passionate players in the early tango period known as the *guardia vieja*. Juan Maglio ("Pacho," 1881–1934) recorded the first solo bandoneón "La sonámbula" ("The [Female] Sleepwalker") in 1913 (WL 2.2). In this recording, Maglio plays a *habanera* accompaniment providing harmonic support in the left hand and a legato melody with small embellishments in the right hand; later, the left hand plays the melody in the lower register. While there is no audible vibrato or staccato in this recording, one can hear the soulful phrasing of typical tango. Arturo Bernstein (1882–1935) advanced the standard of playing with his immaculate technique and profound musical knowledge. Domingo Santa Cruz (1884–1931), known for his amazing dexterity, created *variaciones* (variations) – a key melodic feature of tango, typically played by bandoneones, that embellishes the main melody with fast passagework.

Eduardo Arolas (1892–1924), known as "El Tigre del bandoneón" ("The Tiger of the Bandoneón") stands out as perhaps the greatest *guardia vieja* icon. Arolas was not a virtuoso performer, yet he created a style of playing that had a distinct influence on the sound of the tango orchestra. Eliminating the shrill tones and the monotonous marking of sharp rhythm, he strived for a sensitive and clear sound in favor of legato phrasing and more dynamics.[23] Arolas banished the widespread showy way some players handled the bandoneón that inevitably distorted its noble sound. He introduced *fraseo octavado* (phrasing/playing in octaves) and playing passages in thirds with both hands.[24] He also introduced the *arrastre* (drag) technique,[25] which became a characteristic tango feature. The tango historian Marcelo Solis aptly describes the bandoneón's sound in the hand of Arolas:

As a musician, he gave the strength of his emotion to his performances, breaking his instrument on many occasions, leaving it like an umbrella inverted by a strong wind. . . . His musical language, as a composer and as a player, was purely tango, a language that the people of the neighborhoods of Río de la Plata understand, a language that flows effortlessly like spring water. His performance was vibrantly brilliant, simple, without variations, very nuanced and colorful.[26]

Arolas's 1913 bandoneón solo in the tango *vals* (waltz) "Arancetti" (It., "Oranges") illustrates the early maestro's sound (WL 2.3).

The Guardia Nueva *(New Guard)*

Innovations for the bandoneón's technique and sound continued into the era of the *guardia nueva* (New Guard). Two remarkable players, both named Pedro and of Julio De Caro's Sextet,[27] brought bandoneón technique to a new level: Pedro Maffia (1899–1967) and Pedro Laurenz (1902–1972). While both strengthened bandoneón *arrastres*, Maffia created a more strident and aggressive sonority by his way of opening the bellows and mastered a velvety sound with his soft and legato playing, as heard in his performance of "Heliotropo" ("Heliotrope," type of flower, WL 2.4) from the film *Fuelle querido* (*Dear Bellows*, Mauricio Berú, 1966).[28] Laurenz projected a brilliant sound with his vigorous yet expressive playing couched in eloquent, fluid *fraseos*, heard in "Orgullo criollo" ("Creole Pride," WL 2.5). He also mastered the variation technique with both hands, as heard in "Amurado" ("Abandoned" in *Lunfardo*, WL 2.6). Their impact on bandoneonists was so significant that many tangos have been composed in homage to them, including "Pedro y Pedro" (Piazzolla),

"A Pedro Maffia" (Aníbal Troilo), and "Tocá el bandoneón, Pedrito!" ("Play the Bandoneón, Little Pedro!" Raúl Garello). Ciriaco Ortiz (1905–1970), another bandoneonist who has found a permanent place in the instrument's history, is known for his highly personal phrasing utilizing both hands and his octave appoggiaturas. Ortiz's performance of "El Marne" ("The Marne," referencing the WWI battle, WL 2.7) with his trio illustrates his full range of colors and his rich expressive sound. As innovators of the *guardia nueva*, Maffia, Láurenz, and Ortiz prepared the new era of bandoneón playing.[29]

The Golden Age

Of the many marvelous bandoneón virtuosos from tango's Golden Age (1930s to the mid–1950s), one has been regarded by all *tangueros* as "el bandoneón mayor de Buenos Aires" ("the greatest bandoneón of Buenos Aires"): Aníbal Troilo (1914–1975), nicknamed "El Gordo" ("The Chubby") and "Pichuco."[30] Sierra describes Troilo's sound as a "synthesis of the sonoric delicacy of Maffia, the harmonic brilliance of Láurenz, and the distinctive *fraseo octavado* of Ortiz"[31] – a synthesis of the *guardia nueva* bandoneón school. Tango historian Néstor Pinsón explains why:

He [Troilo] was one of those few artists who made us wonder what mystery, what magic produced such a rapport with people. As a bandoneón player, he was neither a stylist like Pedro Maffia, nor a virtuoso like Carlos Marcucci, nor a multiple creator like Pedro Láurenz, nor a phrasing player like Ciriaco Ortiz. But he had something of them all and he was, precisely, a master of personality and feeling in his expression.[32]

Troilo produced his masterful sound from the *fueye* through his touch, phrasing, ornamentation, use of dynamics, left-hand solos, and inimitable vibrato. All these hallmarks can be heard in his recording of "La cachila" ("The Little Bird," WL 2.8) with guitarist Roberto Grela, where, as another tango's title describes, "Pichuco le canta a su bandoneón" ("Pichuco sings to his bandoneón").

The Post–Golden Age

In the late 1940s, Astor Piazzolla (1921–1992) emerged as a young, brilliant bandoneonist through innovative performance practices, and as an outstanding composer with his new compositional concept of tango called *nuevo tango* (New Tango). In terms of performance, Piazzolla uniquely played the bandoneón in a standing position, propping one foot up to support the instrument's weight. He chose the standing position for both artistic and acoustic reasons: "for many years I played it sitting down, like most of my colleagues, until I became a soloist. Then I felt the need to look for a different position, more in tune with my personality. Sitting down I felt tied down."[33] As the soloist-leader in his band, he wanted to be seen clearly by both the audience and members of the group. The standing position additionally allowed him to use gravity to produce a more powerful sound when opening the bellows (despite the less convenient action of pushing against gravity when closing the bellows).

Piazzolla also introduced the important feature of improvisation to bandoneón playing. Although bandoneonists had already been using their own interpretive ornamentations such as mordents, appoggiaturas, grace notes, chromatic passing notes, and rhythmic elasticity in *fraseos*, Piazzolla took such improvisational elements to a new level. As a soloist in his own ensemble, Piazzolla had the freedom to improvise by adding more notes like *grupettos* (turns), scalar/interscalar passages, repetitions of a note or a figure, and playing outside the fundamental melody. He also frequently gave space to the other musicians to improvise.

Piazzolla's famous tango, "Adiós Nonino" ("Goodbye Nonino," a name of endearment for the composer's father), illustrates his improvisational style. Even though one may hear the melody as a free tango *fraseo*, it is closer to a jazz improvisation. Example 2.2, a transcription of "Adiós Nonino," shows how he would choose between which structural notes to play and which to elaborate, similar to how a jazz player embellishes the main notes of a tune. Furthermore, Piazzolla's execution of a melody often differed from one performance to another. With such melodic innovations, he influenced *tangueros*, who mostly played traditional *fraseo*. Thus, he opened another path to the next generation of bandoneonists for ways to improvise a solo part.[34]

Piazzolla not only made such innovations in his style of playing tango music, but he was also the most prominent *tanguero* to bring tango music and the bandoneón to concert halls. In his hands on stage, the *fueye* was always playing the leading role. Furthermore, he composed pieces in more classical forms, from operatic works like *María de Buenos Aires* to solo and orchestral works such as the bandoneón concerto *Aconcagua* (named for the highest Andean peak, located in Mendoza, Argentina), and cyclical collections like the famous *Las cuatro estaciones porteñas* (*The Four Seasons of Buenos Aires*). For the first time in history, the magical squeezebox of tango became a soloist in the classical world as it took the stage in the most prestigious concert halls of the world.

Example 2.2 "Adiós Nonino" ("Goodbye Nonino") transcription, mm. 86–89 (see audio, WL 2.9).

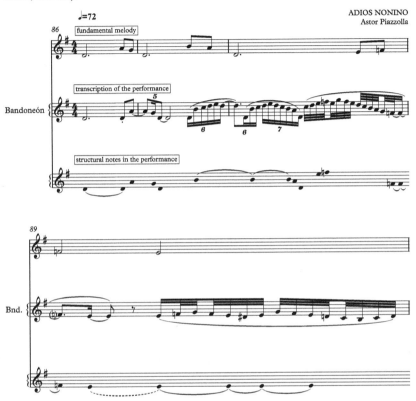

Other post–Golden Age bandoneonists made their mark in tango history through their compositions, arrangements, and performances. For instance, in line with Maffia, Laurenz, Ortiz, Troilo, and Piazzolla, many tango aficionados consider Leopoldo Federico (1927–2014) to be the most consummate modern bandoneonist of tango with his excellent playing skills.[35] In addition, other bandoneón masters expanded their technical and musical abilities through improvisation,[36] as well as their own distinctive solo arrangements and harmonizations.[37] For that reason, almost all the 1950s generation of bandoneonists who led their own orchestras were also arrangers, such as Osvaldo Ruggiero (1922–1994) and Víctor Lavallén (b. 1935). Even bandoneonists Emilio Balcarce (1918–2011) and Julián Plaza (1928–2003), who formed Sexteto Tango, and José Libertella (1933–2004) and Luis Stazo (1930–2016), who formed Sexteto Mayor, were arrangers as well as performers. Younger *maestros* also have made arrangements and recordings for solo bandoneón and brought the *fueye*

from an ensemble instrument to a solo recital instrument, such as Raúl Garello (1936–2016), Rodolfo Mederos (b. 1940), Néstor Marconi (b. 1942), Walter Ríos (b. 1942), and Juan José Mosalini (1943–2022). Dino Saluzzi (b. 1935) composes and plays in folklore and jazz styles as a soloist and with his band; thus, he has opened another new path for the bandoneón.

The New Generation

The new generation of bandoneonists, dating from 2000 to the present, is furthering tango's musical and artistic heritage. Three players, namely Víctor Hugo Villena (b. 1979), Lautaro Greco (b. 1987), and Santiago Segret (b. 1988), are not only advancing bandoneón playing technically and music-ally, but they are expanding the international profile of bandoneonists. Villena, a young Argentine living in Europe, is one of the most sought-after virtuoso bandoneonists. His career and musical language lean toward modern and new compositions for solo bandoneón and tango ensemble projects. He has brought a new expressive style of playing that combines modern-classical (avant-garde) music and tango, heard in his performance of "Bandoneón Legüero" (the title is a word game between a bandoneón and a bombo legüero, a traditional Argentine drum, WL 2.10). Even at his young age, Greco is already considered a genius of the contemporary tango world with his technical mastery, strong sound, and vast repertory. On the other hand, Segret applies his brilliant talent, technique, and sonority to combine his classical, folklore, and tango background, exemplified in his performance of "Tanguera" (female tango musician, WL 2.11).

Bandoneón players today come not only from Argentina but also from Europe, North America, and Asia. For example, Dutch bandoneonist Carel Kraayenhof (b. 1958) founded the Sexteto Canyengue in 1988 in the Netherlands; Japanese bandoneonist Ryōta Komatsu (b. 1973) has collab-orated with the Argentine contemporary tango group Bajofondo; Swiss/Argentinian bandoneonist Michael Zisman (b. 1982) also plays jazz; and I, a Turkish bandoneonist, have led my orchestra TangEsta since 2012.

The Bandoneón in the Tango Orchestra: Colors and Function

In early tango, before the bandoneón came to Argentina, musicians played with crisp staccato articulation in fast tempos. When the bandoneón became part of the ensembles, it provided another sonic way to play longer legato lines as it influenced the slower tempos. One may say that as the bandoneón integrated into tango, it gave the art form a soulful element it was missing. And, perhaps, the bandoneón simultaneously found the music for which it seemed to be created.

The distinct sound colors of the bandoneón enable musicians to play tango, expressing different emotional qualities. Through the instrument, bandoneonists convey both sadness and joy with expressive, legato playing and sparkling, staccato notes, respectively. One may describe the bandoneón as having an overall velvet-like sound with a more mellow lower register and a brighter higher register. Bandoneonists often describe the instrument's three main melodic colors as *canta* (treble/descant), *bajo* (bass), and *dos manos* (a combination of both hands).[38] Interestingly, upon the request of tango bandoneonists, German producers expanded the bass range of the instrument, and perhaps the darker colors heightened the tango's soulful sound.

As a popular-music genre, tango typically uses song forms in a melody-accompaniment texture.[39] While the piano and bass often form the accompaniment group and the strings usually function as melodic instruments, the colorful and versatile bandoneón effectively functions in both melodic and accompaniment roles. Further, the bandoneones are even able to play two roles at the same time, as in "La yumba" (referencing Pugliese's signature rhythmic technique, WE 2.1, WL 2.12).[40]

Variations at the end of pieces allow the bandoneones to shine. The small buttons of the bandoneón keyboard enable musicians to play very quick, bright notes to show the virtuosity and the joyful character of tango. The disjunct pitch layout of the keyboard also lends itself to playing leaps or large intervals notes rapidly. According to Sierra, variations by the bandoneones, along with other musical elements like *fraseos*, signified a few of the most valuable contributions made by Julio de Caro (1899–1980) and his "two Pedros" playing tango.[41] In the Golden Age, bandoneón variations became crucial to project the climax of a piece, as in the style of Juan D'Arienzo (1900–1976). Frequently, bandoneón variations are played *soli* and in parts. In fact, sometimes the bandoneón variations might be more famous and recognizable than the tango itself, as in "Canaro en París" ("Canaro in Paris," WL 2.13),[42] "Quejas de bandoneón" ("Wail of the Bandoneón," WL 2.14) with variations by Feliciano Brunelli, and "La cumparsita" ("The Little Parade," WL 2.15) with the famous variations of Louis Moresco.

In the *orquesta típica* (typical tango orchestra), the bandoneón *fila* (line) generally consists of four bandoneones sitting in front of the violins, and, as the leader of the *fila*, the first bandoneonist plays the solo parts. The standard seating (from the audience's perspective left to right) is Bnd. 4 (Bnd. 1B) – Bnd. 1 (Bnd. 1A) – Bnd. 2 – Bnd. 3. The fourth bandoneonist commonly doubles the first bandoneonist in unison or octaves; therefore, they share the same part, and composers notate it as "Bnd. 1A" and "1B."[43] When the first bandoneonist plays a melodic solo, they deepen the sadness and nostalgia associated with tango by expressively pulling or pushing sound out of the instrument's bellows to create long legato lines. Troilo beautifully illustrates this in "Quejas de bandoneón" (WE 2.2, WL 2.16). Also note, he plays the solo line in his left hand in the tenor register, a hallmark of his style.

Right-hand bandoneón solos in the treble register are also a frequent feature in tango. As Sierra mentions, "Ciriaco Ortiz brought from his native Cordoba a different way of phrasing … although in a plane of less harmonic ornamentation than the previous ones."[44] His very personal *fraseos octavados* (phrasings in octaves) in the right hand, full of color and deep essence of tango, found a permanent place in the instrument's technical canon, as can be seen especially in Troilo's phrasings. Ortiz's 1936 trio recording of "Inspiración" ("Inspiration," WL 2.17) provides an excellent example of *fraseos octavados* in both manners, that is playing the melody with both hands at the same time or with an octave appoggiatura ornamentation. The appoggiatura ornamentation preceding the upper octave is a very characteristic performance practice of the phrasing, especially in solos, as heard in "A Evaristo Carriego" ("To Evaristo Carriego," WE 2.3, WL 2.18).

Playing a melody with both hands in octaves or intervals, such as thirds or sixths, is another common feature of bandoneón arranging in tango, especially for ensembles with a single bandoneón. It can be executed as a duet, as in "Café Domínguez" ("Cafe Dominguez," WL 2.19), or as a dialog between two hands in *soli*, as in "Recuerdo" ("Remembrance," WE 2.4, WL 2.20). The left-hand *soli* part in voices creates another color, as heard in Pugliese's 1972 recording of "El andariego" ("The Walker," WL 2.21). Besides these colors of the bandoneón in the melodic role in the tango orchestra, the *fueye*, as a polyphonic instrument capable of playing multiple parts at the same time, is also played as a solo instrument, as heard in Federico's performance of "Che bandoneón" ("Hey, Bandoneón," WL 2.22).

In the accompaniment role, the bandoneón can play open-spaced chords to produce a rich harmony and sound, even with four fingers in one hand. With its expressive and flexible sound possibilities, the instrument also provides a perfect accompaniment when other instruments play the melody. It can support passionate melodies by producing a sound like a plucked instrument with a sharp attack; it can play long-held notes with vibrato as in the string instruments; or it can produce a *subito* (sudden) dynamic change and *crescendo* or *decrescendo* rapidly like a horn section. When in the accompaniment role, bandoneonists may interpret the execution of a given harmonic and rhythmic structure differently if it is written only with chord symbols.

The bandoneón also helped shape the tango sound in general as other instruments developed *yeites* (percussive instrumental tango techniques) to imitate its distinctive colors. For instance, string players and pianists invented unconventional techniques to imitate the very sharp and strong *staccatissimo* accompaniment sound a bandoneón player executes on one thigh, called *bien marcato* (literally "well marked," but describes an accompaniment style of playing chords *forte* and *marcato* on each beat to strongly emphasize the rhythm, as heard in D'Arienzo's style). Other techniques have been developed for the instruments of the tango orchestra to produce *arrastre*, which is a natural sound for the *fueye*. Since no percussion instruments exist in the classical tango orchestra, musicians found ways to produce percussive rhythmic effects. The *fueye* especially lends itself to such effects, as performers can use almost any part of the instrument percussively. They may hit behind the buttons on the left keyboard or employ several specific techniques like *raspado* (scraping, scratching the buttons with fingers), *vómito* (vomit, a violent *arrastre* with clusters while closing the bellows), *marcato sin altura* (marked without pitch, the gesture of *marcato* but the actual percussive sound comes from the air moving through the bellows).[45]

With all these features and functional possibilities, the bandoneón established itself as a standard sound in tango music. Well-suited to the music of Buenos Aires, its timbre conveys a wide range of expressions and emotions, from lyrical to dramatic and from melancholic to joyful. One may even say its sounds and colors capture the rapid emotional changes of *porteños*, as it breathes and responds like a human. Since its first appearance in tango orchestras, the bandoneón has become an indispensable instrument and the iconic sound of tango.

Although the bandoneón's story began in Europe, where it was played in churches or upper-class house parties, it migrated to South America. As an exile in this new continent, the instrument found itself playing in the brothels of Buenos Aires for lower-class immigrant entertainment. Then, in the hands of highly gifted and passionate musicians, the *fueye* rose to become a respected instrument – even the star of the most prestigious concert halls. Yet, its sound is bittersweet, perhaps representing the same sentiment of *porteños* as they share the instrument's immigrant destiny. With its exuberant joy and contrastingly mournful sadness, the bandoneón remembers its past inside its bellows, which eternally emit its bohemian essence creating the magical sound and soul of the tango.

Notes

1. Mike Dibb, director, *Astor Piazzolla: In Portrait* (Opus Arte, 2005).
2. For further discussion about the invention of bandoneón, see Gorka Hermosa, *The Accordion in the 19th Century* (Santander, Spain: Editorial Kattigara, 2013), 19.
3. For more information, see Janine Krüger, *Heinrich Band* (Essen, Germany: Klartext Verlag, 2020), 54.
4. Krüger, *Heinrich Band*, 54.
5. For the layout of the pitches, see Krüger, *Heinrich Band*, 59–60.
6. Oscar Zucchi, "The bandoneón, name, origin and manufacturers," *Todotango*, www.todotango.com/english/history/chronicle/149/The-bandoneon-name-origin-and-manufacturers/.
7. "History: Extract from the history of Carlsfeld," *Carlsfeld*, www.carlsfeld.com/history.html.
8. Oscar Zucchi, "The Bandoneon in the River Plate, Part II," *Todotango*, www.todotango.com/english/history/chronicle/202/The-Bandoneon-in-the-River-Plate-Part-II/.
9. Ibid.
10. Zucchi, "The bandoneon, name, origin, and manufacturers."
11. Editors' Note: in Spanish, the term *teclado* (keyboard) refers to the buttonboard/keyboard, and *teclas* (keys) refer to the individual buttons/keys. In English, they are referred to as "buttons," not "keys."
12. For further information, see Carsten Heveling, *Bandoneon*, https://bando-bando.de/kontakt.html.
13. Ertuğrul Sevsay, *The Cambridge Guide to Orchestration* (New York: Cambridge University Press, 2013), 136.
14. Burak Şendağ, *Bandoneon: Play, learn and practise*, iPhone and iPad application, https://apps.apple.com/tr/app/bandoneon/id546330120.
15. Mike Dibb, *Astor Piazzolla*. See also the live interview at the BBC Bristol Studios in June 1989, www.youtube.com/watch?v=dt5pQqxWlaE&t=134s.
16. For further information see Eva Wolff, *El bandoneón en el tango/The Bandoneón in Tango* (Buenos Aires: Tango Sin Fin, 2018): 15–16.

17. "Tango y bandonéon vivieron juntos su bohemia." Luis A. Sierra, *Historia de la orquesta típica: Evolución instrumental del tango* (Buenos Aires: Peña Lillo, 1984), 28.

18. Sierra, *Historia de la orquesta típica*, 29.

19. Ibid., 27–32. See also Zucchi, "The Bandoneon in the River Plate, Part II"; Marcelo Solis, "History of Tango – Part 5: The Appearance of the Bandoneon in Tango," *Argentine Tango School*, https://escuelatangoba.com/marcelosolis/history-of-tango-part-5/.

20. Robert Farris Thompson, *Tango: The Art History of Love* (New York: Vintage Books, 2005), 178.

21. Enrique Cadícamo, *Poemas del bajo fondo; viento que lleva y trae* (Buenos Aires: Peña Lillo, 1964).

22. Sierra, *Historia de la orquesta típica*, 30.

23. Sierra, *Historia de la orquesta típica*, 56.

24. Sierra credits Arolas for *fraseos octavados*, *Historia de la orquesta típica*, 43, 56. However, Salgán mentions Ortiz as the creator of *fraseos octavados*, *Curso de Tango*, 99. In Salgán's example, he refers to an ornamentation technique (explained later in the chapter), but Sierra is probably referring to a technique of playing either in octaves or thirds with both hands at the same time. Both techniques are called *fraseo octavado*.

25. For further discussions about the inventor of *arrastre*, see Kacey Link and Kristin Wendland, *Tracing Tangueros* (New York: Oxford University Press, 2016), 50, 95.

26. Solis, "History of Tango – Part 5."

27. Link and Wendland, *Tracing Tangueros*, 59, 144–145.

28. Sierra, *Historia de la orquesta típica*, 72–73.

29. These three maestros, as well as Troilo and Piazzolla, play solos in Berú's 1966 film *Fuelle querido*. See WL 2.4.

30. Link and Wendland cite that "Pichuco" means "little dog" in *Lunfardo* (*Tracing Tangueros*, 158). Thompson notes that "Pichuco" is a 1940s Argentine comic strip character. *Tango: The Art History of Love*, 192. In addition, Lavocah notes: "He acquired his nickname as an infant. The word is likely a variant of *picciuso*, which means cry-baby in the Neapolitan dialect. His father would pick him up and say: Don't cry, pichuco!" Michael Lavocah, *Tango Masters: Aníbal Troilo* (Norwich: Milonga Press), 149.

31. Sierra, *Historia de la orquesta típica*, 96.

32. Néstor Pinsón, "Aníbal Troilo," *Todotango*, www.todotango.com/english/artists/biography/50/Anibal-Troilo/.

33. Natailo Gorin, *Astor Piazzolla: A Memoir* (Portland, OR: Amadeus Press, 2001), 142.

34. For a more detailed study of improvisation on bandoneón playing of modern bandoneonists, see Santiago Cimadevilla, "Construction of Bandoneón Solos in Argentine Tango Music" (unpublished master's thesis, Artistic Research

Case Study, Codarts World Music Academy, Rotterdam, Netherlands, 2012); see also Martín Kutnowski, "Instrumental Rubato and Phrase Structure in Astor Piazzolla's Music," *Latin American Music Review* 23, no. 1 (2002): 106–113. www.jstor.org/stable/780427.

35. Link and Wendland, *Tracing* Tangueros, 275.

36. For more on bandoneón improvisation, see Rubén Juárez's discussion of "Malena," www.youtube.com/watch?v=8RfHEOQi89E.

37. Standard bandoneón solo arrangements were not widely circulated or published during this period. For a compilation of fourteen arrangements of tangos by Troilo, see the homage collection *Troilo Compositor*, Discos Río de la Plata / CD 78190014, 2012, and Walter Ríos' performance of his arrangement of Troilo's "Garua" ("Drizzle"), www.youtube.com/watch?v=KPwL85SAZqk.

38. Playing in both hands is indicated as "*C y B*" or a trill-like symbol after writing the beginning of the phrase in intended octave.

39. For further information, see Ortaç Aydınoğlu, "Arjantin Tango Müziğinde Orkestrasyon Stilleri (Orchestration Styles in Argentine Tango Music)" (PhD diss., İstanbul Technical University, 2019); Julián Peralta, *La orquesta típica: mecánica y aplicación de los fundamentos técnicos del tango* (Buenos Aires: Editorial de Puerto, 2013); Horacio Salgán, *Curso de Tango* (Buenos Aires: Pablo J. Polidoro, 2001), translated into English by Will Genz and Harisa Hurtado as *Tango Course*, 2nd ed., 2001; and Pascual Mamone, with Diego Sauchelli and Julián Hasse, *Tratado de Orquestación en Estilos Tangueros* (Buenos Aires: Altavoz Ediciones Musicales, 2011).

40. Aydınoğlu, "Arjantin Tango Müziğinde Orkestrasyon Stilleri," 79.

41. Sierra, *Historia de la orquesta típica*, 71.

42. Also listen to how this variation itself becomes a theme to be embellished.

43. According to the improvements in notation software, it is easier to separate the fourth bandoneón part, and arrangers now prefer calling the part Bnd. 4 instead of 1B.

44. Sierra, *Historia de la orquesta típica*, 75.

45. Peralta, *La orquesta típica*, 189.

Further Reading

Ahrens, Christian. "Free Reed." In *The Organ: An Encyclopedia*, edited by Douglas E. Bush and Richard Kassel, 210–211. New York: Routledge Taylor & Francis Group, 2006.

Bush, Douglas E., and Richard Kassel. *The Organ: An Encyclopedia*. New York: Routledge Taylor & Francis Group, 2006.

Heveling, Carsten. "Das Bandoneon." *Bandoneon*, accessed July 27, 2021, https://bando-bando.de/verschiedenes/foto.html.

"History," *Accordions Worldwide*, accessed July 24, 2021. www.accordions.com/history/acc_his.aspx.

Kerimov, Rauf. "Akordiyon ve Benzeri Armonikaların Tarihsel Gelişimi Üzerine Bir İnceleme." *Porte Akademik* (Spring 2018): 87–101.

Krapovickas, Mercedes. "Organografía del bandoneón y prácticas musicales: Lógica dispositiva de los teclados del bandoneón rheinische Tonlage 38/33 y la escritura ideográfica." *Latin American Music Review* (Fall/Winter 2012): 157–185.

Montagu, Jeremy. "Concertina." In *The Oxford Companion to Music*, edited by Alison Latham, 288. New York: Oxford University Press, 2002.

Montagu, Jeremy. "Reed." In *The Oxford Companion to Music*, edited by Alison Latham, 1038. New York: Oxford University Press, 2002.

Sachs, Curt. *The History of Musical Instruments*. New York: Dover Publications, 2006.

Solis, Marcelo. "History of Tango – Part 5: The Appearance of the Bandoneon in Tango." *Argentine Tango School*, accessed July 27, 2021, https://escuelatangoba.com/marcelosolis/history-of-tango-part-5.

3 | Ángel Villoldo and Early Sound Recordings

MORGAN JAMES LUKER

How Should One Listen to Historical Sound Recordings?

Historical sound recordings are a curiously underutilized source in the study of tango and other genres of transnational popular music. This applies particularly to sound recordings made during the so-called acoustic era, that is, before microphones and electrical amplification became widely used after 1925. This underutilization is partly because acoustic-era sound recordings are now genuinely rare objects. They mostly reside in the specialized domain of dedicated private collectors or institutional sound collections, despite the increased circulation of these recordings in remediated digital contexts like YouTube and elsewhere in recent years. Another cause of their underutilization is the fact that many contemporary listeners feel an uneasy disconnect when listening to acoustic-era recordings, the sonic quality of which can make listeners feel as if they are encountering something not only from the distant past but from another world entirely.[1] Nevertheless, acoustic-era sound recordings have made constitutive contributions to the organization of contemporary musical culture and the sensorium through which music as such is conceived, engaged, and understood today. This is especially true regarding tango, the historical emergence of which coincides with the development of sound reproduction technologies in the late nineteenth century and the initial efforts and eventual consolidation of the transnational commercial recorded sound industry in the early twentieth century.[2]

Despite these practical and aesthetic barriers to engagement, historical sound recordings also receive limited scholarly attention today because of how researchers listen to them. Conventional modes of musical listening almost immediately categorize whatever it is that one hears into what are now largely predetermined narratives of musical style, genre, and history. This is an extended version of Michel Chion's famous notion of "causal listening," where the goal of listening is "to gather information" about a sound and its source.[3] The listener uses that information to answer what Nina Sun Eidsheim calls "the acousmatic question," namely, "Who [or what] is this?"[4] The answer, in most instances of listening to recorded popular music, is as simple as deciding whether a given example is or is not an instance of whatever style, genre, or history is under consideration, in this case "tango" or "not tango."

At the same time, it is important to note that this type of causal listening is not necessarily a problem in and of itself. In most contexts, being a knowledgeable listener means being able to understand and appreciate how a given recorded example fits within the much larger puzzle of musical style, genre, and history.[5] In other words, developing mastery of this type of causal listening is a primary means through which conventional modes of both committed fandom and scholarly authority are cultivated within genre-specific contexts, including tango. But notice how this type of listening both meaningfully expands and concretely limits what one can learn from any given instance of recorded sound. On the one hand, it uses what is heard to help "complete the picture" of generic knowledge. On the other hand, it simultaneously puts those same recordings "in their place." In the realm of tango, when a composer's piece does not quite fit the hegemonic "tango" narrative, it will often be excluded entirely as "not tango."

Pushing back against such a narrative-driven way of listening, this chapter investigates what one can learn by cultivating a different approach to engaging with recorded sound. I call this alternative approach "matrix listening." A matrix number is an alphanumeric code that is inscribed into the run-out area of a gramophone disc. Commercial sound recording companies and manufacturing facilities used such codes for internal documentation purposes. They are not immediately relevant to the conventional listening experience and are, indeed, inaudible. Nevertheless, by orienting our listening around matrix numbers, and other modes of industrial organization within the early commercial recorded sound industry, one can newly attune ourselves to the materiality of sound recordings. Such materials are physically bounded things, though chained complexly, not technologies that simply contain "music" as a purified or transcendent domain.[6]

In that sense, matrix listening resonates with a growing interest in what is called "new materialism" on the part of music scholars and many others in recent years. This work examines the ways musical and other things are not only the objects of human agency but are themselves a kind of acting subject. Echoing these much larger debates, this chapter shows how historical sound recordings themselves do not simply document or reflect an already existing narrative of musical history. Rather, they actively shape one's understanding and engagement with historical processes, telling their own stories as much as one uses them to tell theirs. Matrix listening serves as a way to move the conventional concerns of causal listening, including macro-level issues of musical style, genre, and history, to the background of our attention. Instead, this approach foregrounds the materiality of individual recorded sound objects as inanimate but nevertheless agentive "things."[7] In other words, matrix listening sidesteps the narrative-driven modes of causal listening, which often end up reducing sound recordings, and especially historical sound recordings, to nothing more than supporting evidence for (re)telling predetermined stories about musical style, genre, and history.

In this chapter, I explore how such a matrix listening approach applies to the early history of tango music via an examination of the recorded work of Ángel Villoldo (1861–1919, WP 3.1). Villoldo was a popular Argentine lyricist, composer, writer, stage actor, circus clown, day laborer, and general man about town in turn-of-the-century Buenos Aires. Villoldo is now firmly canonized as a foundational figure in the history of tango,[8] having written dozens of songs that have made significant contributions to the thematic tropes and stylistic range of early tango music. Several of these songs remain a part of the common tango repertory, most notably "El choclo" ("The Corncob," 1903), which, alongside Matos Rodríguez's "La cumparsita" ("The Little Carnival March," 1916), is one of the two most famous and recognizable tangos of all time.

While he is mostly known as a composer today, Villoldo was also a prominent performer in both musical and nonmusical contexts during his lifetime. He was one of the first Argentine performing artists to be documented by the then-emerging commercial recorded sound industries, producing some seventy-one known sound recordings as both a soloist and ensemble member across a variety of genres for at least three different record labels (primarily Victor and Columbia) beginning around 1905.[9] These recordings were manufactured as either single- or (more commonly) double-sided, ten-inch, 78 RPM discs, which were marketed and sold to listening consumers in Argentina and elsewhere, though they are exceedingly rare today. Indeed, Villoldo's recorded work has been made generally accessible only relatively recently, due to the efforts of the staff and curators at the department of special collections at the University of California, Santa Barbara (UCSB) and their public-facing initiatives such as the Discography of American Historical Recordings (DAHR). As of this writing, the DAHR website provides information and, in some cases, digitized audio surrogates for more than 300,000 historical sound recordings, including many of Villoldo's.[10]

I begin this chapter with an interpretive and contextual discussion of "El choclo." I frame it as both a singular composition and a vehicle for a hugely diverse history of performances, comparing and contrasting the insights provided by causal and matrix approaches to listening. I then discuss Villoldo's own recorded rendition of his famous piece from a matrix listening perspective, highlighting its complicated position vis-à-vis larger tropes of place, style, genre, and history. Connecting these themes to a discussion of Villoldo's broader recorded output, I argue that matrix listening draws our attention to features that conventional modes of narrative, causal listening not only ignore but actively silence. I conclude with some brief reflections on what matrix listening can teach us about the early history of tango specifically and the world of recorded sound in general.

Villoldo's "El choclo": Causal versus Matrix Listening Approaches

While Villoldo – although historically significant – may not be a household name, most tango listeners have almost certainly heard his emblematic piece "El choclo" (WL 3.1). But what makes "El choclo" so emblematic of tango? From a causal listening perspective, one can ascertain certain musical features. For example, the piece includes three distinct musical sections based on harmonic modulations and contrasting tunes. The highly repetitive, motive-driven opening melody incorporates intervallic leaps and arpeggios that feel idiomatic for instrumental performance, which is how the piece is most commonly heard. One may also notice the near-ubiquitous use of standard rhythmic accompaniment patterns throughout the piece (the *habanera*, in this case), which is one of the key features of tango as a musical genre.[11] Beyond these broad musical features, the piece also serves as a vehicle for lyrics, making it an early instance of *tango canción* (tango song), which would become a core component of the overall genre culture of tango over the course of the subsequent years.[12]

Equally important to the basic musical features and lyrics of "El choclo" is the medium through which the piece was initially published and circulated: sheet music. Villoldo's famous piece was published in Buenos Aires in 1903, a moment that coincided with the very earliest efforts of the commercial recorded sound industries in Argentina and preceded the first Argentine radio broadcast by some two decades. Therefore, the piece began its trajectory toward ubiquity via the live interpretation of notated music, be it in the hands of amateur musicians playing in private settings or public renditions in a variety of commercial contexts. Any and all of these settings represented both a coherent articulation of "El choclo" as a distinct piece of popular music and a unique instance of musical performance.[13] And while the same could be said of nearly all commercial music-making before the widespread dissemination of sound recordings, this emphasis on performance also foreshadows the later centrality of arranging within the larger tradition of tango music specifically.

Indeed, arranging is another defining feature of creative engagement and artistic expression in tango, both past and present, and is in large part how and why a distinct canon of tango repertory has emerged and consolidated over the past century.[14] "El choclo" is at the center of that canon, with famous arranged renditions running the gamut from the Orquesta Típica Victor in 1928 to Juan D'Arienzo in 1963 to El Arranque in 2002 and far, far beyond. Different arrangers of the famous tango work with its defining musical elements yet overlay their own unique interpretation of the melody, harmony, rhythm, and instrumentation. It is in expressing those unique interpretations of a shared repertory, rather than in the production of genuinely new and original compositions, that much of the artistic focus and pleasure of making tango music lies, at least historically.

But notice how the discussion here has shifted from a causal listening focus on "El choclo" as a self-contained musical piece to specific arranged renditions of Villoldo's famous tango as documented in a variety of distinct recorded sound performances over the course of time. Recognizing this subtle but important turn toward sound recordings rather than compositions and arrangements as the primary point of historical reference can help move one's understanding of tango away from cataloging formal features and toward a more expansive understanding of musical practice over the course of time and space. This is precisely what matrix listening encourages one to do.

From a matrix listening perspective, the history of "El choclo" does not begin with Villoldo in Buenos Aires but in a New York recording session sometime between 1903 and 1908, where the Banda Española recorded an instrumental arrangement of "El choclo" for a Sousa-style symphonic wind ensemble (WL 3.2). A spoken introduction to the recording announces, in Spanish, that the piece is a "*tango criollo*" (creole, or local Argentine, tango) by the "renowned Argentine songwriter Ángel Villolo, performed by the famous Columbia Band directed by the maestro Charles Prince."[15] Originally released on the Columbia "C" series, which was targeted toward

Spanish-speaking markets within the United States and across the Americas,[16] the Banda Española recording highlights a seeming disconnect between person/genre/place and instrumental forces/industrial structure/ musical aesthetics. On the one hand, Villoldo is a singular composer; tango is a singular genre; and Argentina is a singular place; all three are brought forth and reinforced within a causal listening paradigm. On the other hand, the symphonic wind ensemble is an iconic instance of a musical empire at the global level; the fundamentally transnational workings of the commercial recorded sound industry and the medium and materiality of recorded sound are the epicenter of musical attention and engagement; all three areas are highlighted from the perspective of matrix listening.

This disjuncture is only compounded by subsequent recordings of Villoldo's famous piece by a variety of performing forces over the course of the next century. These include, among many others: the Hurtado Brothers Royal Marimba Band of Guatemala (1916, WL 3.3), the International Novelty Orchestra directed by Nat Shilkret (1928, WL 3.4), the Pietro Deiro Accordion Trio (1932, WL 3.5), a solo electric organ rendition by Vernon Geyer (1937), the jazzy polka stylings of Curly Hicks and His Taproom Boys (1940), and a swinging version by the Stan Kenton Orchestra (1942, WL 3.6). Nat King Cole recorded "El choclo" in Spanish on his 1959 album *A Mis Amigos* (WL 3.7). In 1952, Louis Armstrong released a recording of "El choclo" using alternative, English language lyrics by Lester Allen and Robert Hill, who renamed the piece "Kiss of Fire" (WL 3.8). Singer Georgia Gibbs's version of "Kiss of Fire" reached number one on the Billboard pop music charts in May of that same year (WL 3.9). Somewhat more recently, the avant-garde improvising electronic musician Ikue Mori recorded "Kiss of Fire" with experimental vocalist Catherine Jauniaux on the 1995 album *Hex Kitchen*, and the English actor and entertainer Hugh Laurie recorded a bilingual version of the piece in duet with Guatemalan singer-songwriter Gaby Moreno in 2013 (WL 3.10). The list could go on and on.

Some of these recordings demonstrate awareness of the musical traits that have come to be associated with tango as a genre, of which "El choclo" is a cornerstone. These are the features, such as harmony, melody, and rhythm, that causal listening is most attuned to, making categorical judgments regarding "tango" or "not tango" feel both confident and authoritative. Others depart from these features in what sound like self-conscious ways, creating idiosyncratic but seemingly deliberate juxtapositions between the rhythmic accompaniment patterns of tango and the swinging rhythmic sensibility associated with straight-ahead jazz, for example.

Still, others appear entirely unaware of tango beyond the most egregious stereotypes regarding some vaguely "Latin" notion of sexualized difference, just like "those devil lips that know so well the art of lying" in the opening stanza of the "Kiss of Fire" lyrics.

Listening to them today, it can be easy to criticize, judge, or otherwise dismiss these and the many other recordings of "El choclo" made along similar lines as decidedly not tango, or at least not "real" tango. That is what causal listening within a genre-centric narrative frame is asking of us. But one should be careful not to quickly reject these or any other renditions of "El choclo," and not only because such a judgmental disposition makes it more difficult to engage with whatever it is that we actually hear in these recordings. On the contrary, I believe that the kind of stylistic, generic, and historical diversity that can be heard in this ballooning accumulation of recordings – from the Banda Española to Hugh Laurie and beyond – does not represent an anomalous departure from what we might imagine as real or correct tango but a fundamental feature of tango as such. Villoldo's own recorded rendition of "El choclo" points us in precisely this direction.

Matrix Listening to Villoldo's Recording of "El choclo"

Recorded in 1909 or 1910 for the Columbia Phonograph Company (matrix number 55286, label number T158), Villoldo's recorded performance of his already famous composition confounds the causal listening urge to hear it as a foundational document in any coherently linear narrative of tango's musical history.[17] The recording is three minutes and fifteen seconds long and features Villoldo accompanying himself on guitar. It opens with a few seconds of spoken dialogue in Spanish, in which an unnamed speaker approaches Villoldo and requests that he "sing that little tango 'El choclo' that you composed." Villoldo, in a comedically nonchalant tone of voice, responds "I'm going to see if I remember it, guys." This spoken prelude is more of a theatrical curtain rising than a simple announcement of titles, composers, and performers that opens many commercial sound recordings from this period (such as the Banda Española example cited earlier here). It frames everything that follows with a comedic self-consciousness, comedic, in part, because it positions the song as something Villoldo needs to excavate from his hazy memory of some distant musical past rather than the modern hit that it very much was at the time.

Villoldo establishes the minor key with a few strums through an introductory i-iv-V-i harmonic progression and then launches into the first verse, using his original lyrics.[18] The lyrics are organized into five stanzas, one for the A section and two each for the B and C sections. Villoldo proceeds through them in order, creating an overall ABBCC lyrical form that he goes through twice, using the B^1 and C^1 lyrics the first time and the B^2 and C^2 lyrics on the repetition (due to internal repetitions within the B and C sections, the overall musical form is ABCABC). So far so good, but what we actually hear is by no means a straightforward rendition of the piece. For example, Villoldo drops the lyrics entirely in the second half of the C section during the first time through the form, inserting another quasi-theatrical spoken interjection, this one a meta-commentary on the performance in progress, along the lines of "Hey, good job! This isn't so bad is it?" Villoldo inserts another interlude covering only the second half of the A section, following the second repetition of the overall form. This is where one would expect the performance to end, but instead, he presents the listener with a brief passage of virtuosic whistling set to guitar accompaniment. This leads to a restatement of the A section with lyrics, followed by a B^1 verse as if Villoldo was starting through the full form for a third time. But instead of continuing to the second half of the B section, the recording abruptly ends following one rendition of the B^1 verse, leaving the overall performance unresolved both melodically and harmonically.

It is hard not to hear this awkward ending as a mistake, and I imagine that the nonchalant-sounding Villoldo may have actually been feeling rather nonchalant in the recording studio on that day back in 1909 or 1910, losing track of how much time/space was left on the wax master disc his performance was being inscribed upon.[19] That said, this recording was obviously approved for manufacture and sale by the record company, so maybe the unusual ending was not a mistake at all. It was certainly not considered enough of a mistake to make the recording unsellable. Either way, the abrupt ending of the recording, like the backward-looking theatrical dialogue that opens it, upsets whatever desire causal listening might instill in us to locate the recording as a stylistic and conceptual starting point for a coherent narrative of tango's musical history. It stands, instead, as the material document of a singular performative moment (or performative mishap!) that both contains and exceeds "El choclo" as a musical work.

The recording's complex relationship to time and history is further compounded by the way Villoldo incorporates elements from a variety of styles and genres current at the time into his performance. In terms of tango melodic practices, Villoldo does not exceed the work as much as reduce it, rendering what is notated in the sheet music as an arpeggiated gesture covering nearly an octave and a half to a repetitive semitone.

A similar reduction occurs with the melodic rhythm, which is notated as a near-constant stream of sixteenth notes and sixteenth-note triplets, the volume and rapidity of which curiously exceeds the syllabic rhythm of the original lyrics. Villoldo, therefore, reduces the melodic rhythm to units of three sixteenth notes leading to two eighth notes to make the melody "fit" the lyrics. Meanwhile, Villoldo's guitar strums away at the *habanera* rhythmic accompaniment pattern with little variation throughout the recorded performance, as was typical of tango music then. But this very tango accompaniment pattern also gestures toward Argentine folkloric genres like the *milonga campera*, whose 3-3-2 rhythmic organization of eighth-note groupings syncopates the 3-1-2-2 pattern of the *habanera*. The same is true regarding the harmonic vocabulary of the piece, which includes features associated with Argentine folkloric music genres like *zamba*, such as the i-V-i harmonic motion that opens "El choclo." This heard relationship between genres is only reinforced by the sparse instrumentation used in the recording, just voice and guitar, which is emblematic of both Argentine folkloric music and the then-emerging form of *tango canción*.

None of this is to say that Villoldo's recorded rendition of "El choclo" is somehow not tango. It is announced as such on the recording, though the disc's label itself provides no genre designation, as will be discussed in more detail later. Still, it also clearly includes the performative style, sound, and sensibility of a whole suite of musical practices and genres in and beyond tango. In that sense, it invites us to reconsider what the scope and range of tango even are. In the case of Villoldo's "El choclo," tango certainly includes things like three-part forms, motivic melodies, rhythmic accompaniment patterns, and a suite of interpretive performance practices that both adhere to and depart from the notated version of a piece, among others. In addition, and most immediately, it includes styles that influenced early tango, such as Argentine folkloric music and the transnational *habanera*. But it also includes things like theatrical self-consciousness and dramatic presentational strategies via the introductory spoken dialog and other vocal interjections, which makes the listener feel as if they are observing a dramatic scene rather than listening to a self-contained performance of a musical work.

Villoldo's recording of "El choclo" furthermore engages with the technological medium of sound recording and the "mistakes" that resulted from that then-emergent setting. For example, the abrupt and unresolved ending of this recording brings the very medium of recorded sound as the vehicle and focus of musical practice above and beyond the composed work to the foreground of one's listening. This is true of recorded sound by definition, but it is further highlighted here by the brief passage of whistling, which is typically not thought of as part of the composition itself. Taken together, these features suggest that this recording should not be heard so much as a historical document – a foundational moment in the linear, coherent history of tango as a self-contained genre – but as a document of history. It is a singular encounter between a multitude of ideas, influences, and attitudes regarding style, genre, and history simultaneously, brought forth through the medium and materiality of recorded sound itself.

Ángel Villoldo, Recording Artist

Matrix listening to a broader array of Villoldo's recorded work brings these tendencies even more clearly to the surface. They reveal how framing Villoldo as a tango artist and composer, or even as a musical artist in general, does not really portray an adequate understanding of his work and influence, recorded and otherwise. Villoldo made his seventy-one recordings for no less than three different commercial sound recording companies during his lifetime, beginning as early as (approximately) 1905 with a recorded performance of his composition "El Porteñito" ("The Little Guy from Buenos Aires") for the UK label Zonophone (matrix 13443). The vast majority of his recordings were released either by the US-based labels Victor or Columbia, the former with fifty-two total recordings (thirty of which were recorded in March 1910), and the latter with nineteen total recordings.[20] Of these seventy-one recordings, forty-four (approximately 62%) are sung vocal performances, while twenty-seven (38%) are spoken word performances.

Of the twenty sung recordings that include title descriptors on their labels, only two are explicitly labeled as tangos: "Soy tremendo" ("I'm Tremendous," Columbia matrix 55376) and "El pechador" ("The Moocher" or "The Swindler," Columbia 55380), both of which Villoldo recorded with the accompaniment of the Orquesta Heyberger in 1909 or 1910. The other title descriptors featured on Villoldo's sung recordings are notably diverse. They include *canción* (song, such as Victor matrix numbers F-3, F-6, F-10, F-15, and F-23), *canción cómica* (comic song, Victor R-751 and R-753), *canto popular argentino* (Argentine popular song, Zonophone 13443), *característico* (literally "characteristic," the name of an Argentine folkloric genre, Columbia 55377), *copla picaresca* (roughly "picaresque folk song," Columbia 55379), *cordobés* (meaning from Córdoba, an Argentine province, Victor R-622), *estilo* (literally "style," another Argentine folkloric genre, Columbia 55042), *parodia* (parody, Victor R-750), *parodia morocha* (brunette parody,[21] Victor R-619), *recitado y cantado* (recited and sung, Victor R-616), *reminiscencia patriotica* [sic] (patriotic reminiscence, Columbia 55382), *serenata* (serenade, Victor R-620), and *vals cantado* (sung waltz, Victor F-11).

These title descriptors point not only to the sheer diversity of Villoldo's recorded work, but to the multiple frameworks through which both the then-emergent medium of commercially recorded sound and the scope of modern musical culture were coming to be understood at the time. Note that title descriptors are not simply genre designations. Some, such as *canción* or *recitado y cantado*, frame what one will hear on the disc in broadly descriptive terms, with little or no indication of genre or even general content beyond small gestures such as the descriptor *canción cómico* or comic song.

Other title descriptors explicitly frame the recordings within the national space of Argentina, even though the recordings were often recorded (and before 1919 were always manufactured) outside of Argentina by truly transnational recorded sound companies based in the United States or Europe. This is implicit in the descriptor *reminescencia patriotica* [sic] (patriotic reminiscence) for the piece "El soldado de la independencia" ("The Soldier of Independence," Columbia 55382). This disc recounts the grueling but ultimately heroic exploits of an infantry soldier who served under the military leader Manuel Belgrano (1770–1820) during the Argentine wars for independence, set to a dirge-like melody with the accompaniment of a small wind ensemble. The same is true of the descriptor *cordobés*, which highlights how the city and the province of Córdoba were coming to be seen as a rustic alternative to the more cosmopolitan city and province of Buenos Aires in the Argentine national imagination at the time.[22] It is even implicit in descriptors, such as in the *parodia morocha*, which uses the Argentine slang word *morocha* to reference a biracial female to frame the type of parody song the listener will encounter on the disc.

Others go in the opposite direction, framing something that could be more specific in terms of local context and/or style and genre into a more general descriptor that could be understood and appreciated by a broader audience of listeners. For example, the recording of "El Porteñito," though not nearly as well known and widely performed as "El choclo," made similar contributions to the early formation of tango as a genre and has remained a part of the common tango repertory. Like "El choclo," "El Porteñito" first appeared in published sheet-music form in 1903 with the explicit genre designation *tango criollo*. However, the label on the 1905 Zonophone recording, likely one of the first commercial recordings of "El Porteñito" ever to be made, describes it not as tango or *tango criollo* but as *canto popular argentino*. At the same time, several of Villoldo's sung recordings do use genre names in their title descriptors, including tango but also *característico*, *estilo*, *serenata*, and *vals cantado*. Most of these diverse genres of Argentine folkloric music would go on to have elaborate histories of cultural and commercial development similar to that of tango, both as distinct genres and under the collective rubric of "folklore."[23]

One can take away two noteworthy points regarding the early history of tango from this otherwise seemingly arcane discussion of title descriptors and other physical features of historical sound recordings as material things. First, tango is included among these other genres as just one among many, suggesting that the boundaries between different genres were much more fluid than we might imagine today, both in terms of Villoldo's repertory and in terms of what consumers of commercially recorded sound encountered and enjoyed at the time. Second, it is striking that only two of Villoldo's seventy-odd sound recordings – less than 3 percent of his recorded output – feature tango as a title descriptor or genre designation. Even knowing that several of these recordings were, in fact, tangos regardless of their descriptors, it is nevertheless striking that this foundational figure in the history of tango simply did not record many designated tangos.

True to Villoldo's vocation as a theatrical entertainer as well as a musical composer, some 40 percent of his recorded output was not music at all but spoken-word vocal performances, including recitations, monologues, comic monologues, comic dialogues, and comic scenes, according to their title descriptors. Many of these are solo vocal performances, though Villoldo did record nonmusical material with contemporaries such as the Argentine singer and actor Linda Thelma (1884–1939) and Alfredo Eusebio Gobbi (1877–1938).[24] And while these recordings are not musical in any conventional sense of the term, they are elaborate sonic performances that creatively utilize and exploit the medium of recorded sound for expressive and entertaining purposes.

For example, Villoldo's recording of "La sirvienta gangosa" ("The Nasal Servant Girl," Columbia 55276) presents a recitation of a bawdy original poem in which Villoldo relates a comical encounter between himself and the daughter of an upper-class household as mediated by her "nasal servant girl." Told in the first person over twelve verses organized in an ABBACCCA rhyme scheme, the text is virtuosic in its poetically rigorous hilarity. Even more impressive is Villoldo's tour de force performance as a comic vocal actor, heard in his enunciation, timing, and over-the-top renditions of the story's several speaking characters, including the pinched-nosed squawk of the servant girl. Villoldo's recording of his monologue "Arturito el risueño" ("Cheerful Little Arthur," Columbia 55259) takes this performative emphasis on the nonsemantic sound of the human voice even further. Roughly half of the recording's three minutes and twenty-one seconds features only the sound of Villoldo's intense laughter, foreshadowing the famous novelty *discos de la risa* (laughing records) that would come to pepper the catalogs of commercial sound recording companies the world over following the surprise success of the so-called Okeh laughing record in 1922.[25] However, not all these recordings are fun and games. Villoldo's patriotic declamation "A San Martín" ("To San Martín," Columbia 55398) conveys a melodramatically somber homage to José de San Martín (1778–1850), a central figure in the South American independence movement and a national hero in Argentina.

Whether comedic or dramatic, the unmistakable theatricality of these spoken-word recordings go far beyond the semantic content of their words. They are compelling and dynamic largely due to their sonic features, that is, to the medium of recorded sound and the full range of theatrical performativity that it allows listeners to reproduce. The fact that some 40 percent of Villoldo's recorded output represents spoken-word performances of this type can help one appreciate the heterogeneity of his artistry and the performative diversity from which tango emerged – a vaudeville-style world of entertainment that included tango but also many other forms and genres of music alongside comedy, drama, recitations, and other nonmusical performances. That is exactly what one hears when we apply matrix listening to Villoldo's recorded work, much of which would be ignored from a causal listening perspective. Taken as a whole, Villoldo's recordings do not represent the foundational moment of tango as much as the diverse milieu of commercial entertainment that shaped the contours of everyday life in Argentina at the time. It would be hard to make sense of the theatrical framing of Villoldo's recording of "El choclo" outside of these considerations.

The then-emergent medium of commercial sound recording did not so much determine these performances as take advantage of already existing practices of sonic expression and performative entertainment. This is true of what Villoldo knew and did as an early recording artist, since his diverse career as an entertainer began well before the commercial sound recording industry gained a viable foothold in the Argentine markets in the first decade of the twentieth century. Likewise, it is also true of how listening audiences engaged and understood commercial sound reproduction technologies as they began to encounter them in everyday contexts during this same period. Sound recording and reproduction technologies, despite their genuine newness, did not disrupt already existing modes of listening and performance as much as extend them into different contexts and markets.[26] It was those existing contexts – listening to theatrical entertainments, including music – that framed the sound and meaning of the emergent medium of commercially recorded sound. It is within this context, not as the foundational moment of tango as a distinct genre culture that the full scope of Villoldo's recorded work can best be accounted for and heard.

Finding Musical Meaning in Historical Sound Recordings

Listening to Villoldo's recordings from the perspective I outline here – moving beyond causal listening to recorded sound performances via matrix listening – reveals new insights into the composer and his time. It expands our understanding of Villoldo as both an artist and a historical person, widening his narrow canonization as a foundational figure in the early history of tango. It enriches our knowledge of the tremendously diverse musical and performative milieu that early tango emerged from and operated within, thereby deepening our sense of how tango relates to other forms and genres. It reexamines the role that media technologies and other products of the commercial recorded sound industries played not only in the documentation of early tango music but in its dissemination and development. And finally, it revises some of the core tropes that have become a kind of narrative second nature in the telling of tango history as a distinct genre culture – narrative tropes that conceal as much as they illuminate.

This way of listening to Villoldo's recorded sound discs also helps us better account for the peculiarity of historical sound recordings as primary sources and the complexities of the scholarly listening experience. Historical recordings reproduce sound information generally heard as being about the past, if not directly coming from it, disrupting conventional experiences of place and time via the materiality of the recorded sound object. This perceived disruption accounts for much of the allure of sound recording as a media technology and mediated listening as a cultural practice. It also underscores the basic fact that historical sound recordings are – first and foremost – material objects. They are physical things whose managed materiality both conjures and disrupts listening as a mode of knowledge and the multitude of ideological and institutional structures that frame it. The challenge, then, is to more carefully think through what sound recordings actually do, that is, what role sound recordings play in historical processes and our understanding of or engagement with those processes.

Beyond the details of this case study, I hope to have shown why and how scholars should recenter listening as a method of historical inquiry regarding tango and, indeed, any recorded sound phenomena. My emphasis on listening may feel like it goes without saying, especially regarding a genre of popular music like tango that is typically experienced and understood via embodied engagements with sound recordings, such as social dancing at milongas, rather than through live performances or notated scores. What I am calling for, then, is not just a return to listening per se but the cultivation of a particular approach to listening. This approach – matrix listening – situates sound recordings as the locus and material limit of historical knowledge, not as transparently knowable documents of the musical past or straightforward representations of cultural differences. Not surprisingly, this is easier said than done.

Notes

1. Michael Denning, *Noise Uprising: The Audiopolitics of a World Musical Revolution* (New York: Verso, 2015), 3.
2. Marina Cañardo, *Fábricas de músicas: Comienzos de la industria discográfica en la Argentina (1919–1930)* (Buenos Aires: Gourmet Musical, 2017), 13–25.
3. Michel Chion, *Audio-Vision: Sound on Screen* (New York: Columbia University Press, 1994), 25–34.
4. Nina Sun Eidsheim, *The Race of Sound: Listening, Timbre, and Vocality in African American Music* (Durham: Duke University Press, 2019), 1–37.
5. David Novak, "2.5 x 6 meters of space: Japanese music coffeehouses and experimental practices of listening," *Popular Music* 27, no. 1 (January 2008): 15–34.
6. Morgan James Luker, "Matrix Listening, or, What and How We Can Learn from Historical Sound Recordings," *Ethnomusicology* 66, no. 2 (Summer 2022): 290–318.
7. Bill Brown, *Other Things* (Chicago: University of Chicago Press, 2015), 17–48.

8. For more information, see Tito Rivadeneira, *Ángel Villoldo en el inicio del tango y de los varietés* (Buenos Aires: Editorial Dunken, 2014).

9. "Angel Gregorio Villoldo," *Discography of American Historical Recordings*, https://adp.library.ucsb.edu/names/116562.

10. See *Discography of American Historical Recordings*, https://adp.library.ucsb .edu.

11. Hernán Possetti, *The Piano in Tango* (Buenos Aires: Fondo Nacional de las Artes, 2014), 10–14.

12. Though note that Villoldo's original, double entendre–laden lyrics are now almost always substituted for the later lyrics written by Enrique Santos Discépolo (1901–1951) in 1947, which self-referentially use "El choclo" as (by then) a canonized musical composition for the elaborate poetic evocation and celebration of tango's historical origins.

13. David Suisman, *Selling Sounds: The Commercial Revolution in American Music* (Cambridge, MA: Harvard University Press, 2009), 56–89. See especially chapter two on the marketing of sheet music during this period in the US context.

14. Kacey Link and Kristin Wendland, *Tracing Tangueros: Argentine Tango Instrumental Music* (New York: Oxford University Press, 2016), 87–133.

15. Charles Prince (1869–1937) was a musical director and ensemble conductor for the US label Columbia Records (founded in 1889 and currently owned by Sony Music Entertainment) between 1904 and 1922.

16. Dick Spotswood, *Columbia Records C Series, 1908–1923: A Draft Numerical List, Including All Known Releases* (Highlands Ranch, CO: Mainspring Press, 2017), 3.

17. "Columbia matrix 55286. El choclo / Angel Gregorio Villoldo," *Discography of American Historical Recordings*, https://adp.library.ucsb.edu/index.php/matrix/ detail/2000085801/55286-El_choclo.

18. See *Todotango* for the full text of Villoldo's original lyrics to "El choclo," www .todotango.com/musica/tema/595/El-choclo-[Villoldo]/.

19. Michael B. Silvers, *Voices of Drought: The Politics of Music and Environment in Northeastern Brazil* (Champaign, IL: University of Illinois Press, 2018), 29–47; see chapter one on the materiality of carnauba wax in early recording contexts. At the time, disc-based acoustic sound recording technologies like the one used in this case could typically document a maximum of three to four minutes of continuous sound.

20. With "recording" here meaning a single documented performance, two of which would be included on any double-sided 78 RPM disc "record," one on each side.

21. *Morocha* is a racialized and gendered Argentine slang word that could be translated as "brunette," but refers more broadly to women of mixed racial ancestry.

22. Ana Belén Disandro, "El tango en Córdoba: Lo provinciano y lo porteño en la historia de la construcción de un género (1900–1950)" (PhD diss., Universidad Nacional de Córdoba, 2020), 377–428.

23. Oscar Chamosa, *The Argentine Folklore Movement: Sugar Elites, Criollo Workers, and the Politics of Cultural Nationalism*, 1900–1955, 2nd ed. (Tucson, AZ: University of Arizona Press, 2010), 157–182.

24. Along with his performing partner and wife Flora Rodríguez de Gobbi, Alfredo Eusebio Gobbi made up half of the duo "Los Gobbi," who, alongside Villoldo, were among the earliest and most successful Argentine recording artists. Their son Alfredo Gobbi (1912–1965) would become one of the most significant figures of tango's later Golden Age in the 1940s and 1950s.

25. Cary O'Dell, "The OKeh Laughing Record (1922)," *Library of Congress* (2003), www.loc.gov/static/programs/national-recording-preservation-board/documents/OKEH%20LAUGHING%20RECORD.pdf.

26. For further reading about this idea demonstrated in other contexts, see Johnathan Sterne, *The Audible Past: Cultural Origins of Sound Reproduction* (Durham, NC: Duke University Press, 2003), 215–286.

Further Reading

Brown, Bill. 2015. *Other Things*. Chicago: University of Chicago Press.

Cañardo, Marina. 2017. *Fábricas de músicas: Comienzos de la industria discográfica en la Argentina (1919-1930)*. Buenos Aires: Gourmet Musical.

Denning, Michael. 2015. *Noise Uprising: The Audiopolitics of a World Musical Revolution*. New York: Verso.

Eidsheim, Nina Sun. 2019. *The Race of Sound: Listening, Timbre, and Vocality in African American Music*. Durham: Duke University Press.

Luker, Morgan James. 2022. "Matrix Listening; or, What and How We Can Learn from Historical Sound Recordings." *Ethnomusicology*, Vol. 66, No. 2, pp. 290-318.

Possetti, Hernán. 2014. *The Piano in Tango*. Buenos Aires: Fondo Nacional de las Artes.

Rivadeneira, Tito. 2014. *Ángel Villoldo en el inicio del tango y de los varietés*. Buenos Aires: Editorial Dunken.

Silvers, Michael B. 2018. *Voices of Drought: The Politics of Music and Environment in Northeastern Brazil*. Champaign: University of Illinois Press.

Sterne, Johnathan. 2003. *The Audible Past: Cultural Origins of Sound Reproduction*. Durham: Duke University Press.

Suisman, David. 2009. *Selling Sounds: The Commercial Revolution in American Music*. Cambridge: Harvard University Press.

4 | Orchestral Rhythmic Designs and Performance Practices: Juan D'Arienzo and Aníbal Troilo

IGNACIO VARCHAUSKY
TRANSLATED FROM SPANISH BY ADAM TULLY

The stylistic development of tango orchestras in the Golden Age of the 1940s and '50s is a universe in and of itself. The totality of interpretive details that define the most important orchestras of this period is a compendium of beautiful and intricately subjective material, and it enriches tango's language in an extraordinary and definitive way. In listening to *orquestas típicas* (typical tango orchestras), it is important to observe and define the differences between musical and stylistic aspects. Musical aspects are the elements that define the music: rhythm, melody, accompaniment, harmony, and different textures created by various combinations of timbres. In other words, musical aspects are everything written in the score, essentially, the "what." On the other hand, stylistic aspects are the interpretation of the musical score, in other words, the "how." For example, written rhythmic patterns sound one way when played by a particular orchestra, but the same patterns sound very different when played by another orchestra. In this case, the musical aspect is the same for both orchestras, but the stylistic aspect differs. Thus, what one sees in a written score is basic and preliminary, but the possibilities for interpreting the notation are many, varied, and often personal.

In this chapter, I identify and contrast stylistic traits between two orchestras that are as emblematic as they are different – the orchestras of Juan D'Arienzo (1934–1975) and Aníbal Troilo (1937–1975). These orchestras are two of the most popular tango ensembles of all time, and they remain beloved by tango audiences today. In analyzing their interpretive approaches, I focus on their use of tempo, *marcato* (marked) in 4, and *síncopa* (syncopation). These three elements define a large part of the personality of the two orchestras as well as any tango group; they are the essence of tango's rhythmic language. From a performance viewpoint, it is essential to understand these fundamental elements and their stylistic possibilities. As a double bass player who has played in a wide variety of tango styles alongside tango legends, I am keenly aware of these principles; therefore, I also provide performance techniques for the different styles. My goal in contrasting these two distinct styles is to aid in one's listening to and performance of their differences, as well as to help deepen one's overall understanding of the language of tango.

Fundamental Tango Rhythmic Elements

Tempo

When listening to a tango orchestra, the first element one generally observes is the tempo (velocity) and how it behaves throughout a piece. Within orchestral styles, Argentine tango musicians define three approaches to tempo: *tempo fijo* (fixed tempo), *tempo flexible* (flexible tempo), and *tempo variable* (variable tempo). Each approach has its own logic and creates an enormous impact on both the musical and the stylistic aspects.

Tempo fijo orchestras develop their musical discourse within a constant pulse, with some exceptions or minimal changes. They begin, develop, and end each piece at the same speed. Primarily, these orchestras focus on playing for dancing and base the blueprint of their style on the performance practices of Francisco Canaro (1888–1964) and his orchestra. Other Golden-age orchestras in this category are those of D'Arienzo, Carlos Di Sarli (1903–1960), Alfredo De Angelis (1910–1992), Ricardo Tanturi (1905–1973), Ricardo Malerba (1905–1974), and Francisco Lomuto (1893–1950). Some of the later, more musically developed orchestras but perhaps not dance orchestras, like those of Osmar Maderna (1918–1951) or Astor Piazzolla (1921–1992), are also in this tempo classification. One example of this *tempo fijo* style is "Una fija" ("A Fixed One," WL 4.1) performed by Di Sarli and his *orquesta típica*.

Tempo flexible orchestras frequently increase and decrease the tempo for expressive purposes. Yet, they do this without losing the pulse – the pulse is always present. In other words, these orchestras play with the concept of speeding up or slowing down based on what the musical phrase or context might suggest, and they always have the same rationale – to be expressive. Mostly, these are musically advanced orchestras that seek to move the listener rather than drive the dancers, whose origins are in the blueprint of Julio De Caro (1899–1980) and his sextet. Other orchestras of this style include those of Troilo, Alfredo Gobbi (1912–1965), Mario Demarco (1917–1970), José Basso (1919–1993), and Leopoldo Federico (1927–2014). "Fraternal" ("Brotherly," WL 4.2), played by Gobbi and his *orquesta típica,* provides an excellent example of *tempo flexible.*

Tempo variable orchestras choose a freer approach in which the pulse eventually disappears, and every note and phrase lives and breathes within a personal, whimsical logic. This can lead to extraordinary effects that, again, are made at the service of expressivity. This concept might be present during one or several moments of a piece, but it will never last throughout. If it were to do so, one might consider it a type of experimental tango; traditional tango demands a certain rhythmic continuity, without which it turns into something else altogether. One could say that Osvaldo Pugliese (1905–1995) and his orchestra has an almost outright exclusivity in this category. It is hard to find other orchestras that use this concept as continuously and consistently as his orchestra. Just as with the *tempo flexible* orchestras, the goal with *tempo variable* orchestras is to be expressive, although, at times, the approach is used for special sonic effects. "Don Agustín Bardi" (referring to the early tango musician) played by Pugliese and his *orquesta típica* offers a good example of *tempo variable* style (WL 4.3).

Time-Marking Models

When one listens to tango, one should never lose sight of its original essence – tango is music for social dancing that does not use a drum set or percussion instruments. Following this logic, the rhythmic leader of a tango orchestra is usually the piano, which works in tandem with the bass as the rhythm section, and both use different rhythmic patterns that musicians call "time-marking models." There are a variety of time-marking models, and depending on the situation, they may be played alternately by the bandoneón section and/or the string section along with the piano and/or bass. It is important to understand that both the piano and bass have a foundational rhythmic role in the tango ensemble; they are the rhythmic and percussive force that drive the tango orchestra in all styles. This is why the performance practices of these two instruments are highlighted throughout this chapter.

The lack of a drum set or percussion instruments led tango musicians to develop a percussive approach to playing their instruments, creating endless articulations and effects to reach the goal of sounding rhythmic enough to motivate dancers. There are exceptions, of course, like Osvaldo Fresedo (1897–1984) and his orchestra or Piazzolla's Conjunto 9, which both contain percussion, but like all exceptions, they prove the rule. As a bass player, I know that the rhythm section must always drive the orchestra – that is its primary function. But this function can have many different approaches that eventually have a considerable impact, stylistically speaking. This is where any tango style starts developing its swing and overall sound. The steadiness of the rhythm and the group's swing largely depend on the clarity and precision with which the rhythm section plays each note of a piece. It is not only what they play but also how they play it. That is how the dissimilar practices of each orchestra eventually create contrasting tango styles. Next, I dive into the two main time-marking models, easily recognizable when listening to any tango orchestra.

Marcato *in 4*

Marcato in 4 is the essence of tango rhythm. It is the time-marking model that defines an immense part of tango's musical and stylistic universe. Beginning in the late 1910s and especially the early 1920s, *marcato* in 4 replaced the *habanera* once and for all as the rhythmic basis for tango. Orchestras such as those of Alonso-Minotto, Roberto Firpo (1884–1969), La Típica Select, and Juan Carlos Cobián (1896–1953) and his sextet clearly illustrate this transformation. Although there are many varieties of *marcato* in 4, in this chapter, I describe its most important types.

There are two basic ways to accent *marcato* in 4: accenting all four beats equally (Ex. 4.1a) or accenting the strong beats (beats 1 and 3) only while playing the weak beats (beats 2 and 4) with less emphasis (Ex. 4.1b). "Gitana rusa" ("Russian Gypsy," WL 4.4), performed by Ricardo Malerba and his *orquesta típica*, offers an excellent example of accenting four beats, while "El pollito" ("The Little Chicken," WL 4.5) by Di Sarli and his *orquesta típica* provides an example of accenting the strong beats. To distinguish between these two types of *marcato* in 4, pay attention to the pulse and listen to which beats are accented and which are not. Both approaches are prevalent. Although the choice of accent pattern does not make a style danceable or not, it does give an orchestra a particular rhythmic contour; accenting all four beats is a little more forced than respecting the natural gravitation of accents toward the strong beats in 4/4 time. Of course, there are many subtle differences between the various ways of accenting. Not all orchestras accent the same way; therein lies a good part of their personalities.

Marcato in 4 bass lines played by the piano and the bass mark a clear difference between styles. The significant stylistic difference comes from the duration of the notes: whether they are *staccato* (short and separated) or *legato* (long and connected). In general, the orchestras that are cut out for dancing play bass lines with short notes and without much melodic development, using basic triads and even repeating notes (WE 4.1a), as heard in D'Arienzo's recording of "La cumparsita" ("The Little Carnival March," WL 4.6); the orchestras with more significant musical development choose to play legato bass lines using a richer melodic development or more chord tones (WE 4.1b), as heard in Troilo's recording of "La cumparsita" (WL 4.7). As with everything, this is not an undisputed rule, and there are many exceptions, but there is a clear tendency.

Example 4.1 *Marcato* in 4 for piano. a. Accenting all four beats equally. b. Accenting the strong beats (beats 1 and 3) only while playing the weak beats (beats 2 and 4) with less emphasis.

Arrastre

Arrastre (drag) is in anticipation of the written or arrival note. In *marcato* in 4, *arrastre* is used to emphasize the arrival on the accented notes, typically on beats 1 and 3. While some orchestras like those of Di Sarli and Gobbi consistently use this device (primarily in the bass and the left hand of the bandoneones), others like those of D'Arienzo or Ángel D'Agostino (1900–1991) hardly use it at all. To hear an orchestra with a clear *arrastre*, listen to a recording of "La viruta" ("The Wood Chip," WL 4.8) by Gobbi and his *orquesta típica*. Contrastingly, to hear an orchestra play *marcato* in 4 without an *arrastre*, listen to a recording of "Manoblanca" (name of a horse, WL 4.9) by D'Agostino and his *orquesta típica*.

Síncopa

Síncopa, along with *marcato* in 4, is the most utilized time-marking model in tango. As an integral part of the genre's musical language, it is present in all tango styles. When one talks about "syncopation" in tango, one is specifically talking about this characteristic time-marking model. *Síncopa* always has at least one note shifted outside the normal accent pattern. There are many different types of *síncopas*, but there are two categories from which the rest are derived: *síncopa a tierra* (downbeat syncopation, Ex. 4.2a) and *síncopa anticipada* (anticipated syncopation, Ex. 4.2b).

Example 4.2 Types of *síncopa* for piano. a. *Síncopa a tierra* (downbeat syncopation). b. *Síncopa anticipada* (anticipated syncopation).

With *síncopa a tierra*, one can always hear the first eighth note of the downbeat (first beat of the measure), with a varying degree of accent, but it is always there. This type of rhythm coincides perfectly with one's foot tapping, if tapping along with the pulse. Troilo and his orchestra's recording of "Danzarín" ("Dancer," WL 4.10) offers an excellent example. Even though orchestras frequently play *síncopa a tierra* with an anticipation (generally a half beat and sometimes a full beat), one may call it "*a tierra*" if the first eighth note of beat 1 is played. This is by far the most common type of syncopation in tango. While the execution may vary, it can be heard in all the orchestral styles, ranging from the orchestras of Canaro, D'Agostino, and Enrique Rodríguez (1901–1971) to those of Pugliese, Troilo, and Piazzolla.

As opposed to downbeat syncopation, *síncopa anticipada* is where the accent is placed on the anticipation to the downbeat (specifically, on the last eighth note of the previous measure), and the first eighth note of the downbeat is not played or is played very softly. This type of *síncopa* can be heard in many orchestras, such as those of Horacio Salgán (1916–2016), Troilo, Francini-Pontier, and Basso. One can especially hear it in "Una carta" ("A Letter," WL 4.11) by Salgán and his *orquesta típica*.

Comparison of D'Arienzo's and Troilo's Orchestral Styles

After this brief introduction to tango rhythmic elements, I now focus on how the orchestras of D'Arienzo and Troilo treat tempo, *marcato*, and *síncopa*. As these orchestras represent two of the most widespread and popular styles in tango history, they also have immense symbolic importance. While D'Arienzo's orchestra is considered the peak of the most conservative and highly danceable tango tradition, Troilo's orchestra is appraised as the pinnacle of the more musically developed tango orchestral language, filled with expression and emotion. In this paradigm, D'Arienzo's orchestra represents similar orchestras, like those of De Angelis, Tanturi, Rodolfo Biagi (1906–1969), and D'Agostino, while Troilo's orchestra represents other orchestras like those of Gobbi, Pugliese, Piazzolla, and Francini-Pontier. In a way, comparing D'Arienzo's and Troilo's orchestral styles is like comparing two distinct schools of performance practices within the tango orchestral language.

Tempo

Juan D'Arienzo

The orchestra of D'Arienzo is a *tempo fijo* orchestra, unchanging from beginning to end. Moreover, almost without exception, D'Arienzo rarely changes tempo throughout his nearly 1,000 recordings. The ability of his musicians to maintain such a stable and tight tempo is more than worthy of mention. In many cases, one can put a metronome over the recording and see that the tempo is perfectly steady, for example, in his recording of "Bien pulenta" ("Very Strong," WL 4.12). To play with such precision is as difficult as it is surprising.

Aníbal Troilo

As with many styles that originated at the end of the 1930s, Troilo's orchestra gradually decreased its tempo over the years. Nevertheless, the most striking thing is not the change in speed over time but rather the treatment of tempo as an extraordinary expressive tool. This transformation can be heard by comparing the recordings made during each period. While he utilizes *tempo fijo* during the early '40s, Troilo slowly abandons this paradigm to make room for *tempo flexible*, the goal of which is to be as expressive as possible. Eventually, he arrives at *tempo variable* in the final years of his orchestra in the '50s and '60s. For example, his recording of "Piropos" ("Compliments," WL 4.13) of the 1940s has a *tempo fijo*; his recording of "El Pollo Ricardo" ("Richard The Chicken," WL 4.14) of the 1950s has a *tempo flexible*; and his recording of "Danzarín" from the 1960s has a more *tempo variable* (WL 4.15). A good way to detect at least some

tempo changes is to pay special attention to the fills played by the bandoneones when they are left on their own without the rhythm section. This is
usually the moment when the bandoneones (and sometimes only Troilo
with his bandoneón) pull back and slow down the tempo of the whole
orchestra, such as in "Tinta verde" ("Green Ink," WL 4.16).

Marcato *in 4*

Juan D'Arienzo

Marcato in 4 is by far the time-marking model most utilized by D'Arienzo.
It is present in every tango from start to finish and uses very little back-and-
forth with other *síncopa* rhythmic models. In his orchestra, the instruments
playing *marcato* in 4 execute a very percussive and, at times, almost
hammer-like style. One can hear this style in his recording of "Derecho
viejo" ("Straight Forward," WL 4.17). Occasionally, the rhythm section of
D'Arienzo's orchestra will exaggeratedly accent the weak beats when
accompanying rhythmic melodies. In this case, the idea is to create
a contrast that will surprise and stimulate the listener as well as to provide
some relief to the monotony of *marcato* in 4. As heard in "No mientas"
("Don't Lie," WL 4.18), it is a simple device but very effective.

Generally speaking, most of D'Arienzo's bass *marcato* notes, played in
the piano and bass, are short, accented, and *staccato*. This articulation
generates a sense of urgency, a key element in understanding the general
mood of this style. One can hear this in his "Tierrita" ("Little Dirt," WL
4.19). Less frequently, the bass notes in the piano's left hand are played
legato, while the right hand continues to play *staccato* chords. According to
the period and the piece, the orchestra alternates to a greater or lesser
extent between this double articulation and the one that is entirely *staccato*,
creating subtle changes in mood and texture, for example, in "Don
Orlando" (name of a distinguished man, WL 4.20). Also, when the piano
plays a solo or fill, the bandoneones and the bass continue with the constant
marcato pulse. As heard in "Una y mil noches" ("One and a Thousand
Nights," WL 4.21), this creates a different yet just as powerful texture.

D'Arienzo's bassists play exclusively pizzicato. The bow has no place in
this style. It is a well-known anecdote that D'Arienzo would get mad if he saw
a bassist pick up the bow. Always using a big sound and clear articulation, the
rhythm section resembles a bass drum conducting the orchestra – without
rests or subtlety. One may hear this in D'Arienzo's recording of "Mandria"
("Pusillanimous," WL 4.22). Another striking characteristic of the bass in

D'Arienzo's style is the use of snap pizzicato. This is a very percussive effect, in which the bassist hooks the right-hand fingers around the string, with either the pointer or middle finger, or both simultaneously, and when they release it, the strings bounce off the fingerboard (the wood beneath the strings). This bounce creates a very particular snapping sound, contributing to the general texture and adding percussive emphasis to the note in question. One may hear this effect in his recording of "Yapeyú" (name of a city in the province of Corrientes, Argentina, WL 4.23) or hear snap pizzicato in his recording of "El chupete" ("The Pacifier," WL 4.24). Despite D'Arienzo's rule that the bass play only pizzicato, a minimal number of exceptions occur in passages or long *tutti* chords played *arco* (with the bow), such as in "Bailate un tango Ricardo" ("Dance a Tango, Ricardo," WL 4.25).

Aníbal Troilo

The personalized sound of Troilo's *marcato* is defined by the type of accentuation, the way of articulating, and other interpretive details such as the *legato* bass lines. Although in its early period, the orchestra generally accented the four beats of *marcato* equally, as in "Toda mi vida" ("All My Life," WL 4.26), little by little, this idea began to change, and the orchestra started accenting the strong beats as in "Quejas de bandoneón" ("Wail of the Bandoneón," WL 4.27). When considering this change, it is important to remember that many of the orchestras that were formed at the end of the 1930s (in large part thanks to the dance furor sparked by D'Arienzo's style) started to play more slowly over time, eventually finding the appropriate tempo for their style and sensibility. Troilo made this change in the early years of his orchestra, a fact that can be appreciated by comparing the recordings he made between 1941 and 1944.

Occasionally, Troilo's orchestra employed "Gobbi-style" *marcato*, named after violinist and orchestra leader Alfredo Gobbi. This type of *marcato* consists of playing accented chords on the weak beats in the context of *marcato* in 4, and always playing the second eighth note of the strong beats. The bandoneones usually play this *marcato* for only one measure, generally at the end of phrases or sections. To hear the "Gobbi-style" *marcato*, listen to Troilo's orchestra playing "Cenizas" ("Ashes," WL 4.28).

In terms of how the orchestra plays *marcato*, the bandoneones are a trademark of the Troilean sound. Troilo's style consists of a short but not hammered accent, without *arrastre*. He is known for his light touch, without much air pressure, producing an elegant sound. This can be heard in his recording of "Mi castigo" ("My Punishment," WL 4.29).

In addition to the transition regarding the *marcato* accentuation, there was also a transition in the articulation of *marcato* bass lines in the piano and bass. In the orchestra's early recordings, the bass notes are almost always played *staccato*. Over time (and above all, starting in 1943), bass lines began to be played *legato* and remained a defining trademark of his style. This is exemplified in "Garúa" ("Drizzle," WL 4.30).

The pianist Orlando Goñi (1914–1945) created the double articulation during his years with Troilo between 1937 and 1943. Ever since then, it's been present in all modern tango, regardless of style. This way of playing *marcato* combines two articulations that are contrary in character – the left hand connects the bass notes and holds each for its full value, and the right hand plays very short percussive chords. The effect created by this double articulation is reinforced by the double bass, which imitates the piano but articulates each note with a short, percussive strike of the bow. In this type of *marcato*, the piano's right hand usually plays all four beats on the beat, coinciding with the left hand. However, it often separates from the left hand and plays a 3-3-2 (eight-note groupings of three, three, and two) pattern creating a very interesting polyrhythm (Ex. 4.3). "Bien porteño" ("Truly porteño" [one from Buenos Aires]) offers an excellent example of this polyrhythm (WL 4.31). One can also hear this variant of double articulation in orchestras established under Troilo's influence in the mid-1940s, like those of Francini-Pontier and Piazzolla.

In Troilo's style, the bassist plays *marcato* mainly with the bow, although pizzicato is used when the situation calls for more thrust or a change in timbre. That being said, there is an apparent contrast between the early period of the orchestra and what comes later since, in the first period, almost everything is played pizzicato (another intersection between early Troilo and D'Arienzo's style). For example, one can hear the bass play arco in Troilo's 1943 recording of "La cumparsita" (WL 4.32) and can

Example 4.3 Double articulation in the piano, creating a polyrhythm through blending left-hand *marcato* and right-hand 3-3-2.

contrastingly hear pizzicato in his 1941 recording of "Milongueando en el cuarenta" ("Milonga-ing in the '40s," WL 4.33).

The orchestra had three great bassists throughout its discography: Enrique "Kicho" Díaz (1918–1992) from 1937 and 1959, Alcides Rossi (b. 1927) from 1959 to 1961, and finally, Rafael Del Bagno (1915–1995) from 1961 to 1975. Kicho laid the foundation for the language and development of countless other *arrastres*, chords, and effects that every tango bass player would later use. "De muy adentro" ("From Deep Inside," WL 4.34) offers an example of Kicho's *arrastre* with Troilo's orchestra. Rossi and Del Bagno respected this legacy, each with his own sound and personality.

Síncopa

Juan D'Arienzo

D'Arienzo's *síncopas* are the most personal ones in the language of tango. Their presence is crucial when it comes to providing some variety to the eternal *marcato* in 4 implemented by this style, and although the *síncopas* are not abundant, their use is very effective. A deep dive into D'Arienzo's discography confirms that there are not more than four to six measures of *síncopas* per tango in a sea of *marcato* in 4, where arrangements average between 70 and 80 measures. The other measures either do not have any *marcato*, or the whole orchestra plays a rhythmic tutti. "El africano" ("The African," WL 4.35) offers a simple and clear example of *síncopas a tierra* from the first incarnation of the orchestra.

Sometimes the listener may have difficulty discerning whether a *síncopa* is *anticipada* or *a tierra*. It may not be easy to distinguish since it is not always evident how the first part of the *síncopa* is accented; therefore, it is not always simply one or the other. This is exactly what happens with D'Arienzo's *síncopas*, at least with his main interpretive approach to this time-marking model, because he superimposes two accents: one on the anticipation and one on the downbeat. To understand what this *síncopa* is made of and to better hear it, one must atomize it, observe it in detail, and then put it back together. The following outlines a common approach in D'Arienzo's *síncopa anticipada*: the technique begins in the piano with a very low note eighth note before the downbeat; the piano may or may not play the downbeat, but it will definitely place a strong accent on the second eighth note of beat 1, and it may or may not play a chord on beat 3. The bass does not play the anticipation with the piano but instead plays the down-beat softly, without an accent, and with accents on the second eighth note of beat 1 along with the piano. The bandoneones play the downbeat, usually as part of a rhythmic articulation melody, and sometimes simply with chords as an accompaniment. Like the piano and the bass, the bandoneones also strongly accentuate the second eighth note of beat 1. Web Example 4.2 and Web Link 4.36 illustrate such a typical D'Arienzo *síncopa anticipada*, heard in "Siete leguas" ("Seven Leagues"). While the exaggerated accent gives this off-beat the type of prominence that leads one to identify it as the heart of D'Arienzo's *síncopa*, the recipe is still missing a fundamental ingredient.

D'Arienzo's little formula adds another accent on the last beat of a *síncopa* measure, which, combined with the second eighth note of beat 1, puts the icing on the cake of the unmistakable personality of his *síncopas*. Although it is not a rule, the last beat of each measure is also accented vigorously in the rhythm section and the rhythmic melody. His performance of "Tucumán" (province in Argentina, WL 4.37) exemplifies this hallmark of D'Arienzo's rhythmic style.

It is to be expected that in almost 1,000 recordings over forty years, there are some variants. Some examples of minor differences in the first part of the pattern, but always with a strong accent on the second eighth note of beat 1 include "Chiqué" ("Elegant," WL 4.38), with piano pickup notes; "Don Orlando," which has an almost imperceptible downbeat (WL 4.39), and "Mi parejero" ("My Fast Horse," WL 4.40), which also features *arrastre* in the bandoneones on the downbeat and without an accent on beat four.

Aníbal Troilo

Like D'Arienzo, Troilo's style also incorporates a distinctive use of *síncopa*. One such feature is how he often uses successive *síncopas*. In this model, the first part of the *síncopa* is repeated in the second part of the measure, followed by a normal measure of *síncopa*. Troilo's recording of "Pablo" illustrates his successive *síncopas* (WL 4.41).

Troilo uses *síncopa a tierra* as much as *síncopa anticipada*, with different versions depending on the context. Regarding *síncopa a tierra*, it's worth remembering that although a *síncopa* may have a very prominent anticipation in the piano and other instruments, by definition, the first eighth note of the downbeat is played, even if it is not accented. Troilo's recording of "Don Juan" illustrates his approach to this category of *síncopa a tierra* (WL 4.42).

In its variants, *síncopa a tierra* may feature differences in the strength of the accents on the anticipation and the downbeat, according to the taste or personality of the performers. I identify three such varieties in Troilo's style. First, the piano and the bass play two ascending sixteen notes as pick-up notes, usually playing an accent on the second eighth note of beat 1. This variety is very typical in *milonguero* (dance-oriented) styles like those of Tanturi, Miguel Caló (1907–1972), or D'Arienzo explained earlier, as heard in "Para lucirse" ("To Show Off," WL 4.43). In another version, the bass plays everything pizzicato, using anticipated descending or ascending sixteenth notes. An attractive and rather mysterious rhythmic effect is created by the change in timbre and by a certain intentional imprecision, as heard in "El africano" (WL 4.44). A third variant uses *arrastre* in the bass, where the sliding technique has a dual role. On the one hand, it anticipates the *síncopa a tierra* with subtlety and authority to help the whole orchestra clearly understand where to accent. On the other hand, the friction created by the bow on the string adds a timbre that enriches the overall sonority. Troilo's recording of "Color de rosa" ("Pink Colored," WL 4.45) illustrates this third variant using *arrastre*.

Troilo's use of *síncopa anticipada* also distinguishes his rhythmic style. As previously explained, only the anticipation is played in this *síncopa*, not the downbeat. To accomplish the effect, all the musicians must follow this premise to a "T" and avoid playing the downbeat to achieve a total rhythmic clarity that leads, rather than confuses, the rest of the orchestra. Here, the bass must imitate the mechanics of the piano precisely, copying the effect of the hammer striking the string with a strong, single accent followed by a natural decay in the intensity of the volume of the accented note. To achieve this, the bassist must strongly articulate the anticipation of the *síncopa* and immediately lower the volume applying less pressure to the bow. This important performance practice, which is not always well understood, may be heard in Troilo's recording of "Luna llena" ("Full Moon," WL 4.46).

Concluding Thoughts

The three fundamental rhythmic elements in tango – tempo, *marcato*, and *síncopa* – offer a key perspective to compare the orchestral styles of D'Arienzo and Troilo, where every interpretive detail is crucial to the sound of both orchestras. This straightforward comparison between Troilo's and D'Arienzo's styles, focusing on these three core tango rhythmic elements, makes evident why these two orchestras sound so different, both rhythmically and expressively. While D'Arienzo's orchestra consistently plays with a *tempo fijo*, exaggerates accents in the four beats of the *marcato*, and uses *síncopa a tierra* exclusively, Troilo's orchestra plays with a *tempo flexible*, mainly accents the strong beats in *marcato*, and alternates between different types of *síncopa* depending on the context. In short, while D'Arienzo's orchestra is a seamless, unstoppable rhythmical machine beloved by all tango dancers around the world, Troilo's orchestra takes its time to narrate a story, using different tools to create a rich and expressive narrative that touches the audience emotionally.

The treatment of the tempo and the described stylistic details on how to play *marcatos* and *síncopas* are key to discerning the differences between these two emblematic Golden-age orchestras and defining any tango style more broadly. Using this logic, one can understand how the sum of the different details in every orchestra's rhythmic treatment defines part of the infinite richness of tango as a popular art form. I hope this chapter provides an incentive for readers to become interested in continuing their discovery of the subtleties that make up the beauty and depth of this musical genre.[1]

Notes

1. Editors' note: for further study of tango orchestral styles, see the author's seminars "Los Estilos Fundamentales del Tango" on his website www.ignaciovarchausky.com.

Further Reading

Cadícamo, Enrique, and Luis Adolfo Sierra. *La Historia del tango: La época Decareana*. Buenos Aires: Corregidor, 1977.

Del Priore, Oscar. *El Tango: De Villoldo a Piazzolla*. Buenos Aires: Editorial del Noroeste, 1975.

  Toda mi vida (Aníbal Troilo). Buenos Aires: JVE, 2003.

Ferrer, Horacio, *El libro del tango: Arte popular de Buenos Aires*. Three volumes. Barcelona: Antonio Tersol, 1980.

Gobello, José. *Breve historia crítica del tango*. Buenos Aires: Corregidor, 1999.

  Crónica general del tango. Buenos Aires: Fraterna, 1980.

Loriente, Horacio. *Ochenta notas de tango: Perfiles biográficos*. Montevideo: Ediciones de la Plaza, 1998.

Possetti, Hernán. *El piano en el tango*. Buenos Aires: Ediciones Tango Sin Fin, 2015.

Sierra, Luis Adolfo. *Historia de la orquesta típica*. Buenos Aires: A. Peña Lillo, 1976.

Zucchi, Oscar. *El Tango, el bandoneón y sus intérpretes*. Buenos Aires: Corregidor, 1998.

5 | Guitar Heroes: Roberto Grela and Aníbal Arias

ERIC JOHNS

Histories of tango often emphasize the guitar's role in the early tango by portraying scenes of the instrument, maybe with a flute and violin, accompanying a couple dancing in a close embrace and romantically illuminated by a gas lamp. While stylistic changes have led the guitar's relegation to the outside of the *orquesta típica* (typical tango orchestra), the guitar has maintained a constant presence in the history of tango. Today tango guitar builds on a variety of traditions, most prominently the *tango canción* (tango song), but also classical guitar, jazz, and Rioplatense (from the Río de la Plata region) folk traditions.

In this chapter, I examine the historical and stylistic lineage of tango guitar practice through the influence of two leading figures: Roberto Grela (1913–1992) and Aníbal Arias (1922–2010). While I could have chosen many other guitarists,[1] I decided to focus on Grela and Arias because they are the most consistently referenced inspirations in my personal conversations and interviews with tango guitarists and aficionados. Furthermore, I argue that they are a part of a significant historical trajectory, which I trace in this chapter. I base my research for this chapter on formal and informal interviews, musical transcription, extant literature, and my personal experiences as a student of Aníbal Arias between 2007 and 2009.

Roberto Grela

Roberto León Grela was born into a musical family on June 28, 1913, at Cochabamba 773 in the San Telmo neighborhood of Buenos Aires. His father and uncle formed the duo Hermanos Delpaso, and tango guitarist and composer Manuel Parada (1902–1980) regularly visited the family's jam sessions. While Grela first learned to play the mandolin at home with his uncles, his admiration for Parada led him to switch to the guitar. He first performed publicly on the guitar with tango ensembles that included a singer inspired by the success of *cantores nacionales* (national singers), who used guitar accompaniment like Agustín Magaldi (1898–1938) and

Carlos Gardel (1890–1935).[2] Grela's brother Héctor introduced the young musician to guitarist and composer Avelino Casao, with whom he began to accompany the famous *cantor nacional* Charlo (1905–1990) in 1931.[3]

The foundations of Grela's style have much in common with other guitarists working with singers in the *tango canción* between the late 1910s to the mid-1930s.[4] Initially, it was most common for one or two guitarists to accompany a singer, though often the singer was a guitarist themselves. By the late 1920s, the most common grouping of guitarists accompanying singers was a quartet.[5] The *tango canción* genre is closely connected to Gardel and the guitarists who accompanied him throughout his career: José Ricardo (1888?–1937), Guillermo Barbieri (1894–1935), José María Aguilar (1891–1951), Ángel Domingo Riverol (1893–1935), Julio Vivas (1895–1952), and Horacio Pettorossi (1896–1960). Gardel and his contemporary guitarists, who are particularly associated with instruments made by Antigua Casa Nuñez,[6] primarily used classical guitar technique and posture. They performed seated in chairs, occasionally using footstools and PIMA digitization techniques.[7] In the 1930s, Aguilar began using a pick, an innovation that would forever change the sound of tango guitar.

In general, the early *tango canción* was cast in a two-part (AB) form, with the contrasting sections alternating between major and minor keys. Typically, simple chord progressions of I-V-I and I-IV-V-I harmonized the melody, occasionally adding the minor seventh to the V chord. The guitar primarily played an accompanimental role, using *barrido* (sweep) or *rasqueo* (strum) techniques, moving consecutively from the lowest to the highest notes of the chord with a single quick motion. Rather than sounding all notes at once, a *barrido* is similar to an appoggiatura in that it anticipates the beat and then arrives on the downbeat. Additionally, each note of the chord is performed tenuto.

The accompanimental rhythmic patterns common to the early *tango canción*, which still apply to tango guitar today, were *marcato* (marked), emphasizing beats one and three, and the less-common *síncopa a tierra* (downbeat syncopation) performed in 4/4 meter as two eighth notes, eighth-note rest, eighth note, quarter note, and quarter note. Common variations on the *marcato* pattern included adding two eighth notes to either the weaker second or fourth beats of the measure, where the guitarists often only performed the bass note on the second eighth note. The downbeat of these rhythmic patterns was sometimes approached with an *arrastre* (from the Spanish verb *arrastrar*, to drag) in which the guitarist literally dragged the fretting hand up to the intended chord. Stylistically, it was common to drag the entire chord shape in an *arrastre*.

In addition to the chordal accompanimental patterns, many melodic resources were available to *tango canción* guitarists. They often provided introductory material and melodic fills, sometimes harmonized in thirds or sixths. *Bordoneos* (patterns using the lowest three guitar strings, referred to as *la bordona*) filled in melodic content in the lower register, sometimes as an arpeggio embellishing chord tones chromatically, and occasionally coupling the voice in unison or thirds. Typically, guitarists of this period used *fraseo* (phrasing) that, while notated as four straight eighth notes, was performed more loosely as either eighth note, quarter, and two sixteenths, or as a quarter-note triplet of two quarter notes and two eighth notes.[8] They used other techniques for textural and aesthetic effects, such as *campanella* (little bell)[9] and tremolo, either outlining chord tones or emphasizing leading tones.[10]

Grela not only began his career but developed his style within this milieu. His earliest recordings in 1934 with Charlo for Discos Criollos Odeon incorporate many characteristics of the late *tango canción* period. In "Juan Manuel," for example, Grela and the other guitarists harmonize a quick introduction in thirds, then transition to a slow *milonga campera* (country milonga) section using tremolo to outline chord tones. In the faster sections of the recording, they employ Grela's characteristic all down-stroke picking technique, referred to as either "*ida*" (one-way) or "*directo*" (direct). Grela's influences at this time are not limited to tango with guitars. In an interview, he referred to Julio De Caro (1899–1980), the famous *guardia nueva* (New Guard) violinist and *orquesta típica* director, as his musical guide for the period.[11] After his time playing with Charlo, Grela accompanied Fernando Díaz (1903–1981), Alberto Serna (1900–1983), Agustín Irusta (1903–1987), and many other later *cantores nacionales*.

Grela was not exclusively interested in the tango. In 1938, he joined up with Los Escuadrones de Fleury (The Squadrons of Fleury), a guitar group specializing in arrangements of Rioplatense folk music led by the Argentine guitarist and composer Abel Fleury (1903–1958). Grela attributes this time with Fleury as critical in his development as a guitar player. In an interview printed in the magazine *Tango*, Grela states:

I couldn't play the way I had accompanied before. The harmonic part was different. Technically there was a great improvement. Guitaristically, it was Abel Fleury who reassured my ideas. With him, we rehearsed and rehearsed. That's why I think I can't play as I did in earlier times. I would be outdated.[12]

In the 1940s, Grela's interest in jazz and Brazilian music led him to form the group American Fire, and then two years later, his Sexteto de Jazz. The February 10, 1945, edition of the newspaper *El Mundo* includes an announcement for Grela's *orquesta de jazz* in the Carnival celebration *Flores que surgen* (Flowers that Emerge). The following year Grela performed for the Carnival celebrations in the El Liberal club for the Nueva Chicago football club (today known as Club Atlético Nueva Chicago). Both American Fire and his Sexteto de Jazz regularly performed on the radio, and the latter made four recordings.

Grela's full-time return to tango came in 1952 when he was invited to participate in bandoneón player and composer Aníbal Troilo (1914–1975) and poet Cátulo Castillo's (1906–1975) show *El patio de la morocha* (*The Patio of the Morocha*).[13] In this lyric *sainete* (a theatrical musical genre), Troilo played the role of the *guardia vieja* (Old Guard) bandoneonist Eduardo Arolas (1892–1924), and Grela played a fictional character named Pacífico Taboada on Arolas's tango "La cachila" ("The Little Bird"). The two performed standing, each with a single foot resting on a single chair. The success of *El patio de la morocha* led to the TK label's offer to record the duo. For the recording, the duo expanded into the Cuarteto Troilo-Grela,[14] which included Kicho Díaz (1918–1992) on bass and Edmundo P. Zaldívar (1917–1978) on guitarrón (baritone guitar).[15] After an initial 78 RPM recording, Díaz was replaced by Eugenio Pro and Zaldívar with Ernesto Báez (1925–1974, WP 5.1). Along with Domingo Láinez, the group recorded under the name Troilo-Grela, performing on radio and television as well as in nightclubs and touring internationally, including a 1954 tour to Japan. The group also accompanied numerous singers, many of whom had previously performed with Troilo's orchestra, including Edmundo Rivero (1911–1986).

Grela's work with Troilo was not limited to the quartet. In 1953, Troilo and Grela performed as a quintet with Enrique Mario Francini (1916–1978), Horacio Salgán (1916–2016), and Díaz in a homage concert to the *guardia nueva* tango musician Juan Carlos Cobián (1896–1953). In 1956, he recorded with Troilo's *orquesta típica* for the TK label.[16] After his split from Troilo, Grela formed El Cuarteto San Telmo with the bandoneonist Leopoldo Federico (1927–2014), Báez on guitar, and Román Arias on bass in 1966.

The introduction of the guitarrón into tango was critical in developing the modern tango guitar sound. Musicians from the Cuyo region in central-west Argentina developed the instrument and brought it to Buenos Aires during a period of internal migration in the 1940s. A coinciding explosion of folk genres meant that *porteño* musicians, like Zaldívar, also adapted the instrument. The instrument is slightly bigger than the guitar and is tuned down a fourth (B-E-A-D-F#-B). In some cases, guitarists restring their guitars using the low B-string from a seven-string guitar to imitate the sound and affectionately call it *guitarrón trucho* (fake or knockoff guitarrón). When written, music for guitarrón can be notated in concert pitch, though transposed up an octave for easier reading in the treble clef or transposed to facilitate guitarists' ease in performing the instrument. In Grela, and other tango guitar ensembles, the guitarrón primarily shares an accompanimental role playing chords, often also played by another guitarist, and *bordoneos*. The lower pitch of the guitarrón gives the ensemble a greater range and denser texture.

The influence and overlap of jazz and Rioplatense folk on tango guitar players is not limited to Grela. Guitarronist Zaldívar is perhaps most famous as the composer of the *carnavalito* "El humauaqueño" (a person from the city of Humahuaca in the Argentine province of Jujuy).[17] Ernesto Villavencio, another guitarist in Grela's ensembles, came from the Cuyo region and also performed folk repertory in addition to tango. In 1961, Grela himself was asked to rerecord the guitar parts of a number of *estilos* (a Rioplatense folk genre associated with the countryside) recorded by Carlos Gardel for CBS.[18] Grela's contemporary José Canet is well known for accompanying the tango singer Nelly Omar (1911–2013), who regularly incorporated Rioplatense folk genres into her repertory,[19] and he also briefly led jazz ensembles in the 1940s. In 1953, Ubaldo De Lío formed the Quinteto del Hot Club de Buenos Aires with composer and jazz pianist Lalo Schifrin (b. 1932).

The classic tango guitar ensemble of the late 1950s to the present day expands on the same instrumentation and performance-practice techniques that Grela drew from the *tango canción* of the 1920s and '30s. Trios, quartets, and quintets of guitars could include the guitarrón, and guitarists expanded upon the rhythmic patterns of *marcato* and *síncopa* by including *milonga* and the 3-3-2 pattern. The basic *milonga* pattern, like its antecedent, the Cuban *habanera*, is a dotted eighth, sixteenth, dotted eighth, and sixteenth, with full chords played on the strong beats and a single note, often the bass, played on the weak beats. The 3-3-2 pattern derives from the *milonga campera* (country milonga) by converting the bass notes to chords, which are played in the eighth-note groupings of dotted quarter, dotted quarter, and quarter. Guitarists also began to perform standing upright, either using neck straps or propping a leg on a stool as Grela did when he first performed with Troilo, in addition to classically sitting with or without the use of footstools. The increased use of picks in this period and the change from "gut" to nylon strings allowed for a greater volume level. While guitarists continued to accompany singers, guitar ensembles began to perform instrumental works more often.

Grela formed his first guitar quartet in 1958 with Laine, Báez, Ayala, and Pro on double bass. These quartets recorded and performed both instrumental works and accompanied *cantores nacionales*. For many years, Grela and his ensemble famously accompanied Edmundo Rivero at El Viejo Almacén, a famed tango venue in the San Telmo neighborhood of Buenos Aires.

Grela's use of chromaticism and swing belies his jazz background. When comparing Grela's performance to written scores, he uses various elements to elaborate the melody by including mordents, appoggiaturas, and chromatic runs between notes. These chromatic runs do not necessarily begin on melody notes. For example, in his 1964 version of "Los mareados" ("The Drunkards," WL 5.1), the original melody is completely displaced. In this recording, Grela often approaches the first notes of melodies and other accented notes using glissandi or *arrastres* from an undetermined starting point. He also shortens appoggiaturas to be effectively performed as a minor second.

Rhythmic alteration to melodies was also a regular feature in Grela's playing. Throughout "Los mareados," for example, Grela often anticipates or delays a melodic note by up to an eighth note or with a swung *fraseo* triplet, while at other times he anticipates the downbeat of *síncopa a tierra* rhythmic cells by an eighth note with single-note *arrastres*. He also creates a sense of beat displacement for entire measures by using repeated syncopations.

Grela's ensembles broke from the traditional arranging methods of harmonizing melodies in parallel thirds, sixths, and octaves to make regular use of countermelodies. At times elaborate countermelodies sound between the other guitar voices, as in "Gallo ciego" ("Blind Rooster," WL 5.2),[20] and other times they weave in and out of the vocal melody, as in "Cambalache" ("Hodgepodge," as in a junk shop, WL 5.3). Solo lines could include dissonant harmonies, including minor seconds.

Grela's ensembles expanded upon the accompaniment resources of the generation before. In addition to employing the standard rhythmic patterns of *marcato* and *síncopa*, Grela's ensembles would temporarily invert the accented beats in both patterns by shifting the accents from one and three to two and four, as heard in Troilo-Grela's recording of "Ivette" (1962). *Pesantes* (literally "heavies") are a rhythmic variation on the *marcato* in 4 pattern where all chords are given equal weight and their full value. Grela ingeniously incorporated *pesantes* as harmonic connectors, using parallel chromatic motion to move from one key to another. Similarly, Grela uses *blanca* (half-note) chords in Alfredo Sadi's 1982 version of "Las cuarenta" (literally "The Forties," but more poetically "The Harsh Truths," WL 5.4)[21] with a *coral* (choral) technique in *blancas*, where each voice moves independently.

The *gran tremolo-batido* (great shaking tremolo) technique extends the tremolo to entire chords. Arpeggiated chords also occasionally use minor seconds. An example of this can be heard in Nelly Omar's 1969 recording of "Muchacho" ("Young Boy," WL 5.5), where Grela and Máximo Barbieri outline Am and E^7 chords using minor seconds. This example also uses *células acéfalas* (groups of notes beginning with a rest), where Grela rests for the first eighth note and plays an accented minor second on the next.

Grela projects an expanded harmonic sound in his ensembles. Chords can be extended similarly to jazz, yet with much less frequency. However, most chords are still performed as triads. In Grela's style, the chords are often played without the doubling of notes.

Guitarists today regularly imitate critical elements of Grela's style, such as his all-down picking technique and wide vibrato. Additionally, the master's chord voicings that often lack the doubling of notes are popular among guitarists. While Grela's level of virtuosity is difficult to attain, particularly his down-picking speed, Grela remains an important influence on performance and arrangement style among guitarists performing today.

Aníbal Arias

Much like Grela, Aníbal Arias's influence on today's guitarists is as a performing and recording artist. While Arias's style drastically differs from Grela's, it also builds upon past connections to the tango guitar tradition. Arias has made a more direct impact, however, as a renowned guitar instructor.

Arias was born in Buenos Aires on July 25, 1922, to a musical family from the northwestern province of Catamarca, Argentina. His father was once a guitarist and singer for Manuel Acosta Villafañe's (1902–1956) folk

Figure 5.1 Aníbal Arias and the author at the Academia Nacional del Tango in Buenos Aires, 2007.

ensemble. As a child, Aníbal participated in his family's folk ensemble, Los Catamarqueñitos (The Catamarcans), where he accompanied his older sister Amanda in guitar duets. At age nine, he began to study classical guitar with Pedro Ramírez Sánchez (1885–1959). His studies of Francisco Tárrega's technique with Ramírez Sánchez would significantly influence his playing and teaching for the rest of his life. In the 1940s, Arias began giving recitals performing selections from the classical guitar repertory.

As a recitalist, Arias soon returned to performing a variety of popular music. In the 1940s, he joined the folk group Los Arrieros Cuyanos (The Mule Drivers from Cuyo). This group drew upon and contributed to the popularity of the *folklore cuyano* genre that helped influence the incorporation of the guitarrón into tango guitar ensembles. During this period, Arias accompanied several prominent folklore singers, including Virignia Vera, Alberto Castelar, and Waldo Belloso. In 1949, Arias joined the singer Alberto Ortiz's quartet, where he began accompanying tango singers such as Ángel Reco, Héctor Mauré, Ángel Cárdenas, Libertad Lamarque, and Raúl Berón. Outside of his work with Ortiz's quartet, he also accompanied singers such as Jorge Casal, Oscar Alonso, Rogelio Araya, Aída Denis, Olga Cabrera, and Edmundo Rivero. Like many tango musicians of the time,

Arias played a variety of popular musics and did not exclusively dedicate himself to tango. He played requinto, a small guitar-like instrument, in Los Pregoneros de América (The Town Criers of America), toured with comedic shows featuring the actor Ricardo Pimentel, and composed and performed Greek music as a part of the Ballet Friego Lambrinis.

Like Grela, Arias is most well-known for his time playing with Aníbal Troilo. In 1969, Arias joined Troilo's quartet with Rafael Del Bagno on bass and José Colángelo on piano, whom he accompanied on electric guitar until Troilo's death in 1975.[22] Arias also appeared with Troilo's *orquesta típica* on several occasions, including the ensemble's final performance on May 17, 1975, at the Teatro Odeón (WL 5.6). In 1980, Arias was invited to join the Orquesta de Tango de Buenos Aires (Tango Orchestra of Buenos Aires) under the direction of Carlos García and Raúl Garello.

Many radio stations that employed tango musicians, including guitarists, began to close in the late 1960s and early '70s. These closures, coupled with restrictions on nightlife imposed by the military junta, made professional musicians' lives difficult. However, the 1980s brought educational institutions as a new avenue for employment. Arias initially gave guitar lessons in his apartment on Perón Street. In 1986, Arias joined the inaugural staff of the Escuela de Música Popular de Avellaneda (School of Popular Music of Avelleneda, just south of the city of Buenos Aires).

With an increasing number of students coming to focus on tango guitar specifically, Arias began to write arrangements of over a hundred classic tangos as pedagogical tools. These arrangements were subsequently published by Editorial Melos (formerly Ricordi) and have been widely passed among tango guitarists. Many of the arrangements are currently available online.[23] In addition to the numerous arrangements available to guitarists today, Editorial Melos has also published a book of arrangements for beginners that includes simple melodies and bass lines.[24]

Despite Arias's meticulous arrangements, he did not perform his tangos precisely as written. Tango guitarist and arranger Javier Alem (1959–2021) compares the published arrangement and 1995 recording of the Osvaldo Fresedo and Edmundo Bianchi tango "Pampero" (name for a burst of cold polar air from the west, southwest, or south on the Pampas, WL 5.7). Throughout the performance, Arias plays written block chords as arpeggios, expands the melody with melodic fills, plays alternate bass lines, and displaces the rhythm throughout.[25] Arias was capable of performing solo guitar versions of tangos in almost any key. Many students of Arias, including myself, have shared their experiences of asking Arias to perform a tango in a specific key, only to be surprised by his ability to do so (Figure 5.1).

Arias's style is rooted in the classical guitar tradition. He often assigned classical studies, such as the Tárrega arpeggio studies, to his students. Arias performed using classical guitar posture, a footstool, and right-hand PIMA digitization. Unlike many contemporary classical guitarists, Arias performed without nails yet could still produce a loud and robust sound.[26] Particularly vital in Arias's playing is the concept of *mugre*, literally meaning "dirt." *Mugre* can be any sort of percussive or noisy sound, but in Arias's playing, it is most specifically the noise produced by the strings. This is a significant departure from classical performers who strive for purity of tone. An essential part of Arias's technique was how he used his thumb. He would dig his thumb deep into the strings yet still be able to play entire chords, strumming from the sixth to the third string with his thumb.

Similar to Grela's style of building upon performance practices of guitarists of the *tango canción* period, the crossover of classical guitar and tango has historical antecedents as well. One early crossover guitarist, Domingo Prat arrived in Buenos Aires in 1907, where he both taught and concertized. Prat had been a student of Miguel Llobet, who himself had been a student of Tárrega's. Llobet, along with Josefina Robledo (1897–1972) and Emilio Pujol (1886–1980), helped further spread the popularity of the so-called "Tárrega School" through concertizing in Buenos Aires. The Tárrega technique is based on the studies and methods of classical guitarists/composers Fernando Sor and Dionisio Aguado yet adjusts the right hand's position to allow for a more perpendicular attack on the string and the resting of the finger on an unsounded string immediately after playing.

The use of classical guitar technique in the performance of tango did not begin with Arias. Domingo Prat and Melanie Plesch have noted the overlap between academic and popular guitarists at events held at the Almacén de Raconi and La Berbenita.[27] At the turn of the twentieth century, classical guitarists like Gaspar Sagreras, Julio Sagreras, and Daniel Fortea published transcriptions of tangos for solo guitar, while Vicente Caprino Maineri, Pedro Quijano Mansilla, Fortea, and Julio Sagreras (under the pseudonym Resgrasa), composed original tangos for solo guitar as well.[28]

Tango and classical guitar continued to overlap during tango's *guardia nueva* and Golden Age (1930s–1955). As early as 1914, a concert in Buenos Aires at the Teatro Moderno, today Liceo, included popular music and classical guitar when the Paraguayan composer and guitarist Agustín Barrios (1885–1944) shared a stage with the Carlos Gardel-José Razzano duo.[29] The *cantor nacional* Edmundo Rivero and one-time professional guitar accompanist studied guitar and voice at the Conservatorio Nacional Superior de Música (Argentine National Conservatory).[30] The tango guitar even reached the hallowed halls of the Teatro Colón. On December 13, 1930, an orchestra of forty guitar players, under the direction of De Caro, took the stage of the Colón to perform tangos for La Fiesta del Tango (The Tango Festival), sponsored by the magazine *Comedia*.[31] The guitarist and composer Manuel Parada, who was a frequent guest in the childhood home of Grela, accompanied tango singers, participated in mixed-instrument trios such as his trio with the pianist Enrique Delfino and violinist Antonio Rodio, and recorded and composed tangos for solo guitar with an impeccable technique.

While Arias's solo performances have received the most attention, his time in Troilo's quartet and orchestra deserves a special note. Alem recalls Arias's first rehearsal with the quartet when he replaced De Lío. When Arias arrived with his parts written out, Troilo asked what he had with him. When Arias responded that it was his parts for the quartet, Troilo replied that the quartet did not have written parts. Arias had transcribed his parts from the recordings. After rehearsing two songs, Troilo was content with the results, called the rehearsal off, and invited the musicians to have a drink instead.[32] A recently uncovered recording of Troilo's final performance reveals the musical ways the orchestra navigated the difficulties of integrating a nylon-string guitar into its ranks. While Arias performs throughout, his artistry shines when the orchestra reduces its volume and allows Arias to perform brief passages that would not be out of place in the classical guitar repertory.

Grela and Arias's Legacy

The legacy of Grela and Arias today is a powerful testament to the continuities and on-going story of the guitar in tango. Grela began his career during the *guardia nueva* and Arias during the Golden Age. And while Grela's notoriety waned in his final years, Arias remained an important figure in the Buenos Aires performing scene until 2009, when his health declined. After his passing in 2010, his legacy has been carried on by his many students. Both guitarists expanded on the traditions and techniques set by the guitarists of previous generations. Grela expanded upon the techniques of the guitarists of *tango canción*, and Arias continued the long history of tango and the classical guitar. Neither started their careers as tango guitarists. And while Arias never played jazz, both spent considerable time performing Rioplatense folk music. In my interviews with thirty-six guitarists, all mentioned Grela, and twenty-two of them mentioned Arias. Guitarists who cited Grela's influence on their playing often referred to his down-stroke picking style. Seven of those interviewed were direct students of Arias. The former students commonly commented on Arias' essentially unstructured and informal lessons of teaching by rote. As one of those students myself, I learned by listening and observing him. Grela and Arias are *maestros* (teachers/masters) of the guitar, in both meanings of the word. Their direct and indirect influence can be heard throughout the soundscape of contemporary tango guitar, giving testament to their enduring legacies.

Notes

1. Other prominent guitarists cited by contemporary guitarists as influences not discussed in depth in this chapter include José Canet (1915–1984), Bartolomé Palermo (1936–2015), Tito Francia (1926–2004), Ubaldo De Lío (1929–2012), Horacio Malvicino (1929–2023), Oscar López Ruiz (1938–2021), Cacho Tirao (1941–2007), and Juanjo Domínguez (1951–2019).
2. "La guitarra mayor del tango," *Los grandes del tango* 1, no. 52 (October 1991): 8–12.
3. Lorena Burec, *Estilos guitarrísticos del tango en el Río de la Plata: Un siglo de historia* (Buenos Aires, Argentina: Editorial Autores de Argentina, 2015), 186; and Omar García Brunelli, "Grela, Roberto," in *Diccionario de la música española e hispanoamericana* (Madrid: Sociedad General de Autores y Editores, 1999), 896.
4. Lorena Burec divides *tango canción* into two sub-periods, the first from 1917 to 1925/26, and the second beginning in 1926/27 until 1935. The second period's division coincides with the advent of electronic sound recording in Argentina and Carlos Gardel's death in 1935. In this chapter, when I refer to *tango canción*, I am referencing sung tango between 1917 and 1935. Burec, *Estilos guitarrísticos del tango*, 67.
5. Outside of sung tango, guitarists performed in various ensembles, including trios with bandoneón and piano.
6. A guitar and luthier shop based in Buenos Aires started by the Spanish immigrant Francisco Nuñez (1841–1919) in 1870.
7. PIMA is an acronym standing for *pulgar* (thumb), *indice* (index finger), *medio* (middle finger), and *anular* (ring finger).
8. The rhythmic technique *fraseo* is similar to the concept of "swing" in jazz.

9. *Campanella* is a bell-like effect produced by playing scalar melodies across several strings instead of on a single string.
10. Burec, *Estilos guitarrísticos del tango*, 67–148; Julián Graciano, *Método de Guitarra Tango* (Buenos Aires: Melos, 2016), 119–127; Sebastián Henríguez, *La Guitarra En El Tango: Método Fundamental Para Aprender a Tocar Tango* (Buenos Aires: Tango sin fin, 2018), 20–41.
11. "La guitarra mayor del tango," 12.
12. Gaspar J. Astarita, *Abel Fleury: Vida y obra* (Chivilcoy, Argentina: Editorial GraFer, 1995), 45. "Como yo acompañaba antes no se podría tocar. Varió mucho la parte armónica. Técnicamente hubo una gran superación. Guitarrísticamente quien me renovó en mis conceptos fue Abel Fleury. Con él todas las tardes ensayábamos y ensayábamos. Por eso pienso que ya no puedo tocar como en los primeros tiempos. Estaría fuera de época."
13. *Morocha* is an ambiguous term that can either be a racialized reference to a person with a dark complexion or a brunette. For a discussion on the history and multiple meanings of the word in Argentina, see Ezequiel Adamovsky, "A Strange Emblem for a (Not So) White Nation: *La Morocha* Argentina in the Latin American Racial Context, c. 1900–2015," *Journal of Social History* 50, no. 2 (Winter 2016): 386–410.
14. According to Grela, Troilo wanted to form a trio with two guitars as early as 1933 when performing with Elvino Vardaro's sextet. The most notable trio of this type was Trio Ciriaco Ortiz, formed in 1929. "La guitarra mayor del tango," 20–21.
15. Oscar del Priore, *Toda Mi Vida: Aníbal Troilo* (Buenos Aires: JVE Ediciones, 2003), 85–86.
16. Grela also recorded solos with the *orquestas típicas* of José Basso in 1967 for Music Hall, and Alberto Castillo in 1959 for Odeón. In 1979, he joined the house orchestra for Canal II directed by Osvaldo Requena.
17. The *carnavalito* is a traditional collective dance from the Argentine province of Jujuy. Despite the genre's indigenous origins, the Buenos Aires-born Zaldívar composed *El humauaqueño* on his way to work at Radio El Mundo in Buenos Aires in 1941.
18. In addition to the "technical reconstruction" of these *estilos*, several rereleased versions of Gardel's records erased and replaced the sounds of the original guitar players with an *orquesta típica*.
19. Pablo Buffa, "Tango y jazz: Cuando Carlos García, Roberto Grela y José Canet dirigían sus orquestas de jazz," *La Campaña*, December 16, 1996, sec. Suplemento de tango y lunfardo.
20. As Bardi's tango is an instrumental arrangement, it is difficult to know the intent behind the title. But "Gallo ciego" may also reference a blindfolded tag game called "gallina ciega" ("blind man's bluff").

21. The song title "Las cuarenta" references the *Lunfardo* (Rioplatense slang) reprimand "*cantar las cuarenta*," meaning "to tell the truth harshly." The phrase comes from the card game *tute cabrero*, which has forty cards.

22. Burec, *Estilos guitarrísticos del tango*, 295; Horacio Ferrer, *El Libro del tango. Arte popular de Buenos Aires*, 2nd ed., vol. 2 (Buenos Aires: Antonio Tersol, 1980), 43; Sara Ribot, "Aníbal Arias: La guitarra ha llegado a la Academia Nacional del Tango," *La Campaña*, September 17, 1992, sec. Suplemento de tango y lunfardo.

23. "ARREGLOS PARA GUITARRA SOLA," *Aníbal Arias* (blog), May 26, 2012, https://anibalarias.wordpress.com/sheet-music.

24. Arias is said to not have liked these simplified arrangements. However, they continue to serve a pedagogical function as students can add chords to the basslines and melodies creating their own arrangements in the process.

25. Javier Alem, "Pampero" (Tango). "Arreglo Para Guitarra de Aníbal Arias. Copia, Revisión y Desgrabación de Javier Alem," provided to the author via email, August 23, 2019.

26. Arias's reason for performing without nails was more practical than aesthetic; he had difficulty constantly breaking them.

27. Domingo Prat, *A Biographical, Bibliographical, Historical, Critical Dictionary of Guitars (Related Instruments), Guitarists (Teachers, Composers, Performers, Lutenists, Amateurs), Guitar-Makers (Luthiers), Dances and Songs, Terminology* (Columbus, OH: Editions Orphée, 1986), 18, 119, 254, and 295; Melanie Plesch, "The Guitar in Nineteenth-Century Buenos Aires: Towards a Cultural History of an Argentine Musical Emblem" (PhD diss., University of Melbourne, 1998), 260–264.

28. Lorena Burec, "El tango académico para guitarra sus antecedents, recursos técnicos y expresivos (notación y forma, género y estilo); análisis de algunas obras" (Universidad Nacional de Cuyo, 2009), 32, and 58–60; Burec, *Estilos guitarrísticos del tango*, 33.

29. It should be noted that the dúo Gardel-Razzano did not yet perform tangos in 1914. Horacio Arturo Ferrer, *Inventario del tango*, vol. 1 (Buenos Aires: Fondo Nacional de las Artes, 1999), 118.

30. Horacio Ferrer, *El Libro del tango. Arte popular de Buenos Aires*, 2nd ed., vol. 1 (Buenos Aires: Antonio Tersol, 1980), 510.

31. Lois Reynaldo, "La Fiesta del tango en el Teatro Colón," *La Campaña*, April 12, 1987, sec. Suplemento de tango y lunfardo.

32. Javier Alem, interviewed by José Sebastián Barrera, "La guitarra en el tango" (Trabajo final, Argentina, Facultad Latinoamericana de Ciencias Sociales, 2016), 100.

Further Reading

Astarita, Gaspar J. *Abel Fleury: Vida y obra*. Chivilcoy, Argentina: Editorial GraFer, 1995.

Barrera, José Sebastián. "La guitarra en el tango." Trabajo final, Facultad Latinoamericana de Ciencias Sociales, 2016.

Burec, Lorena. *Estilos guitarrísticos del tango en el Río de la Plata: Un siglo de historia*. Buenos Aires, Argentina: Editorial Autores de Argentina, 2015.

Graciano, Julián. *Método de Guitarra Tango*. Buenos Aires: Melos, 2016.

Henríguez, Sebastián. *La Guitarra En El Tango: Método Fundamental Para Aprender a Tocar Tango*. Buenos Aires: Tango sin fin, 2018.

"La guitarra mayor del tango." *Los grandes del tango* 1, no. 52 (October 1991): 6–35.

Plesch, Melanie. "The Guitar in Nineteenth-Century Buenos Aires: Towards a Cultural History of an Argentine Musical Emblem." PhD diss., University of Melbourne, 1998.

Prat, Domingo. *A Biographical, Bibliographical, Historical, Critical Dictionary of Guitars (Related Instruments), Guitarists (Teachers, Composers, Performers, Lutenists, Amateurs), Guitar-Makers (Luthiers), Dances and Songs, Terminology*. Columbus, Ohio: Editions Orphée, 1986.

Priore, Oscar del. *Toda Mi Vida: Aníbal Troilo*. Buenos Aires: JVE Ediciones, 2003.

Ribot, Sara. "Aníbal Arias: La guitarra ha llegado a la Academia Nacional del Tango." *La Campaña*. September 17, 1992, sec. Suplemento de tango y lunfardo.

6 | Post–Golden Age Pillars: Horacio Salgán and Astor Piazzolla

KRISTIN WENDLAND AND KACEY LINK

Introduction

When engaging with tango music from the second half of the twentieth century, two towering figures immediately emerge: pianist/composer Horacio Salgán (1916–2016) and bandoneonist/composer Astor Piazzolla (1921–1992). These two musical pillars laid their respective foundations in the art form during its Golden Age (1930s–1955); upheld tango through its popular decline in the post–Golden Age with their artistic visions; and then moved the genre forward into the twenty-first century through their inspiration to others. Yet during their artistic pursuits, these *tangueros* (Argentine tango musicians) traveled on two distinct paths both in the trajectory of their careers and the development of their styles. In this chapter, we compare the lives of Salgán and Piazzolla and the characteristics of their music. We provide biographical backgrounds and in-depth analyses of their compositional styles and performance practices. Finally, we offer insight into how these *tangueros* became revered *maestros* that shaped the next generation and kept the flame of tango burning into the twenty-first century.

During tango's Golden Age, the art form flourished with musicians and poets creating a constant stream of new tangos and a multitude of large ensembles performing for eager dancers and audiences throughout Buenos Aires. Then, with the ousting of Juan Perón in 1955, life in Argentina changed. The country went through decades of instability due to political chaos, military dictatorships, and economic volatility. Simultaneously, rock music began to sweep the world, and by the mid-1970s, *rock nacional* (Argentine rock music) was all the rage. As a result of these shifts, tango declined, venues where people danced closed, and orchestras disbanded. In 1955, Salgán and Piazzolla – both at the beginning of their careers – were faced with a daunting question: how do they continue a livelihood in tango when the art form was quickly becoming passé?[1]

One might say that the answer was simple: stop chasing tango and pursue another musical genre. Yet, Salgán and Piazzolla were, in a sense, bound to their heritage in tango. When studying with the esteemed classical composition teacher Nadia Boulanger, Piazzolla played his tango "Triunfal" ("Triumphal") for her, and she replied: "Astor, this is beautiful. I like it a lot. Here is the true Piazzolla – do not ever leave it."[2] Salgán, too, had a strong connection to his tango heritage, as he states in his *Tango Course*: " ... music, is a consequence of the lifestyle of people living in a specific place and time."[3]

Salgán and Piazzolla were definitely cultural products of living in a specific place and time. Salgán, born in Buenos Aires in 1916, was raised by a musical family, and he studied piano and classical music at the Conservatorio Municipal. As a budding musician, he listened to ensembles that accompanied silent films, such as that of Julio De Caro, and began doing such work himself at age fourteen. Then, at twenty years old, his profession in tango commenced by joining the famous tango orchestra of Roberto Firpo. For the next eight years, Salgán performed and arranged for a variety of ensembles until 1944, when he formed his first orchestra. When tango declined in the mid-1950s, he formed smaller ensembles, namely, a duo with guitarist Ubaldo De Lío (1929–2012) and then his famous Quinteto Real in 1960 (WP 6.1).

The Quinteto Real performed in Buenos Aires as well as Europe and Japan, recording thirty-five tangos between 1960 and 1961.[4] Salgán took a short hiatus from performing in the 1970s during Argentina's tumultuous political climate and later formed his Nuevo Quinteto Real in the 1980s. This ensemble, comprised of bandoneón, violin, electric guitar, piano, and bass, prospered through both performing and recording, and the musicians were even featured in Carlos Saura's Oscar-nominated film *Tango* (1998). In 2003, Salgán retired from the stage, yet his ensemble continued to carry on his legacy under the direction of his son César Salgán. In 2005, Horacio Salgán received the Diamond Konex Award, as one of Argentina's most important personalities in popular music.

Piazzolla was born in Mar del Plata, Argentina in 1921, but at the age of four, he immigrated with his family to New York City. There, he was exposed to his Italian immigrant heritage, Jewish and Irish cultures,[5] and American jazz. At age eight, he began playing the bandoneón and later worked with the famed tango singer Carlos Gardel (1890–1935). In 1936, the family returned to Argentina, and at age eighteen, Piazzolla began chasing a career in tango. He had his "tango baptism"[6] with Aníbal Troilo's orchestra, where he first subbed and then became a bandoneón player and arranger. He studied classical music while working in tango during the 1940s and 1950s, and he took lessons with the celebrated Argentine composer Alberto Ginastera (1916–1983). His work *Sinfonía Buenos Aires* won a national grand prize that afforded him the opportunity to study composition with Boulanger in Paris. Then, when he returned to Buenos Aires in 1955, Piazzolla formed his Octeto Buenos Aires – the ensemble in which he forged his own tango voice. He called this new style *nuevo tango* (New Tango), in simple terms, a combination of tango, jazz, and classical music.

From this point forward, Piazzolla became a nomad seeking to play his music throughout the world. He lived in the United States, Argentina, France, and Italy and regularly toured internationally. Piazzolla experimented with a variety of projects composing for various ensemble formations, such as his quintets, an electronic octet, and a nonet, as well as for opera and film (WP 6.2). He worked with musicians of different genres, including jazz saxophonist Gerry Mulligan, to create their album *Summit* (1974). Formed in 1978 and touring for approximately ten years, one of his most successful ensembles was his second quintet, comprised of bandoneón, violin, electric guitar, piano, and bass. In 1990, he suffered a cerebral hemorrhage and passed away two years later. Yet, Piazzolla's music continues to spread as musicians worldwide perform his works regularly. In fact, in some communities, his name is now synonymous with the tango, and posthumously, he achieved the fame that he had perhaps desired.[7]

Analysis of Style and Sound

Horacio Salgán

Whether writing for large orchestras or smaller ensembles, such as his Quinteto Real, Salgán's finely crafted tango compositions generally adhere to the tango stylistic elements he inherited from previous generations of *tangueros*. They feature elegant melodies and crisp rhythms, while also incorporating jazz-like chromatic harmonies and expanded three-part formal structures. He favors lively syncopated *rítmico* (rhythmic) melodies that often spin out from short motivic cells ornamented with chromatic neighbor tone figures, typically in the A section of his pieces, while his lyrical *cantando* (singing) melodies, typically in the B sections, feature written-out *fraseos* (literally phrasing, and used as a performance-practice term for playing a tango melody in a flexible, elastic, and loose rhythmic manner relative to the beat, similar to "swing" in jazz). In either style, his masterful melodies tend to weave together and form contrapuntal webs, rather than thick chordal textures. Salgán draws on standard tango accompanimental rhythms like *marcato* (marked), *síncopa* (syncopated), and the 3-3-2 grouping, all often preceded by the anticipatory sliding technique *arrastre* (drag).[8] He enlarged such standard tango accompanimental patterns with his signature off-beat rhythm called *umpa-umpa*, a syncopated rhythm that accentuates the "&" of beats 2 and 3 in *marcato* in 4, then accents beat 4 and typically with an *arrastre* leading into the next downbeat (WE 6.1).

Salgán colors his rich harmonic palette with augmented and extended chords, modal mixture, and sudden tonal shifts. Even as he creates standard two-, four-, and eight-bar phrases combined into standard sixteen-, twenty-four-, and thirty-two-bar sections, Salgán's compositions typically elaborate the *guardia vieja* (Old Guard) three-part da capo design.

As a pianist and ensemble leader, Salgán's performance style throughout his career was as elegant as his compositional style. From his time as a duo partner with guitarist De Lío to his orchestra and quintet formations, melody always prevails within the texture. He is known for gracefully bringing out melodies through subtly nuanced changes in the registers of the piano or instruments of the ensemble. Like many other *tangueros* stemming from the *guardia nueva* (New Guard), Salgán and his ensembles frequently employed *yeites* (percussive instrumental tango techniques) to accent rhythmic accompaniments and to add an element of spice to melodies. Lastly, Salgán's playing is characterized by his technical precision, lightness of passagework, and refined phrasing. The following analyses of "Don Agustín Bardi" (referring to the *guardia vieja tanguero*) and "Grillito" ("Little Cricket") reveal many of these compositional and performance practice features of Salgán's music.[9]

"Don Agustín Bardi" (1947)

Cast in an ABCBA arch form with a coda, this lively tango in G minor features mostly contrapuntal textures (WL 6.1).[10] Each symmetrical sixteen-bar section contains two repeated and overlapped phrases. While the repeated phrase in the A section is clearly discernible, Salgán varies the repeated phrases in the B and C sections.

In the A section (0:00–0:30), the piano first states the sprightly *rítmico* melody (0:00–0:14), and the bandoneón repeats it (0:15–0:30), beginning hesitantly and then moving forward. The phrase, cast in a 2+2+4 measure classical sentence structure, features a chromatic double neighbor motive around $\hat{5}$ that leaps up to $\hat{3}$ in m.1, followed by a descending chromatic fill in m. 2, as shown in WE 6.2.

The bass accompanies lightly first in *síncopa*, then with *marcato* leading to the cadence. The middle part of each phrase adds a standard violin tango *yeite*, *chicharra* (literally cricket, for the sound produced by bowing behind the bridge). While Salgán's harmonic framework uses a standard tonic-predominant-dominant-tonic progression, the harmony is enriched with secondary dominants and chromaticism in the melody.[11] At the return of A (2:10–2:25), Salgán repeats the first eight-bar phrase exactly, but then inserts a coda in place of the second phrase.

Salgán moves to the relative major in the B section (0:31–1:04). The first phrase features a contrasting *cantando* melody with expressive *fraseos* in a *tango romanza* (romantic tango) style. The piano initiates the section in a fluid tempo, then the strings take up the melody (WE 6.3). The bando-neones follow, supported by a *marcato* accompanimental rhythm in an accelerating tempo. The second phrase of the B section provides a *tutti* restatement of the first but in a stricter tempo, creating an echo of the section's melodic idea in a *rítmico* setting, a *síncopa* accompanimental rhythm with strong *arrastres*, and an enriched chromatic harmonization. Salgán extends the cadential dominant as he evokes the chromatic double neighbor figure around $\hat{5}$, highlighted with reverse *látigo* (whip) *yeite* in the violin, followed by a chromatic wedge fill ending on $\hat{1}$. When Salgán returns to the B section (1:40–2:09), he does so exactly at first, but then varies the last four bars with chromatic runs, first in the piano, then the bandoneón, in place of the chromatic double neighbor figures. He then reverts to the same cadential pattern to close the section.

The C section (1:05–1:39) (marked "Trio" in the published piano sheet music), returns to G minor. The strings play the first *rítmico* statement of the phrase supported with *marcato*, and the bandoneones continue it as the strings take a new countermelody and the accompaniment rhythm changes to *síncopa*. A short piano solo highlighting Salgán's precise technique initiates the beginning of the repeated phrase, then the bandoneón returns in the second part of the phrase with a new *cantando* idea played *tutti* in a *rallentando* that closes the section.

The coda (2:26–2:28) begins with the bandoneón on the main melody, but then a new *cantando* and chromatic countermelody with emotive slides or portamenti sounds against it in the strings. In the second part of the phrase, the bandoneón breaks into virtuosic *variaciones* (variations, a standard tango feature that reiterates the main melody within the original phrase and harmonic framework embellished with running passagework), supported first by driving *marcato* then *síncopa* accompaniment. A *rallentando*, embellished with a violin reverse *látigo* in double stops, brings the tango to a close with a reminder of the chromatic double neighbor figure from the B section in the final cadence. The tango ends with the classic "chan-chan" V (played *forte*) – i (played *piano*) tango cadence.

"Grillito" (1954)

Salgán's elegantly composed tango in G minor expands a standard three-part form into ABCAB with a coda, each sixteen-bar section constructed with repeated four- and eight-bar phrases (WL 6.2).[12] The A section consists of two repeated eight-bar phrases (0:00–0:16 and 0:17–0:34) cast in 2+2+4 classical sentence structure (like "Don Agustín Bardi") in a *rítmico* melodic style. The piano states the opening two-bar group – a playful, chirping motive in thirds with chromatic neighbor tones, and then embellishes it sequentially up a step in the next two bars (WE 6.4). From the opening motive, one immediately hears Salgán's classic light and precise playing style. The following four-bar group of the sentence spins out the incomplete chromatic neighbor idea and leads with a chromatic run to a cadential pattern around $\hat{5}$ (also very similar to that in "Don Agustín Bardi"). Throughout the A section, the bass provides heavy *arrastres* with buoyant *síncopa* accompaniment. Harmonically, Salgán enriches a diatonic frame-work with chromatic neighbor and passing chords, and an augmented sixth chord preceding the cadential dominant.[13] Throughout this A section, Salgán incorporates *yeites* to enhance the complexity and texture, including *golpes* (hitting the instrument) and *chicharra*. In the repetition, Salgán adds imitative fragments of the piano melody in the bandoneón.

Salgán links to the contrasting B section (0:35–1:09), in the key of the submediant E♭ rather than the more standard relative major, with a series of chromatic passing chords. He constructs this section with four four-bar phrases – the first three are similar, while the final is contrasting. The first and second phrases present a lush *cantando* melody with *fraseos* in the piano and strings, including *campanas* (bells) in rising broken octaves in the piano, and the third phrase changes to *rítmico* with a *síncopa* accompaniment. Salgán splits the final phrase into two *cantando* bars and then changes to *rítmico* at the cadence. In this *cantando* B section, one may notice Salgán's elegant phrasing, both with the timing of the *fraseos* as well as the subtle crescendos and diminuendos with the rise and the fall of the melodic lines.

Salgán continues in Eb major in the C section (1:09–1:42), where he constructs another sixteen-bar section but now in four similar four-bar phrases united by a repeated rhythmic motive (WE 6.5). He maintains a steady *rítmico* style supported mostly by driving *marcato* accompaniment with *arrastres*. Salgán's sophisticated harmonic palette comes into play most prominently in this section, most notably by his use of a tonic chord with an added sixth in the first phrase; a chromatic descending bass, an augmented sixth chord and a modulation to G minor in the second phrase; a chromatic countermelody in the third phrase; and then an intensely chromatic final phrase that moves through a chromatic descending fifth sequence to the Neapolitan before arriving at the dominant harmony for the cadence.[14]

The return of the A section (1:43–2:18) follows a standard da capo repeat of the first A, and the return of B (2:18–3:03) at first seems like it will also continue an exact return. But, after the first four bars, Salgán takes a surprising turn to integrate musical ideas from the C section. He cuts to the final four-bar phrase of C with the chromatic sequence (2:26–2:35), then repeats it twice in varied repetition with piano *campanas* and chromatic runs (2:36–2:43 and 2:44–2:52). Then, on the third repetition, the bandoneón extends the phrase as a coda with variations, while the piano leads a *rallentando* with strong *marcato* chords to the end (2:53–3:03).

Astor Piazzolla

Piazzolla's *nuevo tango*, a fusion of tango, jazz, and classical music, pushed the boundaries of every musical element in the tango genre. Rhythm dominates Piazzolla's music, with his signature 3-3-2 and bass-line *marcato* accompanimental patterns, yet also with more complex ostinatos, layers, and cross-rhythms. Within these accompanimental patterns, he is known for performing with heavy accents and powerful *arrastres*. His slow sections and *milongas lentas* (slow milongas) utilize the steady syncopated *milonga campera* (country milonga) accompaniment, providing a subtle heartbeat-like pulse for the melody above. When shifting between rhythmic styles, he often accentuates the abrupt mood changes with heavy *tutti arrastres*. Piazzolla's melodies develop the contrasting *rítmico* and *cantando* styles of traditional tango, incorporating short jazz-like syncopated motives and fast scalar fills in the former, while drawing out long melodic notes with *adornos* (ornaments) in the latter. Piazzolla's harmonic style favors heavy blocks of sound in a slow or even static harmonic rhythm, which then often accelerate through harmonic sequences. He frequently colors a core diatonic framework with extended chords and added notes along with chromatic harmonies, and more radically, with nonfunctional chords, polychords, and abrupt tonal shifts. Piazzolla punctuates his musical texture with an extensive use of *yeites*, ranging from *chicharra* to *látigo* to even human vocal sounds.

In general, Piazzolla constructs phrases in standard four- and eight-bar groups, although occasionally, he expands them with advanced phrase development techniques like extensions and overlaps. He often includes extended introductions, codas, and improvisational sections, while he avoids the standard tango "chan-chan" final harmonic tag in favor of heavy glissandos or accented repeated chords. His formal designs, too, expand traditional tango structures to include elaborate three-part forms with a fast-slow-fast alternation of sections, imitative counterpoint, and continuous variations on a fixed harmonic idea.

With his heavy accents, dark harmonic palate, and extensive use of *yeites*, especially in the second quintet, Piazzolla's performance style evokes a violent side of tango. As he states in Gorin's memoir: "In that neighborhood [Greenwich Village, New York City] the clash was between gangster gangs ... I grew up in that climate ... Perhaps that also marked my music."[15] In line with the images of fighting and dominance, Piazzolla typically stands while playing the bandoneón. This is a striking difference between Piazzolla and every bandoneonist that preceded him, but it is now standard performance practice when playing contemporary tango and Piazzolla's music. This is no small feat in strength and endurance, as bandoneones weigh between twenty and thirty pounds and concerts are generally one to two hours long. The following analyses of "Milonga del ángel" ("Angel Milonga," 1973) and "La camorra I" ("The Duel I," 1988) point to many of Piazzolla's characteristic compositional and performance practices.[16]

"Milonga del ángel" (1973)

Piazzolla's haunting *milonga lenta* typifies the slow and lyrical style he brings to this tango subgenre.[17] Structured in an ABA form, he expands the design with an introduction, phrase overlaps and extensions, and transitional passages (WL 6.3). The Introduction (0:00–0:40) sets up a dreamy mood with slow-moving extended chromatic chords in the piano and violin over a repeated bass line outlining the B minor tonic. In the second phrase, the violin shifts to playing exaggerated, short-ranged sigh-like glissandi on the G-string. Then, as the guitar enters with a more active repeated melodic fragment, Piazzolla sneaks in the long first note of the opening melody a bit early metrically, and so creates a smooth connection into the first main section.

Piazzolla structures the A section (0:41–2:26) with two contrasting melodies, each repeated in a slightly varied form. He anchors the poignant first melody (0:41–1:07) in long sustained notes with *adornos* and *fraseos*; while the guitar continues the melodic fragments from the end of the Introduction, the violin expressively reacts to the shape of the overall phrase created by the bandoneón with a languid countermelody, and the bass provides the *milonga* rhythmic support.[18] The second phrase (1:08–1:33) continues this texture, although the guitar pulses to the cadence with steady eighth notes. In the varied repetition, Piazzolla thickens the texture and activates the rhythm by adding the piano in repeated chords to the guitar's same pulsing rhythm in the first phrase (1:34–1:59). The bandoneón plays many jazz-like melodic improvisations as the violin shifts the tessitura to the E-string to outline the melody, and both instruments increase the intensity of the overall sound. Then in the second phrase (2:00–2:26), Piazzolla reverts back to melodic fragments in the accompaniment and the *milonga* rhythm in the bass.

Piazzolla organizes the contrasting B section (2:27–3:59) into three subsections. The first (2:27–2:57) pushes the tempo as the bandoneón, violin, and piano play a rising chordal figure, repeated sequentially, while the bass and guitar maintain an elaborated *milonga* rhythmic accompaniment. In the fifth iteration of the figure, Piazzolla pushes the tempo even more and increases the dynamic level while moving to the remote A minor harmony. This, in turn, abruptly moves to the unrelated key of C minor to launch the second transitional subsection (2:58–3:25). Piazzolla sustains this C minor harmony as the violin solo sounds another melodic idea; hauntingly reminiscent of its earlier countermelody, it is filled with expressive slides and mordents, but now with bass syncopated *milonga campera* rhythmic support. In the third phrase (3:26–3:59), the violin solo continues, supported by a 3-3-2 accompaniment in the bass and guitar. Piazzolla then recalls the guitar melodic fragments from the Introduction as a phrase extension to set up the return of the opening section.

Piazzolla ingeniously recomposes and expands the return of A (4:00–end). First, as in the piece's opening, he sneaks in on the first note, even as the harmony again shifts up a step to C♯ minor. He extends and develops the second phrase (4:26–5:21), still with the violin countermelody and rhythmic support in the guitar and bass. But a heavy *tutti arrastre* sets up a dramatic mood change in a transformed repetition of the first phrase with yet another abrupt tonal shift to F minor (5:22). Piazzolla sounds the now anguished melody *forte* and continues the dramatic *arrastres*, then releases the tension in the second phrase into a deceptive cadence. A coda of sustained tenuto-sounding chords, with the violin emerging prominently in the top line, brings the piece to a mournful close, ending on a sustained F-minor extended chord with a downward arpeggio in the guitar and upward flourish in the piano.

"La camorra I" (1988)

"La camorra I" typifies Piazzolla's mature *nuevo tango* style,[19] as it is grounded in clear tango rhythms, a solid linear relationship between the bass line and the melody or top line of the chords, and a mostly jazz-inspired harmonic framework (WL 6.4).[20] An elaborately worked-out composition in D minor, Piazzolla casts this dark tango in an extended three-part form with an introduction, a "fuga" in the middle section, and a long coda. It features extreme fluctuations in dynamics and moods and favors a *tutti* sound in the quintet formation, as the bandoneón and violin primarily carry the melody while the piano, bass, and guitar mostly form the rhythm section.

The Introduction (0:00–0:18) presents a forceful chordal *tutti* block of sound with heavy *arrastres*. It establishes a two-bar rhythmic ostinato, repeated exactly as a fixed harmonic element, as the main musical idea of the work. Piazzolla employs a wide range of *yeites* within the first fourteen seconds, including *lija* ("sandpaper," the same technique as *chicharra*) and *látigo* in the violin, and *strappata* (from the Italian word *strappare* meaning "to tear") in the bass. Complex rhythmic layering intensifies the drive to a cadence with cross-rhythms between the steady sixteenth note in the melody and the 3-3-2 and *síncopa* layers in the accompaniment. As the cross-rhythms stabilize into a regular *marcato* within a rapid descending fifth progression, the bandoneón and violin dissipate the terse syncopated rhythm with fast scalar runs. The A section proper (0:19–1:36) features sophisticated irregular phrase rhythms that result from phrase expansions and sequential extensions that elaborate the opening repeated two-bar rhythmic pattern into a syncopated melody initiated with dissonant minor seconds (WE 6.6).

Látigos emphasize the unison syncopated rhythm in the violin, guitar, bandoneón, and piano. Then, the solo bandoneón relaxes the mood with a secondary theme (1:07–1:36), while the bass changes to *marcato* and the harmony wanders sequentially.

A transitional passage (1:37–2:07) links to the B section with a lyrical duet between the bandoneón and violin, where the bandoneón explores the melodic possibilities of a minor second through *fraseo*, and the violin offers a countermelody through sustained harmonics. Both are supported by running arpeggios in the guitar and a continued pulsing pizzicato *marcato* in the bass. A descending fifth progression seems to carry the key from D minor to F minor, but then the piece abruptly changes key.

The B section (2:08–4:22) begins down a half step in the unrelated key of E minor. Piazzolla first sets two contrasting lyrical phrases played by the bandoneón and violin (2:08–2:34 and 2:35–2:59) in a *milonga lenta* style. An ascending step sequence supports the surging melody in the second phrase, then the driving rhythmic two-bar motive returns (3:00–3:08). Piazzolla next spins out a fugal section (3:09–4:12) with a "subject" based on the main syncopated A motive for the second portion of the B section (WE 6.7). The bandoneón begins (3:09), followed by the violin (3:25), and guitar (3:42), where all three highlight the accent pattern and articulation of the phrase. The fugal section concludes with a varied statement in the bandoneón (3:58), followed by a transitional passage in running sixteenth notes in the bandoneón (4:13–4:22), punctuated by a strong vocalized grunt (perhaps insinuating the "duel" of the title) that leads to the return of A.

Piazzolla recomposes the A section (4:23–6:39) to alternate between the rhythmic "theme" and rhapsodic solo, jazz-like improvisational passages. Following the *tutti* return (4:23–4:40), Piazzolla dissipates the dark tension with a bandoneón solo filled with improvised ornamentation and *fraseo*. It is supported by countermelodies in the violin, guitar, and piano, and *marcato* in 2 in the bass – all held together by two descending-fifth progressions to D major (4:41–5:17). Piazzolla reverts to D minor and a thinner texture (5:17–5:45), as the bandoneón continues the main melody and the bass now pulses a pizzicato *marcato* in 4. A *pesante* piano solo abruptly drives back to the A motive (5:45–6:15) and develops it in parallel 6/3 chords offset by chromatic descending fifths. The violin adds to the rhythmic complexity and intensity with various *yeites*, including *tambor*, *lija*, and *látigo*, while the bass stresses the *marcato* in 2 accompaniment with *strappata*. A four-bar sequential passage sets up the virtuoso bandoneón cadenza (6:16–6:39), where Piazzolla continues the thick parallel 6/3 chords and a piano *arrastre* launches the extended coda.

Piazzolla builds his complex coda (6:40–9:26), which is longer than any of the main sections, with additive layers of improvisations on a sixteen-bar group of two repeated eight-bar phrases. Based on the main two-bar rhythmic motive, a heavy *marcato* bass line outlines the harmony with walking thirds followed by descending fifths in each phrase. The bandoneón begins (6:40–7:15), the piano joins (7:16) as the violin adds *lija* (7:50), then the guitar joins (8:23) as the violin adds *látigo*. Piazzolla begins to dissolve the intense energy for one last repetition (8:56) but now reduces to four statements of the essential two-bar motive. On the fifth iteration (9:13), Piazzolla dissipates the energy by softening to *pianissimo* and stabilizing the syncopated minor-second motive to sound on the downbeats. The release of tension concludes the piece with an unusual soft ending on a sustained Dm^9 chord.

Conclusion: Tradition versus Innovation

While both Salgán and Piazzolla helped shape the direction of tango following the Golden Age, it is evident that their styles are distinct – Salgán maintained a traditional approach, and Piazzolla led the avant-garde. In general, Salgán's tango style projects a cool, light, and elegant sound, while Piazzolla's tango style conveys a dark, heavy, and ponderous sound. Piazzolla purposely sought to renovate tango as he created his *tango nuevo* in a fusion of musical styles, drawing on his background working with Troilo, studying with Ginastera and Boulanger, and listening to and working with jazz musicians such as Mulligan. Salgán saw himself as a traditional *tanguero* in the long line of his predecessors like Arolas, Bardi, Cobián, and the De Caros,[21] and he was influenced especially by the older tango melodies and the *tango romanza*.

The two composers' tango styles also emphasize different distinct musical elements. Whereas melody reigns supreme in the texture of Salgán's music, rhythm is the primary element that drives Piazzolla's music. Furthermore, even within standard ABA designs, Piazzolla pushes such restrictions of form to incorporate core melodic/rhythmic ostinatos and contrapuntal sections. While Salgán's arrangements of tango standards adhere mostly to the traditional two-part or three-part forms, the large-scale designs of his original compositions take on more complex structures with returning sections like ABCBA and ABCAB.

Despite their stylistic differences, these *tangueros* were born just five years apart. They came of age at the end of tango's Golden Age in the late 1940s and early 1950s, working as composers and arrangers in the traditional instrumental medium of the large tango orchestra. In this musical environment, they absorbed essential elements of the tango style, and one can recognize standard tango *cantando* and *rítmico* melodic styles in their compositions and arrangements, as well as the standard tango accompanimental rhythms of *marcato*, *síncopa*, 3-3-2, and the anticipatory *arrastre* sliding technique.

Still, they became innovators in their own right within the genre. While both composers were rooted in classical training, each moved tango forward with their distinctive style. Even as they remained grounded in the essential elements that characterize the genre in the broad areas of instrumentation, melody, and rhythm, they pushed traditional harmonic boundaries by incorporating extended harmonies from jazz influences and experimented with more complex musical designs. As tango evolved from dance music into music for listening, both *tangueros* experimented with new instrumentation within the standard tango formation. Salgán, for example, incorporated the bass clarinet, while Piazzolla used the saxophone. Eventually, each *tanguero* settled on the same quintet formation of bandoneón, violin, electric guitar, piano, and bass.

Salgán and Piazzolla have also left the next generation of *tangueros* tremendous artistic legacies with which to grapple. Salgán's ethos carries enormous weight in Argentina as he is revered as a father-like figure of the genre. In addition to his son continuing the tradition of his music through the quintet, many of the *tangueros* who have belonged to the ensemble or have studied with the maestro carry his stylistic torch. For instance, pianist/composer Sonia Possetti, one prominent *tanguera* who studied with Salgán, follows the maestro's path with her light and virtuosic sound, elegant compositional style, and clearly developed motives.

Piazzolla, on the other hand, is an international icon of tango. His music today is featured around the world regularly. For example, Sergei Tumas' *Tango: The Musical*, which has been performed internationally, features only the music of Piazzolla, despite the show's title reflecting the entire art form.[22] Many *tangueros* face the dilemma of what to do next after Piazzolla's tango; one might compare this to Beethoven's legacy in eighteenth-century Vienna as many composers struggled under the *maestro's* shadow. Other *tangueros* view Piazzolla's legacy as opening the door to experimentation in tango, such as incorporating more jazz or rock into tango. For example, Julián Peralta explores a darker rock sound in tango with his group Astillero, and Diego Schissi and Julián Graciano integrate tango and jazz with their chamber ensembles.

Regarding both legacies, the new generation faces a similar question to what Salgán and Piazzolla confronted at the beginning of their careers. In their case, the question was how to move forward after tango's Golden Age, and now it is how to progress after these towering figures of the post–Golden Age. Perhaps the answer lies in the balancing of these two pillars, Salgán of tradition and Piazzolla of innovation, but we, as scholars, will have to wait for the next generation to analyze fully the contributions and transformations of our present.

Notes

1. Kacey Link and Kristin Wendland, *Tracing Tangueros: Argentine Tango Instrumental Music* (New York: Oxford University Press, 2016), 64.
2. Natalio Gorin, *Astor Piazzolla: A Memoir*, translated, annotated, and expanded by Fernando Gonzalez (Portland, OR: Amadeus Press, 2001), 74.
3. " . . . la música, son un reflejo, una consecuencia de la manera de vivir de un grupo humano situado en un lugar y un tiempo determinados."
   Horacio Salgán, *Curso de Tango/ Tango Course* (Buenos Aires: Pablo J. Polidoro, 2001), 29.
4. Omar García Brunelli, *Discografía básica del tango, 1905–2010: su historia a través de las grabaciones* (Buenos Aires: Gourmet Musical Ediciones, 2010), 127.
5. Gorin, *Piazzolla*, 30.
6. Gorin, *Piazzolla*, 61.
7. Link and Wendland, *Tracing Tangueros*, 226.
8. See Varchausky's Chapter 4 and Graciano's Chapter 7 for further explanation of these accompanimental rhythms.
9. See also the case study of Salgán in Link and Wendland, *Tracing Tangueros*, 200–219, including a close reading of "A fuego lento," 213–219. Furthermore, these two manuscripts and six other orchestral arrangements may be found in Horacio Salgán, *Arreglos para orquesta típica: tradición e innovación en manuscritos originales* (Buenos Aires: Biblioteca Nacional and TangoVia, 2008).
10. The description provided here follows the recording of WL 6.1. For the simplified piano sheet music version of "Don Agustín Bardi," which does not exactly match the recording, see *Todotango*, www.todotango.com/musica/tema/1448/Don-Agustin-Bardi.
11. The elaborated progression is i-V^7/iv-iv-ii°6/5-V^7/V-C6/4-V-i.

12. The description provided here follows the recording of WL 6.2. For the simplified piano sheet music version of "Grillito," see *Todotango*, www.todotango.com/musica/tema/3248/Grillito.
13. In this instance, and frequently in all tango music, the augmented-sixth chord is spelled as $\flat VI^7$, and is sometimes referred to as an *apoyatura*. See Link and Wendland, *Tracing* Tangueros, 105–106.
14. The Neapolitan is spelled enharmonically as an E^7 in the sheet music.
15. Gorin, *Piazzolla*, 30.
16. See also the case study of Piazzolla in Link/Wendland, *Tracing* Tangueros, 220–246, including a close reading of "Michelangelo 70," 241–246.
17. See the published quintet version *Milonga del ángel* (Buenos Aires: Editorial Lagos, 1968). For a piano score, see *Piazzolla: Serie de ángel* (Buenos Aires: Melos de Ricordi Americana, 2002).
18. See Aydınoğlu's Chapter 2 for an example of Piazzolla's application of *fraseo* in his "Adiós Nonino."
19. For a detailed analysis of this work, see Omar García Brunelli, "De Woodstock a B.A.: análisis de Camorra I, II, y II," in *Estudios sobre la obra de Astor Piazzolla*, ed. Omar García Brunelli (Buenos Aires: Gourmet Musical, 2008), 109–126.
20. The Piazzolla Library in Mar de Plata, Argentina, holds the manuscript copy by José Bragato.
21. Oscar Himschoot, "Salgán – Interview to Horacio Salgán," *Todotango.com*, accessed September 24, 2022, www.todotango.com/english/history/chronicle/5/Salgan-Interview-to-Horacio-Salgan.
22. As of this writing, *Tango: The Musical* is currently being performed in Los Angeles, CA at the Saban Theatre in Beverly Hills, October 29–30, 2023.

Further Reading

Azzi, María Susana. "The Tango, Peronism, and Astor Piazzolla during the 1940s and 1950s." In *From Tejano to Tango*, edited by Walter Aaron Clark, 25–40. New York: Routledge, 2002.

Azzi, María Susana, and Simon Collier. *Le Grand Tango: The Life and Music of Astor Piazzolla*. New York: Oxford University Press, 2000.

García Brunelli, Omar, ed. *Estudios sobre la obra de Astor Piazzolla*. Buenos Aires: Gourmet Musical, 2008.

Gorin, Natalio. *Astor Piazzolla: A Memoir*. Translated, annotated, and expanded by Fernando Gonzalez. Portland, OR: Amadeus Press, 2001.

Himshoot, Oscar. "Salgán – Interview to Horacio Salgán." *Todotango.com*. Accessed September 24, 2022. www.todotango.com/english/history/chronicle/5/Salgan-Interview-to-Horacio-Salgan.

Piazzolla, Diana. *Astor*. Buenos Aires: Corregidor, 2005.

Salgán, Horacio. *Arreglos para orquesta típica: tradición e innovación en manuscritos originales*. Buenos Aires: Biblioteca Nacional and TangoVia, 2008.

Curso de Tango / Tango Course. Buenos Aires: Pablo J. Polidoro, 2001.

Sierra, Luis Adolfo. *El tango romanza. Enrique Delfino, Juan Carlos Cobián, Francisco de Caro, Lucio Demare, Joaquí Mora, and Horacio Salgán*. Buenos Aires: Academia Porteña del Lunfardo, 1987.

Ursini, Sonia. *Horacio Salgán: la supervivencia de un artista en el tiempo*. Buenos Aires: Corregidor, 1993.

JULIÁN GRACIANO

From the soulful improvisations of the bandoneón playing of Astor Piazzolla (1921–1992) to the raspy sounds of Louis Armstrong (1901–1971) singing "Kiss of Fire," tango and jazz always have had an intertwined relationship. In this chapter, I first explore the connection and development of both genres from their origins at the turn of the twentieth century. Then, I examine how musicians of tango and jazz have crossed national borders and genre-defining boundaries to gain inspiration and innovation in their respective art forms. Last, as a tango and jazz practitioner, I offer insight into how I specifically create a tango-jazz hybrid through composition, arranging, and performance practices.

Historical Overview of Tango and Jazz

Parallels between Tango and Jazz Development

Tango has always had a close relationship with jazz due to the genres' parallel evolutionary histories. From their origins at the turn of the twentieth century, both genres developed from popular music and dance forms that descended from the African diaspora, specifically the *candombe* of Argentina and Uruguay and ragtime of the United States. Also similarly, they drew from improvised singing traditions, namely those of the *payadores* (Argentine folk singers/guitarists), such as Gabino Ezeiza (1858–1916) in "Saludo a Paysandú" ("A Tribute to Paysandú," WL 7.1), and bluesmen such as W. C. Handy (1873–1958) in "St. Louis Blues" (WL 7.2).

As both genres crystalized in the first decades of the twentieth century, they established standard ensemble sizes and instrumentation while continuing to be musical genres for a dancing public and drawing from improvisational roots. The first ensembles of tango were known as *orquestas típicas criollas* (typical creole orchestras), consisting of guitar, bandoneón, flute, and violin as heard in "Don Juan" recorded by the Orquesta Típica Criolla Vicente Greco (WL 7.3). Then, the ensembles standardized into the *sextetos típicos* (typical sextets), which included two

violins, two bandoneones, piano, and bass. In early tango, the improvisational style was known as "*a la parrilla*," which literally means "on the
grill." This term compared a music stand to a grill due to its shape – an
editorial piano score was placed on a music stand, like food on a grill, and
each musician spontaneously created their part, contributing to the final
shape of a tango, like in an *asado* (Argentine barbecue). In this style, the
guitar takes an accompanimental role by improvising bass lines, while the
bandoneón, violin, and/or flute play the melody or, like the trombone in
early jazz, improvised countermelody. The first groups of early jazz, or
Dixieland jazz bands from New Orleans, included trumpet, clarinet, trombone, piano, string bass, drums, and banjo or guitar. As demonstrated by
the New Orleans Rhythm Kings in "Bugle Call Blues," they employed
"collective improvisation," where the ensemble improvised simultaneously
(WL 7.4).

By the 1920s, two great artists emerged, Julio De Caro (1899–1980) of
tango and Armstrong of jazz, both making their stamp on the evolutions of
their respective genres. De Caro established a style of phrasing, arranging,
marcato (marked) in the accompanimental rhythm,[1] and even virtuosity in
coda-like variations. Referred to as the *epoca decareana* (De Caro age), all
of these elements, as heard in "El monito" ("The Little Monkey," WL 7.5),
shaped the development of tango. Armstrong's "hot jazz" defined "swing"
and began spontaneous variations on the melody, such as in "Muggles"
(WL 7.6). His band members executed more complex walking bass lines
and utilized the drum set, which set the stage for the future of jazz.

Both tango and jazz experienced a Golden Age in the 1930s and 1940s
characterized by large venues, sizable orchestras, dancing audiences, abundant recordings, and published sheet music.[2] In tango, there was the birth
of the *orquesta típica* (typical tango orchestra). *Tangueros* (tango musicians) such as Juan D'Arienzo (1900–1976), Aníbal Troilo (1914–1975),
and Osvaldo Pugliese (1905–1995) formed expanded orchestras to perform
in dance halls throughout Buenos Aires. Trolio's *orquesta típica* demonstrates this sizable orchestra with his piece "Toda mi vida" ("All My Life,"
WL 7.7). In jazz, big bands performing in a swing style became prominent,
and the instrumentation was increased to meet the acoustic needs of the
large dancing venues in numerous cities throughout the United States. The
greatest exponents of this style included Duke Ellington (1899–1974),
Fletcher Henderson (1897–1952), and Count Basie (1904–1984).
Ellington's big band recording of "Mood Indigo" exemplifies this style
(WL 7.8). During this time, both tango and jazz musicians clung to the

roots of improvisation while creating their own compositional imprint and orchestral aesthetic.

The 1950s marked a change in both genres as they searched for music for music's sake – not music for the dancer, but music for the listener. In Argentina and the United States, performance venues reduced in quantity and size, causing musicians to form smaller ensembles from trios to octets. Musically, the genres are characterized by melodic chromatism, extended phrases in sixteenth notes, and extended chord harmonizations. Notable artists of this stylistic transformation included Piazzolla and Eduardo Rovira (1925–1980) of tango, and Charlie Parker (1920–1955) and Dizzy Gillespie (1917–1993) of jazz. One could compare and contrast Piazzolla's "Tangology" (WL 7.9) with Parker and Gillespie's "Anthropology" (WL 7.10).

Rock music heavily influenced both genres in the 1970s to create a form of "fusion music." In tango, rhythmic elements of rock, like the backbeat, and instruments, such as drums, electric guitar, and electric bass, appeared in the music of Rovira, for example, in his "Sónico" ("Sonic," WL 7.11), Piazzolla's Electronic Octet, and Rodolfo Mederos' (b. 1940) group Generación Cero with his "Todo ayer" ("All Yesterday," WL 7.12). Miles Davis (1926–1991) introduced rock into jazz with his album *Bitches Brew* (1970, WL 7.13), and musicians like Chick Corea (1941–2021) followed down the fusion path with his band Return to Forever in pieces such as "Spain" (WL 7.14). Still, even amid their experimentations, both genres always retained their characteristic instruments, namely the saxophone or the trumpet in jazz and the bandoneón in tango.

Through the last decades of the twentieth century, tango and jazz have had moments of decline and struggle, but today they are thriving. Both genres are practiced by highly trained musicians with exceptional technique and creative skills while being academically grounded in the roots of each genre.[3] Instrumentalists, singers, composers, and even orchestras of all styles perform around the world and online for engaged audiences.

Tango and Jazz Musicians

As tango and jazz developed simultaneously in South and North America, respectively, their musicians drew from each other for musical inspiration, innovation, and even, in some cases, duplication to create a cross-country, cross-cultural, and cross-genre dialogue. As early as 1910, Argentine musicians began traveling to the United States, namely pianist/composer Enrique Delfino (1895–1967), bandoneonist Osvaldo Fresedo (1897–1984), and violinist Tito Rocatagliata (1891–1925). Composer/pianist Juan Carlos Cobián (1896–1953) worked in the United States on two different occasions (1923–1928 and 1937–1943) and led not only tango ensembles but also conducted jazz orchestras. From an orchestral perspective, one may hear the influence of George Gershwin (1898–1937) on musicians like De Caro and Francisco Canaro (1888–1964) in the writing of tango fantasies, such as Canaro's "Halcón negro," ("Black Hawk," WL 7.15) arranged by Héctor Artola (1903–1982).

Perhaps early tango's most important international star was the great Carlos Gardel (1890–1935). His career skyrocketed with radio performances, recordings, and films in Argentina, the United States, and France. His most famous films included *Cuesta abajo* (*Down Hill*, 1934), *El tango en Broadway* (1934), *El día que me quieras* (*The Day You Loved Me*, 1935), and *Tango Bar* (1935). In addition to bringing tango to the world, Gardel also gained inspiration from popular genres in New York City, as evidenced by his 1934 fox trot "Rubias de New York" ("New York Blondes," WL 7.16).

By the 1940s, tango and jazz flourished, and the musicians began to demonstrate a fluidity between the genres and borrow musical elements from each other. In Buenos Aires, it was very common in the milongas (dance venues for tango) for "la Jazz" and "la Tango" orchestras to share the stage with each performing forty-minute sets. Arrangers began incorporating jazz sounds, like 4ths in melodies and ♭5, ♯5, ♭9, and ♯9 in extended chords, as in the style of Paul Whiteman (1890–1967) or Ellington. Argentino Galván's (1913–1960) arrangement of "Recuerdos de bohemia" ("Bohemian Memories," WL 7.17) for Troilo's orchestra exemplifies such dissonances. Some Argentine guitarists played both tango and jazz, like Oscar Alemán (1909–1980), who played tango with the Trío Víctor in addition to becoming one of the most important musicians of Argentine swing as heard in "Página gris" ("Gray Page," WL 7.18). In the 1950s, guitarist Roberto Grela (1913–1992) formed a Gypsy jazz sextet and recorded two jazz tunes, "Singin' in the Rain" and "Dinah," for the TK label.[4] Additionally, pianist Osvaldo Berlingieri (1928–2015) used elements from jazz such as the "blue note," phrase fills, and pentatonic scales. For example, his tango "Ritual," recorded in 1966 with the Orquesta Típica Baffa-Berlinghieri, contained a bridge based on the "blue note" of an augmented fourth over a minor chord (WL 7.19). Composer/pianist Horacio Salgán (1916–2016) integrated jazz elements with more chromaticism in the harmony, tritone substitutions, and the chromatic writing of the double bass line as exemplified in "A fuego lento" ("At a Low Heat," WL 7.20), "Don Agustín Bardi," and "Grillito" ("Little Cricket").

In the tango world, the year 1956 marked the establishment of a significant gateway between tango and modern jazz with the beginning of Piazzolla's Octeto Buenos Aires. With this ensemble, Piazzolla made a conscious effort to combine the musical elements of tango and jazz, as heard in his "Marrón y azul" ("Brown and Blue," WL 7.21). Not only did he incorporate Horacio Malvicino (1929–2023) on the electric guitar (called the "American guitar" in Argentina), but he added space for improvisation in traditional works during "vamps" (usually two repetitive chords), entire sections of the theme, or during the endings with improvised guitar solos. In 1959, Piazzolla experimented with combining the tango and jazz repertory on the albums *An Evening in Buenos Aires* and *Take Me Dancing* with tango works such as "Adiós muchachos" ("Bye Guys") and "Derecho viejo" ("Straightforward"), and jazz works such as "Lullaby of Birdland" (WL 7.22) and "Sophisticated Lady." Then in 1963, Piazzolla began utilizing modes common in jazz in his works, such as the Dorian mode in "Buenos Aires hora cero" ("Buenos Aires Zero Hour") and the Phrygian mode in "Zum."

On the other hand, many jazz musicians from the United States were interested in tango repertory during the 1950s and 1960s. In one landmark session in Buenos Aires, also in 1956, Gillespie worked with Fresedo's Orquesta Típica and recorded "Vida mía" ("My Life," WL 7.23), "Adiós muchachos," "Preludio No. 3," and "Capricho de amor" ("Whim of Love"). In each piece, Gillespie displayed moments of improvisation in a bebop language that achieved a beautiful and historic intersection of the genres. Additionally, Armstrong recorded "El choclo" ("The Corn") with the title "Kiss of Fire" (WL 7.24) as well as "Adiós muchachos." Nat King Cole (1919–1965) then went on to record a Spanish version of "El choclo" in 1959 and "A media luz" ("At Half Light") in 1962. Lastly, pianist Gil Evans (1919–1988) even composed his own tango in 1964 with "Las Vegas Tango" (WL 7.25).

Since the 1970s, tango and jazz musicians have been working together and crossing genres. In 1974, Piazzolla worked with jazz saxophonist Gerry Mulligan (1927–1996), and they recorded the album *Summit* with works by each musician, for example, "Aire de Buenos Aires" ("Buenos Aires Air," WL 7.26). Also in 1974, swing violinist Hernán Oliva (1913–1988) and jazz pianist Mito García recorded the album *Nieblas del Riachuelo* with the title song, which united jazz and tango with a fresh interpretation (WL 7.27). Then in 1987, jazz vibraphonist Gary Burton joined forces with Piazzolla's quintet to record *The New Tango*. Argentine pianists like Pablo Ziegler (b. 1944) have found mirrors in Americans Bill Evans (1929–1980) and Oscar Peterson (1925–2007), two jazz pianists admired by many tango musicians. In the tango "Chin-chin" ("Cheers," WL 7.28) performed live at the Montreal Jazz Festival by Piazzolla's quintet, Ziegler developed a free improvisation with solo piano where one can hear how the melodic phrasing and harmonic language is close to that of modern jazz, yet the rhythmic pulse is that of Piazzolla's tango style.

Other pianists show their inclination toward jazz elements in their improvisation, but with a tango phraseology, like Osvaldo Tarantino's solo piano tangos or his participation in Pizzolla's nonet. In one of his most emblematic performances, Tarantino displays his capacity for improvisation in the tango that Piazzolla wrote especially for him, "Onda 9" ("Style 9," WL 7.29), where the pianist improvises in the introduction over the tango chord changes and then improvises again later in the piece. Additionally, in the vein of Piazzolla, jazz guitarist Al Di Meola (b. 1954) recorded an album completely dedicated to Piazzolla, *Di Meola Plays Piazzolla*, and it also included his own work, "Last Tango for Astor" (WL 7.30).

Coming closer to contemporary times, the tango-jazz musician relationship has remained strong. Tango double bassist Pablo Aslan recorded the album *Y en el 2000 también* with his group Avantango, consisting of jazz pianist Ethan Iverson and jazz saxophonist Thomas Chapin. This album begins with tango standards such as "Don Agustín Bardi" (WL 7.31), then transforms them into a jazz improvisation. Ziegler has continued to work with tango-jazz fusions with his album *Jazz Tango*, which won the 2018 Latin Grammy Award for Best Latin Jazz Album. It also is noteworthy that pedagogical works on the execution of tango have begun appearing for instruments closely linked to jazz, such as the saxophone manuals by Jorge Retamoza (*El tango desde el saxo*) and Bernardo Monk (*The Tango Saxophone Book*).[5] Today, the story continues in real time, and one could cite many tango-jazz musicians and many jazz-tango musicians, on both shores using repertory, instruments, or rhythmic elements of each genre, all of which their grandfathers found as a common point in Africa.

Tango and Jazz in Practice

As a guitarist and composer from Buenos Aires, Argentina, I grew up with the sounds of tango. Like many *tangueros*, I also studied jazz, in my case, at the Berklee College of Music in Boston. As evidenced by my ensembles

Tango en Tres and Graciano 4, I have found my musical voice by combining tango and jazz in my compositions, arrangements, and performance practices. Here, I offer a detailed description of my approach to creating a tango-jazz hybrid in terms of instrumentation and scoring techniques, arranging, harmony, and melody and improvisation as well as a guide to performance practice.

Instrumentation and Scoring Techniques

Through the years, I have experimented with composing and arranging for different instrumentations, such as jazz horns, guitar ensembles, singers and various instruments, string quartets, symphonic orchestras, jazz "power trios" including guitar, double bass, and drums (Tango en Tres), and my current group (Graciano 4) with two guitars, bandoneón, and bass. Here, I develop my vision of a tango-jazz hybrid utilizing the guitar, bandoneón, double bass and drums. I continually use these instruments to apply a jazz language with scalar phrasing, chromaticism, extended chords in the guitar and bandoneón, a walking bass line, and varied rhythmic patterns within a measure, like those on jazz snare and bass drums.

Bandoneón

The bandoneón is the iconic instrument associated with tango. In tango-jazz hybrids, I like to think of this instrument as a jazz horn section – the right keyboard of the bandoneón functions as the trumpets and the alto saxophone, and the left keyboard functions as the trombones, tenor saxophone, and baritone saxophone. This association allows me to use jazz voicing, such as spreading the parts in open harmony. Further, by the nature of its construction, the bandoneón projects its sound in a stereo way, which allows for an aurally clear separation of the sides and gives the impression of a jazz horn section.

I score melodies in unison to imitate the jazz sound of such groups as the Charlie Parker and Dizzy Gillespie Quintets, where the trumpet and alto saxophone play a complete melody in unison. Melodic writing in unison is possible on the bandoneón between the pitches A3 and A4, since they are present on both keyboards, as in my "A tus pies" ("To Your Dancing Feet," WE 7.1). In my "Mandinga" (a name for a South American devil, derived from West African culture WE 7.2), I also recreate the color of jazz melodies by scoring in octaves, similar to phrases played between trumpet and tenor sax in the famous Miles Davis Quintet with John Coltrane (1926–1967).

When I use the bandoneón in an accompaniment role, I usually score the chords in open spacing in a jazz horn section style. I place the root, third, and seventh of each chord in the left keyboard, while using available extended chord tones or writing in triads on the right keyboard. Additionally, on the right side of the bandoneón, I utilize left-hand voicings of jazz pianists, like Evans and his famous voicing of three notes arranged by an interval of 2nd and another of 4th in my "Trasnochado" ("Night Owl," WE 7.3).

In chromatic writing for the bandoneón, I incorporate elements of the bebop style, as in "Donna Lee" by Charlie Parker (WL 7.32), by using "enclosure tones" (chromatic double neighbors around the main note), seventh- and ninth-chord arpeggios, and rhythmic 16th notes to create bebop's double-time feel, for example, in my "Tres + uno" ("Three Plus One," WE 7.4). With its expansive pitch range, the bandoneón can also capture chromatic tension with jazz-like extended chords, or what jazz musicians call "tension chords," added tones as in "Eduardo y Eduardo" ("Eduardo and Eduardo," WE 7.5), and polychords as in "Puntos cardinales" ("Cardinal Points," WE 7.6).

Drums

Although the drums appeared in early tango in 1913, even before the use of the double bass, the instrument became marginalized within the genre. It notably reappeared in the orchestras of Fresedo, Canaro, and Francisco Lomuto (1893–1950) and later the ensembles of Mariano Mores (1918–2016), Piazzolla, and Raúl Garello (1936–2016). One drummer, José "Pepe" Corriale (1915–1997), who recorded the variation of "Canaro en París" ("Canaro in Paris") with Garello, stands out with his use of roto toms to achieve different pitch levels. I have worked with drums for many years to develop a tango-jazz vocabulary with my ensemble Tango en Tres.

I connect tango and jazz drum styles by copying how jazz drummers follow a constant rhythmic pattern in the ride and the hi-hat, while disrupting the set pattern, or "time feel," with improvised rhythmic bursts on the snare drum. Correlating this practice with traditional tango *marcato*, I use the hi-hat on beats 1 and 3, which contrasts the typical jazz pattern marking beats 2 and 4, to maintain the tango time feel, as in my "De tanguistas" ("A Tango Player's Way," WE 7.7, WL 7.33). As in jazz, however, I write the word "fill" on the score every 4 or 8 bars, indicating to the performer to play a short, virtuosic improvised passage to complete a musical idea. I also include the jazz idea of "stop time," a one- or two-bar rhythmic notation that indicates isolated, free accents on the drum or cymbals of the player's choice that are not incorporated into the set time feel. I call this type of almost melodic drum writing "cantabile" drumming. It creates a kind of symphonic percussion pattern, in both solos and as melodic support, and gives the drummer the freedom to play and orchestrate according to their preference. My piece "Tango Ritual 1" illustrates this drumming style (WE 7.8, WL 7.34). Last, I use the jazz concept of "kick over," which indicates a rhythmic accent to be incorporated into the indicated time feel, by notating a cymbal hit on the upbeats with small note heads, stems up, above the staff. I allow the drummer to do it on the ride, crash, splash, or any other cymbal within the criteria of the instrumentalist's good taste.

Guitar

As I incorporate the guitar into my music, I meld the elements of tango and jazz by using the classical guitar and pick combined with fingers to recreate the phraseology of Troilo, and the typical jazz guitar fingerings, closed chords, voicings with tension/extended chords, and chromaticism in the vocabulary of Parker's bebop. The addition of the seventh string (low B) allows me to reinforce the bass. This not only aids in longer notes but also as an expressive element of "*yumbado*,"[6] played on the open lower strings on beats 2 and 4, and open voicing, which combines very high notes with low ones.

One important guitar arrangement technique is "chord melody," a technique ingeniously developed by jazz musician Joe Pass by playing the melody simultaneously above the chord. I demonstrate this in my "Déjà vu" ("Already Seen," WE 7.9). Conversely, a linear solo strips the guitar of all chords and brings it to a melodic performance as if it were a sax or a trumpet. In "Ocaso en la ciudad" ("Rush Hour in the City," WE 7.10), I incorporate purely melodic-line patterns in Coltrane's style and add chromaticism in Parker's style. Influenced by the great jazz guitarist George Van Eps, who added the seventh low string as heard in "A Foggy Day" (WL 7.35), I can match this sound in the lower bandoneón register as exemplified in my "Al gran capitán" ("To the Great Captain," WE 7.11). When I work with two guitars, rather than separate them into traditional melody and accompaniment roles, I emulate a piano writing style with one as the left hand and the other as the right hand. With this technique, I can create open-voiced chords like Evans that are impossible to play on a single guitar. I use the same approach when I want a voicing in quarters in the style of the pianist McCoy Tyner's piano solo in "My Favorite Things" with Coltrane (WL 7.36), in my "Medianoche la ciudad" ("Midnight in the City," WE 7.12) for two guitars. Lastly as seen in my "Un tal Gardel" ("A Man Called Gardel," WE 7.13), the *soli a 2* scoring technique is ideal for playing very fast phrases in 3rds or 6ths in the manner of the trumpet and alto duo.

Double Bass

From the tango's beginning, the double bass has been used to reinforce the harmonic foundation along with the piano. Leopoldo Thompson, an Afro-Argentine guitarist and bassist, introduced the instrument to tango. He combined pizzicato (plucking the string) with the use of the bow, a very characteristic yet executively complex technique. My compositional style is to think of the pizzicato of the jazz double bass and the arco (bowed) techniques of the European classical school, and thus I achieve an amalgam of technical elements that produce both traditional and contemporary sound.

The most traditional form of the *marcato* technique uses the bow to play the notes of the chord in quarter notes, as in "Un tal Gardel" (WE 7.14). I draw on jazz techniques to transform this traditional *marcato* with chromatic ornaments outside the chord and play in double time with eighth notes in *pizzicato*, as in "Ocaso en la ciudad" (WE 7.15). Another jazz-influenced bass technique creates a repetitive groove of notes, as in the introduction of "Autumn Leaves" by Davis with Cannonball Adderley on their 1958 album *Blues and Ballads* (WL 7.37). Piazzolla was one of the first tango musicians to adopt this technique for the bass, as in "Buenos Aires hora cero" ("Buenos Aires Zero Hour," WL 7.38) recorded by his quintet five years later in 1963. My use of this technique is illustrated in Web Examples 7.16a "Tango en negro" ("Tango in Black") and 7.16b "Caminos" ("Paths"). To maintain the balance of tango with the influence of jazz and to create the fusion of both sound worlds, the double bass line also combines techniques of the traditional *marcato* with the eighth-note pizzicato added to the *arrastre* (drag), as in "A tus pies" (WE 7.17). Finally, the double bass may be used in its high range like a cello, as explored by jazz bassists from Jimmy Blanton to Neil Pedersen. Frequently, I ask the double bass player to use this register, marked *alla cello*, to provide them with melodies within the ensemble, like in "Eduardo y Eduardo" (WE 7.18), as a solo in "Puntos cardinales" (WE 7.19), and to create the sound of multiple parts also in "Puntos cardinales" (WE 7.20).

Arrangements

From the early days of tango, arrangers have commonly based their work on published piano sheet music. During my jazz studies at Berklee, I noticed how easy it was to work from repertory in the famous *Real Book of Jazz* lead sheets as I honed my arranging techniques. While this process is typical in jazz, lead sheets had not been strongly developed in tango other than occasional chord symbols in the published sheet music. I began to transfer many tangos to the lead-sheet format, and to date, I have compiled more than 700 tangos, waltzes, and *milongas* in my collection *El Libro Real del Tango*.[7]

Now in my tango arranging, I apply the jazz approach in terms of thought, logical processes, and ordering of work. These steps include evaluating the tonality; determining the instrumentation; and adding introductions, bridges between sections, and extended endings. I often take the last four or eight bars as an introduction, add a short two-bar transitional bridge between sections, and extend the ending with the last four bars of the work. This way of working is also prevalent in the *a la parrilla* way of playing tango.

As in jazz, it is crucial to know the characteristic meters to determine appropriate accompanimental rhythms of the standard repertory. I illustrate lead sheets for each of the tango genre's *tres ritmos* (three rhythms): tango, *milonga*, and *vals* (waltz). The first, Salgán's "Don Agustín Bardi," shows how tango writing has been standardized since the 1950s in 4/4 (WE 7.21, WL 7.39). The second, "Milonga de mis amores" ("My Beloved Milonga"), exemplifies the *milonga* as the predecessor rhythm of tango written in 2/4 (WE 7.22, WL 7.40). Many tango musicians feel a connection between the *milonga* and the blues for their harmonic simplicity and melodic vigor. Interestingly, in a typical *milonga* bass line of $\hat{1}$-♭$\hat{6}$-$\hat{5}$, like in the example, tango musicians commonly speak of the ♭6 as the "green note" in a play on words with the ♯4 "blue note" from the blues. The third rhythm, the *porteño* (from Buenos Aires) *vals*, like all types of waltzes, maintains a 3/4 meter. It can be categorized into *criollo* (creole) when its title or lyrics refer to rural themes, and *urbano* (urban) when it deals with problems in the city or love conflicts, as in "Palomita blanca" ("Little White Dove," WE 7.23, WL 7.41). It shares an accompanying rhythmic pattern with jazz, where beat one is a dotted half note in the bass, and a half-note chord is played on beat two.

Form and Improvisation

Tango and jazz share many similarities in form, both in large-scale and small-scale designs. Beyond the traditional large-scale tango forms of AB and ABABCA, I usually use fugue as in "Un tal Bach" ("A Man Called Bach," WE 7.24) and free form as in "Ocaso en la ciudad" (WE 7.25), similar to earlier composers who integrated jazz and tango in these two structural frameworks. For example, Piazzolla builds the fugue exposition in "Fuga y Misterio" ("Fugue and Mystery," WL 7.42), "Fuga 9" ("Fugue 9"), and "Fugata" (as in the classical name for a fugue exposition) on the 12-bar minor blues form, and both Chick Corea and Rovira used free or expanded forms in "Señor Mouse" (WL 7.43) and "Sónico" ("Sonic," WL 7.44), respectively. Using the ending tag over the last four bars of the work is a common arranging technique in both styles of music. There is also a remarkable similarity in the construction of introductions on the bass-line, as in "A Night in Tunisia" (WL 7.45) compared to "Percal" ("Percale," WL 7.46).

Just as jazz typically follows the age-old formal principle of exposition, development, and return (or recapitulation, like the classical sonata form), I always maintain a formal balance. I apply the same principles from the organization of a jazz standard, which begins with an exposition on the thirty-two bar "head" (theme), moves to a development based on improvisation, usually on the chord changes of the thirty-two-bar theme, and concludes with a recapitulation of the original head and often a coda based on the repeat of the last four bars. I also determine a clear thematic exposition; think about the development, in which an improvisation section on chord changes may be included; and restore the original theme in a recapitulation that includes a coda with a new theme to find the ending, whether the work is tonal or moves away from the tonal system.

In jazz, a musician does not always improvise on the complete form, as in "Spain" (WL 7.47) by Chick Corea, where the improvisation occurs over just twelve bars of the composition, and in "A Night in Tunisia" (WL 7.48), where the improvisation occurs only over the first twenty-four bars. In complex works such as "Five" by Evans, the improvisation section occurs over the traditional "rhythm and changes" – a standard thirty-two bar AABA form but with harmonic chord changes relative to Gerswhin's "I

Got Rhythm" – rather than Evans's own changes (WL 7.49). Many of my solos are written specifically for my musicians as in "Mandinga" (WE 7.26), but other solos, usually on the guitar, are based on improvisation over chord changes that vary between four, eight, or sixteen bars, or in the entire form of the head like jazz music as in "Bien de abajo" ("From the Roots," WE 7.27).

Harmony

Tango and jazz draw on similar harmonic progressions and techniques, ranging from standard major/minor tonal progressions to modal, chromatic, and even atonal harmonies. Basic harmonic progressions in each style range from I-V^7-I with one chord per measure to the classic ii-V^7 and the standard jazz I-V/II-II-V^7 turnaround that leads back to the beginning of the tune (e.g., in C Major, C-A^7-Dm^7-G^7). I use a harmony close to the "rhythm and changes" approach in Gershwin's "I Got Rhythm" (WL 7.50), Parker's "Anthropology" (WL 7.51), and Sonny Rollins' "Oleo" (WL 7.52) in the first eight bars of my "De tanguistas" ("A Tango Player's Way," WE 7.28, WL 7.53). I apply the multitonic concept like the famous "Coltrane changes" heard in his "Giant Steps" (WL 7.54), which moves through the keys of B, G, and E♭ over the 16-bar form, to my "Amanece la ciudad" ("The City Awakes"), where the Am-Fm-D♭m harmonic changes and the minor keys give it the intense dark color of tango (WE 7.29, WL 7.55).

Just as jazz draws on modal scales and harmonies in pieces like "So What" on the Davis album *Kind of Blue* (WL 7.56) or in Coltrane's "Acknowledgement" on the album *A Love Supreme* (WL 7.57), I use modal passages in many segments of my works. In "Tres + Uno" ("Three Plus One"), for example, I use the Japanese scale *hirajōshi*, a pentatonic scale built on scale degrees 1–♭2–4–♭5–♭7 (WE 7.30). I also reinforce the modal sonority with quartal harmonies in favor of functional tertian harmony, in the manner of McCoy Tyner's accompaniment with Coltrane on "Afro Blues" (WL 7.58). In "Caminos," I explore the main motif in F Dorian mode with the blue note raised $\hat{4}$ (WE 7.31).

Throughout tango's development, composers have made extensive use of chromatic harmonies, yet some tango composers utilize chromatic techniques more specific to jazz, such as tritone substitution, advanced modal exchanges, hybrid chords, and constant structures (a series of chords that are of the same quality moving in a pattern, which may be tonally functional or nonfunctional). For example, Piazzolla's

"Decarísimo" (a superlative for De Caro, WL 7.59) uses constant structures, like Coltrane's "Like Sonny" (WL 7.60). Hybrid chords are very characteristic of Weather Report's jazz-rock "Birdland" (WL 7.61) and Rovira's 1962 contemporary tango "Sónico" ("Sonic," WL 7.62). In the 1960s, Rovira and Piazzolla applied more complex approaches to harmony and introduced non-functional chords and atonality. I follow such practices and explore polychords for two guitars by generating different tonal chords to harmonize the same melody in "Medianoche la ciudad" (WE 7.32).

Both jazz and tango have even used the twelve-tone technique. Evans employed it as a melodic series in "Twelve Tone Tune" in 1971 and in "Twelve Tone Tune Two" in 1973 (WL 7.63). Rovira was the first tango composer to apply this technique in "Supersónico" ("Supersonic," WL 7.64), where he executes a serial line supported by a constant harmonic structure on a minor chord, and more systematically in his 1963 "Serial docecafónico" ("Twelve-Tone Serialism," WL 7.65). I use the rigorous twelve-tone technique in my work for two guitars, "Gran ciudad" ("Big City"), and as a two-bar bridge within the tonal work "Trasnochado" (WE 7.33). In "Eduardo y Eduardo" (WE 7.34), dedicated to Rovira, I use a four-bar series to recreate Rovira's aesthetic.

Melody and Improvisation

Although both tango and jazz incorporate the element of improvisation, they evolved differently. In jazz, improvisation was based on variations on the given melody in early Dixieland, the notes of the chord changes in the Swing Era, the relationship between chords and scales in bebop, and finally, an avant-garde approach in free jazz. In the traditional tango *a la parrilla*, musicians who knew some tango repertory got together and started "improvising" by adding their own passages, melodic phrasing, harmonization, and variations. This tradition continued for tango musicians to "play by ear" without having to play a tune exactly the same each time. Some modern tango composers have borrowed jazz approaches. For example, Piazzolla used the bebop improvisational style on harmonic changes toward the end of his 1956 Octeto Buenos Aires piece "Marrón y azul" ("Brown and Blue," WL 7.66), where the guitar improvises on a two-chord vamp Em^9-F^9 (a similar progression to the introduction of Dizzy Gillespie's "A Night in Tunisia," WL 7.67).

In my music, I create space for improvisation in various ways. I cue an open moment for free improvisation over a progression of eighteen bars and the regular *milonga* rhythm in "Buenos Aires negra" ("Black Buenos Aires," WE 7.35), where I also experiment with 3/4 meter from the traditional *milonga* 2/4 meter. Within my tango "Para quién escribo" ("For Whom I Write," WE 7.36), the first guitar improvises on a repeated two-chord vamp Ab^{Maj7} and Cm^7. To create the spirit and feeling of improvisation, I often write a guide melody for the musicians and ask them to paraphrase it expressively while in rehearsal as in "En silencio" ("In Silence," WE 7.37). Even with written solos, I apply techniques such as indirect resolutions, guide tones lines, and chromaticism in arpeggios to generate a fresh musical line and to give a feeling of spontaneous improvisation, for example, in "Tango en negro" (WE 7.38). In all these approaches to improvisation, the "gesture" should always focus on creating a tango sound through rhythmic, melodic, and harmonic elements.

Thoughts on Performance Practice and Genre Tradition

In order to incorporate jazz elements into tango, a musician must possess a solid working knowledge of each genre's technical elements. One must study characteristic rhythmic, melodic, and harmonic elements to understand which are constitutive of tango and which are borrowed from jazz. To understand what musicians call "style," I always propose to my students to take the same composition, listen to three or four different performers, and compare which elements vary to make each orchestra or soloist distinguishable. If they want to understand a musical genre, it is crucial to listen to as much music as possible, and even transcribe and play it on their instrument.

First, I encourage students to differentiate the characteristic rhythm of one interpreter from another. Once they can understand different rhythmic aspects through comparison, they can move on to listening to the melodic element. Next, if one presents a coherent rhythm of the tango and maintains the melodic intention, then they can exercise harmonic freedom that has been adapted from the knowledge of tango composers, be it tonal, atonal, modal, or twelve-tone. Harmony will be able to amalgamate with the other elements.

Many tango musicians refer to "*el toque*" (the touch) when describing performance practices, like having "swing" in jazz or "style" in tango. It is the way of articulating and accentuating a phrase. For example, a jazz guitarist seeks to articulate like a saxophone, that is, lightly and with many slurred notes, flexibility, and speed. Conversely, a tango guitarist articulates in a more accentuated way, using expressive vibrato in long notes and only slurring the mordents. It is essential to listen to all types of instrumentalists and singers to understand the genre, or what we usually say in tango "*yeite*" (a *Lunfardo* word like "lick" or "trick" that means a "secret" resource to understand how to perform something in a certain way).

Finally, one practice I always do to integrate the two genres is to take jazz works and play them as if they were tangos. In this process, I call "tango in jazz," I only alter the intention of the melody with accents and tango articulations supported by the original harmonies, but with tango rhythmic cells. Sometimes I do the reverse process, that is, "jazz in tango." Based on this idea, I have developed a series of videos with a jazz and tango repertory on internet platforms called "Argentine Jazz."

Integrating Tango and Jazz in Practice

This final section illustrates my practical approach to integrating tango and jazz. I aim to help increase one's ability to control the "style" of each genre while creating aesthetic criteria. Following the points explained earlier, the conjunction of written music and moments of improvisation, or *a la parrilla*, will always maintain a clear "tango" line. Without generating "collage" spaces, a coherent and natural amalgam of both types of music will emerge. I summarize this integration below and offer a video to demonstrate my process based on my lead sheet of Ángel Villoldo's "El choclo" ("The Corncob," WV 7.1 and WS 7.1).

Integrating the Melody

1. Take a lead sheet from the classic tango repertory.
2. Play four bars of the original phrased melody followed by four bars of improvisation on the chord changes.
3. Play two bars of the original phrased melody followed by two bars of improvised melody over the chord changes.
4. Play one bar of the original phrased melody and one bar of improvisation on the harmonic chord changes.
5. Reverse the order of processes (steps 2, 3, through 4).

Integrating the Harmony

1. Memorize the original harmonic progression.
2. Complement the chord changes with bass inversions.
3. Add different reharmonization techniques, such as dominant/tritonal substitutions and chromatic chords.

Integrating the Rhythm

1. Make a plan for the rhythmic accompaniment, noting which type of pattern and tango style to use on each harmonic change.
2. Practice playing the same tune in two different compositional/arranging tango styles. For example, interpret a tango in the style of Gardel, then transform it into the style of Salgán.
3. Experiment with this practice by drawing on other compositional/arranging tango styles.

Conclusion

Jazz and tango have been two of the most important genres of popular music since their origins in the early twentieth century to today. This is true not only because of their musical complexity but also because of their early acceptance and popularity that, despite fashion changes, has continued in force. Comparing these two genres shows that both were initially created by Afro-descendants and Creoles in rural settings. Then, the musics grew up in large cosmopolitan cities like New York and Buenos Aires, influenced by immigration and a confluence of cultures. The parallelism shows the similarity of blues singers with *payadores*, Dixieland ensembles with *orquestas típicas criollas*, the hot jazz of Louis Armstrong with the *epoca decareana*, the big bands with the *orquestas típicas* of tango's Golden age, Bebop and Hard bop with the vanguard groups of Piazzolla and Rovira, the jazz-rock of Davis with tango-rock experimentations by Rodolfo Mederos with Generación Cero, and the arrival of acid jazz and electronic tango. Undoubtedly with all of these transformations through time, both genres have maintained their unique swing and style, even though many musicians feel an almost natural interconnection to play both musics and create crossovers. Today musicians, like myself, relish composing, arranging, and performing in a tango-jazz hybrid style, and thus the tradition of influencing and intertwining musical ideas continues in a cross-cultural dialogue.

Notes

1. Editors' note: for details on *marcato* and other key tango performance techniques, see Varchausky's Chapter 4.
2. The Golden Age of tango lasts slightly longer than jazz and extends into the 1950s. The Golden Age of Jazz is a less standard term than for tango, but for photographic documentation, see William P. Gottlieb, *The Golden Age of Jazz: On-Location Portraits, in Words and Pictures, of More Than 200 Outstanding Musicians from the Late '30s through the '40s* (New York: Simon and Schuster, 1979).
3. Two notable academic institutions of tango and jazz include, respectively, Escuela de Música Popular de Avellaneda (EMPA) in Buenos Aires and Berklee College of Music in Boston.
4. Editors' note: for details on Grela, see John's Chapter 5.
5. Jorge Retamoza, *El tango desde el saxo* (Buenos Aires: Editorial Melos, 2014) and Bernardo Monk, *The Tango Saxophone Book: A Method for Playing Saxophone in Argentine Tango* (Mainz: Advance Music, 2014).
6. Rhythm derived from *marcato* in 4, introduced by Pugliese's orchestra from his composition "La yumba," in which a cluster in the lower register of the piano is played on the weak beats 2 and 4.
7. Julian Graciano, *El Libro Real del Tango*, 3 vols. (Buenos Aires: Melos Ediciones Musicales, 2022).

Further Reading

Baker, David. *How to Play Bebop*. Vol. 1–3. Van Nuys, CA: Alfred Publishing Co., 1987. *Jazz Improvisation*. Van Nuys, CA: Alfred Publishing Co, 1983.

Bergonzi, Jerry. *Inside Improvisation Series*. Vol. 1–7. Rottenburg: Advance Music, 1994.

Coker, Jerry, James Casale, Gary Campbell, and Jerry Greene. *Patterns for Jazz*. Miami, FL: Studio P/R, 1970.

Goldstein, Gil. *Jazz Composer's Companion*. New York: Consolidated Music Publishers, 1981.

Graciano, Julián. *El libro Real del Tango*. Vol. 1–6. Buenos Aires: Melos Ediciones Musicales, 2020.

Pease, Ted. *Jazz Composition: Theory and Practice*. Boston: Berklee Press, 2003.

Rawlins, Robert, and Nor Eddine Bahha. *Jazzology: The Encyclopedia of Jazz Theory for All Musicians*. Milwaukee, WI: Hal Leonard Co., 2005.

Reilly, Jack. *The Harmony of Bill Evans*. Brooklyn, NY: Unichrom Ltd., 1992–3.

Salgán, Horacio. *Curso de Tango*. Buenos Aires: Pablo J. Polidoro, 2001. Translated into English by Will Genz and Marisa Hurtado as *Tango Course*, 2nd ed., 2001.

PART II

Tango Song

8 | Audacious Women: Profiles of Early *Cancionistas*

ROMINA DEZILLIO[*]

Introduction: About Women and Tango

The history of tango in Argentina has involved women for more than a century. From the beginning of the 1900s, women have struggled to remove their marginalized status from public consideration, and yet they have created their own remarkable place in tango's development as singers, or *cancionistas*. Facing bias and underestimation was not an easy thing for women. The practice of tango – as a popular dance and musical genre – had built its paradigm upon a categoric division of genders, in which men were subjects and women were considered objects for men's amusement. Despite such challenges, astute and audacious women found ways to subvert this narrative by making their own opportunities within tango.

In this chapter, I focus on tango *cancionistas* and the implications of their professionalization through a feminist musicological perspective that includes the examination of differences in gender and sexuality, and the reexamination of sociocultural possibilities according to women's history.[1] While famous tango *cancionistas* embrace a variety of tango vocal styles, from Tita Merello to Ada Falcón and Mercedes Simone to Tania, I narrow my discussion to the figures who *first* printed their own and long-lasting female stamp onto a masculine and *machista*[2] genre. I begin with some considerations concerning female singers from the *guardia vieja* (Old Guard). Then I examine the personal styles of three tango *cancionistas* who started their careers in the 1920s and 1930s and became stars within the tango mainstream: Rosita Quiroga (1896–1984), Azucena Maizani (1902–1970), and Libertad Lamarque (1908–2000). Each of their distinctive styles took advantage of a different development in the leisure and entertainment industry, boosted by radio broadcasting, that paralleled the expansion of tango. Quiroga, who was spontaneous and casual but easily intimidated by the presence of large audiences, preferred making phonographic recordings; Maizani found a way to exploit her dramatic streak singing tangos as part of theatrical plays; and Lamarque took her voice to the cinema and became a diva of international recognition.

These tango *cancionistas*, in general, were young, modern women. They came from low-income urban areas, and the sociocultural changes in the city further shaped their subjective experiences. They conjointly engaged in public spaces by becoming members of the cultural industry and participating in the consumer economy. As they put new social norms into practice and contributed to new recreational conventions, they adopted changes in fashion and body habits like smoking, drinking, and dancing as they helped transform the criteria for sexual morality.[3] Thus, their lifestyle implied overcoming social restraints as a part of the pendular process between inclusion and exclusion of women's emancipation.[4] With charming personalities and determination to face the demands of artistic careers at every step of their professional development, the *cancionistas* were not afraid of negotiating their possibilities on the edge of norms for the female gender.

Literature Review: Close Up from Afar

Research on women in tango is not new. The gender perspective in tango scholarship dates to 1972 with Estela dos Santos's historical and biographical research that focused not only on *cancionistas* but also on female instrumental musicians and dancers.[5] Since the 1990s, critical revisionism has examined the alliances between musical practices and the established dictates of twentieth-century patriarchy. Scholars have raised legitimate concerns about such issues as the widespread machismo of tango lyrics;[6] the "unvirtuous" feminine stereotypes portrayed by theatrical dramaturgy and cinematic narrative;[7] and the sorrows of love due to "illegitimate" real-life relationships between tango artists.[8] However, by only highlighting the struggles and sufferings of tango *cancionistas*, scholars have tended to promote the *cancionistas'* victimization, which ultimately overshadows their most important achievements and underlines their defeat rather than success. Only recently have Argentine scholars begun to explore how tango *cancionistas* defied these established gender roles and to consider how they contributed to the emergence of new feminine subjectivities by challenging the ideology of the eternal feminine.[9] These new approaches not only confront women's oppression and difficulty but also celebrate their accomplishments and gestures of emancipation, while encouraging a fairer recognition within the cultural hierarchy.[10] In line with this discourse, I demonstrate in this chapter how *cancionistas* have crossed over the limitations of their female gender to make a legitimate profession for women in a male-centric genre, and show how they have contributed to a progressive cultural transformation of tango.

In the Beginning Was "La Morocha"

> I will tell you. One evening the meeting was extremely lively, with the *muchachos* [male fellows] Victorica, Argerich, the congressman Félix Rivas, and others. As they noticed, I was very enthusiastic about Lola, who was an exquisite brunette, they touched my self-esteem, assuring me that I was not capable of writing a tango piece that she could sing successfully.
>
> Enrique Saborido, *Caras y Caretas* (1928)[11]

The first tangos sung on stage were part of the *criollo* (creole, or local Argentine) circus as well as musical numbers in variety shows and theatrical musical genres like revues, *sainetes*, and *zarzuelas*. *Tonadilleras* (singers of the Spanish *tonadilla* song form) and *cupletistas* (singers of *cuplé*, a type of light, sometimes risqué song sung in variety shows)[12] had also been increasingly incorporated into these stage genres since the beginning of the twentieth century with their light, provocative, and humorous styles. Early tangos were a hybrid of these genres, half Spanish and half *criollo*, sung by attractive female singers with a suggestive and erotic performance. Pepita Avellaneda, Rosita Miramar, Linda Thelma, Lea Conti, Andreé Vivianne, Lola Membrives, and Lola Candales were the first women to perform tangos in this context. Well known for their licensed and eccentric way of life, these singers were typically sopranos who were influenced by Hispanic genres such as the *sainete* and *zarzuela*. They had their own repertory marked by the feminine gender of the lyrics through which the singer and the character of the song identified with each other. They sang simple *coplas*, a verse form of Hispanic origin in a cocky tone, that usually introduced the name of the singer and boasted their graces in a provocative way.[13] Dos Santos quotes the *copla* that Avellaneda used to introduce herself on stage:[14]

A mi me llaman Pepita, jai, jai.	They call me Pepita, ha, ha.
De apellido Avellaneda, jai, jai,	My surname is Avellaneda, ha, ha,
cuando canto la milonga,	when I sing the milonga,
conmigo no hay quien pueda.	nobody can beat me.

These kinds of pieces were the predecessors to "La Morocha" ("The Brunette," music by Enrique Saborido and words by Ángel Villoldo), which was "the first one [tango *criollo*] especially composed to be performed by a female voice."[15] In his 1928 anecdote about the piece's creation cited in the above epigraph, Saborido describes how he was "with the *muchachos*" (guys) at the Reconquista bar in 1906, and, when they saw him yearning for the Uruguayan dancer/singer Lola Candales, they challenged him to write a hit tango that she could sing well.[16] He worked through the night, and in the morning he took the new tango to his friend Villoldo to add the verses. Villoldo, then, expressly tried to write polished and well-mannered lyrics that could be sung without shyness by any woman. Like the *cuplé*, the first stanza begins in the first person singular with an amusing self-description:

Yo soy la Morocha,	I am the Brunette,
La más agraciada,	The most graceful,
La más renombrada	The most renowned
De esta población.	Of this town.

In the third-stanza refrain, the lyrics of "La Morocha" build the main character around the stereotypical features of an Argentine woman, not just any type, but the *criolla*:

Soy la morocha argentina,	I am the Argentine brunette,
la que no siente pesares	the one who feels no regrets
y alegre pasa la vida	and joyfully spends her life
con sus cantares.	with her songs.
Soy la gentil compañera	I am the gentle companion
del noble gaucho porteño,	of the noble gaucho [cowboy/horseman] from Buenos Aires,
la que conserva el cariño	the one who preserves her affection
para su dueño.	for her owner.

One could say, then, that the first female *subject* created in tango was the singer. Although she was imagined with ideal features of a female partner – she was brunette, Argentine, and faithful to her *porteño* (someone from Buenos Aires) man – this *morocha* opened the door for women to participate in tango on their own terms and with the stamp of their own personalities in the future.

Candales also set a precedent when she performed this song. The anecdote goes: "She learned it by heart, rehearsed it, and that night *in the presence of all that memorable crew*, she sang it for the first time. *An absolute triumph*. It was repeated eight times to the applause of the audience, and Congressman Rivas sent Lola two hundred pesos as a reward for her success."[17] The story confirms, after a century of elaborations, the exercise in sociability based on differences in class, gender, and power, which articulate a complicity among males and their "productive" consumption of women. For the record, the "memorable crew" included [Benjamín] Victorica, [Juan] Argerich, and the congressman Félix Rivas. They were all public servants representing the ruling conservative political hegemony at the time, and the two hundred pesos that Rivas gave Candales was the highest salary a working woman could earn as a shirtmaker in a month.[18] Although this beginning of the female self in tango lyrics had much to say about male privilege, it also meant an undeniable milestone for women.

Two crucial factors boosted the circulation of "La Morocha." One was the published sheet music edition for voice and piano that enabled in-home use of the tango (WP 8.1), and the other was the new technology of phonographic recordings. The first recording of "La Morocha" appeared around 1908 in France by the Chilean performer Flora Hortensia Rodríguez (WL 8.1).[19] This recording of "La Morocha" reached unprecedented popularity, conquered the private sphere for the first time, and was heard widely in Europe. Flora Gobbi, who had earlier married singer, director, and composer Alfredo Eusebio Gobbi in Buenos Aires, went on to become one of the most popular variety artists in the early twentieth century.[20]

"La Morocha" claims a past for women within tango. It illuminates bits and pieces of history for *cancionistas* of the 1920s through the first written, printed, and phonographically recorded piece about them. While this tango did not arise from a change in the conditions of tango production, its emergence promoted a change in its consumption through the female self in the lyrics, a printed edition for home use, and a phonographic recording by a well-known female artist. Therefore, "La Morocha" made the first crack in a male-centered tango repertory resistant to the participation of women as subjects in the first person.

Women Speak of Men, Love, and Tango

By the 1920s, *guardia vieja* lyrics that closed the *cuplé* were left behind with the rise of the *tango canción* (tango song).[21] When Carlos Gardel decided to change his repertory from *criollo* styles to tango, he not only took the riskiest step in his career but reoriented the tango style completely. Gardel set a standard for tango singing by transforming tango's poetry as well as its expression.[22] The new style, which turned into the sentimental song of Buenos Aires, recast tango *criollo*'s light and risqué lyrics into those of love and suffering, and created one of the genre's great themes: *amor desdichado* (lost love).[23] Women now had a leading presence in tango lyrics in this paradigm shift to a deeper level of lament. On the one hand, they became the cause of men's pain and suffering, as in the lyrics of "Mi noche triste" ("My Sad Night"): "Woman you left me in the best of my life, leaving my soul wounded and [a] thorn in my heart."[24] On the other hand, women sang about their own painful love to men, as in the lyrics of "Julián": "I had a sweetheart who left me abandoned, and in my hours of sadness I remember him in my soul."[25]

Almost immediately theater and radio audiences adored *cancionistas*, and critics acclaimed them. Such an incipient star system, strengthened by the boom of mass media, shaped and fictionalized these singers' careers and lives. Their undeniable success, together with stories of their personal lives, infiltrated the tango world with female agency. From then on, tango, as a chosen artistic and life experience for both men *and* women, reframed and expanded feminine sensibility. In this context of half-fiction and half-truth where transgression was possible, female discretion and modesty (the supreme bastions of the bourgeoisie) found their outlets in natural ease and self-assurance.

During this process during the 1920s, discussions referencing gender representation began to appear in tango's narrative world. *La canción moderna*, a periodical devoted to tango culture that appeared in 1928, included an interview section with fixed questions addressed to different tango personalities (WP 8.2). Personal opinions on tango and the opposite sex were the main subjects. Regarding women, men generally boasted their unprejudiced taste for them with phrases such as "bring them all to me,"[26] "if they are pretty ... give them to me,"[27] or "I love them all without loving any of them."[28] Yet, there was also room for sentimental expressions, such as "they have been the ones who inspired all my songs."[29] When referring to men, women were elusive of commitment. For example, Quiroga defied convention, "I open myself up, *compañero* [male partner]";[30] La Porteñita confessed, "I don't know how to eat it [love]";[31] and Sofía Bozán commented provocatively, "I like men a lot."[32]

While using wit and mischievousness to characterize references to love and the opposite sex had been usual gestures among men, such allusions were deemed subversive coming from women. Inversely proportional to their independence from men, women expressed their passion for tango in a more serious way: "It is the most beautiful thing known. Tango is for me, when I perform it, as if it were life itself," said Simone;[33] Bozán expressed, "To hear a tango is to feel deep in the soul, the pain and joy of all my *criollo* people . . ."[34] and Virginia Vera synthesized emotion and performance by saying "[the person who] does not feel it will never be able to sing it well."[35] Men also began to soften their tone when referring to tango: bandoneonist Pedro Maffia summarized that tango "is, par excellence, the song of the people,"[36] and singer Ignacio Corsini was confident that "tango will not die as long as there is only one *criollo* to sing it."[37]

These testimonies reveal some aspects of the new sensibilities that tango modelled in the 1920s, namely expanding old customs and traditions of gender relations. In this context, female tango singers achieved visibility and legitimate public consideration as artists of popular culture. Although they had antecedents as actresses, they established their own place as tango *cancionistas*.

The "*Arrabalera*" Affability of Rosita Quiroga: From Lyrical Pretentiousness to Suburban *Chamuyo*

> My voice? What does it matter! I never had a great voice. To sing tango it is the least important. The soprano, the tenor, they stop singing eventually. The *cantor* and the *cancionista* always sing.
>
> Rosita Quiroga[38]

Unlike most *cancionistas* who were also actresses, Rosita Quiroga began her career at a record company. Her story portrays a self-determined and daring young woman from the suburbs who auditioned at Argentina's first recording studio installed by the Victor Label in 1922. Almost by chance, she began recording at the Victor studio and went on to become one of the studio's most successful figures.[39] Her unique way of *singing* tango lyrics also quickly established her career on the radio.

Quiroga was born in La Boca (a south-side neighborhood near Buenos Aires's harbor), which contained *conventillos* (collective urban tenements) filled with Italian immigrants, *criollos*, and rural people who had moved to the city. Since she was a child, Quiroga had been fond of singing and playing the guitar. Though completely self-taught in singing, she first studied guitar with the tango composer and conductor Juan de Dios Filiberto, a neighbor and a family friend.

In the early 1920s when she began to record and participate in radio auditions, Quiroga performed a repertory of *criollo* folk styles, including *milongas, estilos, zambas,* and *vidalitas.* "Later I turned to tango, but to *arrabalero* [neighborhood] tango," she recalled in 1976 (WL 8.2).[40] This transition from *criollo* styles to tango was not unique to Quiroga.[41] In the first decades of the twentieth century, her neighborhood of La Boca was properly an *arrabal* (a border area between the city and the countryside), where preferences and traditions coexisted by alternating between country rhythms and tango. Her singing expression included, as no other *cancionista* did, the *canyengue* accent – a characteristic cadence of dragging the beat and a manner of speech emphasizing the letter "s" from the *arrabales* – and a genuine use of the Buenos Aires slang *Lunfardo.*[42] Interviews recorded in later decades confirm a common characteristic regarding Quiroga's style: she sang the same way as she spoke. Regarding this, dos Santos notes how Quiroga was never interested in learning vocal technique or diction, and how this led to her temporary departure from tango as it conformed to the cultural industry and star system of the 1930s.[43]

Being a prominent figure for the Victor label allowed Quiroga to make crucial decisions over her repertory – a significant gesture, during this foundational time, of autonomy (and power), as women usually sang what they were asked. Quiroga's determination compelled one of her biggest moves to engage the prominent poet of *Lunfardo* verses, Celedonio Flores, who was writing for Gardel at the time. She stated: "When I heard the tangos by Flores that Gardel had recorded [for Odeon], we wrote to Flores from the Victor Company and I offered him a five-year contract" (WL 8.3). Quiroga premiered and recorded twenty-five tangos with lyrics by Flores, many of which he wrote exclusively for her.[44] One of the most characteristic was "Muchacho," a moralizing biographical sketch of a wealthy young man who lives in a luxurious way, spending money on women and vices, but does not know what love is. Another tango titled "La musa mistonga" ("The Poor Muse," WL 8.4) set a milestone in 1926 as the first commercial recording with a microphone for Victor in Argentina.[45] That same year, the Uruguayan composer and singer Ramón Collazo dedicated his tango "Pato" (*Lunfardo* for a destitute person) – a story of a poor man who, after a stroke of luck, earns some money and forgets about his humble origins – to "the queen of tango Rosita Quiroga." She immediately recorded the tango, and the sheet music appeared that same year, bearing Collazo's dedication (WP 8.3).

With her repertory, Quiroga never got away from the popular canon as she devoted herself to the oral expression of working-class people and street language. She did not seek to refine tango, nor did she try to feminize its rhetoric. Rather, she kept close to her intimate and *chamuyado* (conversational) style, maintaining a typical *criollo* guitar accompaniment. Despite the cosmopolitan gentrification of tango during the 1920s, Quiroga built her artistic identity by highlighting the early yet marginalized idiosyncrasies of tango and eternalized them with the new technology of recorded sound.

Azucena Maizani, "The Soul of Tango": Sensibility and Toughness

> Buenos Aires, where tango was born,
> my beloved land,
> I wish I could offer you
> all my soul in my singing.
>
> > "La canción de Buenos Aires" (1933)[46]

Azucena Maizani highlights a different tango scene from Quiroga's. Her scene sublimated the tango of the rough suburbs into the socially acceptable *el centro* (the center) of Buenos Aires around the bustling Avenida Corrientes (see WL 8.5 for her "La canción de Buenos Aires"). Famously known as the street "que nunca duerme" ("that never sleeps"), Corrientes exhibits a concentrated world of show business in its theatres, displays luxury and pleasure in its cabarets, and reflects a bohemian subculture in its cafes.

Maizani felt the call of tango when she was seventeen years old and working as a dressmaker in Buenos Aires. She was born in Palermo (a northern neighborhood of Buenos Aires) in 1902, and she lived there until age five when she moved to Martín García Island (in the Río de la Plata) to live with her aunt and uncle. She moved back to Buenos Aires at the end of the 1910s and began her tango career. Unlike Quiroga's ascent, Maizani was alone when she approached and sang for the tango band leader Francisco Canaro at the cabaret Royal Pigall. Canaro describes in his *Memorias* how that day, after a test, he and his orchestra accompanied her in two of Gardel's songs.[47] Although Maizani returned to her day job the following morning, she developed an unwavering desire to sing tangos. This desire, along with a vocation for acting, led her to her first step as a *particina* (supporting role singer) at the Teatro Apolo on Corrientes in actors Cesar and Pepe Ratti's company.

In the early twenties, when broadcasting was in its infant stage and the path of tango proliferated in the direction of "the sentimental song," the *sainete criollo* scene in Buenos Aires gave tango great cultural advancement.[48] *Sainete criollo* and tango drank from the same waters; they shared the linguistic variable of *Lunfardo*, and playwrights were often tango lyricists. Against the demands of "high" culture, the *sainete criollo* elaborated the world view of urban and popular people. It included codified characters or social "types" that exemplified figures from the city's immediate reality. Thus, tango music and its typical male and female social actors were an unavoidable part of its narrative structure. Characters such as *compadritos* and *malevos* (both are male *criollo* ruffians and pimps well known for their knife duels) and *grelas*, *milonguitas*, and *paicas* (all women close to prostitution) were a usual presence among other gender stereotypes.

In 1923, the playwright and poet Alberto Vacarezza wrote the lyrics of a tango especially for Maizani, after hearing her on tango composer Enrique Delfino's recommendation. With a musical setting by Delfino, Vacarezza created the tango "Padre nuestro" ("Our Father," WP 8.4, WL 8.6), which premiered on June 23, 1923, in the *sainete criollo A mí no me hablen de penas* at the El Nacional theatre. This first success of Maizani constituted an inaugural moment for tango *cancionistas*: it was the first tango written in the theatre for a female singer, not only to fit within the drama but also to portray Maizani's own character. The resulting progressive professionalization of *cantores* and *cancionistas* would come to replace the performances by actors and actresses.[49]

With his exceptionally fine intuition for portraying social "types," Vacarezza noticed Maizani's non-*femme fatale* character and dramatic disposition, and so wrote a lamentation for her. In this song, a woman, abandoned by her beloved man, begs God to bring him back while waiting and agonizing: "Our Father, who art in heaven, you the Almighty who sees all things; Why do you abandon me in this agony? Why do you not remember to bring him back?"[50] Maizani exaltingly leads the performance, seizing the tempo to the point of suspending the rhythm. Rubato, syncopation, and permanent *rallentandi* – all her way of interpreting the melody – leave the orchestra subordinated to the rhythm of her suffering (compare WL 8.6 to WL 8.7). Dos Santos affirms that "the triumph was so instantaneous the night of the premiere Azucena had to repeat the tango five times."[51] While engagements with broadcasting and record companies immediately followed her success with "Padre nuestro," Maizani's performances at the theatre did not stop. She continued at El Nacional for the following season, and from then on, she toured different theatres on the commercial circuit premiering tangos with great success.

Following "Padre nuestro," Maizani pointed out in 1928, "I definitely became famous with "Organito de la tarde" ("Little Street Organ of the Evening").[52] This tango, along with "Silbando" ("Whistling"), both with lyrics by José González Castillo, were premiered by Maizani in the revue *La octava maravilla* in 1925. With these pieces, Maizani started a characteristic feature of her artistic identity: dressing in performance as a *compadre* (the most respected male figure of authority in suburban neighborhoods, WP 8.5).[53] Cross-dressing earned her the nickname of "Ñata Gaucha" (to signify a "noble girl").[54] The name was immortalized in the song "Milonga del novecientos" ("Milonga of the 900") from the last scene of the film *¡Tango!* (1933), the first Argentine sound movie by Luis J. Moglia Barth (WL 8.8). Although this attire was not an exclusive feature of Maizani,[55] her repeated wearing of it turned into a style demarcation. Further, her association with González Castillo, who suggested this change of clothes, added other cultural and sexual resonances. For example, González Castillo was famous for his work *Los invertidos* (*The Inverted*), a tale of secret passions between two men, which had premiered ten years earlier. *Los invertidos* opened the stage to representations of the queer world – a gesture considered both anarchic and revolutionary by critical homosexual revisionism.[56]

Maizani's cross-dressing had its limit on stage, and, even though alluded to, there are no specific indicators of lesbian sexuality. However, she was deeply aware of the social meaning behind gender differences as well as the effects of her gender transgression, and so was the audience. Far from being "the gentle companion of the noble *gaucho porteño*," as "La morocha" describes herself, Maizani chose the commanding character of the *compadre*. This figure recalls another *tango criollo*, "El Porteñito" by Villoldo, where the lyrics describe the social and cultural male counterpoint of "La morocha" as "the most *compadrito* among *criollo* men born in this land" (see the character depicted on the sheet music cover, WP 8.6). With the attributes of pride, courage, freedom, and self-sufficiency, Maizani penetrated the representations of those lyrics about *reos* (convicts) and *malevos* (ruffians), *criollo* duels, and stories of the *arrabales* that were the core of her repertory. In 1925, the male costume also allowed Maizani to whistle at the end of her performance of "Silbando" (WL 8.9), an exclusively widespread practice among men. This tango tells the story of a crime of passion in a cinematographic description through four stanzas and two musical sections. The second stanza (refrain) describes the murderer coming, "whistling a song" in the night, and the third stanza describes the fatal scene:

Una calle . . . Un farol . . . Ella y él . . .	A street . . . A street lamp . . . Her and him . . .
y, llegando sigilosa,	and, creeping up,
la sombra del hombre aquel	the shadow of the man
a quien lo traicionó una vez la ingrata	who was once betrayed by the ungrateful
moza	wench
Un quejido y un grito mortal	A moan and a mortal scream
y, brillando entre la sombra,	and, shining through the shadow,
el relumbrón	the glint
con que un facón	with which a gaucho knife
da su tajo fatal . . .	gives its fatal slash . . .

After the last stanza and as a kind of coda, Maizani introduces the whistling to end the song.

In 1931, Maizani embarked on a European tour as both the main headliner and the sole investor. With an unexpected success, the company performed in Spain, visited several cities in Portugal, and ended its tour with a several-week stay in the brand-new casino of Biarritz, France. Meanwhile, in Buenos Aires, a 1931 contest to choose the Queen of Tango was held at the Teatro Colón. Although the prize went to Libertad Lamarque, tango representatives from the media claimed that Maizani deserved it.[57] This controversy gave rise to a dichotomy between the two *cancionistas* in the characterization of their styles and representations: manly toughness versus sweet femininity.[58]

Libertad Lamarque: Romantic Femininity, Suffering Passion, and Renouncement

Libertad Lamarque was not a native *porteña* but rather was born in 1909 in Rosario (a city northwest of Buenos Aires in the Argentine province of Santa Fe). As a little girl, she began developing her singing and acting skills in carnivals. When she was a teenager, she took part in a theatre company touring small villages of Santa Fe and Buenos Aires provinces and learned songs by ear to build her repertory.

In 1926, she left her hometown and settled in Buenos Aires with her parents to pursue a career as a singer and actress. Like Maizana three years before, the impresario and director of El Nacional gave Lamarque her first theatrical opportunities with small roles. After just two months, Lamarque made her debut as a *cancionista* with the tango "Mocosita" ("Little Kid Girl"). She then quickly expanded her repertory, began recording with the Victor label (the same as Quiroga), and started auditioning for the radio. In 1929, she was in the cast of the most successful *sainete criollo, El conventillo de la paloma* (*The Tenement of the Dove*) by Vacarezza (the same author of "Padre nuestro"). She stayed in the theatrical company for two years until she left to focus on her singing career. Although Lamarque's path to success had the traces of her predecessors, it would expand much further through the development of the film industry.

As aforementioned, the audience of a full Teatro Colón crowned Lamarque the "Queen of Tango" in 1931. Although they had expected the most famous *cancionistas* to participate in the competition, neither Maizani, Merello, Simone, Tania, nor Falcón appeared. Surrounded by mostly amateurs, this context left Lamarque as the only professional figure of the night and explains why the contest did not have much legitimacy among tango enthusiasts. Nevertheless, gaining the title "Queen of Tango" enabled her to be recognized as an outstanding *cancionista* by the public and allowed her to pursue her own tango style through the selection of a repertory far from *Lunfardo, malevos*, and knife fights. Lamarque's light soprano voice resumed the legacy of the *cupletistas* that had sunk into oblivion with the *criollo* influence in the styles of Quiroga and Maizani. The tangos she performed the night of the competition were "Si supieras" ("If You Knew," a 1924 version of "La cumparsita" with words by Pascual Contursi and Enrique Maroni) and "Taconeando" ("Tap Dancing"). "Si supieras" had earlier marked Lamarque's beginning on Radio Prieto in 1926, and this piece had also been one of her first tangos as a *cancionista* at El Nacional.

Although originally thought to be from a male suffering perspective, "Si supieras" works for both genders with small adjustments (WL 8.10). Such modifications allowed Lamarque to explore romantic femininity and to passionately embody the sufferings of the woman – legitimately – in love by inverting the roles of the story inaugurated by Contursi with "Mi noche triste."[59] From the first stanza, the lyrics express nostalgia and long-lasting love:

Si supieras,	If you knew,
que aún dentro de mi alma,	that deep in my soul,
conservo aquel cariño	I still keep that affection
que tuve para ti . . .	I had for you . . .
Quién sabe si supieras	Who knows if you knew
que nunca te he olvidado,	that I have never forgotten you,
volviendo a tu pasado	revisiting your past
te acordarás de mí . . .	you will remember me . . .

Through pieces like "Si supieras," Lamarque evaded the male self that prevailed in most tango lyrics without subverting the convention of romantic love. The heteropatriarchal family model had been reinstalled as the hegemonic social and cultural narrative since the 1930 military coup in Argentina, and the reactionary context gradually subdued the independence that women had achieved in the 1920s. A sector of the film industry became in charge of reordering the agency of genders within its representations.

The exemplifying morality in cinema's petty-bourgeois melodramas also replaced the picturesque and popular characters of *sainete criollo*. Along with the cross-dressed Maizani, Lamarque debuted in the film *¡Tango!*, but in the part of Elena who represents the renouncement of the beloved object/subject.[60] From this role forward, Lamarque further shaped her tango persona to include a "melodramatic profile of the lonely diva"[61] and a "grieving heroine."[62] In this persona, she assumed the restoration of the old conservative order with the mask of modesty, abnegation, and passionate suffering for love, and she clearly embodied a counterpart of the defiant and autonomous cross-dressed *cancionista*.

Lamarque's role in *¡Tango!* awarded her another inaugural moment for a *cancionista* – a tango written especially for her character titled "Noviecita" ("Little Girlfriend," WL 8.11). Beginning in the 1930s, a long list of subsequent successful movies included other pieces composed especially for her, tracing Lamarque's development with tango for many decades. Such tangos include "Ayúdame a vivir" ("Help Me to Live," 1936, WL 8.12)[63] and "Besos brujos" ("Haunted Kisses," 1938) from the films with the same name, and a homage version of "La Morocha" in Luis Saslavsky's movie *Puerta cerrada* (*Closed Door*, 1939, WP 8.7, WL 8.13).

Conclusion: Feminine Singular

Tango discourse around vocal performers has concerned itself with distinguishing singers according to their gender. First, the male *cantor* was born; then, as heir of the female *cupletista* and later of the *estilista* (singer of a folk repertory including *cifras*, *estilos*, *zambas*, *milongas*), the "female vocal performer of tango" arose and was called a *cancionista*.[64] The historical category of *cancionista* bears the mark of the professionalization of women within tango when, with few exceptions, female instrumentalists were minimal. *Cancionistas* negotiated and won their unique place within tango through the force of difference – their own struggles, their own bodies, and their own voices.

The *cancionistas* in the 1920s and 1930s were women who achieved unprecedented visibility in the public eye, not only to fulfill stereotypical female duties but to exercise their right to desire, to be acknowledged, and to be successful. A particular emotion of the tango scene during these two decades resounds with its own timbre in each of the *cancionistas* studied in this chapter. The voices of Quiroga, Maizani, and Lamarque modeled and expanded tango styles as they participated in the projection of the genre as a mass phenomenon and a promotional point of the Argentine cultural industry.

Seizing the moment of the 1920s and 1930s, tango *cancionistas* possessed the courage, intuition, and talent to answer the call of the sentimental song and take what they rightfully deserved. Now, looking back, we see that each of these singers represents a different way of living and feeling tango. Quiroga's affective dimension appeared simple, intimate, and natural; Maizani projected a transgressive, strong, and unconditional persona; and Lamarque illustrated a long-suffering and passionate image. Their singular vibrations do not play in unison, but their combined emotions allow us to appreciate their influence on tango through their stamps of audacity.

Notes

* I would like to give thanks to Vera Wolkowicz (Instituto de Artes del Espectáculo–Universidad de Buenos Aires) for her help with the translation of the text and her insights; Julia Kratje (Instituto Interdisciplinario de Estudios de Género–Universidad de Buenos Aires/Consejo Nacional de Investigaciones Científicas y Técnicas (UBA/CONICET)), Daniela Anabel González (Instituto de Ciencias Antropológicas–UBA/CONICET) for their feedback during the elaboration of this chapter, and Omar García Brunelli (Instituto Nacional de Musicología "Carlos Vega") and Soledad Venegas (Instituto de Investigación en Etnomusicología) for sharing their own research sources to help me complete this investigation during periods of isolation in the Covid-19 pandemic.

1. For further discussion, see Pilar Ramos López, "Hacia una historia de las mujeres intérpretes," *Quadrivium* 5 (2014), available online at *Fundación Dialnet*, https://dialnet.unirioja.es/ejemplar/492382.

2. A form of sexism based on the social, economic, and political oppression and domination of women – as a human group – by men within patriarchy.

3. For further discussion, see Dora Barrancos, "Moral sexual, sexualidad y mujeres trabajadoras en el período de entreguerras," in *Dora Barrancos: Devenir feminista. Una trayectoria político-intelectual*, comp. Ana Laura Martín and Adriana María Valobra (Buenos Aires: Editorial de la Facultad de Filosofía y Letras, 2019), 397–424.

4. For further discussion, see Dora Barrancos, *Inclusión exclusión: Historia con mujeres* (Buenos Aires: Fondo de Cultura Económica, 2002).

5. Estela dos Santos has three seminal books on the subject matter: *Las mujeres del tango* (Buenos Aires: Centro Editor de América Latina, 1972); *La historia del tango: Las cantantes* (Buenos Aires: Corregidor, 1978); *Damas y milongueras del tango* (Buenos Aires: Corregidor, 2001).

6. Such scholars include Irene López, "Morochas, milongueras y percantas. Representaciones de la mujer en las letras de tango," *Espéculo* 45 (2010): 1–14, and Dulce María Dalbosco, "Préstame tu voz: acerca de la enunciación femenina en las letras de tango," *Chasqui. : Revista de literatura latinoamericana* XLIV (2015): 180–195.

7. For further discussion, see Fernanda Gil Lozano, "Género y representaciones femeninas en el cine sonoro argentino," in *Historia de luchas, resistencias y representaciones. Mujeres en la Argentina, siglo XIX y XX*, ed. María Celia Bravo, Fernanda Gil Lozano and Valeria Silvina Pita (San Miguel de Tucumán: Edunt, 2008), 391–406.

8. For example, the relationship between Merello and Luis Sandrini is depicted in the film by Teresa Constantini, *Yo soy así. Tita de Buenos Aires* (Buenos Aires Producciones, 2017); and the relationship between Falcón and Francisco Canaro is depicted in Sergio Wolf and Lorena Muñoz, *No sé qué me habrán hecho tus ojos* (S/R, 2003).

9. For further discussion, see María Aimaretti, "Sutiles astucias de la voz: potencia y fragilidad en la representación de las cancionistas Libertad Lamarque y Tita Merello en dos films argentinos," *Imagofagia* 15 (2017): 1–35; Florencia Calzón Flores, "El sistema de estrellas en Argentina durante los cuarenta y cincuenta: el caso de Tita Merello," *Montajes: Revista de Análisis Cinematográfico*, Vol. 2 (2013): 53–73.

10. Mercedes Liska, "'Se dice de 'ella.' Sentidos de género en los discursos biográficos sobre Tita Merello," *Revista Argentina de Musicología* 22, no. 1 (2021): 103–104.

11. "Le diré. Una noche la reunión estaba sumamente animada, figurando en ella los muchachos Victorica, Argerich, el diputado Rivas y otros. Como notaran que yo estaba muy entusiasmado con Lola, que era una morocha exquisita, me tocaron el amor propio asegurando que no era capaz de escribir un tango que ella pudiera cantar con éxito." Ernesto E. de la Fuente, "De cómo Enrique Saborido compuso su tango 'La morocha,' hace 22 años," insert "Los reyes del tango" in *Caras y Caretas* (September 1, 1928).

12. Although the word *cuplé* derives from the French *couplet*, in this context it describes a musical genre widespread in Spain that developed from the traditional *tonadilla* at the end of the nineteenth century and later as a synonym for song. Its most popular performers have always been women. For further discussion, see María Baliñas, "Cuplé [Couplet]" in *Diccionario de la Música Española e Hispanoamericana*, dir. Emilio Casares Rodicio, Vol. IV, 317–325 (Madrid: SGAE, 1999).

13. *Coplas* were often improvised and they "relate humorous incidents, amorous sentiments, current or historical events or merely comment on daily life or the natural environment of the singer. Witty use of slang expressions and double meanings add to their often-erotic nature." William Gradante, "Copla," *Grove Music Online*, 2001, www.oxfordmusiconline.com/grovemusic/view/10.1093/gmo/9781561592630.001.0001/omo-9781561592630-e-0000006421.

14. Dos Santos, *Las cantantes*, 2231.

15. Dos Santos, *Las cantantes*, 2235.

16. De la Fuente, "De cómo Enrique Saborido compuso su tango 'La Morocha,' hace 22 años." Other versions present different places and dates of the same anecdote. Saborido himself states in 1936 that he created the tango on Christmas Eve 1905. See Héctor and Luis Bates, *Historia del tango* (Buenos Aires: Authors' edition, 1936), 60. Other sources also change the place. See Oscar Del Priore and Irene Amuchástegui, "La Morocha, un tango de exportación," on *Todotango*, www.todotango.com/historias/cronica/222/La-Morocha-un-tango-de-exportacion.

17. "Lo aprendió de memoria, lo ensayó y esa noche, *en presencia de toda aquella barra memorable*, ella misma lo cantó por primera vez. . . . *[Un triunfo] absoluto*. Fue repetido ocho veces, entre lo aplausos de la concurrencia, y el diputado Rivas envió a Lola 200 pesos como premio por su éxito." De la Fuente, "De cómo Enrique Saborido compuso su tango 'La morocha,' hace 22 años." Italicized words by the author.

18. The minimum wage for a shirtmaker was thirty-five pesos. Mirta Zaida Lobato, *Historia de las trabajadoras en la Argentina (1869–1960)* (Buenos Aires: Edhasa, 2007), 45.

19. Dates vary from 1906 to 1909.

20. For further information about Flora and Alfredo Gobbi, see Omar García Brunelli, "2. Rodríguez, Flora Hortensia," in *Diccionario de la Música Española e Hispanoamericana*, vol. V, dir. Emilio Casares Rodicio (Madrid: SGAE, 1999), 668.

21. Throughout this book, the editors use the term *tango canción* to describe the genre of sung tango and translate it literally throughout for consistency. However, some scholars disagree with this term, and many scholars in Argentina use the terms *tango instrumental* and *tango cantando* to differentiate instrumental tango and sung tango.

22. Omar García Brunelli, "Gardel Músico. Su proyección en la historia del tango," in *El Mudo del tango: ocho estudios sobre Carlos Gardel*, comp. Omar García Brunelli (Buenos Aires: Instituto Nacional de Musicología "Carlo Vega," 2020), 59–76.

23. García Brunelli, "Gardel Músico. Su proyección en la historia del tango," 64.

24. "Percanta que me amuraste en lo mejor de mi vida, dejándome el alma herida y espina en el corazón." "Mi noche triste" (Castriota/Contursi, 1916).

25. "Yo tenía un amorcito que me dejó abandonada, y en mis horas de tristeza lo recuerdo en el alma." "Julián" (Donato/Panizza, 1923).

26. "Que me las traigan todas," "Con Catulo Castillo (compositor), Reportajes a vuela pluma," *La canción moderna*, April 2, 1928.

27. "Si son bonitas … que me las den," "Con Pedro M. Maffia (compositor), Reportajes a vuela pluma," *La canción moderna*, April 16, 1928.

28. "Las amo a todas sin amar a ninguna," "Con Antonio Polito (compositor), Reportajes a vuela pluma," *La canción moderna*, June 18, 1928.

29. "Han sido las que inspiraron todas mis canciones," "Con Ignacio Corsini (cantor), Reportajes a vuela pluma," *La canción moderna*, April 9, 1928.

30. [De los hombres] "me abro, compañero," "Con Rosita Quiroga (cancionista), Reportajes a vuela pluma," *La canción moderna*, April 2, 1928.

31. [El amor] "no sé cómo se come," "Con 'La Porteñita' (bandoneonista), Reportajes a vuela pluma," *La canción moderna*, June 4, 1928.

32. [Los hombres] "me gustan una barbaridad," "Con Sofía Bozán (cancionista), Reportajes a vuela pluma," *La canción moderna*, April 16, 1928.

33. "Es lo más lindo que se conoce. El tango es para mí, al interpretarlo, como si fuera la vida misma," "Mercedes Simone (cancionista), Reportajes a vuela pluma," *La canción moderna*, May 21, 1928.

34. "Oír un tango es sentir en el alma, el dolor y la alegría de todo mi pueblo criollo …" "Con Sofía Bozán (cancionista)."

35. "[Quien] no lo siente nunca podrá llegar a cantarlo bien," "Con Virginia Vera (cancionista y guitarrista), Reportajes a vuela pluma," *La canción moderna*, August 27, 1928.

36. "El tango es, por excelencia, la canción del pueblo," "Con Pedro M. Maffia (compositor), Reportajes a vuela pluma," *La canción moderna*, April 16, 1928.

37. "El tango no morirá mientras exista un solo criollo para cantarlo," "Con Ignacio Corsini (cantor), Reportajes a vuela de pluma," *La canción moderna*, April 9, 1928.

38. "¿Mi voz? ¡Qué importa! Yo nunca tuve gran voz. Para cantar el tango es lo menos necesario. La soprano, el tenor, alguna vez dejan de cantar. El cantor y la cancionista cantan siempre." Quoted in dos Santos, *Damas y milongueras del tango*, 38.

39. Dos Santos states that Rosita accompanied a friend on guitar for a private recording at Victor's house. It was a fashionable practice at the time to record

greetings, recitations, or songs to give as gifts. She was immediately granted a recording contract. *Las cantantes*, 2247.

40. Excerpt from the film *El canto cuenta su historia* (15:07–17:57). With the expression "*arrabalero*," Rosita emphasizes the "authentic" character of tango. Adjectives such as *arrabalero*, *orillero*, and *canyengue* originally referred to a way of dancing tango before its stylization and internationalization as a ballroom dance. In their reference to sung tango, these adjectives allude both to its themes, relating to the *arrabal*, and to its expressive modes, such as the use of *Lunfardo* words in the lyrics and the *porteño* accent in the pronunciation.

41. García Brunelli studies this switch in Gardel's repertory and its implications in the development of tango, "Gardel Músico. Su proyección en la historia del tango," 59–76.

42. *Lunfardo* is the lexicon born from a blend of interlanguages that boomed in the city of Buenos Aires between the 1870s and 1940s due to the great wave of immigration. It was progressively incorporated into mass circulation through writing, and many consider its integration into tango lyrics begins with "Mi noche triste" (Castriota/Contursi) in 1916. Lila Caimari, "Buenos Aires. Mezclas puras: lunfardo y cultura urbana (años 1920 y 1930)," in *Ciudades sudamericanas como arenas culturales*, comp. Adrián Gorelik and Fernanda Arêas Peixoto (Buenos Aires: Siglo Veintiuno, 2016), 155–173.

43. Dos Santos, *Las cantantes*, 2247 and 2249.

44. Marina Cañardo, *Fábricas de músicas. Comienzos de la industria discográfica en la Argentina (1919–1930)* (Buenos Aires: Gourmet Musical, 2017), 164.

45. Cañardo, *Fábricas de músicas*, 55.

46. "Buenos Aires, donde el tango nació, / tierra mía querida, / yo quisiera poderte ofrendar / toda el alma en mi cantar." Music by Azucena Maizani and Orestes Cúfaro and lyrics by Alberto Romero. From the opening scene of the film *¡Tango!*, see WL 8.5.

47. Quoted in dos Santos, *Las cantantes*, 2255.

48. While the *sainete* came originally from Spain, by the last decades of the nineteenth century many theatre companies started to develop a local or "*criollo*" version of this theatrical genre. Jorge Dubatti defines it as a short theatrical piece (in a single act divided into two or three scenes) of popular characters, who are generally comic but include dramatic or tragic qualities. Jorge Dubatti, "Estudio crítico," in Alberto Vacarezza, *El conventillo de la paloma y otros textos* (Buenos Aires: Colihue, 2013), 239.

49. Premiere performances that stand out include Manolita Poli of "Mi noche triste" in the *sainete Los dientes del perro*; Iris Marga of *Julián* in the revue *¿Quién dijo miedo?* and *Milonguita* by María Esther Podestá in the *sainete Delikatessen Haus*.

50. "Padre nuestro, que estás en el cielo que todo lo puedes, que todo lo ves; ¿Por qué me abandonas en esta agonía? ¿Por qué no te acuerdas de hacerlo volver?" (Vacarezza).

51. Dos Santos, *Las cantantes*, 2256.

52. "Me consagré definitivamente con Organito de la tarde," "Con Azucena Maizani (cancionista), Reportajes a vuelta de pluma," *La canción moderna*, April 23, 1928.

53. Later on, she would alternate between *compadre* and *gaucho* clothing.

54. Literally, *ñata* means short or small nose, and *gaucho/a* may be used as an adjective to mean a noble and trustworthy person. In this case, *gaucha* is also a play on words with the noun, since Maizani dressed in *gaucho* clothes.

55. Male attire worn by women had already been done by Pepita Avellaneda as well as Mercedes Simone.

56. Diego Trerotola, "Transgénero criollo," *Soy* in *Página 12*, March 18, 2011.

57. For further discussion, see Romina Dezillio, "'¿Qué hacemos con la "Corona" si la Reina está en España?' Controversias en torno a la elección de la Reina del Tango en el Teatro Colón en 1931," paper presented at the *III Jornadas de cine, teatro y género del Instituto de Artes del Espectáculo*, Centro Cultural de la Cooperación Floreal Gorini, CABA, November 2, 2018.

58. For further discussion, see Romina Dezillio, "'No se nace cancionista, se llega a serlo.' Estudio sobre el proceso de consolidación de las cancionistas de tango durante la década de 1930," paper presented at the *XIV Jornadas Nacionales de Historia de las Mujeres y IX Congreso Iberoamericano de Estudios de Género*, Universidad Nacional de Mar del Plata, July 29–August 1, 2019.

59. In this 1970 performance of "Si supieras" (the only one phonographically available), as part of the Mexican film *Rosas blancas para mi hermana negra* directed by Abel Salazar, Lamarque changes the reference to a woman with the words "Decí, percanta, ¿qué has hecho de mi pobre corazón?" ("Say woman, what have you done to my poor heart?") to that of a male addressee, "Decí mi negro ¿qué has hecho de mi pobre corazón?" (Say my *negro* [used colloquially as a term of endearment among *porteños*] what have you done to my poor heart?).

60. Ricardo Manetti, "Aprender y consumir, legitimación de un modelo estelar," in *30-50-70. Conformación, crisis y renovación del cine industrial argentino y latinoamericano*, comp. Ricardo Manetti and Lucía Rodríguez Riva (Buenos Aires: Editorial de la Facultad de Filosofía y Letras Universidad de Buenos Aires, 2014), 36.

61. Gil Lozano, "Género y representaciones femeninas en el cine sonoro argentino," 405.

62. Aimaretti, "Sutiles astucias de la voz," 5.

63. The pathos of these verses by Atilio Supparo highlight tango's pathos: "¡Toma, ruin! / abre esta herida / saca el corazón de aquí, / dame al menos la alegría / de morir." ("Here, you wretch! / open this wound, / get the heart out of here, / give me at least the joy / of dying.")

64. Horacio Ferrer, "Cancionista," *El libro del tango. Crónica & diccionario 1850–1977* (Buenos Aires: Editorial Galerna, 1977), 321.

Further Reading

Aimaretti, María. "Sutiles astucias de la voz: potencia y fragilidad en la representación de las cancionistas Libertad Lamarque y Tita Merello en dos films argentinos." *Imagofagia* 15 (2017): 1–35.

Barrancos, Dora. "Moral sexual, sexualidad y mujeres trabajadoras en el período de entreguerras." In *Dora Barrancos: Devenir feminista. Una trayectoria político-intelectual*, compiled by Ana Laura Martín and Adriana María Valobra, 397–424. Buenos Aires: Editorial de la Facultad de Filosofía y Letras, 2019.

Calzón Flores, Florencia. "El sistema de estrellas en Argentina durante los cuarenta y cincuenta: el caso de Tita Merello." *Montajes: Revista de Análisis Cinematográfico*, Vol. 2 (2013): 53–73.

Dalbosco, Dulce María. "Préstame tu voz: acerca de la enunciación femenina en las letras de tango." *Chasqui. Revista de literatura latinoamericana* XLIV (2015): 180–195.

Dos Santos, Estela. *Las mujeres del tango*. Buenos Aires: Centro Editor de América Latina, 1972.

Gil Lozano, Fernanda. "Género y representaciones femeninas en el cine sonoro argentino." In *Historia de luchas, resistencias y representaciones. Mujeres en la Argentina, siglo XIX y XX*, edited by María Celia Bravo, Fernanda Gil Lozano, and Valeria Silvina Pita, 391–406. San Miguel de Tucumán: Edunt, 2008.

Gil Mariño, Cecilia. *El mercado del deseo. Tango, cine y cultura de masas en la Argentina de los '30*. Buenos Aires: Teseo, 2015.

Liska, Mercedes. "Se dice de 'ella'. Sentidos de género en los discursos biográficos sobre Tita Merello." *Revista Argentina de Musicología* 22, no. 1 (2021): 101–144. https://ojs.aamusicologia.ar/index.php/ram/article/view/350.

Ramos López, Pilar. "Escribir hoy sobre la historia, la música y las mujeres." *Música e Investigación* 30 (2022): 79–102. https://inmcv.cultura.gob.ar/noticia/musica-e-investigacion-30-2022/.

Venegas, Soledad. "Narrativas de nación: tango y género en los años veinte." *Revista Argentina de Musicología* 23, no. 1 (2022): 180–205. https://ojs.aamusicologia.ar/index.php/ram/article/view/402.

9 | The Poetics of Golden Age Tango

PABLO PALOMINO*

Introduction

Tango's Golden Age was the years when a distinct form of tango dance and music became mainstream in the Río de la Plata region, expanded nationally in Argentina, acquired global fame, shaped a modern media business, and, as this chapter discusses, writing *lyrics* became a professional endeavor. While early tango lyrics were often accessories to the music – which in turn was mainly intended to produce the dance – by the Golden Age, spanning from the 1930s to the mid-1950s, lyrics shaped through memorable *verses* the collective imagination. They were passed on across generations by media systems and family transmission, feeding personal memories, literary and song traditions, and today's urban heritage and tourism industry. If, internationally, tango became a fancy dance, a musical tradition, and a global symbol of cosmopolitan nostalgia, it also became a *poetic* identity in Buenos Aires.

The precise chronology of the Golden Age has been richly discussed among tango scholars.[1] Tango's poetic stages do not exactly match those of music composition and performance practices or its social dance form. Since its nineteenth-century origins and well into the first two decades of the twentieth, tango either lacked lyrics or incorporated improvised words. The few exceptions to the rule – tangos with recognized authorship – had quite simple verses. For example, Ángel Villoldo's famous "La Morocha" ("The Brunette," 1905) celebrates an archetypical *criolla* (creole, or local Argentine) woman as the *morocha* (ambiguously brunette or dark-skinned) in first-person. She is a passionate lover and loyal wife to her man, the *gaucho porteño* (a figure that conflates the *gaucho*, or rural man, with the *porteño* or port-city urban man), and she sings to him and her country in her "beloved ranch" and "under the silver night." While this figure became a national symbol rich in cultural complexities, the poetry of this tango is like that of the early times of the genre: a simple, joyful boast of oneself as a fighter, lover, or dancer.[2]

Tango poetics changed in 1917, when Carlos Gardel performed the first *tango canción* (tango song) "Mi noche triste" ("My Sad Night," WL 9.1),[3] with which the poet Pascual Contursi "inaugurated the disgusting theme of the crying pimp, abandoned by his beloved prostitute."[4] Metaphors of conflict and pain began to appear in the new songs after this pivotal year. The *tango canción* led to a powerful stream of songs whose verses became Buenos Aires' classic poetry, influential nationally and also in many Spanish-speaking Latin American cities, especially in the 1930s.

By the 1950s, Buenos Aires' musical and cultural habits began to shift to other genres, and the tango world began to close in on itself and lose popularity. Post–Golden Age exquisite tango writers like the Uruguayan–Argentine Horacio Ferrer elaborated classic themes in new ways. In his innovative style, Ferrer drew on the speech-song recitative technique, often collaborating with modern tango composers like Astor Piazzolla.[5] But tango's declining popularity limited its poetic impact. Interestingly, when new generations of *tangueros* revamped the genre at the turn of the twenty-first century, they found inspiration in the early Golden Age poetry.[6]

Golden Age tango poetics were the fruit of exceptional lyricists. They were numerous, and any selection and analysis would be unfair to the poets themselves and to generations of listeners, writers, and cultural critics. Still, with the dash of the *compadrito* (the archetypical brave man of the early tangos), I present a selection of tango's classical poetry through lyrics penned by Alfredo Le Pera (1900–1935), Enrique Cadícamo (1900–1999), Enrique Santos Discépolo (1901–1951), Pascual Contursi (1888–1932) and his son José María Contursi (1911–1972), Homero Manzi (1907–1951), and two of the few women in this rather masculine world: Azucena Maizani (1902–1970) and Mercedes Simone (1904–1990). I organize the poetry around three central themes that emerged in the Golden Age: the urban space, the sociological and poetic issue of the relationship between *love* and *self*, and the modern experience itself. But first, I will consider the historical context in which, through a unique mix of modernism and vernacular speech, tango lyrics became a sentimental, philosophical, and aesthetic lens for several generations of listeners in Argentina and beyond.

The Context

Many of these and other tango poets were first- and second-generation Argentines from Italian immigrant families, as well as *criollo* (older population of mixed indigenous, African, and Iberian descent) families and other immigrants from Eastern and Western Europe and the Mediterranean world. They were either born in the city of Buenos Aires or migrated there. Their poetry reflected and reshaped the peculiar Spanish (or more accurately, Castilian) of the Río de la Plata region, with its slang, its *voseo* (*vos* instead of *tú*, conjugating the present tense of the poetically crucial second person – *you* – differently than most of the Spanish-speaking world), its aspirated *s*, and its *sh* sound (*yeísmo*, an old Iberian and Romance tradition). The stylistic sources were varied: *cuplés*, songs by Spanish theater companies; oral verses of the countryside *payadores* (minstrels or troubadours who played the guitar and deftly improvised verses to challenge each other); and above all, works by Argentine modernist poets of the beginning of the century, like Evaristo Carriego (1883–1912). These poetic sources converged in tango lyrics that fed the sentimental education of a growing and cosmopolitan audience of *criollos*, newcomers, and children of migrants. Growing literacy rates, music business opportunities, and print culture turned Buenos Aires and Montevideo into cultural hubs. Tango lyrics – danced to in salons, clubs, and brothels, sung in theaters and films, read in magazines, and orally disseminated – became their modern folklore.

Since Buenos Aires was Argentina's most influential literary and musical center, its popular poetry threatened the linguistic nationalism of the *hispanistas*. These traditionalists valorized the colonial linguistic legacy, like Eusebio Castex, who stated: "When we say Argentine popular poetry we don't include the barbarous slang of *Lunfardo*, so fashionable, alas, in these calamitous times of tango *arrabalero*."[7] *Lunfardo* was a popular vocabulary created in the late nineteenth century (still integral to colloquial Spanish in the Río de la Plata region),[8] and the *arrabal* was the "uncivilized" city outskirt. In 1931 the Argentine Academy of Letters was created to police public texts and discourses from the kinds of linguistic uses disseminated by tango lyrics.[9] But *Lunfardo* thrived anyway. Its prohibition and vindication were a part of a broader debate around the very definition of what constitutes "folk" and "national" language and culture in Argentina. The question, therefore, about tango's cultural legitimacy during its very Golden Age became: did the tango belong to a *cosmopolitan* (i.e., immigrant), *folkloric* (i.e., *criollo*), or *Castilian* (i.e., Hispanic) linguistic tradition?[10] Tango lyrics, like Rioplatense language, have elements of all three, representing a unique, delicate, and expressive merging of literary modernism and folk speech informed by urban *Lunfardo*. They shaped not just the city's musical culture but the Rioplatense linguistic identity.

Tango's Golden Age encompassed decades of political changes in Argentina. While the modern form of tango emerged at a time of political democratization (1916–1930), the Golden Age was concocted in a cycle of coups d'état and political fraud (1930–1946), democratic populism (1946–1955), and military and liberal authoritarianism (1955–1958). These decades witnessed the decline of European mass immigration by the 1930s, the rise of domestic mass migration to the Buenos Aires area, and periods of rising salaries and full employment alternating with those of economic hardship. Inclusive state policies like public schooling and a vibrant public and media culture coexisted with repression and censorship. A manifold current of progressive political forces pushed to democratize the liberal order through social legislation, suffrage equality, and divorce laws, against varied forms of liberal, conservative, and Catholic activism. These conflicts directly affected the subjective experiences elaborated by tango lyricists. The cultural climate during tango's Golden Age was thus a complex and changing one. But two disparate social traits remained constant: on the one hand, upward mobility, with economic growth sustaining an attainable ideal of a modern, middle-class (a term that became widespread precisely in these decades) lifestyle for many citizens; on the other hand, the underside of modernity, those migrants or *criollos* who could not move past precarious jobs, abandoned in the shadow of progress. While political and social critique did appear in tangos and popular songbooks, as in the anarchist, radical, unionist, nationalist, and Peronist tangos that animated the social world of working-class organizations,[11] lyrics became to its listeners less a political than a poetic guide. Golden Age tango's dominant theme was the subjectivity shaped by the uncertainties of the modern experience.

The Urban Space as Poetic Geography

The geographic span of the Golden Age tango is vast. To start with, the genre itself, tango, has a long global history, rooted in the Atlantic musical exchanges among Africa, Iberia, and the cities of the Americas and the

Caribbean. By the 1880s, Argentine tango became an autonomous tradition not just musically, but as a specific poetic style, both in Buenos Aires and Montevideo. Because these were busy port cities – hence the adjective *porteña/o* to refer to the people of Buenos Aires – growing at the pace of the meat and grain exports, their cultural life was shaped by musical trade with other urban cultures, especially European ones, from where immigrants, refugees, investments, and musical scores and instruments arrived. This, in turn, enticed local performers to cross the Atlantic in the opposite direction to pursue opportunities. For example, "Volver" ("To Return," WL 9.2), penned by Alfredo Le Pera in 1935, depicts this musical trade by immortalizing Gardel on a ship deck crossing the Atlantic, and singing that, "even if I didn't want to come back," he will return to Buenos Aires "under the scornful sight of the stars." Golden Age poetics also revealed the geography of Buenos Aires and Montevideo's surroundings, namely the *arrabal*, the semi-urbanized, porous borderlands between the consolidated city and the agricultural areas, with their slaughterhouses, slums, unpaved roads, brothels, and fairs. And tangos reflected as well the far-removed inner lands, away from the port cities and the *arrabal*, the rural bygone worlds many urbanites left behind in their provincial origins epitomized by "Caminito" ("Country Road," 1926, by Gabino Coria Peñaloza, 1881–1975, WL 9.3), in which the poet evokes his own past in the form of a slim country road of his youth, "a shadow soon you'll be, a shadow just like me."

A particular poetic space laid at the core of this genre. The endpoint of migration, the cradle of the Río de la Plata's cultural melting pot, the ultimate node of its global entanglements, and the key artifact of its urban modernity and demographic growth was the *barrio*, both a physical neighborhood and a spiritual atmosphere. The Buenos Aires' *barrios* were residential and commercial areas, formed by a variable number of blocks, and extended from the colonial downtown by the riverside to the sprawling metropolis that hosted two million inhabitants by 1920 and five million by 1950 (the largest in Latin America during this period). In the absence of a geographic barrier to its expansion, the metropolis grew by creating new *barrios* in a territory that simply spilled over into the Pampa, that endless grassland that the city continuously pushed farther and blended with. All *barrios* were, as writer and witness of Buenos Aires' transformations Jorge Luis Borges (1899–1986) put it, in a *mythical* sense, the same one: the old *barrio* of the *sur*, the South, a place that was neither the downtown nor the countryside, but a perennial and heroic border.[12]

The opening verses of the tango "Sur" ("South," 1948, WL 9.4) by poet Homero Manzi evoke a symbolic South by describing two Southern *barrios*, Boedo and Nueva Pompeya (New Pompeii), with a series of images/concepts (see WP 9.1 for an aerial image of the Nueva Pompeya *barrio* from 1940 and Figure 9.1 of Café "Esquina Homero Manzi" in the Boedo neighborhood).

First, an old intersection in Boedo under the infinite sky (*San Juan y Boedo antigua / y todo el cielo*), and then Pompeya as the prelude to the end of the city and, through a flood, the end of the world (*Pompeya y más allá la inundación*). These verses are followed by a memory of youth and love (*tu melena de novia en el recuerdo / y tu nombre florando en el adiós*). In "Melodía de arrabal" ("Outskirt Melody," 1932, WL 9.5), Alfredo Le Pera and Mario Battistella wrote a paean to an unnamed, ideal-type *barrio*, presented as intimate but also liminal, by weaving the *arrabal* into it: "throughout the tough *barrio*, an *outskirt* melody." This tango is dense in visual and sonic images: silvered by the moon, all its fortune are the rumors of *milonga* dance steps and a grumbling bandoneón in a miserable corner. A beautiful woman in her prime vainly combs her hair, under the fixed

Figure 9.1 Café "Esquina Homero Manzi" at the corner of San Juan and Boedo streets in the Boedo neighborhood of Buenos Aires. The original café opened in 1927.

light of a streetlamp. Crucially, the poet praises not the moon, nor the woman, nor the melody, but the *barrio* itself: "you old 'hood, anxious soul of a sentimental sparrow ... Forgive me if, as I evoke you, I fail to contain a tear, which rolling over your cobblestones becomes a way for my heart to long-kiss you." (*Barrio, barrio / que tenés el alma inquieta de un gorrión sentimental ... Perdoná si al evocarte / se me pianta un lagrimón / Que al rodar en tu empedrao / es un beso prolongado / que te da mi corazón.*)

The *barrio* often stands for a bygone world, as in the lines by Manzi set to music by Aníbal Troilo: "*Barrio* of tango / moon and mystery / From the vantage point of my memories / I'm seeing you again" ("Barrio de tango," "Tango Neighborhood," 1942, WL 9.6). The theme of the *barrio* emerged and exploded in media and cultural commentary precisely when the city's expansion was blurring the differences among the actual *barrios*, therefore erasing their autonomy as the metropolis became a rationally planned urban totality, without significant physical variations nor ghettos.[13] Hence, "lyricists and playwrights ... collectively imagined the *arrabales* of the tango ... [and] were not reporting on the world around them; they were engaged in creative invention."[14]

The inhabitants of Buenos Aires thus grew up learning to love their neighborhood through nostalgic tangos that, by evoking a paradise lost but poetically retrieved, gave a mythical meaning to the new urban experience. Like the *potrero* in Argentine football (the empty spaces between blocks where kids improvise football [soccer], turning their dribbling into symbols of national magic and creativity), an ordinary *barrio* corner or café was infused with mythical meanings by tango lyrics. They resonated not just in Buenos Aires and Montevideo via cinema, radio, tours, and local adaptations, but in other cities like Valparaíso (Chile), Medellín (Colombia), and Mexico City, where the *barrio* became a metaphor of the urban experience, too.[15]

Love and Self

Tango lyricists continuously evoked love, but lamented its failure to redeem the absurd and cruel experience of the self in modern life. Love was an old philosophical theme and central to nineteenth-century European bourgeois culture, and it became a major topic in virtually all popular music traditions under commercial media in the twentieth century.[16] But tango poets gave particularly existentialist, fatalist, and nihilist meanings to the quest for romantic love.

Nostalgia for an irretrievable past was perhaps the most pervasive vehicle for tango lyrics to address the irony of love and reflect on the self. It began before the Golden Age, with Contursi's words to "Mi noche triste," sung by Gardel at the Cine Teatro Empire on Corrientes Avenue and also recorded with guitar accompaniment in 1917 on Max Glucksman's label. The main character in this tango is a *proxeneta* or *compadrito* (pimp), a dominant figure in the popular imaginary around 1900, for example in Villoldo's 1903 tango "El Porteñito," where this "son of Buenos Aires" exhibits with joy and pride his ability to seduce women and live off their money. But in "Mi noche triste," the dominant feeling is not pride but sadness and disorientation. This is perhaps one of the greatest sorrows in the history of tango: nothing, not even crying, alcohol, resting in bed, playing the guitar, nor drinking some *matecitos* (a traditional South American herbs infusion, in this song a symbol of a personal sobering and relaxing ritual) can alleviate the absence of the loved one.

In tango lyrics, scholars have found a romantic challenge posed to young men by a demographic imbalance during mass immigration to Buenos Aires: women's relative shortage and their ability to abandon their partners. By the 1930s and afterward, once the gender distribution in the population was balanced again, Golden Age lyrics maintained the old poetic focus on the independent woman, as women kept widening their autonomy in both public and private spheres.[17] Gardel's career, from his rise to stardom in 1917 to his tragic death in 1935, encompasses both periods, and a statistical study of his songs reveals, as Donna Guy points out, "a deep discontent and anxiety expressed in his most popular tangos."[18] More than half of the songs from a representative selection are about love and hatred. In these songs, a woman frequently leaves a man, who then may feel betrayed and end up murdering or hurting the woman or her new lover. In other narratives, the man simply laments about being abandoned. And in very few cases, the man celebrates the woman's new life. This portrait of Buenos Aires men in tango songs points to "a feeling of loss of control in their affective relations" in contrast with "more pleasant memories of the infancy" in several songs.[19]

While Argentine women increasingly benefitted from an expansive public educational system that improved labor markets and conditions (especially with Peronist labor legislation since the mid-1940s), and political equality (women suffrage was established in 1947), many tangos continued to present a woman's youth as an idealized period of life. Only this stage allowed her dignity and power. "Esta noche me emborracho" ("Tonight I'll Get Drunk," Discépolo, 1928, WL 9.7) shows a woman past her youth who betrays a simple but sincere man for the sake of money and luxury in her pathetic decadence ("*fané y descangayada*," or rotten and hurt, in expressive *Lunfardo*). In "Afiches" ("Street Ads," Homero Expósito, 1956, WL 9.8), a woman abandons the poet "selling the last shred of youth" (*vendiendo el último jirón de juventud*) by becoming a prostitute, now available "to everyone," like a naked mannequin in a shop window (*porque eres algo para todos ya / como un desnudo de vidriera*). Here the poet is a victim: "I gave you a home, blame it on love," but "the truth is then to scratch one's palate with sand, drowning without being able to scream" (*luego la verdad / es restregarse con arena el paladar / y ahogarse sin poder gritar*). The song ends with tango's most concise line about suicide: "it makes one want to hide and shoot oneself" (*dan ganas de balearse en un rincón*).

In other tangos, love is an idyllic state, simple in its wholeness, at once elevated, modest, and sincere, capable of compensating life's precarity ... but irremediably gone. In "Naranjo en flor" ("Flowering Orange Tree," Expósito, 1944, WL 9.9), "she was softer than water, than soft water / She was fresher than the river / flowering orange tree" (*Era más blanda que el agua / que el agua blanda / Era más fresca que el río / naranjo en flor*). Sometimes love offers redemption and a remedy to the ills of modern life (such as syphilis and the sexual diseases that marked the subjectivity of the "modern girls" and working young women),[20] but its dominant mode is sardonic skepticism, a resigned mix of loneliness and pain. In "Yira, yira" ("Spin, Spin," E. Santos Discépolo, 1930, WL 9.10), hopelessness is depicted as the absence of love: "when Fortune, who's a bitch, fails you over and over and leaves you at your own devices," when you are "aimless, desperate," without "faith, even without some yesterday's *yerba mate* leaves drying up for re-use," and when you finally meet "the world's indifference" to realize "that everything is a lie, that nothing is love, that the world doesn't care: it just spins and spins" (*Cuando la suerte, que es grela / fayando y fayando, te large parao / Cuando estés bien en la vía / sin rumbo, desesperao / Cuando no tengas ni fe / ni yerba de ayer / secándose al sol ... La indiferencia del mundo ... recién sentirás / Verás que todo es mentira / verás que nada es amor / Que al mundo nada le importa: ¡yira, yira!*). An empty, indifferent world without love, expressed in *Lunfardo*: grela, fayando, yira.

A few influential female lyricists and singers elaborated as well on love and the self in tangos that set women as protagonists of the poetic experience. In "Pero yo sé" ("But I Know," 1928, WL 9.11) Azucena Maizani inverts the masculine perspective and focuses on the pleasures and arrogance of the Buenos Aires man who can barely hide his inner suffering, and at the end, just cries:

Pero yo sé que metido	But I know that in your heart
vivís penando un querer,	you live in sorrow for a wanting,
que querés hallar olvido	that you want to find oblivion
cambiando tanta mujer...	changing so many women...
Yo sé que en las madrugadas,	I know that in the early mornings,
cuando las farras dejás,	when you leave the parties,
sentís tu pecho oprimido	you feel your chest oppressed
por un recuerdo querido	by a dear memory
y te ponés a llorar	and you start to cry

In "Cantando" ("Singing," 1931, WL 9.12), Mercedes Simone reminds us that the core feeling of loss is shared by women too: "I no longer have the sweetness of those kisses / I wander alone in the world without love / Another happier mouth will be the owner / of those kisses that were all my passion" (*ya no tengo la dulzura de sus besos / vago sola por el mundo sin amor / Otra boca más feliz será la dueña / de sus besos que eran toda mi pasión*).

Life's Been Mixed Up: The Modern Experience

Golden Age tango poets also gave a fresh voice to the timeless trope of the inevitability of time and death, now elaborated through the modern experience of loss and absurdity. Discépolo composed one of tango's most enduring lyrics in 1934, "Cambalache" ("Hodgepodge" or "Junk Shop," WL 9.13), which laugh at the surreal nonsense that, in his view, characterized the twentieth century at the time. This tango argues that while the world has always been lousy, the twentieth century is worse: "a display of shameless evil" in which "it's the same to be rightful and a traitor / ignorant, wise, crook, generous, or fraudster" (*el siglo veinte es un despliegue de maldad insolente ... Hoy resulta que es lo mismo / ser derecho que traidor / Ignorante, sabio, chorro / generoso, estafador*). Today "everything is the same, nothing is better / the same a jackass and a great professor" (*Todo es igual, nada es mejor / Lo mismo un burro que un gran profesor*). Life itself has been mixed up, losing coherence (*se ha mezclao la vida*). In "La última curda" ("The Final Bender" [drinking spree], 1956, WL 9.14), Cátulo Castillo put it bluntly: "I know, don't tell me, you're right: life's an absurd wound" (*ya sé, no me digás, tenés razón: la vida es una herida absurda*).

In "Cafetín de Buenos Aires" ("Buenos Aires Small Coffeeshop," 1948, WL 9.15) Discépolo reached metaphysical heights from the perspective of a key space of male sociability, the café (see Figure 9.2 of a typical Buenos Aires café). Infancy, youth, and adulthood (and afterlife too, through the memory of dead friends) are depicted in this tango from the perspective of the café. Infancy is the café as a forbidden space: "as a kid I stared at you from outside, as those things out of reach." Youth is the café as "as a school of everything . . . smoking, faith in my dreams, and a hope of love," as well as treasured friends, "a golden handful" (*me diste en oro un puñado de amigos*), some living and some gone – like "Abel, who still guides me." Then, desperately, the café of adulthood is where "I discovered grief, drank my years away, and gave up without a fight." Above all, in the refrain, the nostalgia for the *cafetín* becomes a lament for the most cherished and protective space: "how should I evoke you, Buenos Aires coffeeshop, the only thing in life similar to my mother?" (*¿cómo evocarte en esta queja, cafetín de Buenos Aires / si sos lo único en la vida que se pareció a mi vieja?*) Finally, the evocation yearns for those wise but fatalistic Buenos Aires

Figure 9.2 A table at the Café Homero Manzi.

men – "miraculous mix of savants and suicides" (*mezcla milagrosa de sabihondos y suicidas*) – who wasted their days at its tables and taught the poet the most important lessons: "philosophy, gambling, and the cruel poetry / of just stop thinking about myself" (*yo aprendí filosofía, dados, timba y la poesía cruel / de no pensar más en mí*).

In "Naranjo en flor," the memory of a lost lover allows a reflection on what modern life is about. The beloved, that woman depicted as a flowering orange tree, softer and fresher than the softest water, at some point, "in a lost street one summer night / left a piece of life / and went away" (*Y en esa calle de estío / calle perdida / dejó un pedazo de vida y se marchó*). The moral of the story is that first one must know to suffer, then to love, then to depart, and finally wander without any thoughts (*primero hay que saber sufrir, después amar, después partir, y al fin andar sin pensamientos*). Tango lyrics teach, again, a painful vitalism.

Romantic and modernist poetic traditions responded to modernization across Latin America by elaborating on the new subjective experiences in many popular repertories comparable to tango in richness and originality. A vast commercial songbook in Spanish (and Portuguese) of *boleros, sones, rancheras, sambas, cuecas, huaynos,* and *rumbas* also depicted illusions, nostalgias, treasons, migrations, cherished places, and the uncertainty of life and death through the main topic of love. But Golden Age tango poetics did it through a particularly acute sense of the absurdity and instability of the modern experience, which produced a somber take on the sheer passing of time. This somber perspective appears in "Sur" ("South," 1948, Manzi), in which everything – love, one's life, the *barrio* itself – simply vanishes:

Las calles y las lunas suburbanas	Streets and suburban moons
y mi amor y tu ventana	and my love and your window
todo ha muerto, ya lo sé	everything is dead, I already know it
Nostalgias de las cosas que han pasado	Nostalgia of things gone
arena que la vida se llevó	Sand that life blew away
pesadumbre de barrios que han cambiado	Sorrow of neighborhoods that have changed
y amargura del sueño que murió	And bitterness for the dream that died

"Niebla del Riachuelo" ("River Fog," 1937, Cadícamo, WL 9.16) locates us in the old port of Buenos Aires, in a turn of the Riachuelo (the final section of the Matanza river that borders the city to the South and opens as a mouth – La Boca – to the wide Río de la Plata), where one can witness the

remains of old merchant ships stuck on its margins. Cadícamo found in
these ruins a metaphor of life's inevitably unfulfilled dreams. The tango
opens depicting love as a misty and sinister port scene:

Turbio fondeadero donde van a recalar,	Shady anchorage where they land,
barcos que en el muelle para siempre han de quedar	ships that in the dock shall forever remain
Sombras que se alargan en la noche del dolor,	Shadows that lengthen in the night of pain,
náufragos del mundo que han perdido el corzón	castaways of the world who lost their hearts
¡Niebla del Riachuelo!	River fog!
De ese amor para siempre	From that love forever
me vas alejando ...	you are taking me away ...

Modern *porteños*, "castaways of the world who lost their hearts,"
through the sentimental education of tango songs, can evoke in the
Riachuelo the entire city of yore (in 1937 or today) and their own memories
of fulfilled or unfulfilled love, mirroring themselves in the *memento mori* of
a ship that won't ever sail again.

Conclusion: A Cultural Tradition

Poets of tango's Golden Age created a distinctive *porteño* cultural
tradition through their unique poems about nostalgia for bygone
barrios, the meaning of love, and the self through the prism of the
modern experience of loss and absurdity. Their popularity speaks of
a society whose members, by dancing to, singing, or whistling these
tangos, acquired a sentimental and philosophical education, and
accessed a repertory they could call their own. Many decades later,
younger lyricists and poets have created tangos that interweave classic
and contemporary vocabularies and themes, for example challenging
conventional gender and narrative tropes. Interestingly, they see themselves as continuing the Golden Age tango's aesthetics.[21] Even the
poetry of Argentine rock music sometimes echoes the tango poetics
discussed here. More importantly, the urban music scene, nightlife,
gender dynamics, and the subjective experience of the always changing
metropolis keeps the poetics of Golden Age tango relevant to new
generations of *porteñas* and *porteños* as a living cultural tradition.

Notes

* I thank the late Alberto Ferrari Etcheberry and Héctor Palomino for their teachings, the editors of this volume for their feedback, and Valeria Barbuto for introducing me ages ago, through a collection of tangos by Roberto Goyeneche, to many of the topics discussed in this chapter.

1. For example, Oscar Conde points to the verses of "El matasano" by Pascual Contursi in 1914 as the *thematic* watershed between the arrogant poetic self of tango's origins and the suffering man of the Golden Age, while "Mi noche triste" in 1917 produced instead a *stylistic* innovation. On the other end of the story, the decline of the Golden Age was attributed, for example, to the official rhetoric of popular happiness (the "fiesta peronista") of the Perón administrations (1946–1955), a debatable hypothesis that I mention here simply to indicate the political dimension of tango's chronology. See Oscar Conde, "Los temas del *amuro* y la *milonguita*, o de cómo Contursi revolucionó la letra de tango," in *Las poéticas del tango-canción: rupturas y continuidades* (Buenos Aires: Biblos, 2014), 86–87; Emilio De Ipola, "El tango en sus márgenes," *Punto de Vista* 7, no. 25 (1985): 13–16; and Pablo Palomino, "Tango, Samba y Amor," *Apuntes de Investigación del CECYP*, 12 (2007): 81–82.

2. Ezequiel Adamovsky, "A Strange Emblem for a (Not So) White Nation: La Morocha Argentina in the Latin American Racial Context, c. 1900–2015," *Journal of Social History* 50, no. 2 (December 1, 2016): 386–410; Oscar Conde, "*Lunfardo* in Tango. A Way of Speaking that Defines a Way of Being," in Marilyn G. Miller, *Tango Lessons: Movement, Sound, Image, and Text in Contemporary Practice* (Duke University Press, 2014).

3. See the companion website for links to complete translations and audio files of tangos in this chapter.

4. In the condemnatory words of Tallón, "inauguró Contursi el tema repelente del canfinflero que llora abandonado por su querida prostituta." José Sebastián Tallón, *El tango en sus etapas de música prohibida* (Buenos Aires: Instituto Amigos del Libro Argentino, 1959): 81.

5. See Eduardo Pellejero, "Horacio Ferrer, poeta de la redención," in *Poéticas del tango*, ed. Oscar Conde (Buenos Aires: Marcelo Héctor Oliveri Editor, 2003).

6. See Julia Winokur, "'Ahora que lo antiguo se ha vuelto moderno': los pioneros del nuevo tango canción en la década del noventa," *Calle 14* 16, no. 30 (2021): 262–275.

7. "Al decir poesía popular argentina, no comprendemos en ella la bárbara jerga del lunfardo, tan en auge, por desgracia, en estos calamitosos tiempos del tango arrabalero." Eusebio R. Castex, *Cantos populares (Apuntes lexicográficos)* (Buenos Aires: Talleres Gráficos La Lectura, 1923), 5.

8. For further reading, see Oscar Conde, *Lunfardo. Un estudio sobre el habla popular de los argentinos* (Buenos Aires: Taurus, 2011).

9. Mara Glozman, "Combatir y conservar: posiciones y saberes sobre el lenguaje popular en los Boletines de la Academia Argentina de Letras (1933–1943)," *Gragoatá* 17, no. 32 (2012).

10. Pablo Palomino, *The Invention of Latin American Music. A Transnational History* (New York: Oxford University Press, 2020), 71–78.

11. For further reading, see Clara Rey, "Poesía popular libertaria y estética anarquista en el Río de La Plata," *Revista de Crítica Literaria Latinoamericana* 15, no. 29 (1989): 179–206; Avelino Romero Pereira, "Modernidade e transgressão na Buenos Aires dos anos 1920: tango e anarquismo nas páginas de *La Canción Moderna*," *Revista Territórios e Fronteiras* 9, no. 2 (2016): 156–170; Ricardo Horvath, *Esos malditos tangos: apuntes para la otra historia* (Buenos Aires: Editorial Biblos, 2006).

12. Jorge Luis Borges, *El tango: cuatro conferencias* (Buenos Aires: Lumen, 2017).

13. For further reading, see Adrián Gorelik, *La grilla y el parque: espacio público y cultura urbana en Buenos Aires, 1887–1936* (Buenos Aires: Universidad Nacional de Quilmes, 1998).

14. Matthew B. Karush, "The Politics of Tango: A Response to Michael Denning's Noise Uprising," *Journal of Popular Music Studies* 31, no. 4 (2019): 62.

15. For further reading, see Eileen Karmy and Cristian Molina, *Tango viajero: orquestas típicas en Valparaíso (1950–1973)* (Santiago de Chile: Mago Editores, 2012); Carolina Santamaría Delgado, *Vitrolas, rocolas y radioteatros: hábitos de escucha de la música popular en Medellín, 1930–1950* (Bogotá: Editorial Pontificia Universidad Javeriana, 2014); Luis Sandi, "Agustín Lara y la canción mexicana," *Música – Revista Mexicana* 1, nos. 9–10 (December 1930): 46–49.

16. Sérgio Costa, "Amores fáceis: romantismo e consumo na modernidade tardia," *Novos Estudos CEBRAP* 73 (2005): 111–124; Charles Lindholm, "Love and Structure," *Theory, Culture & Society* 15, nos. 3–4 (1998): 243–263.

17. Dora Barrancos, *Mujeres en la sociedad argentina: una historia de cinco siglos* (Buenos Aires: Sudamericana, 2010), 156.

18. Donna Guy, *El sexo peligroso. La prostitución legal en Buenos Aires, 1875–1955* (Buenos Aires: Sudamericana, 1994), 185, and Darío Cantón, *Gardel, ¿a quién le cantás?* (Buenos Aires: Ediciones de la Flor, 1972), 199.

19. Ibid.

20. For further reading, see Cecilia Tossounian, *La Joven Moderna in Interwar Argentina: Gender, Nation, and Popular Culture* (Gainsville: University of Florida Press, 2020); and Diego Arums, "Tango, Gender, and Tuberculosis in Buenos Aires, 1900–1940," in *Disease in the History of Modern Latin America* (New York: Duke University Press, 2003), 101–129.

21. Julia Winokur, "Las pioneras del nuevo tango canción: un panorama de mujeres compositoras a fines de la década de 1990 y comienzos del 2000," *Revista Argentina de Musicología* 22, no. 2 (2021): 101–125.

Further Reading

Archetti, Eduardo. *Masculinities: Football, Polo, and the Tango in Argentina.* New York: Berg, 1999.

Corradi, Juan. "How Many Did It Take to Tango? Voyages of Urban Culture in the Early 1900s." In *Outsider Art: Contesting Boundaries in Contemporary Culture*, 194–214, 1997.

Francfort, Didier. "Le tango, passion allemande et européenne, 1920–1960." In *Littératures et musiques dans la mondialisation: XXe–XXIe siècles*, edited by Anaïs Fléchet and Marie-Françoise Lévy. Paris: Publications de la Sorbonne, 2015.

Garramuño, Florencia. *Modernidades primitivas: tango, samba y nación.* Buenos Aires: Fondo de Cultura Económica, 2007. [*Primitive Modernities: Tango, Samba, and Nation.* Stanford, CA: Stanford University Press, 2011].

Ibarlucía, Ricardo. "La perspectiva del zorzal: Paul Celan y el 'Tango de la muerte.'" *Revista Latinoamericana de Filosofía* 30, no. 2 (2004): 287–312.

Matallana, Andrea. *Qué saben los pitucos: la experiencia del tango entre 1910 y 1940.* Buenos Aires: Prometeo, 2008.

Nudler, Julio. *Tango judío: del ghetto a la milonga.* Buenos Aires: Editorial Sudamericana, 1998.

Salas, Horacio. *El tango.* Buenos Aires: Planeta, 1986.

Santamaría-Delgado, Carolina. "Tango's Reterritorialization in Medellín: Gardel's Myth and the Construction of a Tanguero Local Identity." *The Musical Quarterly* 92, nos. 3–4 (September 21, 2009): 177–209.

Tallón, José Sebastián. *El tango en sus etapas de música prohibida.* Buenos Aires: Instituto Amigos del Libro Argentino, 1959.

PART III

Tango Dance

10 | Tango's Journey from a Río de la Plata Dance to a Globalized Milonga

CHRISTOPHE APPRILL

TRANSLATED FROM FRENCH BY KACEY LINK AND GÉRARD PIGEON

Imagine that you are at a dinner party conversing about tango. Without fail, the same general observations arise: "tango is such a sensual and passionate dance"; "it is beautiful when it is danced well"; and "it used to be danced between men in the *bordellos* (brothels)." Scholars of tango, however, aim to deconstruct such limiting descriptions. In this chapter, I seek to examine tango stereotypes, particularly in relation to tango dance, while opening new perspectives on contemporary dimensions of globalized tango scenes (Figure 10.1).

Brothels and Slums: The Landscape of Despair

In the wake of the importation of frozen beef from Argentina by the commercial boating network, tango disembarked and landed in Europe at the beginning of the twentieth century. Upon its arrival, tango became "Argentine." In the realm of the music, tango scholar Béatrice Humbert underlines the role played by Alfredo Eusebio Gobbi and his wife Flora Rodríguez, who lived in Paris from 1907 to 1914, as transporters of the art form. As for the dance, Humbert notes the uncertainty about who was responsible for its introduction to the aristocracy and "made it pass from the mud of the suburbs to the parquet floors."[1] Since then, throughout the world, the dance and the music have been "naturally" qualified as Argentine.

Yet, during the last twenty years of the nineteenth century, Argentine foundations of national identity were not well established.[2] One must keep in mind that tango developed in the Río de la Plata (River Plate) region of Argentina and Uruguay within the context of mass immigration, port modernization of the harbors, increased trade, a booming livestock industry, and urban demographic and geographic growth in Buenos Aires and Montevideo. In Buenos Aires, a city under construction and transformation, immigrants primarily from Spain and Italy assimilated with *criollos*

173

Figure 10.1 Milonga de la Rue du Tango, Marseille, 2015.

(creole, or local Argentine) as well as Afro-Argentines. Two hundred twenty thousand immigrants settled in Buenos Aires in 1889, and 32 percent of those immigrants were Italian.[3] Within this migratory flow, Buenos Aires became the largest city in Latin America as the urban social fabric profoundly transformed. It is no wonder that from 1880 to 1916, as historian Carmen Bernand notes, Argentina and Buenos Aires became the "*creuset argentin*" ("Argentine melting pot").[4]

From this early period in tango's history, first-hand sources are few and difficult to interpret.[5] The dominant historiography focuses on the description of a typical portrait, which oscillates between caricature and stereotype, and forms a set of representations that has been attractive to scholars.[6] The geographic setting of an urban landscape lends itself to the creation of figures such as the *compadrito* (young ruffian who lives on the city's outskirts), the prostitute, the pimp, and the *gaucho* (cowboy). Together, these figures summarize both the mixing and confrontation of ethnic and cultural Otherness. In this discussion, one must also include the evocative poetry of Jorge Luis Borges. In his *Evaristo Carriego*, the chapter devoted to tango's history in particular presents urban growth as the fertile ground for tango's emergence.[7] Therefore, if one agrees with tango scholar Donald Castro, the meeting and interweaving of the social cultures of the *criollos* and the immigrants, as well as the contrast between the rural and the developing urban environments, permeate Argentina's history and its literature.[8] One may then wonder: is the history of tango, therefore, only an imaginative way of telling the history of Argentina?

The notion that tango was born in the brothels and slums of Buenos Aires and Montevideo gives the art form an aura that combines elegance with depravity, while the social context becomes aestheticized. For example, scholars do not analyze tango in relation to the economics of prostitution at the time in large European cities such as London and Paris. Tango is rather systematically assigned a popular past whose settings emphasize vice, perdition, and misery, as well as feelings of nostalgia, sadness, loneliness, and love. The understanding of these ideas is not without ambiguities, because the value attributed to them today is sometimes a projection on the immigrants of the last century. People often speak about the immigrants as if they had crossed paths with them yesterday. Argentine writer Ernesto Sábato remarks in his introductory essay to Horacio Salas's *El tango*:

> The brothel is sex in the state of (sinister) purity . . . . [And] as Tulio Carella says, the solitary immigrant who entered it solved easily his sexual problem: with tragic ease this problem resolved itself in this gloomy establishment . . . It wasn't, then, what worried the man of Buenos Aires . . . It was precisely the opposite: the nostalgia for communion and love, the yearning for a woman, rather than the presence of an instrument of his lust.[9]

Thus, complex notions, such as joy, melancholy, and anguish that tango music conveys are attributed to these "uprooted people stranded in the Southern capital."[10] One, therefore, ends up ascribing many intentions to the Argentine individual. This approach uses empathy for affects,[11] which are accessible to us today to interpret the complex social and cultural activity that constitutes the emergence of the dance. It does not, however, allow one to account for tango's intermediatory alternative places of diffusion, or its indicators that would counterbalance the idea that tango was "born in the brothels." A quantitative ethnographic methodology has shown that tango's reception is an intimate, complex act that is resistant in a way to sociological analysis.[12] Many survey-like conversations between contemporary *milongueros* (tango dancers) attest to the complexity of their lived experiences in connection with their practice of tango. It seems difficult to base a social history of tango on such anachronistic projections. The purpose of these stories, however, is to make people dream about an ideal world, rather than analyze the economic, intellectual, and sexual misery of Buenos Aires' *suburbios* (poor urban outskirts).

According to historian Roberto Daus, tango's landscape of despair comes from a handful of intellectuals whose cultural benchmark was Europe and who have endeavored to deny the popular character of tango. He recalls that many districts of Buenos Aires where tango was developing (La Boca, Montserrat, San Cristóbal, Recoleta) were close to the city center, not the *suburbios*. Taking into consideration the 18,123 pianos imported into Argentina between 1901 and 1907, and the writing of tangos for the piano, Daus notes that the spread of tango took place very early outside of the marginal circles, and long before its validation by the European bourgeoisies.[13] By recalling the internal movements, and the geographical and social displacements of a budding art form in an emerging city, his analysis qualifies the idea that tango went from a miserable urban and social setting to the golden paneling of Parisian salons.

A Break in the System of Couple Dances

Introduced in France before the beginning of World War I, tango dance was based on improvisation. A variety of different steps, in terms of grandeur, rhythm, and direction, became possible. The dance also created new gender roles.[14] In the typical embrace of traditional couple dances, each person maintains their own space and defined role. However, with tango, there was a break in the system of these norms, which demonstrates the dance's stylistic modernity and helps explain its success and longevity. Whereas the waltz, through its historical evolution, provides a stage for an enchanting partner encounter, the tango places the male and the female face-to-face in a duel. It balances masculine and feminine energy and power as well as oscillates in speed. This creates a force of restraint between the couple and places them "*en majesté*" ("in majesty"): it gives the couple a form of presence and poise.

After World War I, tango dance experienced a Golden Age in Buenos Aires. More than 600 orchestras brought the milongas (tango dance events) to life in the interwar period,[15] and this craze spread throughout the capitals of Western Europe. Afternoon gatherings called "tango teas" were all the rage, and women would attend wearing "tango-colored" skirts (first orange and then red). Among all the exotic dances that crossed the Atlantic and swept through Europe during this period,[16] tango is the one that has lasted over a century and has spread to over five continents.[17] Tango was so popular during the craze that it caused a decline in open dances of the nineteenth century, such as the *quadrille, berlines* (salon dances), and *pas de quatre*.[18] In the interwar period, it was added to the waltz and the French java, and together they constituted the "basis for the musette."[19] After being purified of its sensuality by the incorporation of dance teachers,[20] tango took over the dance halls – temples of worldliness, modernity, and celebrations. It was, therefore, a phenomenon of acculturation of dance and music that occurred during the interwar period and then continued after 1945. Gradually, tango became a form of an eroticized embrace that expressed itself throughout the world.

One may wonder about the vigor of tango's development and even its permanence. But note, tango did not maintain its dominance and craze throughout the twentieth century. It began to decline in the 1960s and 1970s, first in Europe with changes affecting customs, and then in Argentina with dictatorships disrupting political stability. This decline can be observed with all social dances as ballroom dances became outdated and new dances emerged. In line with the musical tastes of the new generations, bebop and rock were among these new dances. Their open structure foreshadowed the separation of the couple in dance, and the move toward individual dances like the twist and the jerk. These new forms of "freestyle" dance allowed dancers to explore other options that featured encounters between the sexes: the "slow dance" is the obvious example.[21]

The Reinvention of the Milonga

A resurgence in the 1980s followed tango's phase of decline, and its revival traveled along multiple trajectories. In Europe, the hit show *Tango Argentino* played a major role in the art form's rebirth.[22] In Argentina, one may see a correlation to tango's renewal and the end of political dictatorships in 1983. These two complementary phenomena took place during a general worldwide cultural movement of interest in dance practices. There was a general craze for body, sex, seduction, and dance in the 1980s, and dance was the catalyst for them all.[23] Several cultural signs bear witness to this, although it is difficult to know whether they are the causes or the effects. For example, the musical and movie *Hair* (Milos Forman, 1979) connects cultural liberation of the body with movement. *Flash Dance* (Adrian Lyne, 1983) exalts the work of the dancer and the social and individual assumptions that result from creative perseverance. Additionally, the emergence of hip-hop dance, driven by the novelty of video, shook up the academic dance traditions and diversified audiences of amateur dancers.

In France, the concomitance of several events reinforced the renewed interest in dance practices. *Grands bals* (large dances), organized as a part of the Lyon Dance Biennale, built bridges between social dances and stage dances. Supported by the cultural policy of Jack Lang (French Minister of Culture, 1981–1986 and 1988–1993),[24] young choreographers began embracing "new dance" and "French dance." The year 1989 was crowned the "Year of the Dance," and the bicentenary celebration of the French Revolution was staged by Jean Paul Goude on the Champs-Élysées. For the opening ceremony of the 1992 Winter Olympic Games in Albertville, France was entrusted to choreographer Philippe Découflé. The explosion of dance also manifested itself in the field of writing – between 1980 and 2000 several works were published which combine dance and thought.[25]

In the context of this renewed interest in dance, tango resurfaced in France and other European nations. Its most widespread places of practice reappeared in revived *guinguettes* (establishments for dance, music, and drinking in the suburbs of Paris), cafés/cabarets, afternoon salon dances or teas, and dance competitions. Tango's restoration and renovation assumed a variety of attributes, including varying styles, relationships between partners, new professionals (dancers, musicians, event organizers, and DJs), and a circulation of both professionals and amateurs. All these attributes are still expressed at the milonga today.

The Passion of Passion

The trajectory of contemporary tango dance oscillates between the milonga and the stage. With the latter, tango benefited from international productions of *Tango Argentino*, other shows such as *Tango Pasion* and *Chantecler Tango*, and reinterpretations by choreographers such as Ana María Stekelman (neoclassical), Catherine Berbessou (contemporary), and Julio Bocca (classical). But, tango is not just for staged productions. If the theatrical stage gives tango volatile legitimacy, the social stage of the milonga gives tango sustainability. Before tango's resurgence, the notion of a milonga did not exist outside of the Río de la Plata region. From Baltimore to Singapore and Beirut to Rome, a reinvention of social dance culture has occurred in a multitude of deterritorialized scenes.[26] One may see the same weakening of cultural ties to a place or location with milongas. Without the milonga, tours of the great tango dance masters, as well as the shows and concerts, would probably not have been enough to ensure the longevity of tango for three decades.

In other publications, I have examined how social tango dancers understand "passion."[27] The word comes up most frequently to describe the practice of tango in the milonga. It is used by both practitioners from the inside and observers from the outside. This generic term has three dimensions of meaning: it refers to a state of the body, it oscillates between valuing and devaluing dance, and it conceals a singular specificity of "the passion of passion." Tango dancers do not share the same degree of passion with ordinary dancers. This difference in depth of passion is especially true for tango's close embrace, which is more erotic than other dance practices. Penetrating more deeply than ordinary passion, "passion of passion" is like an addiction cut from ordinary eroticization. The passion of tango dance merges with the passion for an encounter with another person, hence, the power of this addiction and attachment to tango. When deprived of tango, some social dancers state that they become sad and depressed. But paradoxically, when it comes to speaking of the eroticization of the bodies and the relationship between two people, there is silence. Social tango dancers prefer to simply evoke "the pleasure of dancing."[28]

The Journey of Oneself

Through their investment in the multidimensional aspects of passion, social tango dancers engage in a temporal, geographical, and intimate nontraditional lifestyle characterized by a predominance of nocturnal over daytime sociability. Dancing through the night is not easily compatible with a normal pace of life devoted to work. Such a dance experience brings about an inversion of the industrial revolution's hierarchy of how one spends time, namely the subordination of pleasurable pastimes to work activities. In this inversion of priorities, dancing becomes first through the construction of an idealized rhythm of life, breaking with social conventions, seriousness, and responsibilities.

For Europeans and North Americans, dancing tango undoubtedly appears as a reason for travel. Listening to the stories of those who make a pilgrimage to Buenos Aires exemplifies how tango dance enthusiasts often share common life themes both with each other and tango in general, such as loss, death, mourning, and the search for oblivion. After the death of a loved one or an amorous breakup, tango may offer a way to change the *paysage* (scenery). A pilgrimage then allows one to remove themself from their previous reality that is struggling to flow, and the Rioplatense matrix of the tango becomes a place where one can absolve this former reality. Some familiar attributes of Argentina allow this absolution to occur easily for Europeans and North Americans – the country is in the Southern hemisphere, yet the climate is temperate (also, there are no tarantulas or malaria); the population is primarily white and Catholic; and the cafés serve foreign drinks that are similar enough to those of Europe and North America. All these familiar ingredients combine to set the scene for white exoticism in which the tango fits perfectly. For example, does not the *abrazo* (embrace), one of tango's formal properties, come from the European system of couple dances? Immersion in the Río de la Plata region, therefore, does not constitute a plunge into radical otherness. Yet, upon returning to one's native country, travelers tell stories imbued with an enchanted tone from which it is possible to extract two themes of sensations. One theme is how, as these travelers insist on going to the other side of the world to absorb the Argentine tango culture, they live a lifestyle according to the milonga. A second theme is how in doing so, they create the impression of living and carrying out a collection of experiences with and through their body.

Because one encounters a similar culture to one's home in the milongas, the dance enthusiast experiences only a small change of scenery. But the transition from situations of interactions based on verbal exchanges (and structured by the rationality of language) to that of the milonga causes a powerful change of perspective. Because of this change in perspective or moment of rupture from reality, the experience of the milonga can be considered as an "adequate discharge of pathogenic affects" and a "deliverance from internal conflicts."[29] But it is also an enjoyable experience in the form of a musical *ritornello* (returning theme), where a feeling is accomplished by the body in movement with other bodies. The experience of dance is also a way of filling the void of loneliness, of restoring structure, of getting back into one's body through the presence of another.[30] Through this metaphysical dance journey, *milongueros* examine their existential foundation and rebalance themselves in the milonga's whirlwind of excitement and intensity; therefore, one better understands why tango dancers talk about it so passionately.

A Low-Intensity Trance

Tango dancers can reach a state of being that I call a low-intensity trance.[31] This notion includes the ideas of losing oneself and a suspension of being. Nevertheless, tango is often narrated by some as a modified state of consciousness. On the one hand, they encounter this state of trance at the milonga, although not as anthropologists have analyzed it.[32] On the other hand, it is not identified as a priori, or gaining knowledge independent from experience, as a context where one may glean an instance of a modified state of consciousness.[33]

Despite both losing oneself and finding a suspension of being, tango is nevertheless narrated by some as a modified state of consciousness. This would arise in part from ecstasy in that the atmosphere is completely illuminated by becoming denser, in a back and forth between lightness and gravity, and detachment and reattachment. The dancer Federico Rodríguez Moreno thus describes how improvisation evokes the low-intensity trance state:

Yes, [improvisation] is something that at times you touch in the tango, during a *milonga*, a *práctica* [practice milonga], or an exhibition. It's not common, it's not frequent, but every now and then you touch it. I think that it is a great motor of the passion that there is around the tango, these moments of light, these moments other than the normal experience, which pushes people to try to find it; that's why they're in it and that's why they train more and more, because these are truly magical moments ... It is true for me, I am someone who dances a lot at the milonga, I do not stop myself, and at times, I leave [lose myself] completely.[34]

This beautiful escape resembles abandonment and enjoyment detached from reality and the perception of the world, like the state of Durassian rapture.[35] It is guaranteed by the protective embrace, that is to say, the enveloping presence of the Other (the partner and all those who surround them taking part in the milonga). Once achieved, a tango dancer continues to seek this magic and the accompanying feeling of freedom. But these feelings occur quite rarely, hence the need to return frequently to the milonga. This repetition, in the form of a *ritornello*,[36] follows the pattern of breaking up and reattachment – the enjoyment of the dance is both singular and collective. The description of psychological states experienced by the dancers attests to the importance of their individual dimension. These states are not necessarily shared by others at the same time. Lived in a singular, narcissistic, or even egocentric way, the beautiful escape nevertheless has a timeless character. Additionally, it draws from a communal practice: it is through others that the dancers reach this state. In doing so, they operate a reattachment with the imagery of the milonga as expressed in the song lyrics "which turns, and which carries them," which places them "body against body," "becoming one," "eye to eye,"[37] "blooming, intoxicated, and happy."[38] (See Web Photos 10.1 and 10.2 for images of such states in a milonga.)

Although not directly related to ecstasy or trance, these states require significant concentration. Hungarian psychologist Mihalyi Csikszentmihalyi (1934–2021) formalized them in his 1990 notion of flow,[39] of which one finds the four main characters in the milonga.[40] Achieving this low-intensity trance can be hampered by the stylistic segmentations that run through the milonga.

Nuevo *versus* Milonguero *Styles*

With the development of teaching dance in the Rioplatense matrix during the 1990s and 2000s, two stylistic variations emerged: *nuevo* and *milonguero*. One main figure embodied each style, namely Mariano "Chico" Frumboli for *nuevo* and Suzanna Miller for *milonguero*. The *nuevo* style is carried by the generational renewal that stretches from the tango of the 1990s through today. Next to the first prestigious dancers, such as Pablo Verón, Gustavo Naveira, and Fabián Salas, a new and technically superior generation of dancers is making it possible to analyze the dance structure with influences by other disciplines, such as classical and contemporary dance and tap. This new generation includes Giselle Anne, Catherine Berbessou, Bernadette Doneux, Teresa Cunha, Cecilia Gonzales, Milena Plebs, and Victoria Vieyra. By settling in Europe, or by touring there for several months, these dancers have also distanced themselves from their Rioplatense home.

The resulting transformation recomposes the relationship between partners. In the *nuevo* style, the female dancer no longer typically "follows"; she becomes the dancer's alter ego. She is no longer reduced to the rank of the muse that inspires the "*maestro*"; she becomes a full performer. The fluid *abrazo* varies between open and close, in other words, it can be modified according to the desired combination of steps and figures. In this context, at the beginning of the 2000s in France, dancers acquired an unprecedented recognition that allowed them to break away from certain codes. For example, dressed in pants and sneakers, women could invite "like men." Although still, contrarily, several male dancers persist in claiming their attachment to patriarchal privilege; in their eyes, dancers who dare to issue an invitation to dance are devalued with an attitude of, "But who does she think she is?"

Based on a collection of detailed manners of dancing by the traditional *milongueros*, the *milonguero* style was invented in Paris by Suzanna Miller during a workshop in 1994. It systematizes a teaching method based on a close embrace, where the chests of the dancers are in permanent contact. Compared to the *nuevo* style, the repertory of steps is considerably limited as is the amplitude or height of the movements. On the other hand, this style allows for a search for rhythmic games and an enhancement of sensuality between partners. This style also has several educational advantages. While providing immediate benefits, it is rich in promises of sensuality, and it conveys an image of a fusional couple relationship. It neither challenges stereotypes, particularly in terms of gender roles ("the man guides, and the woman follows"), nor patriarchal codes of the milonga. The ritual of the invitation, including the *mirada* (the exchanging of a glance) and the *cabeceo* (the head nod to express a desire to dance), gives the dancers the impression of parity. Lastly, where the *nuevo* dancers have transgressed dress codes, *milonguero* dancers pay particular attention to their appearance (with women wearing feminine attire, high heels, and slitted skirts). *Milonguero* dancers attach great importance to tradition and believe in the existence of an "authentic Buenos Aires tango."

A Heterosexual Dance

Looking face-to-face, men and women create a traditional male-female tango performance. Opposing certain contemporary choreography, which strives to desexualize the bodies of the performers,[41] such traditional practice highlights gender and sex. At the point of transgression, each person has their own place and plays a role while respecting a constant dissymmetry, particularly among professionals. For example, a man is typically taller so that the average-size female dancer does not become ill at ease. Although, if a tall woman dances in high heels, the eight-to-ten-centimeter height gain from her shoes will give her immediate domination. During demonstrations, a woman rarely leads a man; moreover, women are often younger than their male partners. As one author observes in the process of forming couples, the man, often the expert in the dance, gives the female dancer social status and might even open doors professionally.[42] Younger, less experienced, but well-trained female dancers put their flexibility, technique, and erotic potential at the service of the male dancer. Even while being subjected to this role, the female dancer serves it and ensures its sustainability. Whether in the context of the milonga or a demonstration, the female dancer's erotic aura is directed toward the male dancer and at the service of a flawless performance. By articulating them precisely, communities of practitioners continue the tango social codes and stylistic elements that seem to carry on or pursue a shared purpose – they provide a dynamic way of dancing and being that maintains a tolerance of male superiority over female partners. All these forms of domination are presented as "natural" by many dancers who have internalized this principle.[43] The tango couple thus appears to be normalized. If there are alternative tango scenes, like queer tango,[44] the couple is sometimes overtaken by a prescription of roles – still frequently the guide and the guided in a relationship of subordination.

Made up of transfers, re-compositions, and adaptations, the circulations of tango around the world have not altered the permanence of a system of reference for couple dances founded on a heterosexual historical configuration. This remarkable inertia can be attributed to the engagement of the body. More than in other social places, the moments in the milonga bring to life a different spectrum of relations between genders. Dancers implicitly attempt to express the internalization of social structures. For the researcher, unless one resorts to a quantitative survey, it remains difficult to specify the content of the sexual orientations of the practitioners at a milonga. But it is clear that, unlike some leisure spaces, diversity is the rule at milongas, and statements from those in North America and Europe to those in Buenos Aires show that the heterosexual couple holds the majority. Lived, interpreted, and defended by communities of practitioners, this "tradition," whether right or wrong, is a part of tango's heritage.

Conclusion

The conditions of tango's transnational circulation lead to questioning the meaning of its distinct cultural identity. Is this a macho tradition that offers an additional platform for deploying male domination? Is it a passion where the shared presumption of heterosexuality provides tangible benchmarks in a period marked by multiple forces affecting the redefinition of gender identities and relations? Examined from the angle of a heterosexual dance, the culture of tango seems less researched, whereas this dimension accounts for more than a century of tango's territorialized and deterritorialized properties. Key to the fundamental partnership system, this configuration crystallizes the essential dimensions that make sense beyond the microcosm of the dance. Tango is a heterosexual couple dance, where the eroticization of the relationship (qualified by a presumption of sexual orientation) participates in the making of the act of the dance.

Approaching the distributions of roles in a different way, as in queer tango, goes beyond the simple question of style. Through a partial or total reconfiguration of gender assignments in dance, tango's historical properties are freshly questioned and brought again into play in the globalized milonga.

Notes

1. Béatrice Humbert, "Le tango à Paris de 1907 à 1920," in *Tango nomade*, Ramón Pelinski, ed. (Montréal: Editions Triptyque, 1995), 110–113.

2. Christophe Apprill, "Les métamorphoses d'un havane noir et juteux ... Comment la danse tango se fait 'argentine'," *Volume!: La revue des musiques populaires* 8, no. 1 (2011): 41–67.

3. Gérard-François Dumont, "1492–2006. L'aventure démographique des Amériques," in *Herodote.net: le media de l'histoire*, 1996, accessed April 25, 2022, www.herodote.net/histoire/synthese.php?ID=55&ID_dossier=227.

4. Carmen Bernand, *Histoire de Buenos Aires* (Paris: Fayard, 1997), 207.

5. Donald S. Castro, *The Argentine Tango as Social History (1880–1955): The Soul of the People* (New York: Edwin Mellen Press, 1991), 94.

6. Madeleine Séguin, "Le tango et les jeux de représentations. Vers une déconstruction de son image stéréotypée et érotisée," in *Tango, corps à corps culturel*, France Joyal, ed. (Québec: Presses de l'Université du Québec, 2009), 77–96.

7. Jorge Luis Borges, *Evaristo Carriego* (Paris: Editions du Seuil, 1969).

8. Castro, *The Argentine Tango as Social History*, 94.

9. "El prostíbulo es el sexo al estado de (siniestra) pureza. Y el inmigrante solitario que entraba en él resolvía, como dice tulio Carella, fácilmente su problema sexual: con la trágica facilidad con que ese problema se resuelve en ese sombrío establecimiento. No era, pues, eso lo que al solitario hombre de Buenos Aires podía preocuparle ... Era precisamente lo contrario: la nostalgia de la comunión y del amor, la añoranza de la mujer; no la presencia de un instrumento de su lujuria ... " Ernesto Sábato, "Estudio Preliminar: Tango, canción de Buenos Aires," in Horacio Salas, *El tango* (Buenos Aires: Planeta, 1986), 13. Translated by the editors.

10. Bernand, *Histoire de Buenos Aires*, 199.

11. Max Weber, *Economie et société* (Paris: Plon, 1995), 31.

12. Jean-Claude Passeron and Emmanuel Pedler, "Le temps donné au regard. Enquête sur la réception de la peinture," *Protée* (Chicoutimi, Quebec: Presses de l'Université du Québec, 1999), 94.

13. Roberto Daus, "Homenaje a la Guardia vieja del tango. Banda municipal de la ciudad de Buenos Aires, 1908–1909," *El Bandoneón*, CD 123. Ricardo García

Blaya also disputes this thesis in "Reflexiones sobre los origenes del tango," *Todotango*, accessed July 25, 2022, www.todotango.com/historias/cronica/103/Reflexiones-sobre-los-origenes-del-tango/.

14. Rémi Hess, *Le tango* (Paris: Presses Universitaires de France, 1996), 23–32.

15. The term *milonga* designates both a term for the place where one dances tango and one of the three rhythms of the tango genre, including tango, *milonga*, and *vals*.

16. For more information, see Anne Décoret-Ahiha, *Les danses exotiques en France: 1880–1940* (Paris: Centre national de la danse, 2004).

17. For further reading, see Pelinski, *Tango nomade*.

18. Among the ballroom dances, there are group dances, couple dances, and solo dances. Open dances are in the category of group dances, where the formation of the couple is intermittent.

19. The musette style in dance refers to a musical repertory and style, as well as to a certain type of sociability of the neighborhoods and inhabitants of Paris in the first half of the twentieth century (namely Italians and Auvergnats). According to accordionist Jo Privat, in François Billard and Didier Roussin, *Histoires de l'accordéon* (Paris: Climats, INA, 1991), 25.

20. For more information, see Christophe Apprill, *Sociologie des danses de couple* (Paris: L'Harmattan, 2005).

21. For further reading, see Christophe Apprill, *Slow. Désir et désillusion* (Paris: L'Harmattan, 2021).

22. *Tango Argentino* (1983), directed, stage design, and costumes by Claudio Segovia; dancers include Juan Carlos Copes, Mónica Pelay, María Nieves Rego, Ana María Stekelman, and Carmencita Calderón.

23. For further reading, see Eva Illouz, *La fin de l'amour. Enquête sur un désarroi contemporain* (Paris: Seuil, 2020); and Christophe Apprill, *L'invention politique de la danse contemporaine* (forthcoming, 2024).

24. Philippe Le Moal, *Dictionnaire de la danse* (Paris: Larousse/Bordas, 1999), 765.

25. For further reading, see Niclas Lorrina, ed., *La danse. Naissance d'un mouvement de pensée, ou le complexe de Cunningham* (Paris: Armand Colin, 1989); and Laurence Louppe, *Poétique de la danse contemporaine* (Bruxelles: Editions Contredanse, 1997).

26. Deterritorialization refers to the philosophy of Gilles Deleuze and Félix Guattari, in which cultural, social, and political practices become severed from their native location or territory and a part of another location. Gilles Deleuze and Félix Guattari, *L'anti-Oedipe* (Paris: Editions de Minuit, 1972).

27. Editors' note: see also Davis's Chapter 11 in this volume.

28. Christophe Apprill, "Le plaisir de la danse: des représentations aux propriétés formelles," in *Tango, corps à corps culturel*, France Joyal, ed. (Québec: Presses de l'Université du Québec, 2009), 99–117.

29. Jean Laplanche and Jean-Bertrand Pontalis, *Vocabulaire de la psychanalyse* (Paris: Presses universitaires de France, 2007), 60–61.

30. According to Jean Oury, it is the signifier that will allow for the development of the psyche. Jean Oury, *Création et schizophrénie* (Paris: Galilée, 1989), 145.

31. For further reading, see Christophe Apprill, *Les mondes du bal* (Nanterre: Presses universitaires de Paris Nanterre, 2018).

32. For more information, see Gilbert Rouget, *La musique et la transe. Esquisse d'une théorie générale de la relation de la musique et de la possession* (Paris: Gallimard, 1980).

33. The idea is controversial. Is it the consciousness or the state that changes? What norms serve as a reference to designate an ordinary state of consciousness? Not only is this dichotomy implicitly established between culturally relative ordinary and extra-ordinary situations, but the concept varies according to the individual.

34. Author interview with professor and tango dancer Federico Rodríguez Moreno, 2010.

35. For more information on Durassian rapture, see Marguerite Duras, *Le ravissement de Lol V. Stein* (Paris: Gallimard, 1964).

36. This aspect was noticeably observed in the 1970s with traditional and folk dances. See François Gasnault, "Les enjeux de la danse dans les réseaux 'revivalistes' français," *Recherches en danse: Danse(s) et politique(s)* 4 (2015): 5–6, online, accessed October 1, 2016, http://danse.revues.org/1185, doi: https://doi.org/10.4000/danse.1185.

37. "Le petit bal perdu," (song) by Robert Nyel and Gaby Verlor, sung by Bourvil.

38. "La foule," (song) by Michel Rivgauche, sung by Edith Piaf.

39. For more information, see Mihalyi Csikszentmihalyi, *Flow: The Psychology of Optimal Experience* (New York: Harper & Row, 1990). See also Jean Heutte, "Mise en evidence du flow perçu par des étudiants au cours d'un travail collectif: l'homo sapiens retiolus est-il un épicurien de la connaissance?" Blog, accessed June 28, 2021, http://jean.heutte.free.fr/spip.php?article114.

40. A sense of mastery and control; a perception of altered time, a feeling of detachment from oneself, a feeling of well-being. Jean Heutte and Fabien Fenouillet, "Propositions pour une mesure de l'expérience optimale (état de Flow) en contexte éducatif," paper presented at Actes du congrès de l'Actualité de la recherche en éducation et en formation (AREF), Université de Genève, Geneva, Switzerland (September 2010), available online, https://plone.unige.ch/aref2010/communications-orales/premiers-auteurs-en-h/Propositions%20.pdf/view. This state has been analyzed in the practice of tango by Sabine Zubarik, "Sublime Feelings: The Experience of 'Flow' in Dancing Tango," paper presented at Tango: Creation, Identification, Circulation, organized by Center for Research in Arts and Language, Paris, France, October 26–29, 2011.

41. François Frimat, "Danse avec le genre," *Cités*, 44 (2010): 77–89.

42. Michel Bozon, "Les femmes et l'écart d'âge entre conjoints: une domination consentie, I. Types d'union et attentes en matière d'écart d'âge," *Population*, 45, no. 2 (1990): 327–360.

43. For more information, see Pierre Bourdieu, *La domination masculine* (Paris: Éditions du Seuil, 1998).
44. For more information, see María Mercedes Liska, *Argentine Queer Tango. Dance and Sexuality Politics in Buenos Aires* (Lanham: Lexington Books, 2017).

Further Reading

Apprill, Christophe. "Des nuits à danser: passion ou décentrement?" In *Tango sans frontiers*, edited by France Joyal, 81–113. Québec, Presses de l'Université du Québec, 2010.

"L'hétérosexualité et les danses de couple." In *Hétéros: Discours, lieux, pratiques*, edited by Catherine Deschamps, Laurent Gaissad, and Christelle Taraud, 97–108. Paris: Epel Éditions, 2009.

Ayral, Sylvie and Yves Raibaud, eds. *Pour en finir avec la fabrique des garçons*. Bordeaux: Maison des sciences de l'Homme d'Aquitaine, 2014.

Castro, Donald S. *The Argentine Tango as Social History (1880–1955): The Soul of the People*. New York: Edwin Mellen Press, 1991.

García Blaya, Ricardo. "Reflexiones sobre los origenes del tango." *Todotango*. Accessed July 25, 2022, www.todotango.com/historias/cronica/103/Reflexiones-sobre-los-origenes-del-tango/.

Hess, Rémi. *Le tango*. Paris: Presses universitaires de France, 1996.

Humbert, Béatrice. "Le tango à Paris de 1907 à 1920." In *Tango nomade*, edited by Ramón Pelinski, 109–162. Montréal: Éditions Triptyque, 1995.

Nahoum-Grappe, Véronique. "Le couple en piste." In *Danses latines et identité, d'une rive à l'autre . . .*, edited by Elisabeth Dorier-Apprill, 191–212. Paris: L'Harmattan, 2000.

Salas, Horacio. *Le tango*. Arles: Actes sud, 1989.

Walkowitz, Judit. "Sexualités dangereuses." In *Histoire des femmes. Le XIXème siècle*, edited by George Duby and Michelle Perrot, 390–418. Paris: Plon, 1991.

11 | Tango Lessons: What Research on Tango Dancing Can Teach Us

KATHY DAVIS

Introduction

Tango was first danced in the late nineteenth century in the port cities of the Río de la Plata, Buenos Aires and Montevideo, but it soon became – and continues to be – a global phenomenon.[1] From the outset, the music and the dance "traveled," as tango became popular in many parts of the world and went through many revivals.[2] In the 1930s, it was taken up in Europe and beyond, becoming a rage among the affluent and bohemian classes of the metropolises of Paris, London, Berlin, Warsaw, Istanbul, New York, and Tokyo. From there, tango returned to Buenos Aires where the dance was embraced by well-to-do Argentines who had previously spurned it as a vulgar, immoral dance. Since its Golden Age (1930s–1950s), tango has gone in and out of fashion, entering its most recent worldwide revival in the 1990s. Today it has become a global dance culture with a growing community of dancers willing to spend a considerable part of their daily lives on tango. Many are prepared to travel long distances to participate in tango marathons, tango festivals, and tango vacations. Some even make yearly pilgrimages to Buenos Aires, where tango has become a major tourist industry replete with commercial tango shows, dance venues (salons), tango clothing and shoe stores, and guest houses for tango tourists. Many local dancers there make their living teaching and performing tango for the tourists.[3]

From 2009 to 2012, I conducted a study on tango as a global dance culture which was later published under the title *Dancing Tango: Passionate Encounters in a Globalizing World*.[4] Employing ethnographic fieldwork in Buenos Aires, the undisputed mecca of tango, and in Amsterdam, one of the European tango centers, I interviewed tango dancers for whom dancing tango is more than just a hobby and, at times, even a way of life. I wanted to know why people from very different social, cultural, and geographical backgrounds could become so passionate about

189

a dance from another era (turn of the twentieth century) and another place (Buenos Aires). What were they looking for in tango? What happened to their lives, relationships, and identities as they became involved in this strange and apparently addictive dance culture? In addition to wanting to understand more about what dancing tango meant to the dancers themselves, as a feminist sociologist, I was also curious about how contemporary men and women were able to negotiate the inevitable ambivalences and contradictions of tango that have always been and continue to be shaped by gendered, sexualized, and ethnicized hierarchies of power. Notably, the history of tango is told through representations of knife-wielding *compadritos* (immigrant men living in the slums of Buenos Aires) competing with other men for the attentions of duplicitous women, often prostitutes. While this representation hardly fits the cosmopolitan tango dancers of today, it continues to shape the music to which they dance, the salon culture in which they participate, and, most importantly, their cherished image of so-called authentic tango. But how, I asked the dancers I interviewed in my research, do they reconcile such retro and clearly heterosexist and exoticized notions of tango with their presumably enlightened late-modern personas?

In the course of giving talks about my book, I often found myself having to explain to academic audiences how a researcher like myself could take up such a frivolous topic as tango dancing. My fellow sociologists were accustomed to investigating serious social problems involving inequalities, crises and conflicts, as well as migration and displacement. If they took an interest in body practices at all, they tended to focus on weighty issues like illness or dying, disability, extreme forms of body modification, adventurous leisure-time activities, or dangerous sports. Dancing tango, with its reputation for pleasure and passion, hardly seemed like a suitable research topic for a serious sociologist. My study of tango seemed even more problematic for my feminist colleagues who wondered why I, a critical (postcolonial) scholar, would want to invest her energies in what is arguably one of the most exoticized, heteronormative dances around.[5]

In this chapter, I identify what I believe are the sound sociological reasons for doing research on dancing tango. I argue that there is a lot that we can learn from tango about topics that are, in fact, highly relevant for sociology; namely, the importance of passion in ordinary people's everyday lives, gender relations in late modernity, and the possibilities and pitfalls of transnational encounters in a globalizing world. Lastly, I discuss some of the methodological innovations that I employed, which were necessary for me to understand the broader sociological and cultural significance of tango dancing, and I argue why they deserve to be embraced more broadly and applied more widely to sociological research in general.

Tango Passion

One of the clichés about tango is that it is all about passion. In fact, tango is a metaphor for passion. It can be found in popular discourse, literature, and the media. Just a few strains of tango in a film are enough to announce that a steamy sex scene is coming up (WL 11.1). Passion is what we "see" when tango is performed. We read it in the movements of the dance, in the exaggerated poses of women in slinky dresses swooning in the arms of their sexy Latino partners. We imagine it in the women's closed eyes and the dramatic expressions on the partners' faces (WP 11.1).

Critical feminist and postcolonial scholars have devoted considerable attention to the problematic ways in which passion is mobilized in the popular imagination about tango. The well-known tango scholar Marta Savigliano has argued that contemporary dancers cannot dance tango without drawing upon the exoticized/eroticized images that are a part of tango's imbrications in the gendered, racialized legacies of colonialism. As she puts it, by dancing tango, they "*cultivate* passion, passionately."[6] But passion is not just a metaphor for a performance with eroticized overtones. It is also and, more importantly, an intensely emotional, embodied experience. It is what many dancers say they *feel* when they dance tango in a close embrace. They offer passion as the main reason for their willingness to spend money, time, and effort learning what is generally considered a difficult dance. Their passion for tango is what incites them to practice their steps for hours on end, to attend countless classes, workshops, and *prácticas* (practice milonga), and to venture out – sometimes far away from home – just to dance tango. Their passion accounts for the way tango has taken over their lives, pushing out activities they used to enjoy (such as going to films and listening to other kinds of music) and causing them to neglect their families and (non–tango-dancing) friends. As one of my informants, a tango "exile," as he called himself, who had moved to Buenos Aires to dance, leaving his children and grandchildren in Europe behind, explained: "They [his family members] might have been a reason to stay, but, on the other hand, they have their own lives and don't want me hanging around anyhow. So, I started looking for a place in Buenos Aires and the rest is history."[7] In short, passion explains why tango dancing can become an important – even the most important – part of a person's life.

The cultural and performance studies scholars Celeste Delgado and José Muñoz explain the passion for dancing as a form of resistance that allows people to avoid the drudgery and oppression of everyday life.[8] Passion is what makes life worth living.[9]

Obviously, dancing tango is not the only thing a person can become passionate about. People may develop passions about all kinds of activities, objects, ideas, and other people.[10] Despite the importance of passion in people's everyday lives, however, most sociologists do not know what to make of it. Passion feels unruly, capricious, and out of control. Sociologists are often more comfortable with treating the behavior of their research subjects as more or less intentional, based on choice and capable of being explained or justified. Even for those sociologists who have directed their attention to the role of emotions in social life, they seem to prefer what Sianne Ngai calls the "ugly" emotions – disgust, guilt, and shame, for example.[11] Passion as an emotional experience has largely been ignored.

Understanding the role of passion in social life is essential in order to understand what makes a person's life meaningful. It is, therefore, mandatory for anyone interested in social life to try to understand why people develop passions and what caring passionately about someone or something means to them. To what extent are people prepared to follow their passions? What obstacles do they have to overcome? Which passions does society tolerate and which are subject to sanctions? And, what are the consequences for a person's well-being if their life is devoid of passion? These are all questions begging for serious sociological research and, therefore, became central to my research on tango.

Gender and Tango

The second tango-related topic of interest for a sociologist is gender. Dancing tango offers a site for exploring how gender relations are organized, negotiated, and transformed, historically as well as across national borders. Gender is integral to the lyrics of tango music, the performance of the dance, and the ways dancers encounter one another on and off the dance floor.[12] Many of the most iconic tangos have lyrics full of gender stereotypes and machismo.[13] Women are represented as prostitutes, traitorous femmes fatales, or "rebellious broads," while men are cast as "whiny ruffians" whose machismo causes them to suffer jealousy and engage in extreme acts of violence against their unfaithful lovers.[14] But gender is also embedded in the way the dance itself is performed. Conventionally, it is the man who leads and the woman who follows. He determines the choreography and the moves, while she pays attention (often with her eyes closed) and responds to his signals. Feminists have criticized the gendered-ness of the dance, noting how women are immobilized by impractical clothing and stiletto heels, stifled by being enclosed in a small space (an embrace), and forced to dance backwards without having any control over the dance.[15] In the more traditional tango salons, men are usually the ones who invite a partner to dance, while women have to wait to be invited. This may occur with a *cabeceo*, initiated by the man and accepted or rejected by the woman.[16] In Buenos Aires, the sexes are even seated separately in most traditional milongas (tango salons) with men on one side and women on the other side of the dance floor. Men share a table with their friends, drinking and commenting on the dancers,[17] while women wait anxiously for a dance, often doomed to be a "wallflower" for hours on end.[18]

Tango has been viewed as the embodiment of hyper-heterosexuality, macho masculinity, and subservient femininity. This raises the question of how contemporary dancers who tend, at least in principle, to be committed to egalitarian relations between the sexes reconcile their late-modern identities with the traditional gender hierarchies which are so prevalent in the world of tango. Some tango dancers have balked at what they see as old-fashioned gender roles and have begun looking for new forms of music, like *nuevo tango* (New Tango), to interpret.[19] Or, they have adopted dancing that eliminates fixed gender roles and emphasizes switching positions during the dance, as in queer tango.[20] Many tango salons, both in and outside Buenos Aires, have taken up more relaxed arrangements in terms of seating and invitation rituals. Nevertheless, a considerable group of *milongueros/as* continues to dance tango traditionally, and many of the salons today embrace traditional regimes of male leaders inviting female followers with the *cabeceo* and playing music strictly from tango's Golden Age. This traditional regime not only compels, but also allows these dancers to engage in behaviors that they would normally avoid in their everyday lives. Women can wear ultrafeminine clothing and abandon themselves to their partner, while men can unashamedly take control or explore their "macho side."[21]

Explaining this discrepancy between a late-modern commitment to gender equality and retrograde gender hierarchies in tango provides an interesting challenge for sociological research. Sociologists might wonder how dancers themselves account for and justify their desire for a dance that displays such archaic forms of heterosexual masculinity and femininity. Is it a way for otherwise emancipated and cosmopolitan men and women – the majority of contemporary tango dancers – to engage in an exotic practice, one that will allow them a momentary escape from their everyday routines, if only for a moment? Or does tango provide the possibility for late-modern men and women to experience connection without the complications of a relationship – something that would fit the relational context of liquid modernity?[22] Or does tango address a deeper need for playfulness and ambiguity, which is missing in contemporary gender relations where direct communication and consensuality are the unspoken rules?[23]

These questions suggest that tango dancing might be a fruitful starting point for investigating the contradictions that complicate gender relations in late modernity, providing an opportunity to explore some of the tensions in contemporary discourses and practices of gender equality. Dancing tango thus offers a window into the complexities of contemporary gender relations, something that should be of interest to any sociologist interested in the problems of intimacy and connection as well as the role of fantasy and playfulness in late modernity.

Transnational Encounters through Tango

The most recent global revival of tango in the 1990s made tango dancing available to individuals of different genders and ages, from different classes and ethnic backgrounds, and from urban or rural settings across the globe. By dancing tango, they are able to enter a transnational cultural space, even when they are dancing in their local tango salon. Every tango dancer participates in a global community of dancers, some of whom they may meet face-to-face, but most of whom they will never actually physically encounter.[24] For example, many tango dancers have watched so many videos of dance performances in other parts of the world that these foreign venues feel just as familiar to them as their own home salons. As soon as they enter the transnational cultural space of tango, literally or vicariously, hear the familiar music, and see the other dancers circling the floor locked in a close embrace, they will have the uncanny sense of being both home and elsewhere, neither here nor there, not in the past, but also not entirely in the present – in short, somewhere in between, in a liminal moment of transcendence, lost – as it were – in translation.[25]

Such a transnational culture space is not simply an innocent place to socialize, however. Historical and economic disparities between the Global North and Global South make tango anything but a level playing field.[26] Tango tourists from affluent nations flock to Buenos Aires every year to dance the so-called authentic tango in search of a particular kind of emotional experience and a taste of "authenticity."[27] As Savigliano has convincingly shown, these visitors often draw upon exoticized/eroticized images that are part of tango's imbrication in the gendered, racialized legacies of colonialism.[28] This makes tango literally a love-hate embrace with colonial overtones.

For Argentine dancers, tango has a different meaning. It is not only a symbol of their national identity, something that they feel "belongs" to them,[29] but it is also for some of them a source of income and a way to earn a living in an increasingly precarious economy. They organize milongas, offer dance lessons, provide the escort services of a "taxi dancer" for tourists,[30] sell tango clothing and shoes, and operate tango guest houses. For them, tango is both something ordinary Argentines have listened to and seen their parents dance for most of their lives as well as a profitable export product. In the former, tango is danced according to the traditional codes of "home tango," while the "export tango" financially exploits the hyper-erotic staged performance of professionals.[31]

Clearly the contemporary transnational tango culture has plenty to offer the enterprising sociologist. The effects of globalization on global power relations, worldwide encounters between differently located individuals, and how individuals view themselves and their everyday lives have been well-trodden subjects in contemporary sociology. Across the globe, individuals are increasingly finding ways to connect – literally or through the internet – and many of the communities to be found in the world today are virtual. For sociologists, this raises the question of how to think about the way people participate locally in a global culture and what this means for their lives, their relationships, and their sense of self in the world around them.

Taken together, the significance of passion, the complications of contemporary gender relations, and the emergence of transnational cultural spaces are all phenomena of sociological interest. Tango is the site *par excellence* for exploring how individuals actually negotiate, reconcile, and sometimes transform the differences (of class, ethnicity, and national belonging) that divide them in the interests of sharing a moment of pleasure and connection.

In the final part of this chapter, I take up some of these methodological innovations. I show why they are essential not only for understanding passion and tango dancing but also, more generally, for understanding embodied cultural phenomena in the context of globally structured gender and power relations.

Researching Tango Dancing

Researching tango dancing confronted me with two difficulties that had ramifications for the methodologies I needed to employ to answer my questions. The first involved the problem of how to investigate a *bodily practice* (dancing) that is intensely experienced but difficult to articulate. The second was how to analyze a *dance culture that is local, yet at the same time, global* with dancers who not only travel across borders just to dance but also imaginatively partake in what they see as a global dance culture. To address these issues, I drew on two seemingly disparate and innovative branches of sociological research – carnal sociology and global ethnography.

Carnal sociology emerged in the late 1990s in an attempt to bring the body back into sociological research.[32] While many sociologists were researching *about* the body as an object of specific discourses and practices, carnal sociologists specifically wanted to do research *from* the body. As Wacquant states, researchers need to submerge themselves in the bodily practices they are investigating and find a way to express the "taste and the ache" of the embodied experience.[33] This entails providing visceral accounts of what it actually feels like to engage in a practice, namely to enter the body of people who do it. In my research on dancing tango, I employed this methodology in several ways. First, I drew upon my own experiences as a tango dancer. For example, I used my own experience of entering into a close embrace with a stranger by drawing upon my sense of touch, smell, and sound. This allowed me to convey the sensations of, for example, smelling a partner's freshly laundered shirt, feeling each other's heartbeat, being surprised by the tickle of a strand of hair, or the prickle of an unshaven cheek.[34] Second, I worked interactively with my informants, who often struggled to describe a bodily encounter that was unique and intense – "an intimacy like no other," as one dancer put it – but for which they had no ready-made language. The interviews became themselves embodied occasions, involving listening to tango music together "to get in the mood," my interview partner jumping up to demonstrate a particular step, or showing me with a hug what a good or bad embrace would entail. Given the often joyful nature of their tango experiences, I was frequently surprised when they suddenly began to cry when they recounted a particularly intense dance that reminded them of a lost love, a divorce, a family member who had died, or nostalgia for their homeland. By mobilizing our bodies, a different kind of interview emerged – one which allowed a more profound understanding of what can make dancing tango such a meaningful and moving experience.

But carnal sociology, with its embodied approach to interviewing, was not the only methodological innovation I needed for my research on tango dancing. I also required a more unconventional approach to ethnographical fieldwork, which I found in global ethnography.[35] Traditionally, ethnographies are anything but global. They are microstudies of everyday life in circumscribed localities and bounded communities, full of thick descriptions with intimate details and lots of local flavor. This fieldwork methodology has frequently been used to describe local dance cultures – anything from the Lindy Hop in New York City to a women's *Palo de Mayo* (Maypole) dance in Nicaragua.[36] While dance ethnographies have been particularly suited to understanding the kinesthetic aspects of dancing as well as the gendered and ethnicized dimensions of local dance cultures, they are less suited to understanding how contemporary dance cultures have traveled across the globe, moreover, how these travels have shaped how dance cultures are experienced, organized, and transformed. In contrast, Burawoy and his colleagues take as their starting point that in a globalizing world, like the one we live in, it is impossible to separate the local from the global; rather, the local is permeated by and mutually constituted by global forces, transnational connections between people, and global imaginaries. Therefore, ethnographies need to be "extended out" from the local to the global and vice versa.

This approach to ethnographical fieldwork shaped my understanding of tango dance culture in ways that were both surprising and, at times, disconcerting. For example, I realized that tango tourists in Buenos Aires were not the only ones looking for a special experience with an exotic "other," as Savigliano has argued, but that the Argentine locals, themselves, are also engaged in processes of exoticization.[37] For example, one might hear: "I only dance a tango waltz with a European. They just know how to do it."[38] Similarly, the all-present Global North/Global South divide favored by most globalization scholars for describing power asymmetries in different parts of the world proved unhelpful for explaining the complicated processes I observed in the salons of Buenos Aires, where local dancers skillfully used their contacts with tourists to negotiate the – often fraught – gender and class relations among themselves. Men who were precariously employed outside the milongas could overcome the injuries of class by scoring young tourists anxious to dance with "real" *milongueros*, while local women could alleviate the insults of "wallflowering" by turning up their noses at the local men. I would hear them rave about how "cultured" and educated European men are and how they are much more likely to be able to have a conversation with them.[39] The idea that tango is a global community of dancers is not limited to the affluent North American or European dancers who are able to travel, but includes, in fact, anybody wherever and whenever they dance. Dancing tango means entering a shared transnational space in which every dancer, whether man or woman, unemployed or affluent, white or black, gay or straight, is confronted with structured hierarchies of power and privilege, but also with a passionate desire for connection and pleasure. This does not mean that historical, economic, or geopolitical divisions do not matter. It suggests, however, that a "cosmopolitan disposition rather than the colonizing gaze may more accurately describe what links wildly disparate and differently situated dancers in the world of tango."[40]

Conclusion

In this chapter, I have demonstrated that tango dancing is a serious subject for critical sociological research. I have argued that there are, at least, three reasons why tango is anything but a frivolous topic for sociologists. First, we need to understand the importance of passion in people's everyday lives. Second, we need to understand how men and women negotiate the contradictions of gender relations in late modernity. And finally, we need to understand the transnational cultural space in which differently situated individuals encounter one another, negotiating both the differences that divide them as well as their desires for connection.

These topics are not only what makes tango dancing a worthwhile subject for sociological research. I have also shown why the methodologies from carnal sociology and global ethnography were necessary to understand these phenomena. Such methodological interventions are, of course, not just applicable to investigating the phenomenon of tango dancing. Tango is not the only embodied practice that allows its practitioners a betwixt and between where they can shed their mundane concerns and have a sense of being outside themselves.[41]

Tango dancing belongs to a much broader range of activities that are fervently desired, even when they run counter to the individual's normative or social commitments. In a globalizing world, all of us are connected through travel, the internet, and popular culture, no matter where we live or what our lives look like. These "contact zones"[42] are perfect for exploring the ways differently situated individuals search for connection, while at the same time, negotiating the power differences that divide them. Listening to their stories can help us understand how interwoven our lives are – both in the past and the present.

Notes

1. Ramón Aldolfo Pelinski, *El tango nómade: ensayos sobre la diaspora del tango* (Buenos Aires: Corregidor, 2000), 21.
2. While I focus primarily on tango dancing in this chapter, tango music also has an international trajectory. This has been a fruitful object for many investigations in the field of musicology. See, for example, Robert Farris Thompson, *Tango: The Art History of Love* (New York: Vintage Books, 2005); Janine Krüger, *Cuál es tu Tango? Musikalische Lesarten der argentinischen Tangotradition* (Münster: Waxmann, 2012); Kacey Link and Kristin Wendland, *Tracing* Tangueros: *Argentine Tango Instrumental Music* (New York: Oxford University Press, 2016); Morgan James Luker, *The Tango Machine: Musical Culture in the Age of Expediency* (Chicago: The University of Chicago Press, 2016); and Bárbara Varassi Pega, *The Art of Tango* (Abingdon: Routledge, 2021).
3. Franco Barrionuevo Anzaldi, "The New Tango Era in Buenos Aires: The Transformation of a Popular Culture into a Touristic 'Experience Economy.'" Paper presented at the II ISA Forum of Sociology (Buenos Aires, August 1–4, 2012).
4. Kathy Davis, *Dancing Tango: Passionate Encounters in a Globalizing World* (New York: New York University Press, 2015).
5. See Kathy Davis, "Should a Feminist Dance Tango? The Experience and Politics of Passion," *Feminist Theory* 16, no. 1 (March 2015): 3–21, in which I address these feminist concerns by taking up the (rhetorical) question of whether a feminist should or should not dance tango.
6. Marta E. Savigliano, *Angora Matta: Fatal Acts of North-South Translation* (Middletown: Wesleyan University Press, 2003), 161; see also Savigliano, *Tango and the Political Economy of Passion* (Boulder: Westview Press, 1995).
7. Davis, *Dancing Tango*, 94.
8. Celeste Fraser Delgado and José Muñoz, "Rebellions of Everynight Life," in *Everynight Life: Culture and Dance in Latin/o America*, eds. Celeste Fraser Delgado and José Muñoz (Durham: Duke University Press, 1997), 9–32.
9. Robert J. Vallerand, "On the Psychology of Passion: In Search of What Makes People's Lives Most Worth Living," *Canadian Psychology/Psychologie canadienne* 49, no. 1 (February 2008): 1–13.
10. Cheryl Hall, *The Trouble with Passion. Political Theory beyond the Reign of Reason* (Abingdon: Routledge, 2005), 11.

11. Sianne Ngai, *Ugly Feelings* (Cambridge: Harvard University Press, 2005), 2–8.

12. The best source on gender relations during the early days of tango in Buenos Aires remains Savigliano's *Tango and the Political Economy of Passion*, but see also Jorge Salessi, "Medics, Crooks, and Tango Queens: The National Appropriation of a Gay Tango," in *Everynight Life: Culture and Dance in Latin/o America*, eds. Celeste Fraser Delgado and José Esteban Muñoz (Durham: Duke University Press, 1997), 141–174 and Magali Saikin, *Tango y Género* (Stuttgart: Abrazos Books, 2004) for a historical look at machismo in tango. For the workings of gender in the contemporary tango scene, refer to Julie Taylor, *Paper Tangos* (Durham: Duke University Press, 1998); Eduardo P. Archetti, *Masculinities: Football, Polo, and the Tango in Argentina* (Oxford: Berg, 1999); Sirena Pellarolo, "Queering Tango: Glitches in the Hetero-National Matrix of a Liminal Cultural Production," *Theater Journal* 60, no. 3 (October 2008): 409–431; Jeffrey Tobin, "Models of Machismo: The Troublesome Masculinity of Argentine Male Tango Dancers," in *Tango in Translation. Tanz zwischen Medien, Kulturen, Kunst und Politik*, ed. Gabriele Klein (Bielefeld: transcript Verlag, 2009), 139–169; Paula-Irene Villa, "Bewegte Diskurse, die bewegen. Warum der Tango die (Geschlechter-) Verhältnisse zum Tanzen bringen kann," in *Körper Wissen Geschlecht*, ed. Angelika Wetter (Sulzbach/Taunus: Ulrike Helmer Verlag, 2010), 141–164; María Julia Carozzi, "Light Women Dancing Tango: Gender Images as Allegories of Heterosexual Relationships," *Current Sociology* 61, no. 1 (January 2013): 22–39; Maria Törnqvist, *Tourism and the Globalization of Emotions: The Intimate Economy of Tango* (Abingdon: Routledge, 2013); and Davis, *Dancing Tango*.

13. Anahí Viladrich, "Neither Virgins nor Whores: Tango Lyrics and Gender Representations in the Tango World," *Journal of Popular Culture* 39, no. 2 (April 2006): 272–293.

14. Savigliano, *Tango and the Political Economy of Passion*, 30–72.

15. Paula-Irene Villa, *Sexy Bodies. Eine soziologische Reise durch den Geschlechtskörper* (Opladen: Leske & Budrich, 2001), 239–263.

16. *Cabeceo* literally means a "nod of the head" used as a nonverbal invitation to dance.

17. Tobin, "Models of Machismo," 145–148.

18. Savigliano uses "wallflowering" as a translation of *planchar* to indicate a lack of activity into which dancers have fallen into under certain circumstances rather than an identity with which someone who does not dance is stuck. Savigliano, *Angora Matta*, 166–167.

19. See María Mercedes Liska, "El cuerpo en la música: La propuesta del tango *queer* y su vinculación con el tango electrónico," *Boletín Onteaiken* 8 (2009): 45–52.

20. For more on queer tango, see Salessi, "Medics, Crooks, and Tango Queens"; Saikin, *Tango y Género*; Savigliano, "Notes on Tango (as) Queer

(Commodity)," *Anthropological Notebooks* 16, no. 3 (2010): 135–143; and Mercedes Liska, *Argentine Queer Tango: Dance and Sexuality Politics in Buenos Aires* (Lanham: Lexington Books, 2016).

21. This is how one of my male informants put it: "I guess I do have something macho in myself.... At the same time, I'm not macho at all. I could use a little more of it, in fact ... but the moment I start dancing it comes to the surface.... That's fantastic, don't you think?" in Davis, *Dancing Tango*, 114.

22. Zygmunt Bauman, *Liquid Love* (Cambridge: Polity Press, 2003), vii–xiii.

23. Eva Illouz, *Why Love Hurts: A Sociological Explanation* (Cambridge: Polity, 2012), 156–197.

24. In this sense, tango has all the ingredients of what Benedict Anderson called an "imagined community." It is possible to feel part of the community without actually knowing all of its members. Benedict Anderson, *Imagined Communities: Reflections on the Origin and Spread of Nationalism* (London: Verso, 1983), 6–7.

25. Kathy Davis, "From Transnational Biographies to Transnational Cultural Spaces," in *Handbuch Biografieforschung*, eds. Helma Lutz, Martina Schiebel, and Elisabeth Tuider (Wiesbaden: Springer Verlag, 2018), 659–668.

26. "Global North" and "Global South" are shorthand for the social, economic, and political divisions between wealthy, developed countries (often, but not always, in the Northern Hemisphere) and poorer, developing countries (often, but not always, in the Southern Hemisphere). Contemporary scholars have rightly criticized this terminology, noting that affluence is not limited to the North, nor poverty to the South. However, it remains helpful for understanding the political and economic problems facing Argentina today as well as how it is positioned ideologically by the relatively affluent consumers of tango in Europe, North America, Australia, and parts of Asia. See also Davis, *Dancing Tango*, 193.

27. Franco Barrionuevo Anzaldi, "The new tango era in Buenos Aires: the transformation of a popular culture into a touristic 'experience economy'" (paper presented at the II ISA Forum of Sociology, Buenos Aires, August 1–4, 2012).

28. Savigliano, *Angora Matta*, 209–224.

29. Archetti, *Masculinities*, 17.

30. Maria Törnqvist and Kate Hardy, "Taxi Dancers: Tango Labour and Commercialized Intimacy in Buenos Aires," in *New Sociologies of Sex Work*, eds. Kate Hardy, Sarah Kingston, and Teela Sanders (Farnham: Ashgate, 2010), 137–148.

31. Ana C. Cara, "Entangled Tangos: Passionate Displays, Intimate Dialogues," *Journal of American Folklore* 122, no. 486 (Fall 2009): 438–465.

32. Nick Crossley, "Merleau-Ponty, the Elusive Body and Carnal Sociology," *Body & Sociology* 1, no. 1 (March 1995): 43–63; Loïc Wacquant, "Carnal

Connections: On Embodiment, Apprenticeship, and Membership," *Qualitative Sociology* 28, no. 4 (December 2005): 445–474.

33. Wacquant, "Carnal Connections," 470.
34. Davis, *Dancing Tango*, 57–58.
35. Michael Burawoy, Joseph A. Blum, Sheba George et al., *Global Ethnography: Forces, Connections, and Imaginations in a Postmodern World* (Berkeley: University of California Press, 2000), 1–40.
36. Randal Doane, "The Habitus of Dancing: Notes on the Swing Dance Revival in New York City," *Journal of Contemporary Ethnography* 35, no. 1 (February 2006): 84–116; Maarit E. Ylönen, "Bodily Flashes of Dancing Women: Dance as a Method of Inquiry," *Qualitative Inquiry* 9, no. 4 (August 2003): 554–568.
37. Savigliano, *Tango and the Political Economy of Passion*, 2.
38. Davis, *Dancing Tango*, 172.
39. Ibid.
40. Davis, *Dancing Tango*, 181.
41. For a nice description of this phenomenon of "self-transcendence," see Claudio E. Benzecry, *The Opera Fanatic: Ethnography of an Obsession* (Chicago: The University of Chicago Press, 2011), 5, 126.
42. Mary Louise Pratt. *Imperial Eyes: Travel Writing and Transculturation*, 2nd ed. (Abingdon: Routledge, 1992), 7.

Further Reading

Anzaldi, Franco Barrionuevo. "The New Tango Era in Buenos Aires: The Transformation of a Popular Culture into a Touristic 'Experience Economy'." Paper presented at the II ISA Forum of Sociology, Buenos Aires, August 1–4, 2012.

Appadurai, Arjun. *Modernity at Large: Cultural Dimensions of Globalization*. Minneapolis: University of Minnesota Press, 1996.

Cara, Ana C. "Entangled Tangos: Passionate Displays, Intimate Dialogues." *Journal of American Folklore* 122, no. 486 (Fall 2009): 438–465.

Carozzi, María Julia. "Light Women Dancing Tango: Gender Images as Allegories of Heterosexual Relationships." *Current Sociology* 61, no. 1 (January 2013): 22–39.

Delgado, Celeste Fraser, and José Esteban Muñoz. "Rebellions of Everynight Life." In *Everynight Life: Culture and Dance in Latin/o America*, edited by Celeste Fraser Delgado and José Esteban Muñoz, 9–32. Durham, NC: Duke University Press, 1997.

Pelinski, Ramón Aldolfo. *El tango nómade: ensayos sobre la diáspora del tango*. Buenos Aires: Corregidor, 2000.

Pellarolo, Sirena. "Queering Tango: Glitches in the Hetero-National Matrix of a Liminal Cultural Production." *Theater Journal* 60, no. 3 (October 2008): 409–431.

Savigliano, Marta E. *Tango and the Political Economy of Passion*. Boulder, CO: Westview Press, 1995.

   Angora Matta: Fatal Acts of North-South Translation. Middletown, CT: Wesleyan University Press, 2003.

12 | *Encuentros Milongueros:* Europe's Twenty-First-Century Tango Dance Practice

KENDRA STEPPUTAT

Imagine: it's Friday evening, and you're looking forward to a weekend filled with dancing *tango argentino.*[1] You walk toward a spacious building and hear soft tango music wavering in and out of the entrance door and windows. You recognize the tune; it's Ricardo Tanturi's 1942 recording of "Así se baila el tango" ("This Is How the Tango Is Danced"). This is a classic first song for the DJ to play, and you smile in anticipation of entering the room of fellow dancers. You quickly go to the registration desk and get your bracelet for the weekend. Then, you rush to the wardrobe area, exchange your street shoes for your dancing shoes, and give a last look in the mirror to check your clothes, which are fancy yet comfortable to wear for dancing. On your way to the dance hall, you enthusiastically greet numerous friends – some of whom you haven't seen in months, others whose names you don't remember, and even some whose language you don't speak. But the warm embrace of dancing with these friends is vivid in your memory. Finally, you enter a large hall with high ceilings, a spacious dance floor, and festive lighting. You find a place to put your things on one of the chairs, grouped in rows around the dance floor's perimeter. On one side of the room, you notice a slightly raised table where the DJ sits. Tonight's DJ is well known and experienced. Good, you think; there will be no musical surprises, and the mood is guaranteed to have just the right amount of energy. The next *tanda* (song set) is about to start. You excitedly look around the room to make eye contact with a dance partner. Then, across the empty floor, you spot one of your favorite dancers. Your eyes meet, the music starts, and both of you grin and nod in this mutual invitation to dance. Along with fellow dancers, you meet this partner on the dance floor and gently entangle your bodies into a close embrace. You feel your partner's touch, respiration, and heartbeat. You listen to the music – the marking accompanimental rhythm and the entrancing melodic line of the bandoneón. Then after some moments, you and your partner take your first steps to embody the music. This will be the first of many dances during the weekend dedicated to dancing tango with like-minded enthusiasts. It will be a weekend devoted to experiencing pure tango bliss together.

The above scene, while fictitious, is a typical example of an *encuentro milonguero* – a gathering of tango social dancers to experience *tango*

Figure 12.1 Afternoon milonga at an *encuentro milonguero*.

argentino. In this chapter, I shed light on the rather short history of the *encuentro milonguero* as a cultural phenomenon of tango social dance in Europe (Figure 12.1). I focus on the social, musical, and dance aspects that define and distinguish *encuentros milongueros* from other practices of *tango argentino*. I compare the diametric perspectives of enthusiastic participants and organizers who are convinced that an *encuentro milonguero* is the best way to dance tango in Europe with those perspectives of dancers who are not part of *encuentro milonguero* networks and criticize the practice for its elitist and exclusive qualities. Regardless of the *encuentro milonguero*'s controversial status, I argue that these events demonstrate how *tango argentino* has been adapted to a European translocal tango practice. I show how European dancers have conceptualized the *encuentro milonguero* as a copy of *tango argentino* dance practice from Buenos Aires, while at the same time developing a separate, European *tango argentino* practice.

Introduction to *Tango Argentino* as a Social Dance

Born at the turn of the twentieth century in the Río de la Plata region of Argentina and Uruguay, the tango art form includes music, dance, and lyrics. As a music-dance-poetic genre, it migrated to other countries and continents in the first decade of the twentieth century and took root in Paris and other European cities.[2] In its distinct form back home, *tango argentino* reached its height during its Golden Age from the mid-1930s to early 1950s. The 1980s saw a revival of the art form on both sides of the Atlantic, and since then, the dance practice has gained a growing membership.

Tango dance-movement repertory has developed far from its beginnings, and now dancers practice a wide variety of social tango styles.[3] While these social tango dance styles may possess different movement aesthetics, they all share the most important tango principle: joint movement improvisation. Based on trained embodied movement,[4] one dancer takes on the leader role, initiating the movement, while the other follows, interpreting the leader's movement. The challenge with dancing in such a joint improvisation – in addition to adjusting to different partners' movements and signals – is to dance not only to, but with the music. Many practitioners consider interpreting tango music in this embodied way to be the epiphany of tango dancing. They engage in a never-ending learning endeavor to master the technique, connect with their partner, listen to and creatively interpret the music, and last but not least, navigate the floor and the shared space with other couples safely.

Private and professional dance teachers, along with a wide variety of local and international event organizers, serve the needs and tastes of tango dancers. A dancer trained in *tango argentino* can dance at a milonga (tango dance event) anywhere in the world and be able to find a partner with whom sharing dances is possible. They will know the same basic tango steps and have an idea of how to interpret the music. Tango social dancing in Europe is translocal because it is practiced in many locations that are mutually connected through social media and travel.[5] Because of Europe's scattered tango community, the more experienced dancers are more likely to travel internationally to dance, and this travel may include attending *encuentros milongueros*.

The *Encuentro Milonguero* as a European Tango Tradition

An *encuentro milonguero* is a meeting of experienced tango dancers over the course of one weekend (Friday through Sunday) with up to ten hours of dancing per day. While the Spanish word "*encuentro*" translates quite straightforwardly as "meeting," the term "*milonguero*" warrants explanation. The adjective *milonguero* comes from the term "*milonga*," which has two meanings. First, the term refers to the Argentine dance-music genre that evolved from the Cuban *habanera* and retained the characteristic dotted accompanimental rhythm. Second, milonga refers to any social tango dance event. The adjective *milonguero*, then, generally describes anything related to traditional tango dance. Additionally, the word can function as a noun, where *milonguero* (male) and *milonguera* (female) are people who dance tango at a traditional milonga. Opinions, however, differ on what traditional tango dance encompasses and what being a *milonguero* or *milonguera* means, and all these terms are subject to philosophic, political, and economic discussions and interpretations.[6] In this chapter, I use and define the term *milonguero* as *encuentro* dancers use it. For them, the term *milonguero* represents a way to engage with tango dance and music as a historical practice flourishing today. This practice includes social rules on and off the dance floor that they consider essential for *milonguero* dancing. Although these rules are adopted from historical tango practices in Buenos Aires, *encuentros milongueros* construct and shape an essentially European tradition as they form a significant part of the practice of the European translocal tango community.

History of Encuentros Milongueros

Probably the first *encuentro milonguero* occurred in Italy in 2005. Organized by Tango Firenze, the *encuentro* called Raduno Milonguero took place in Impruneta, a town close to Florence. Thereafter, similar events began to occur throughout Europe, notably Les Cigales in Sainte Colombe, France (2009); Yo Soy Milonguero in Crema, Italy (2008); the Experiencia Milonguera in Pradamano, Italy (2009); the Festivalito con Amigos in Saarbrücken, Germany (2011); and Abrazos de Corazón in Moosburg, Austria (2012).[7] These events were a huge success, and dancers who had experienced them started organizing similar events in their own local surroundings. In a recent interview, tango DJ Paola Nocitango described how this process began in 2011:

There were only festivals at the beginning, you know? Then arrived the *encuentros*. And when you dance the first time in an *encuentro* you fall in love. ... You cannot ... [*sic*] this long year waiting for the other edition ... I remember that we went to Impruneta, it was end of October, and in May, we went to Les Cigales, and I said, "Oh my God, we have to wait until October." And it was too much. You could not resist. So, with some friends we ... said, "Why don't we try to do it, to do it in our town?" And so, we did.[8]

With such enthusiasm, Nocitango started in Noci, Italy, in 2012.[9] In the beginning, the difference between a regular tango festival, which includes live music, classes, and demonstrations, and an *encuentro milonguero* was blurred, but the distinction became clear within the first few years. Whereas a tango festival is open to everyone, an *encuentro milonguero* is an exclusive event for experienced dancers. *Encuentros milongueros* have become so popular that nowadays there is one almost every weekend somewhere in Europe.[10] Most major cities have their own annual *encuentro milonguero*, and some organizers even host more than one regular event per year. They are mostly privately organized by enthusiasts who want to bring the possibility of dancing for a whole weekend in *milonguero* style to their own locale. Organizers focus on providing a valuable tango experience to the participants rather than making a profit. In an interview, Liljana and Sabine, organizers of the Abrazos de Corazón, explain:

It came from the wish to have this great tango feeling which we had in Buenos Aires, and this feeling of being socially accepted as in Buenos Aires here as well. And not only for one milonga, but for a whole weekend.[11]

Since their beginnings, *encuentros milongueros* have featured an important element of travel. Participants enjoy the thrill of a tango journey and the opportunity to meet and dance with people from different regions and backgrounds who share the same passion for dancing tango in *milonguero* style. Martin, a tango blogger, describes the *encuentro milonguero* experience on his website:

I love the concept of *Encuentros*: close embrace, gender balanced, excellent Tango DJs and the best of all, seeing all the lovely places and cities in Europe and meet[ing] people from all over the world [who] have the same interest … *Tango Argentino*. So, I have travelled from the north of Europe (Norway) to the south (Sicily, Italy), [and] from the east (Poland) to the west (Portugal), to meet people with the same passion.[12]

Music, Dance, and Social Aspects of an Encuentro Milonguero

Organizers of *encuentros milongueros* in Europe have a clear idea of the music, dance, and social aspects they want to provide at their event. They often add one or two sentences to their online promotional pages to clarify what kind of tango experience a participant can expect. Not every *encuentro milonguero* mentions all the following distinct features in their advertisement. However, they all include several of them, and in combination they clearly describe not only what *encuentros milongueros* are like in Europe, but also provide insights into what they encompass culturally. These features include participation by invitation; balanced number of leaders and followers; employed *códigos milongueros* (milonga codes) to ask for dances; rules on the dance floor; dancing in close embrace; good (wooden) dance floor; Golden Age tango music; structure of the music played; and a selection of international tango DJs.[13]

Participation by Invitation

Encuentros milongueros restrict access from the beginning of the registration process. Anyone interested in the event must first register to be considered as a participant. Registration usually starts several months before the event, and about 90 percent of interested dancers register within the first two days. From this pool of registrants, organizers select as many participants as they can accommodate, typically between 100 and 250 dancers depending on the size of the dance floor. Each organizer has their own rules and criteria for selecting participants. While this may be, for example, to include a wide variety of dancers from different regions, in general, organizers choose dancers they know and who are integrated into the *encuentro milonguero* community.[14] Beginner dancers are not allowed to participate, as well as those who are known to dance in a way that does not fit with the *milonguero* ethos. While dancers of all levels and styles are welcome at other types of tango events, like local milongas or international weekend festivals, *encuentro milonguero* organizers want to ensure that the level of dancing is high and homogenous at their events. They want to avoid situations that may occur at other tango events, where dancers of all levels mingle and create a hierarchy. Namely, the more advanced a dancer is, the pickier they are about selecting their partners. This causes less dancing for everyone and frustration if the "wrong" partner is selected (because they were unaware of the other's skill level). *Encuentro milonguero* organizers seek to avoid such situations, thereby guaranteeing a good dance experience for everyone involved. In turn, many interested registrants are rejected – not only those of a lower skill level, but also those who are just among the too many or unknown applicants. This pre-selection of dancers is probably one of the most obvious and fundamental differences between *encuentros milongueros* and all other forms of tango dance events.[15]

Balanced Number of Leaders and Followers

At many regular milongas, tango followers considerably outnumber leaders,[16] which in turn creates an imbalance of dancing opportunities. In this case, leaders have many opportunities to select their partners over the entire evening, but followers must wait for dances and, therefore, may sit more than they actually dance. Many followers complain about such situations; likewise, leaders feel equally uncomfortable. Leaders sometimes perceive having to dance as a "pressure to perform" more than they might if there were an equal number of leaders and followers. A pre-selected balance in leader and follower numbers ensures that all dancers have mathematically the same possibilities to dance. This balance, in turn, relaxes the atmosphere of the event. It removes feelings of pressure and disappointment, along with competition among followers, which is ever-present at events with an imbalanced leader-follower ratio.

Mirada *and* Cabeceo

In *tango argentino*, the *mirada* (gaze) and the *cabeceo* (nod) signify an invitation to dance.[17] Instead of the leader approaching the follower and asking directly for a dance as in some social dance forms, *milongueros* employ subtle communication from a distance. First, both leader and follower look around the dance space as they aim to make eye contact with a potential dance partner. If their gazes lock, the leader, and then the follower, nod slightly, and only then does the leader approach the follower. If a dancer meets someone's eye and is not interested in dancing with them, they may simply avert their eyes from the other person's gaze. This advantageous way of asking for dances offers follow-ers an escape route without having to decline verbally and avoids pressure from someone standing in front of them with an extended hand. It also reduces the disgrace leaders might feel if visibly rejected and forced to walk away from a person publicly. However, the game of *mirada* and *cabeceo* has to be learned and mastered, and it is not without problems and miscommunications. Self-consciousness, shyness, or bad eyesight can limit successful communication and an invitation to dance. *Mirada* and *cabeceo* are possibly the most important tango *códigos milongueros* that encompass the rules for social behavior off the dance floor. Their inclusion at *encuentros milongueros* has two reasons. First, it is a pragmatic way to ask for dances, giving both partners the same agency to ask and decline. Second, as a ritual stemming from the historical tango dance practice in Buenos Aires,[18] it adds to the historicity and perceived authenticity of the *tango argentino* event.

Respectful Dancing in the Ronda

The *ronda* (circle) refers to the flow of dancing couples at a milonga, where they move counterclockwise around the dance floor. If the dance floor is crowded, they form several lanes in concentric circles. To respect the flowing *ronda*, the dancing couple neither pushes the couple in front nor blocks the couple behind them. In addition, their movements do not risk hurting themselves or others, and they stay in their lane. The leader generally guides the couple's navigation, yet the follower might help, depending on their mutual preferences for dancing and communicating with their partner. The more crowded the dance floor, the harder it is to navigate in the *ronda*. Tango movements that consume space or bring the heels up are dangerous in such environments. Some *encuentro* organizers explicitly state that they expect dancers to "keep their heels on the floor" or have the ability to "dance in small spaces." Most issue more general statements that they expect dancers not to dance in a space-consuming or imperiling way by using the phrase "respectful dancing in the *ronda*."

Dancing in a Close Embrace

In *tango argentino*, a couple dances in an asymmetric hold. On one side, the partners hold hands; on the other, they embrace with the follower's arm over the leader's arm. Several variants of this hold in tango social dance are mainly differentiated by the distance between the two dancers. In an open embrace, the dancers maintain bodily contact only with their arms; in a semi-open embrace, their arms hold each other's bodies, resting on their partners' back; and in a close embrace, they wrap their embracing arms around their partner as far as they can reach, while maintaining close contact between their torsos from the sternum down to above the hipline. Furthermore, in a close embrace, the partners align their torsos slightly to the left, enabling them to hold their heads side-by-side and even connect with their right temples. A close embrace is the preferred – mainly the only – way of dancing at an *encuentro milonguero*. On a pragmatic level, the couple consumes less space in this hold, even as it limits their movements. It thereby fits ideally with the respectful dancing in the *ronda* and accommodates the limited space available for each couple.

In addition to these practical features, a close embrace facilitates other priorities in dancing, especially how *milongueros* value the intense connection with their partners and the intimate expression of the music together. For them, it is more important that the dancing feels good rather than looks good, and a close embrace enhances the feeling of connection with their partner. Finally, most dancers perceive dancing in a close embrace to be more traditional than any other tango dance style, adding to the felt authenticity and codes expected at an *encuentro milonguero*.[19]

Good (Wooden) Dance Floor

Milongueros prefer dance floors made of wood, which lessens the strain on the body and joints. Dancing for four hours straight at each milonga can cause considerable pain in the feet, legs, and back, especially for women wearing stiletto high-heeled dance shoes.[20] Additionally, the average *milonguero* is of advanced age compared to the average at festivals and marathons. Ideally, they like to dance on a sprung wooden dance floor, which is neither too slippery nor too sticky, to enable easy and safe stepping and pivoting.

Golden Age Tango Music

Dancers within the *tango argentino* practice understand that "traditional" tango music describes music played at milongas in Buenos Aires during the Golden Age.[21] At that time, many *orquestas típicas* (tango orchestras) regularly played live music for a dancing crowd, and they disseminated their 78 RPM recordings (78s) to the public and aired them on Argentine radio stations.[22] As tango declined after 1955, *tango argentino* practice entered a dormant period during which tango music developed into a concert form for a listening, not a dancing, audience.

This division between music and dance practice continued until the 1980s, when the revival of tango dancing in Argentina and Europe started. As a critical number of people began to practice tango music and dance actively, many dancers considered contemporary tango music to be undanceable, while some musicians felt limited in their musical expressions if they had to play for dancers.[23] Therefore, most dancers – particularly those who dance at *encuentros milongueros* – prefer the recorded Golden Age tango music in dance contexts. Additionally, the sounds of these recordings sonically revive the historical time and place in Buenos Aires that *milongueros* see as the cradle and origin of their dancing.[24] Moreover, as they are well acquainted with these recordings, *milongueros* cherish the music they can predict and recognize.

Selected International DJs

Tango DJ'ing is the youngest of all *tango argentino* disciplines and the last to reach Europe. The establishment of professional DJs marks an important element of the European *tango argentino* culture, and it only dates to the 1990s when it was imported directly from Buenos Aires. Although during the Golden Age, recorded dance music on 78s circulated to the public and amplification was strong enough to cover a room when played for a dancing crowd, the art and profession of a tango DJ as a celebrated music expert is a rather recent phenomenon and part of the tango dance revival.

While international tango festivals may include live music played for dancing and exhibitions by the invited tango dance teachers, tango DJs are the only advertised highlights at *encuentros milongueros*. None of the European tango DJs are professional, instead, all have day jobs. Nevertheless, if well established, they can be very busy traveling each weekend to a different event by invitation. Tango DJs come from all European countries, and organizers usually ensure that the DJs at their events are among those known for a good performance, which means primarily serving the crowd well.[25] In the last decade, tango DJs have started specializing in DJ'ing at marathons, festivals, or *encuentros milongueros* – though, of course, many do provide their services at all kinds of events. Being an *encuentro milonguero* DJ means having a thorough knowledge of Golden-age tango music,[26] being well-versed in combining tracks and orchestras into a coherent flow, and having a sense of the dancers' mood.[27] Ultimately, they provide a selection of music that will make the whole room dance continuously and offer something for every taste. Advertising their "selected *encuentro* DJs" helps organizers to lure dancers to an *encuentro milonguero*, because they know they can expect expert Golden Age DJ'ing.

Tandas *and* Cortinas

Typically, DJs organize a *tanda* in groups of four pieces in a row at an *encuentro milonguero*. A *tanda* is comprised of pieces by the same orchestra – often also of the same recording year – and conveys a unified mood or feeling to the dancers. Each *tanda* is followed by a *cortina* (curtain), a piece of music with a fundamentally different character from tango most import-antly, which does not inspire tango dancing. With this clear sonic break, the *cortina* signals the end of one *tanda* and the beginning of a new one. In addition to these sets, the DJ imposes a meta-structure on top of the *tanda-cortina* alteration that embraces the three distinct rhythms of the tango genre: tango in 4/4 meter, *vals* (waltz) in 3/4, and *milonga* in 2/4. After two sets of tango *tandas*, the DJ will play a *milonga tanda*, followed by two more tango *tandas*, and then a *vals tanda*.[28]

Several different theories trace the origins of the *tanda-cortina* structure, including the way tango orchestras were broadcasted in fifteen-minute sets on the radio,[29] the duration of dances men paid for with employed ladies at dance houses,[30] and the number of 78s that could be played in a row (four, counting the front and back sides of two records).[31] Although similar structures of the *tanda-cortina* concept date back to the late 1920s, *tandas*, as used today, most likely originated in the 1960s in Buenos Aires.[32] In Europe, the *tanda-cortina* way of DJ'ing started in the late 1990s and became established at milongas in the first decade of the twenty-first century. This approach to DJ'ing is now seen as the most "traditional" and conventional way to play music at a milonga.[33]

In an interview with Horacio Godoy, the famed tango DJ from Buenos Aires, he conveyed his main reasons for playing tango music in *tandas* with *cortinas*, namely, to ensure diversity in musical styles throughout one evening, to satisfy tango enthusiasts with different tastes, and to enable a transition between different orchestras and their musical styles.[34] These musical reasons closely connect to one important social rule of *milonguero códigos*, which is to change partners regularly. Tango DJ and author Michael Lavocah states that "in a traditional milonga, everyone changes partners when the *cortina* comes, so the length of the *tanda* is social as well as musical – it is the length of time that the couple spends together."[35] Therefore, if *encuentro* organizers advertise that the music will be played in *tandas* and *cortinas* at their events, it conveys information to dancers about how the music will be grouped and how the social norm of changing partners regularly and simultaneously will be applied.

Conclusion: A Matter of (European) Perspective

Many European tango dancers engage in blogs and social media discussion groups around the pros and cons of the *encuentro milonguero*.[36] Critics of the *encuentro milonguero* concept oppose its elitist and exclusive atmosphere. They see the selection of participants and the rather strict application of *códigos milongueros* regarding social, music, and dance aspects as negative factors. They believe that *encuentros milongueros* foster a single way of dancing and practicing tango; therefore, these events diminish alternative dance styles, ways to interact at a milonga, and music choices. In addition, critics view *encuentros milongueros* as a reason why local milongas might decline. Good dancers may stop dancing locally, and less experienced dancers might be cut off in their development because they cannot mingle with experienced dancers at milongas.

Encuentro milonguero organizers and dancers are aware of such criticism and admit to the problems that might derive from their practice. Liljana and Sabine, for instance, see a danger in more experienced dancers not dancing locally anymore, which hinders beginner and intermediate dancers from learning from experienced dancers at local *prácticas* (tango practice sessions) and milongas and might disconnect them from established *milonguero* networks.[37] However, while some tango dancers who regularly attend *encuentros milongueros* have indeed stopped or reduced dancing in their home tango environment, many dancers still practice locally. They may even bring new, promising dancers into *encuentro milonguero* networks by recommending them to organizers for acceptance. In addition, some organizers accept a certain percentage of less experienced dancers to avoid separation between tango dance communities. Some organize open-to-the-public milongas before and after the *encuentro milonguero*, where visitors and local dancers mingle.

While the *encuentro milonguero* practice remains exclusive – and is criticized for it – those who are a part of the *encuentro milonguero* community in Europe consider it to be welcoming and liberating. They appreciate the predictability at *encuentros milongueros*, including the music, the people, the style of dancing, the level of dance experience, and the *códigos*. Such rules offer a structure to navigate socially and aesthetically a milonga without having to experiment or be disappointed. Another liberating aspect discussed by *milonguero* dancers is that they are watched less on the dancefloor at *encuentros milongueros*. Paola believes, "Because ... [at a festival or regular milonga] it's like an exam. I don't dance relaxed, I am watched, and I'm judged, and I don't want to be. I want to be relaxed and dance. I feel that in the *encuentro*; you can do it."[38] Additionally, tango dancers who regularly travel and dance at *encuentros milongueros* know each other well and look forward to meeting again. While the main reason for them to meet is to dance, regardless of whether they speak the same language or remember each other's names, sometimes friendships develop out of tango acquaintances. Of course, dancers at *encuentros milongueros* also dance with others they do not know yet, because part of tango's thrill is to dance with someone unknown and come to know them through embodied communication.

Such differences of perspective between the elitist demeanor and exclusivity, on the one hand, and the relaxed and liberating atmosphere, on the other, naturally depend on whether a dancer is an *encuentro milonguero* dancer or not. The *encuentro milonguero* is either judged as an elitist development in the wrong direction or viewed as a way to connect to like-minded and abled dancers in a nonhierarchical setting. Regardless of what social tango dancers judge it to be, the *encuentro milonguero* tradition has become an important fixture of European *tango argentino* practice in the early twenty-first century. It was conceptualized to bring experienced *milonguero* dancers together who are otherwise scattered in many places all over Europe. Thus, *encuentros milongueros* significantly support the translocal networks of *tango argentino* social dancing in Europe. Through its conceptualization, the *encuentro milonguero* nurtures *tango argentino* dance and music from the Golden Age and Buenos Aires, yet over the years, it has turned into a contemporary and distinctly European tradition. In doing so, the *encuentro milonguero* remains closely connected to Argentine tango practice while expanding the translocal dimension of *tango argentino*.

Notes

1. My own experiences as a tango dancer for two decades, deeply embedded in the central European *tango argentino* dance community, inform my understanding of the phenomena described in this chapter. I want to thank my fellow dancers for their time and enthusiasm, and for sharing their insights, stories, and tango with me. Editors' note: *tango argentino* broadly refers to the traditional tango dance from Argentina.
2. For more information, see Ramón Pelinski, *El tango nomade. Ensayos sobra la diáspora del tango* (Corregidor: Buenos Aires, 2000); and Jo Baim, *Tango: Creation of a Cultural Icon* (Bloomington: Indiana University Press, 2007), 52–86.
3. For the development of social dance styles, see Gustavo Benzecry Sabá, *The Quest for the Embrace: The History of Tango Argentino* (Stuttgart: Abrazos, 2010) and Laura Falcoff, "El Baile del Tango Ayer, Hoy y Mañana," in *El Tango Ayer y Hoy*, ed. Coriún Aharonián (Montevideo: Banda Oriental, 2014), 40–42.

4. Movement researchers generally use the term "embodied movement" to refer to knowledge on a physical level. Here, I refer to how dancers do not think about the interpretation, but rather react physically in response to the music. Such improvisation in dance is based on embodied knowledge that has been acquired with experience and transferred into muscle memory as well as through the trained ability to react physically to outside influences like partner, space, and music. Thus, the movement knowledge necessary to carry out joint improvisation has been "embodied." For more information, see Michael Kimmel, "A Cognitive Theory of Joint Improvisation: The Case of Tango Argentino," in *The Oxford Handbook of Improvisation in Dance*, ed. Vida L. Midgelow (New York: Oxford University Press, 2019).

5. See Kendra Stepputat, "Tango Journeys: Going on a Pilgrimage to Buenos Aires," in *Dance. Senses. Urban Contexts*, ed. Kendra Stepputat (Aachen: Shaker Verlag, 2017); and Kendra Stepputat and Elina Djebbari, "The Separation of Music and Dance in Translocal Contexts," *the world of music (new series)* 9, no. 2 (2020): 5–9.

6. For more information, see María Julia Carrozzi, *Aquí se baila el tango: Una etnografía de las milongas porteñas* (Buenos Aires: Siglo Veintiuno Editores, 2015), 160–164; Christine Denniston, *The Meaning of Tango: The Story of the Argentine Tango* (London: Portico Books, 2007), 200; Carolyn Merritt, *Tango Nuevo* (Gainesville: University Press of Florida, 2012), 75; Elia Petridou, "Experiencing Tango as It Goes Global," in *Tango in Translation*, ed. Gabriele Klein (Bielefeld: transcript Verlag, 2009), 62; Ana C. Cara, "Entangled Tangos: Passionate Displays, Intimate Dialogues," *The Journal of American Folklore* 122, no. 486 (Fall 2009): 440.

7. For related links, see *Tango Florido*, www.scuolatangofirenze.it; *Milongueando France*, www.milongueandofrance.com; *BibleTango*, www.bibletango.com/tangoatlas/tgatlas_detail/detatlas_06/milongueando_france_06_detatlas.htm; and *Tangokombinat*, www.tangokombinat.de.

8. Interview with Paola di Venezia aka Paola Nocitango, Bad Gleichenberg, Austria, August 2019.

9. See *Nocitango*, www.nocitango.it/italiano/eventi-passati/1-raduno-milonguero-6-9dicembre2012.

10. In 2020 and 2021, *encuentros* were canceled due to the COVID-19 pandemic. As vaccination rates have risen since this writing, people have dared to travel and dance in close embrace again.

11. Video interview with Sabine Oberscheider and Lilijana Maric, July 19, 2021, "Entstanden ist es einfach aus dem Wunsch dass wir dieses tolle tango Gefühl was wir in Buenos Aires gehabt haben, und dieses sich sozial so akzeptiert fühlen [. . .] wie in Buenos Aires, uns hergewünscht haben. Und das halt nicht nur für eine milonga, sondern ein ganzes Wochenende."

12. See *Tango-International*, www.tango-international.eu/info.html.

13. While most *encuentros* advertise their event via Facebook, a few have a public website with statements as mentioned above. Examples include La Colmena in Copenhagen (Denmark), La Colmena, www.anem.dk/lacolmena/milonguero-codes; Pequeña in Saarbrücken (Germany), Tangokominat, www.tangokombinat.de; Noches de Invierno in Bad Reichenau (Austria), Noches de Invierno, www.nochesdeinvierno.com; Noche de Pasión in Regensburg (Germany), Noche de Pasion, www.nochedepasion.net; Días de Juventud in Ljubljana (Slovenia), Tango.si, www.tango.si/dias-de-juventud; and Boca in Antwerp (Belgium), Encuentro Boca Antwerp, sites.google.com/view/encuentro-boca-antwerp.

14. For more information, see Kendra Stepputat, Wolfgang Kienreich, and Christopher Dick, "Digital Methods in Intangible Cultural Heritage Research: A Case Study in Tango Argentino," *ACM Journal on Computing and Cultural Heritage* 12, no. 2 (June 2019): 1–22.

15. A tango marathon also has restricted access. The differentiation between a tango marathon and *encuentro milonguero* is blurry; adding to the indistinctness, one could say that an *encuentro* is more "*milonguero.*"

16. For discussions of gender roles, see Kathy Davis, *Dancing Tango: Passionate Encounters in a Globalizing World* (New York: New York University Press, 2015); Jeffrey Tobin, "Models of Machismo: The Troublesome Masculinity of Argentine Male Tango Dancers," in *Tango in Translation*, ed. Gabriele Klein (Bielefeld: transcript Verlag, 2009); and Mercedes Liska, "The Geopolitics of Queer Tango: From Buenos Aires to a Community of Translocal Practice," in *Made in Latin America: Studies in Popular Music*, edited by Julio Mendívil and Christian Spencer Espinosa (New York: Routledge, 2016), 125–134. Though the vast majority at *encuentros milongueros* are male leaders and female followers, a certain percentage does break with the norm. Dancing the opposite role or interchanging roles is welcomed and integrated without hesitation.

17. Gustavo Benzecry Sabá, *New Glossary of Tango Dance: Key Tango Argentino Dance Terms* (Stuttgart: Abrazos, 2010), 20.

18. Merritt, *Tango Nuevo*, 75.

19. Close-embrace tango today is quite different from *tango argentino* during the Golden Age. For insights into the close embrace, "*estilo milonguero,*" and its perceived authenticity, see Petridou, *Experiencing Tango*, 63–64; Janine Krüger, *¿Cuál es tu tango? Musikalische Lesarten der argentinischen Tangotradition* (Münster: Waxmann Verlag GmbH, 2012), 189; and Carozzi, *Aquí se baila el tango*, 139.

20. Interestingly, none of the *códigos* at *encuentros milongueros* concern clothing. For insights into tango fashion, aesthetics, and meaning, see Elia Petridou, "Dancing in High Heels: A Material Culture Approach to Argentine Tango," in *Social Matter(s): Recent Approaches to Materiality*, ed. Tryfon Bampilis and Pieter ter Keurs (Münster: LIT Verlag, 2014), 91–116.

21. For an introduction to tango music and its Golden Age, see Kacey Link and Kristin Wendland, *Tracing* Tangueros: *Argentine Tango Instrumental Music* (New York: Oxford University Press, 2016).

22. See Matthew B. Karush, *Culture of Class: Radio and Cinema in the Making of a Divided Argentina, 1920–1946* (Durham: Duke University Press, 2012), 45–52.

23. For a thorough analysis of the separation and reconnection of tango music and dance in the second half of the twentieth century, see Kendra Stepputat, "Tango Musicality and Tango Danceability: Reconnecting Strategies in Current Cosmopolitan Tango Argentino Practice," *the world of music (new series)* 9, no. 2 (2020): 51–68.

24. See also Stepputat, *Tango Journeys*, for an introduction to the phenomenon of the tango pilgrimage to Buenos Aires. For a critical account of the "sacralization" of the Golden Age music, see Carozzi, *Aquí se baila el tango*, 107–113.

25. Over the last ten years, I have conducted more than twenty interviews with DJs in Europe, in some cases following their development from their first milonga gigs to international fame. One important topic in this ongoing research is how they negotiate their role and position as service provider, performer, and educator. In a recent publication, I also investigate the mechanics of how tango DJs influence the translocal tango networks in Europe concerning taste in music, through the selection of the music they play at a milonga (see Stepputat, *Digital Methods*).

26. Elia Petridou, *Experiencing Tango*, 64.

27. See also Csongor Kicsi, "The Impact of the Golden Age Period on the World of the Argentine Tango Community," *Bulletin of the Transilvania University of Brașov Series VIII: Performing Arts*, 13 (62) no. 1 (2020): 109, doi: https://doi.org/10.31926/but.pa.2020.13.62.1.12.

28. The abbreviation used often to communicate about the structure a DJ plays is "T-T-M-T-T-V."

29. "The Birth of the Tanda: A 'Radial' View (Part 1)," *Tango Decoder*, https://tangodecoder.wordpress.com/2015/10/06/the-birth-of-the-tanda/.

30. "A Note on the Origin of Tandas," *Tango Decoder*, https://tangodecoder.wordpress.com/2015/10/02/a-note-on-the-origin-of-tandas/.

31. See blog "Tango en el Espejo," which delves into tango lyrics about the origins of *tandas* and *cortinas*, https://elespejero.wordpress.com/2015/07/09/tango-stories-la-victrolera-and-danza-maligna.

32. The question "on the origin of *tandas*" by member Olli Eyding in the "Tango DJ Forum" Facebook group (posted May 4, 2019) led to detailed expert discussions among DJs. It featured personal insights and theories as well as pointing to additional material and paraphrasing dancers and DJs who experienced the Golden Age and post–Golden Age milongas.

33. Also see Merritt, *Tango Nuevo*, 75.

34. Interview with Horacio Godoy, Vienna, Austria, May 2014.
35. Michael Lavocah, "Tango DJing – Part 1: Music for dancing," *Todotango*, www.todotango.com/english/history/chronicle/481/Tango-DJing-Part-1:-Music-for-dancing.
36. Since such discussions take place in the safe space of closed groups, I will neither explicitly reference any of these discussions here nor highlight selected personal opinions of individuals that could be perceived as offensive.
37. Video interview with Sabine and Liljana, July 19, 2021.
38. Interview with Paola di Venezia, Bad Gleichenberg, Austria, August 2019.

Further Reading

Benzekry Sabá, Gustavo. 2015. *The Quest for the Embrace: The History of Tango Dance 1800–1983*. Urquillo: Editorial Abrazos.

Carozzi, María Julia. *Aquí se baila el tango: Una etnografía de las milongas porteñas.* Buenos Aires: Siglo Veintiuno Editores, 2015.

Denniston, Christine. *The Meaning of Tango: The Story of the Argentine Tango.* London: Portico Books, 2007.

Kimmel, Michael. "A Cognitive Theory of Joint Improvisation: The Case of Tango Argentino." In *The Oxford Handbook of Improvisation in Dance* edited by Vida L. Midgelow, 563–591. New York: Oxford University Press, 2019.

Lavocah, Michael. *Tango Stories: Musical Secrets.* Norwich: Milonga Press, 2014.

Liska, Mercedes. "The Geopolitics of Queer Tango: From Buenos Aires to a Community of Translocal Practice." In *Made in Latin America: Studies in Popular Music*, edited by Julio Mendívil and Christian Spencer Espinosa, 125–134. New York: Routledge, 2016.

"Dancing in High Heels: A Material Culture Approach to Argentine Tango." In *Social Matter(s): Recent Approaches to Materiality*, edited by Tryfon Bampilis and Pieter ter Keurs, 91–116. Münster: LIT Verlag, 2014.

Stepputat, Kendra. "Tango Musicality and Tango Danceability: Reconnecting Strategies in Current Cosmopolitan Tango Argentino Practice." *the world of music (new series) 9*, no. 2 (2020): 51–68.

"Tango Journeys: Going on a Pilgrimage to Buenos Aires." In *Dance. Senses. Urban Contexts: Proceedings of the 29th Symposium of the ICTM Study Group on Ethnochoreology*, edited by Kendra Stepputat, 195–205. Aachen: Shaker Verlag, 2017.

Stepputat, Kendra, and Elina Djebbari. "The Separation of Music and Dance in Translocal Contexts." *world of music (new series) 9*, no. 2 (2020): 5–30.

13 | Re-imagining the Future of Tango Dance

CAROLYN MERRITT

> However we choose to think of the social body, we are each other's
> environment.
>
> Eula Biss, *On Immunity: An Inoculation*[1]

Moments of passage in our lives, alongside and across boundaries and borders, invite an awareness and openness that transcend the everyday. A year into the COVID-19 pandemic, in April 2021, it surprised me to encounter this feeling at a vaccination hub. I traced the ribbon of its clockwork lines, submitted to ID and temperature checks, and responded to rote interrogations on the state of my health, my social interactions, and my body's response to injections. I did all of this for the promise on the other side of inoculation. When I departed the spaced huddle to stride alone through a cavernous block to the door, my body vibrated with memories of travel – of airports and checkpoints with their strange mix of adventure and bureaucracy, and of passport stamps with their physical mark and cosmic imprint. My skin was alive with its contradictions – the point at which I am me, and where my edges dissolve and open to something larger.

In the pandemic year, I grieved for the milonga, a place where social tango dancers gather with real bodies in real time and space, where I go walking for this sensation. Tango as dance promises little more than potential – for connection, bliss, trance, transcendence, whatever we wish to call these moments that shift our experience of self and bring us into communion. Like oases, these moments bring vibrant life, offering us visions of salvation, but they ultimately evaporate. Even so, their memories take root in the body. They have nourished many of us through the losses of an exceptional year: trips canceled, projects delayed, work gone, tours cut short, and nights on end in isolation; still worse, a year of friends and family lost, and the distant branches of a global family felled.

In this chapter, I consider my two-decade love affair with tango, which began during my first days as an anthropology graduate student in 2002. Tango soon became my work, and through the early aughts, I conducted ethnographic research on contemporary tango dance in the United States and Argentina. Utilizing anthropology's primary methodology of field-work, I became a participant observer in tango's global community, travel-ing to dance tango and conduct research in cities along the US northeast corridor and west coast. I spent two years in its mecca, Buenos Aires, and made subsequent follow-up visits to live tango there. Along the way, I took tango classes and participated in social dance events, collected stories and conducted interviews, and carried out archival research and visual docu-mentation. I navigated the somewhat bipolar existence of an anthropolo-gist, at once immersed inside the community and observing it from the outside as a social scientist. The result of that labor, my book *Tango Nuevo*,[2] reads as both a love letter to and an interrogation of this intimate partner dance.

Years later, in the late 2010s, I was a young mother struggling to fit this nocturnal love into my new reality. With less time to commit, I grew frustrated with the struggles many women face with tango, including ageism and gender imbalance. I dove into lessons in leading, only to pause in the wake of COVID-19. In this interim, the power of tango's suspension gained new meaning. Politically generative, its prolonged colli-sion with other pandemics begs a deeper examination into tango's evolu-tion. To embrace again, we must ask what we owe one another and how we might chart a better future. Or, in the language of anthropology, we must transform tango's culture while preserving its essence.

Leading, Following, and Interrogating Dichotomies

A Philadelphia Milonga and #metoo, 2018

I arrive at the milonga late and tired. It is a quiet night, the leaders I hope to dance with are not there, and I resign myself to socializing. I sit at a table with two women who are older than I. A man I have never seen before appears on the periphery of my vision, and despite my effort to keep talking, his cabeceo (head nod) is unrelenting.[3] After we dance to a song, he places a hand on my waist as we talk. I wiggle away to increase the space between us. He then takes my hand, not to dance but to hold on to me while chatting between songs. I pull my hand away. "Thank you," the polite tango exit strategy, is on the tip of my tongue, but instead I say, "I don't even know your name."

I wonder if the women I chatted with had danced much. If he'd invited them earlier or if he would have asked one of them had I not been there. I wonder what gave him the impression my agreeing to dance meant he could touch me as if I were his date. In a moment, I will embrace this man and rest my chest against his. Perhaps that confuses him, and perhaps confusion is a pretense. The incident itself is nothing. The behavior could have been – has been – much worse. But in the time of #metoo, where women join together to challenge sexual harassment and sexual violence, it nags at me in a way that feels different. My tolerance is low. I have been at this too long. I am too old for this, I think.

After years of dancing and multiple short-lived attempts at leading, I signed on as a leader in the beginner track at the 2018 Philadelphia Tango Festival. From 2019 into early 2020, I gathered a group of women to practice leading together. I discovered momentum and began writing about my experience. Then COVID-19 arrived. Sheltered at home with a partner who towers over me by a foot and nearly twice my weight, and our young homeschooler, I admitted defeat. We dabbled in virtual classes; I attended occasional online lectures, community meetings, music concerts, and virtual milongas. In the extended limbo created by the pandemic, I revisited tango lessons past and pondered the future.

Beginner Intensive, 2018 Philadelphia Tango Festival

Two women, Kristin Balmer and Barbara Kountouzi, lead the beginner track, guiding us through social rules, mechanics, and concepts rather than steps or sequences. We learn the cabeceo. *We partner palm-to-palm to avoid any temptation to push or pull, and to learn how to balance and be responsible for our own weight. We walk in counter-clockwise circles to the tune of floorcraft: no passing, the outer edge of the floor is safest, maintain distance from the next couple as if you're driving a car, and move forward when there is space. We do not embrace until day three; Balmer and Kountouzi take their time and talk explicitly. The leader's right hand rests behind the follower's scapula, not the low back, waist, or butt: "Leaders, do not EVER touch the follower's butt!" It should not wrap fully around the follower's side and inch for more: "Leaders, this is not an opportunity for side boob!" They implore followers not to fall onto the leader, stroke the leader's hair, or use tango to throw themselves at someone. They offer intervention tactics: physically establish more space in the embrace; verbally state "I'd prefer if we open the embrace a little more" when a partner ignores physical cues; say "thank you" and exit the floor when neither of these strategies works and you feel unsafe or too uncomfortable to finish the* tanda (song set).[4]

None of the women raise questions. One man is flummoxed over the prospect of a sloppy follower. This isn't news for many of us, whether we have experience in other partner forms or not. What is new for me, in tango, is a frank discussion of violations that occur all too often, that I figured out through observation, trial and error, conversations on the sidelines, venting sessions with tango friends, and my own maturation in tango and in life.

Being in a beginner class brought back memories of my beginning: when nearly every dance was good, when I wanted miles under my belt, when I struggled to discern what I was experiencing and seeing. And when I was ripe for predators. Over time, I learned what to watch for and avoid. I developed a bit of armor and cultivated an attitude supported less by skill level than by survival instinct. Like most followers, I have wrestled with leaders on the dance floor and in classes. Indeed, like countless others, I've been "dance-raped" in tango: groped, harassed, made to feel uncomfortable or unsafe, and had my physical and verbal cues ignored. I once watched someone give up on tango after her first evening. She was accosted by a man all evening, sought refuge in the bathroom, and asked me to coordinate her exit rather than re-enter the milonga to find her ride home.

I have also been desperate to dance – to lose myself in the moment, to embrace someone on a crowded dance floor, and to move together to music and lyrics from another time and place that I have gradually adopted as my own. That desperation has bred innumerable wonderful dances, countless nights that have lingered past sunrise because the dancing was so good and the evening and the world of the milonga so vibrant. Only years into my practice did I begin to reckon with my capacity for desperation, and my desire for experience for its own sake. I let things roll off me like water because I had arrived remarkably unscathed. From the beginning, I approached tango as a dancer and researcher. I moved to Buenos Aires and embraced the anthropological tenet of cultural relativism.[5] I found value in "meeting people where they are" as I moved through a city and a culture different from my own. My openness opened doors. People invited me into their homes, shared stories of their lives, and taught me to dance, hear, see, and understand tango as a way of life.

I cannot count the number of times I was physically escorted from my seat to the dancefloor and back by a leader in Buenos Aires. Some leaders do it here. We practiced this in the beginner intensive but were also instructed to listen to one another's cues. I find it corny, but do not mind when a friend retains hold of my hand between songs. An Argentine friend often sings in my ear while we dance. I wonder now which came first – our friendship or my love for his singing. I also wonder how others interpret such behaviors. And I wonder where the line is, between embodying culture and co-opting it, to test the waters with a partner in a way that would not be acceptable outside tango.

A Tango Festival on the East Coast of the United States, 2012

Two young men who usually partner with women perform together, exchanging lead and follow roles. All of it leaves me speechless – explosive jumps and turns, subtle weight shifts, the absence of stasis in each pause, the way they devour the space, even in the milliseconds when a leg or foot or a torso hovers above an audience member's head – and a bit discouraged for being so outdone by these men who dabble, at best, in following. They invite a handful of men friends from the audience to join in a song. They sing for two minutes about penises and how blessed they are to have them. Never in question, the masculinity of the man who follows has nonetheless been restored.

This lovely surprise – the possibility of their duet performed with none of the face-saving humor some men scrabble to perform in public moments of same-sex closeness – evaporates with the song. What we are left with is more of the same.

Once labeled "the vertical expression of a horizontal desire,"[6] tango is famously linked to brothels and often reduced to heterosexual passion. This belies its origins among men in late 1800s Buenos Aires and Montevideo (Fig. 13.1). When explaining these roots, historians often emphasize the region's population growth during a period of heightened immigration, when men came in search of work and often left women and families behind, as well as tango's scandalous profile. Men *had* to dance together is the unspoken implication, because it was "unfit for ladies" and there were so few women. But making invisible does not erase. Images from the early 1900s show women dancing together (WP 13.1).[7]

In the mid-1900s, young boys were bodies to be practiced on – they danced with older men and learned to lead after they had mastered following.[8] During tango's Golden Age (1930s–1950s), women interpreted some of the most memorable recordings, some dressed in drag, such as Azucena Maizani.[9]

Modern efforts to transcend tango's stereotypically macho profile include open-role dancing, the exchange of lead and follow roles, gay milongas, and queer tango. In the early aughts in Philadelphia, several men verbally attacked me when a woman friend from out of town "monopolized" their coveted followers once she realized there were few men she wanted to follow. By 2021, Philadelphia's many women teachers were leading in the classroom and on the dance floor, and the ranks of women learning to lead has continued to grow. That men rarely

Figure 13.1 Two men dancing tango together, 1903.

dance together socially, even if they often partner in classes, speaks to the differences in how same-sex couplings are perceived. And as young people embrace fluid and nonbinary identities, simple dichotomies of gender are increasingly outdated if tenacious.

In Buenos Aires, same-sex partnering and role exchange were once relegated to specifically sanctioned gay or queer spaces, or to class and practice settings. By the late 2010s, however, more women began leading socially, teaching, and performing solo – a phenomenon that scholars have attributed to LGBTQ- and trans-positive legislation, globalized tango commerce, and the growing international queer tango movement.[10] Back in the early aughts, the Argentine women I encountered explained leading only as a skill to earn a living, or as a last resort to avoid sitting, while some men disparaged women leaders as "ugly" or unnatural. But, in a recent Zoom chat with professionals Ines Muzzopappa and Gaby Mataloni, they professed no qualms whatsoever about "going out and having a great time following women only."[11]

Once COVID-19 quarantine restrictions were lifted in Spring 2021, I stood on the sidelines of an outdoor milonga with an elegant elder woman who praised my newfound commitment to leading and observed, "many of the women lead better than the men, don't you think?" As I watched her following a woman later, I pondered the paths to transformation. Gender imbalance and ageism have long plagued women in tango – it is still common for women to outnumber men and for older women to sit more at social dance events.[12] Now I wonder if these issues might inspire jettisoning outdated codes. Local dancers Mary Jane Pahls and Bob Bridges began dancing later in life and are learning both roles – Pahls to avoid sitting, and her husband to support her. In the process, Bridges experiences increased "appreciation and empathy for followers."[13] Though Argentina's elder *milongueros/tangueros* do not describe their training with the politicized language of inclusion,[14] the majority would likely see the wisdom of this approach because that was their experience. Indeed, some elder men dancers I met during my early fieldwork questioned why men no longer learn to follow first. They argued that the tradition ensures leaders will be more sensitive to their partners' needs and contributions because they know how it feels to follow.

Nada Nuevo (Nothing New): Philadelphia Tango Festival, 2018

A male MC introduces Gustavo Naveira and Fabián Salas (the festival headliners, along with their partners, Giselle Anne and Lola Diaz). Together, Naveira and Salas were central figures in reviving interest in tango dance in the late 1980s, when it had fallen out of fashion. When I interviewed Naveira years back, he openly acknowledged the role women played in the dance's evolution. Yet, watching the MC introduce the men at the festival opening while ignoring the women seated beside them, I am reminded of the macho culture that still thrives within tango.

On festival websites and in class and workshop advertisements, instructors' names often appear in leader-follower order. Whether alphabetic, established marketing, or random, this tiny fact speaks volumes. In a profile of Tango Hembra, Buenos Aires' first women-only international festival, journalist Charis McGowan underscores inequities that inspired the event:

Men … almost exclusively hold higher-powered positions in the industry, from festival-management to radio-production roles. Women in tango, although integral to performances, are often sidelined; accounting for fewer than 15 percent of those billed on festival lineups.[15]

Similarly inspired, feminist activists created Buenos Aires' milonga La Furiosa, a relaxed event free of social codes like the *cabeceo* and heteronormative pairings, to save tango from becoming a "caricature of the patriarchy."[16] In my conversation with Gaby Mataloni and Ines Muzzopappa, they depicted an industry culture where women depend upon men, in which women must work harder to establish ownership of their careers. Muzzopappa states: "In the beginning, when partnerships dissolved, I had to start over from scratch. Either the men left with the contacts, or if they shared them with me, the organizers wouldn't answer my messages"; and Mataloni states: "It still happens sometimes that the man keeps control of the contacts and takes a certain percentage of the couple's shared income for networking. The networking *is* work, but . . . "[17] They also described a sense of always being on trial as women leaders, a constant pressure to be excellent that is reminiscent of the struggles described by people of color, to always be *better than* in order to be recognized as simply equal, fully human.

In Spring 2020, technology allowed me to study with an intercontinental women-dominant teaching trio – Carla Marano (from Buenos Aires) with Natacha Lockwood and Octavio Fernández (both from Paris). Later I took an online class led by Muzzopappa and Mataloni, and I streamed a concert in which Muzzopappa exchanged lead and follow roles with Corina Herrera (WL 13.1). That the somewhat saturated world of tango accommodates solo and duo women teaching artists exemplifies the ever-shifting terrain.

During my time in Argentina, men dancers occasionally flirted with and infantilized me in interviews and conversations. In one of my first encounters with a mentor I grew to adore, he listened intently as I described my research project and then informed me, he had "never met such a beautiful woman with so many problems." I ate such comments up in the moment, and then jotted them down in my notebook afterward. When I explored these encounters as I pieced together my book, a mentor advised me to consider the cultural contours of Argentine men's behavior and argued that I might have missed out on much had I protested, shown offense, or shut down. Just as male dancers assess their partner's ability and adjust their movements on the dance floor, she argued, they gauged my ability to play along and shared or held back accordingly. I reacted with the humor at my disposal and a certain compassion for these men. To ignore the learned nature of their behaviors, cultivated in response to pressures of culture and economy alike, struck me as unimaginative. Acknowledging the transactional nature of my presence, I have tried to give back as much as I took. Still, I question all this theater with different eyes today.

Followership

> The physical carriage hauls more than its weight.
> Claudia Rankine, *Citizen: An American Lyric*[18]

A lone video on my phone recalls life before COVID-19. In a dark room punctuated by purple, blue, green flashes, I twirl in the arms of someone whose name I forget but whose smile I remember. A Monday night drink with a friend turned into an impulsive cab ride to a salsa club, a pact to leave after the lesson, yet a night of dancing until 2 a.m. A force on the dance floor, my friend does not practice any partner form. At a certain point, she declines repeated invitations, admiring the scene and overwhelmed by how "traditionally gendered" it is. I barely sit all night. A novice with a sense for following, I tell myself I know how to exit a bad situation; I no longer worry about doing it "gracefully."

As the evening progresses, my friend invites partners for me, including the night's very young star. I am disappointed but I don't end our song that borders on dance-rape. Instead, I make excuses: he doesn't like being invited, he doesn't dance with beginners. I leave wanting more; not of that, but everything else.

Nearly two years later, I scroll through my phone and stumble across this reminder of life before COVID-19. My jaw softens and my heart smiles when I encounter myself light and happy, a lifetime younger than the lines that mark my face, flight impulse gripping my nervous system. Now I cross streets to avoid crowds. I bristle when a neighboring patron pushes their chair toward mine at a cafe. I wonder if I'll ever dive in with both feet again, and how I'll react in a similar situation. I also wonder at terms like snowflake, at cruelty in response to the simple desire for safety, autonomy, and dignity.

With my background in ballet and modern dance, I made quick progress in my early tango lessons. I had a tendency to backlead, but I was not interested in leading myself. I liked the scene's embrace of femininity, both throwback and modern – the skirts and dresses, stockings and high heels, the backless shirts and harem pants. On a deeper level, I liked handing over responsibility. I watched skilled followers close their eyes, melt into the arms of accomplished leaders, shut out their surroundings, move effortlessly, and respond seamlessly. In retrospect, this interpretation is overly simplistic and ultimately inaccurate, but it was what I perceived at the time.

An aptitude for following can be confusing for women. In my prior research, I met women who struggled with the idea of following, others who found catharsis in the more "feminine" role, and others still who experienced both feelings and more. In more recent conversations with women who lead, the question of why I have not mastered leading after all these years hung in the air. I discovered a newfound literature on follower-ship in former tango professional Sharna Fabiano's *Lead and Follow*.[19] As Fabiano points out, we glorify leadership to a fault in the United States: advancement in the working world is vertical and pyramid shaped, and moving up almost inevitably means managing others. We have clear language, imagery, role models, and whole libraries dedicated to celebrat-ing leaders, while the skills required to follow elude us. In her new career as a life coach, Fabiano hears countless stories of this imbalance from clients. Tango dancers are "keepers of this wisdom, of the complementarity of both roles," she asserted in our conversation, noting that she wrote the book to "reclaim the value of the follower role, which is often responsible for maintaining the moral center of relationships."[20]

In my attempts at leading, doubt consumed me. The strength I harnessed to peacock my slight frame translated as tension. Once upon a time, my teacher intervened to show how leading should feel and I marveled at the effortlessness. In Spring 2021, as tango gradually reopened in Philadelphia, the lessons I took were words and imagery, demonstration and mimicry, but no contact. That so much translated speaks to the decades I have spent studying movement; that I longed for the hands-on assist, for the words and the sensations to collide in my body, speaks to the particular nature of tango, where the learning is in the doing with someone else. The most useful technique was the most challenging – to go with my mistakes. As I felt my intention derail, I needed to resist the temptation to stop, explain, or ask for a redo. Rather, I learned to go with whatever the follower made of it. I know how it feels when a leader tries to force me into something, whether a misreading on my part or insufficient execution on their part. I have no patience for instruction on the dance floor, and I have endless gratitude to leaders who disregard or make magic with my mistakes.

When I encourage friends to try tango, I emphasize its essence: you hug someone and you walk. I dismiss the idea that you need to do anything fancy. But I have struggled to heed this advice myself. Women leaders reminded me that leading is equal parts technique and navigation: do not wait too long to get on the floor, they warned, or you could fall apart amidst the circling crowd. Yet, I resisted inviting followers out of the fear I would waste their time. Reflecting on Juliet McMains' conversations with women leaders who only invite other women to dance if there are not enough men around,[21] this deferral to men and to the hetero binary of gender balance exasperates me even as I have remained in its grip. It recalls traditional codes like the *cabeceo*, and how they twist me into knots. After two decades, I still rarely verbally invite leaders to dance. There are some I might never ask, even if they would likely say yes, because I know they would not like my asking. That I prefer to be asked and that I will behave according to leaders' preferences – those I want to dance with, regardless of gender identity – is something I cannot ignore, that I struggle to change and to comprehend.

In a conversation with Fabiano, who always taught students to dance both roles, she described the "radically different experience of working with women only in retreats and workshops," where the energy was "totally different" and "mutually supportive."[22] While gender identity alone cannot shape an environment, Fabiano's description evokes the giddy women's practice sessions I held before COVID-19, where we shared excitement at one another's progress. Now I recall the lore of one-upmanship, the stories of men who pushed tango forward through homosocial competition, as I question how we should carry forward tango's past. I think of the leaders I adore and admire from afar, many of whom do not follow, and I wonder if they would not shine even brighter if they learned. I find notes from a conversation I had with a now forgotten *tanguerx* years back, and a line jumps from the page as if in accusation: "Anyone who is serious about the dance needs to know both roles."

Virtual Tango

> Our nervous systems know touch. They know closeness and a hug. And to not be able to do those things when people are really hurting has been a huge loss, and there's much grief there.
>
> Christine Runyan, "What's Happening in Our Nervous Systems?"[23]

Earth Virtual Milonga,[24] *April 2020*

I scroll through Zoom's gallery pages, scanning the squares for a face or name I recognize. A durational event featuring DJs from Los Angeles, Stockholm, Boston, and Tokyo, Earth Virtual Milonga is my first online dance party. Dancers tune in from around the world. I feel like an anthropologist on Mars – a tourist, an onlooker, a confounded participant observer in this mediated rite. Many attendees appear solitary. Several dance alone or substitute a pillow or doll or animal for a partner. A lucky few appear to be sheltering with a partner or friend who dances. The chat space fills with greetings, expressions of gratitude for pets, happiness at seeing other couples embrace in the flesh. It brings a smile to my face even as it breaks my heart.

Soon after the severity of COVID-19 became apparent, tango professionals the world over shifted all manner of activities online. Philadelphia Argentine Tango School (PATS) director Meredith Klein worked tirelessly to keep the community connected. She created work opportunities for tango professionals whose livelihood had disappeared through online classes, a lecture series, music concerts, and virtual festivals. I noticed my capacity for online events wane quickly. I felt resistance to the camera, to the invasion of my home space, to the pressure to consume, and to perform my fealty to tango in this quasi-panoptic space. I ran from oven to makeshift dance space and back as I combined preparing dinner for my family with Zoom tango classes. I tried to weigh the loss of focus and immersion against the benefits of multitasking, but that sort of mental calculus rang absurd.

In a conversation with psychologist and dancer Farrell Silverberg, he suggested that tango's next generation may increasingly look to virtual platforms for technique and practice. At the same time, he questioned the soullessness of virtual tango. Could it ever provide the highs we once chased from club to club and embrace to embrace until the wee hours of the morning, again and again? I am happy these platforms arose to connect dancers and generate modest support for artists who made their living in tango. Perhaps time will soften my resistance and warm me to the healing potential of tango without tactile human connection in real time and space.

I chatted with two couples who participate regularly in PATS online activities. April Dunleavy and Ross Alexander's tango involvement increased nearly twofold during the pandemic. Alexander asserted "tango has been more of a focus than almost anything else."[25] They highlighted silver linings for *tanguerx* living in relative comfort: incomparable access to world-class instructors, concerts, and lectures. Before leaving our Zoom room, they revealed shirts emblazoned with messages of hope and salvation: "We Will Embrace Again" and "Dancing Saved Me in 2020." Similarly, in a phone conversation with me, Mary Jane Pahls and Bob Bridges underscored advantages to online tango: they save hours once lost to commuting; they see instructors' every move clearly; instructors exercise greater clarity with language; and students can video themselves and self-correct by comparing to instructors' videos. While their initial impetus was to maintain momentum, students remain committed to Zoom classes as long as the option continues.

Safety and Inclusivity

Skin Hunger and Distanced Walks, Winter 2020–21

My new tango walk is at a distance. I rotate among tango friends as I once switched partners at the milongas. We meet in groups of two or three in parks, on city sidewalks, and in beautiful graveyards that call to mind pilgrimages to Recoleta and Chacarita cemeteries in Buenos Aires. Swapping stories with a tanguera *one day, we lament the labor of navigating relations with men dancers and teachers. In the pause, she finds clarity, strength, and emotional reserves, and she questions what space tango will occupy in her life going forward. As the pandemic drags on, moving discussions of skin hunger meet illuminating treatises on the preponderance of unwanted touch we are socialized to endure. The open-air strolling sets my mind wandering, and an article I've just read surfaces, in which a woman confesses that she "was very confused for a long time about who [her] body belonged to."[26]*

In the wake of #metoo, I began to notice the appearance in other social dance spaces of community agreements designed to yield safer and more welcoming environments. In Buenos Aires, the Movimiento Feminista del Tango emerged in 2018, taking inspiration from the grassroots Ni una menos (Not one [woman] less) movement that arose in 2015, following the brutal murder of fourteen-year-old Chiara Páez by her boyfriend. The social media hashtag *#NiUnaMenos* went viral, spawning huge demonstrations that spread from Argentina across Latin America, uniting adherents in the fight to end gender-based violence. Movimiento Feminista del Tango stages demonstrations and promotes equity, safety, and inclusivity through protocols designed to curtail physical, mental, and psychological violence in tango spaces.[27] While certain behaviors were always encouraged in Philadelphia – friendliness, dancing with out-of-town visitors and partners of all levels – the community had no code of conduct when I began writing this chapter. Since the book went into production, the Philadelphia Argentine Tango School adopted a Safer Spaces program,[28] which includes guidelines on behavior, coordinators at events, and an online portal for reporting incidents or concerns. Given the intergenerational and international nature of tango, I question the potential for consensus, in particular with regard to sanctioning unwanted behaviors.

In a conversation with Mitra Martin, co-founder of Los Angeles-based Oxygen Tango School and Awaken Tango (a values-centered organization that posits tango as a tool for global connection), she spoke about the capacity-development necessary to actualize positive, meaningful change. Over the decade Martin spent teaching and organizing, she witnessed instances of harm end with incomplete trials on social media platforms (in which community members weighed in on someone's guilt or innocence), broken relationships, and painful silences. She noted that organizers are often overburdened, financially and otherwise. Only after stepping down from her role as organizer did Martin have the time and space to develop a community-agreements template with contributions and feedback from colleagues. Two years later, Martin concluded that:

> ... a document alone cannot ensure a safer community. Without a thoughtful conflict resolution or restorative justice system, such agreements – an important first step – could be useless or even harmful, in the sense that they provide dancers a false sense of security.[29]

Over drinks with two *tangueras*, we contemplated the life's work of finding the path to "no." Mandated cordiality bristles because it recalls the link between manners and madness, especially for marginalized groups who suffer societal strictures and sanctions disproportionately. Such policies rightly interrogate tango's magic exceptionalism, espoused by professional and amateur dancers alike: its accessibility combined with its open-ended structure through improvisation position tango as a unique vehicle for transcending difference through nonverbal communication. At the same time, community agreements may be experienced as unnecessary or infantilizing, even by dancers who support their spirit. A friend who does not dance came to a milonga post–COVID-19 restrictions, where attendees were offered buttons colored to signify openness (or not) to invitations. Community members alerted the organizer when they spotted someone chatting her up, inviting her to dance, despite her red button. She laughed and assured the organizer she did not mind, that she would happily accept after some lessons. She can take care of herself in the meantime.

Despite openness toward dancing the role one wishes to dance, the climate in Philadelphia's scene remains fairly heterosexual, a profile approaching irrelevance for younger generations expanding definitions of sexuality and embracing fluid identities. Women leading more reflects a certain open-mindedness and cultural progress rather than diversity per se. And this mirrors the scene's racial and class makeup. While most *tanguerx* will tout the dance's international profile to cheer its cosmopolitanism, the community remains predominantly middle- to upper-middle class, and the overall vibe is somehow "white." There are exceptions, and tango's working-class roots complicate this scenario in Argentina;

however, the exclusions and segregation in our daily lives permeate tango spaces as well.

In researching community agreements, I found proposed policies on hygiene, attire, equipment, punctuality, and zero net carbon emissions – ideas that suggest respectability politics as they counter pressures to consume authenticity. I attended a Zoom meeting of the Anti-Racist Tango Organizing group, where participants discussed "radical belonging," debated whether traditions like *tandas* and the *cabeceo* reinforce exclusion, and questioned whether cashless payments are liberatory or discriminatory. Suggested strategies for attracting under-represented populations included free teacher training as well as advertisements that subvert "traditional," macho, heteronormative, and white-washed imagery of tango. In the aftermath, I wondered how community agreements and inclusion mesh, if "radical belonging" could ever accommodate all ideas about comfort and safety, and how to cultivate collective buy-in to everyone's autonomy.

Over nearly two decades, I have had countless conversations about how unwelcoming tango spaces can be. *Tanguerx* who practice other partner forms often compare the scenes and lament tango's social and psychological challenges, where visitors, beginners, elders, people of color, queer dancers, and others may be sidelined. I ponder this each time I remember my pre-COVID-19 salsa soirée: in that room full of strangers, I barely sat, and I experienced diversity in a different way than I do among my global tango family. In Spring 2020, I tuned in to a Facebook forum on Racism, Inclusivity & Tango,[30] where women of color shared some of their tango experiences and discussed the need for more altruism to breed greater care and community. Making an analogy to a stay-at-home mother's decision to leave behind a toxic work environment after having children, one participant named Nicole Hill questioned how many people might discover greater peace during COVID-19's tango pause, and simply not return to dancing tango in the aftermath.[31]

Later I chatted with Hill (whom I had known from the many years she lived and danced in Philadelphia), who suggested that tango take a cue from some tech companies adopting metrics and policies to promote inclusion. We discussed tango's elitist culture and how dancers find cover for unfriendliness in purported notions of authenticity. Hill underscored the erasure of tango's African roots as she contrasted the scene to samba, whose Africanist sensibility of inclusion and inviting people in is noteworthy and celebrated. As I recall how welcome I felt from my first tango steps twenty years back, I cannot ignore the facts of my age, race, size, appearance, and ability at that time. Hill questioned whether professionals fear compromising their status or income should they encourage more inclusive and horizontal communities, arguing that such shifts would likely boost growth and stability.[32]

Dancer/writer Misha Agunos is concerned with safety in an inclusive tango space. In a recent article, she asks provocative questions:

> If safety is fundamental to pleasure and connection, and connection is foundational to pleasurable tango experiences, are you even actually dancing if your partner doesn't feel safe? Or if you don't value the well-being of your partner beyond what they can provide for you on the dance floor?[33]

Memories resurfaced, like the time I finally watched videos of a professional who was notorious for abusing his partners. I sat transfixed before the screen, unable to look away. I had recently screened the documentary/musical *Un tango más* (*Our Last Tango*),[34] in which María Nieves Rego (b. 1934) describes the hatred that fueled and empowered her later dancing years with Juan Carlos Copes (1931–2021), the romantic and professional partner who made her life in and love of tango possible, and who betrayed her more than once during their celebrated, decades-long career. That their partnership ends per the ultimatum of Copes' second wife complicates a one-sided take on their story. The young dancers and choreographers who reinterpret Nieves and Copes in the film watch historic footage of the pair, observing their "connection within their disconnection."[35]

Born of pain and sorrow, dislocation, marginalization, nostalgia, and myriad violations and beauties alike, tango transcends these foundations even as the themes reverberate through the mythology of its poetry, music, and history. These reverberations underlie efforts to leave behind sexist and misogynistic tango lyrics, like "Amablemente," in which a man "kindly" stabs his unfaithful lover thirty-four times, as well as feminist music projects like Buenos Aires' La Empoderada Orquesta Atípica (The Empowered Atypical Orchestra),[36] an all-woman orchestra that performs music by women composers. I feel awe before such liberatory projects and questions. Universal well-being and safety ring clear and essential; dismissing violence and maintaining the status quo are not options. Still, I question whether tango's magic, and its confounding potential to bridge fathomless divides in the moment, transcends prescription. As time drags on and I reflect on tango in the abstract, its mysteries and its humanness loom large.

————————

La Pausa (The Pause)

> Choosing to trust others, especially in moments of uncertainty, is
> a courageous act. It orients us in body and mind toward generosity,
> goodwill, and possibility.
>
> Sharna Fabiano, *Lead and Follow*[37]

Philadelphia Suburbs, May 2021

*I attend my first in-person tango party in May 2021. We hug, as our smiles
and laughter border on tears, and we dance – all without masks. Later that
night, I attend the virtual milonga Café Pacífico. I enter to a live-streamed
bandoneón solo from Buenos Aires, marred by interference and delays. Then
Juan Villareal appears with his guitar, also from Argentina, but the internet
connection is solid. The sound is crystal clear, and the distance between his
voice and my heart collapses. His rendition of classic songs unlocks something
inside me. "Yo soy el tango," "Carnaval de mi barrio," "Lejos de Buenos
Aires" ... One after another conjuring the* porteña *in my soul.*

*In the span of a few hours, I experience the power of presence and
technology to facilitate something approximating presence. I witness tango
transcend boundaries but exert little influence over inequities that rage
between. Access to all manner of things – healthcare, internet connectivity,
passports and visas, immunity – remains differential, arbitrary, as COVID-
19 plows on. We tune in for many reasons, not least of which is to support one
another, in whatever tiny ways we can. The hard reality of the insufficiency
remains unnamed, glaring.*

Among the things I love about tango is its intergenerational character.
From the first days of COVID-19, the inevitable loss that I knew was to
come caused me anxiety. It did not take long for society's rifts to surface. By
summer 2020, I heard of people dancing in New York City. In response,
a group of local professionals produced a video, "Too Soon to Tango," in
which they exhorted viewers to "respect the pause" and encouraged other
organizers and dancers to "take care of the common good." "Don't risk
lives for a *tanda*," they pleaded, noting, "we can stay together while apart,
through online events," and *ojalá* (God willing), "we will hug again." Short
and sweet, the video exemplified our incapacity to agree on a definition of
the common good.

In early 2021, the global tango community lost two legends: Copes, who
brought tango to Broadway alongside Nieves, and Latin Grammy-winning
bandoneonist Raúl Jaurena. Copes generously shared his time with me

during my fieldwork, inviting me to his class and gifting me with his biography, a moving account of the power of dance to change a life.[38] To his and Nieves' formidable legacies, Copes added his role in inspiring tango dancers to organize the nonprofit Trabajadores del Tango Danza in 2017;[39] women members of this group in turn spearheaded the aforementioned Movimiento Feminista del Tango in 2018. At the age of 79, Jaurena remained vibrant, his playing stunning; he looked the picture of health when he played at a masked outdoor concert in Philadelphia months prior.

Soon after, I read of underground raves in NYC, a host's defense of the right to dance, especially for burned-out healthcare workers. Despite its recklessness, still something in me softened at the naked human need. My parents cleaned out their attic and I received a pile of letters from a college friend, full of reminiscences of nights dancing together. Memories of pure joy flooded over me. I recalled a chat with a tango friend in COVID-19's early days, in which she projected a breaking point:

If the opportunity arises, I will take it, whether a vaccine comes out or not. For me life is not worth living in such fear and isolation. I fully respect that many people won't want to, but I also believe that people should have the option, as long as they don't put others who have not made the same choice at risk.[40]

In a Zoom chat with renowned tango dance leader Phi Lee Lam, she lauded the potential of our slow emergence. Before the pandemic, Lam organized a women's salon in New York City, where she was surprised by stories of a toxic scene. Noting that tango helped her to identify safe touch and "experience men as human[s],"[41] she is committed to fostering positive change through sessions that explore tango beyond the dichotomies of gender and role and re-imagining tango's past and future through conversation and movement. Responding to the notion that community agreements restrict, Lam argued that "by exposing people to possibility and not framing ideas as punitive," we can build a culture in which "positive experience lives in and nourishes you."[42]

In Spring 2021, Philadelphia experienced a celebratory reopening as access to vaccines became widely available. Meanwhile, in Buenos Aires, elsewhere in Argentina, and in much of the Global South, access to vaccines remained limited – a situation compounded by their inferior efficacy. I wondered if the pause, with its preponderance of virtual activities, would heighten our connection to tango's homeland, and if our relief and concern for our Argentine compatriots would compound our drive to dance. We had barely begun to emerge when the spread of new variants, combined with conflicts around safety protocols and vaccines, threatened and divided the community on the cusp of its resurgence.

If meaning exists in seeing beyond ourselves and finding purpose there, might this prolonged isolation expose our need for connection, and provide nourishment in this space for creative re-imagination? In the work ahead, I see the logic of immunity, the lessons of tango: we need one another.

Notes

1. Eula Biss, *On Immunity: An Inoculation* (Minneapolis: Graywolf Press, 2014), 63.
2. Carolyn Merritt, *Tango Nuevo* (Gainesville: University Press of Florida, 2012).
3. The *cabeceo* is an invitation to dance via eye contact and a subtle head nod.
4. A *tanda* ("batch") is a set of three or four songs, grouped according to the type of music (tango, waltz, or *milonga*), during which a couple typically dances together until the *cortina* (literally "curtain," a 20- to 60-second piece of non-tango music) signals the moment to change partners.
5. A central tenet of anthropology according to which we evaluate aspects of another culture through an understanding of that culture's larger framework and not by comparing to one's own culture. Cultural relativism became enshrined under American anthropology's father figure, Franz Boas, at Columbia University in the early twentieth century, and was then disseminated by his students, including Margaret Mead, Ruth Benedict, Zora Neale Hurston, Edward Sapir, and others.
6. Angela Rippon, "Vertical Expression of a Horizontal Desire," *Tango por dos* (*Tango for Two*) concert program (London: Sadler's Wells, 1993).
7. The Queer Tango Image Archive includes many images of women dancing together in the early twentieth century, mostly from the United States, Western Europe, and Asia. The absence of such images from Argentina likely speaks to the erasure of its lower-class origins (when women dancing together were perhaps prostitutes or lesbians) and the fact that "respectable" women who learned to dance in domestic settings were not photographed engaging in "scandalous" activities like tango. The 1939 Argentine film *Así es la vida* (*Such Is Life*) includes a scene in which two young women dancing together in the home are set straight by their father, who demonstrates that "real" tango is led by a man. See Ray Batchelor, "Women Couples," *The Queer Tango Image Archive*, http://image.queertangobook.org/category/women-couple.
8. Merritt, *Tango Nuevo*, 59–60.
9. See Dezillio's Chapter 8, WP 8.5, for a photo of Maizani.

10. See Juliet McMains, "Rebellious Wallflowers and Queer *Tangueras*: The Rise of Female Leaders in Buenos Aires' Tango Scene," *Dance Research* 36/2 (2018): 173–197.

11. Ines Muzzopappa and Gaby Mataloni, Zoom interview with author, May 20, 2021.

12. I explore this situation in greater depth in my book *Tango Nuevo*, where I discuss tango's embrace of practitioners of all ages, and how mature women experience the freedom to revel in their sexuality in tango spaces. See Merritt, *Tango Nuevo*, 9.

13. Bob Bridges, Zoom interview with author, May 25, 2021.

14. A *milonguero* or *tanguero* is one who attends the milongas frequently, sometimes every night. Historically, the term *milonguero* carried negative connotations, to refer to a man who lived in the milongas, barely held down or had no job, and in many cases was supported by a woman. The term was appropriated by a sector of *porteño* (someone from Buenos Aires) dancers and organizers in the 1990s to brand a style of tango danced in a close or chest-to-chest embrace featuring a simple vocabulary that stresses rhythmic complexity. It was quite successfully marketed locally and abroad as the "real" tango danced in Buenos Aires' milongas, where the crowded dance floors might not permit a more open frame. In this essay, I use the terms *tanguera/o/x* to refer to tango dancers in general.

15. Charis McGowan, "All-Women Argentina Tango Festival Calls for End to Machismo," *Al Jazeera* (March 12, 2019), www.aljazeera.com/news/2019/3/12/all-women-argentina-tango-festival-calls-for-end-to-machismo.

16. Ernesto Londoño, "'A Caricature of the Patriarchy': Argentine Feminists Remake Tango," *New York Times* (October 5, 2019), www.nytimes.com/2019/10/05/world/americas/argentina-tango-gender.html.

17. Muzzopappa and Mataloni, Zoom interview with author, May 20, 2021.

18. Claudia Rankine, *Citizen: An American Lyric* (Minneapolis: Graywolf Press, 2014), 28.

19. Sharna Fabiano, *Lead and Follow: The Dance of Inspired Teamwork* (Virginia Beach: Koehler Books, 2021).

20. Sharna Fabiano, phone interview with author, January 19, 2021.

21. McMains, "Rebellious Wallflowers," 9.

22. Sharna Fabiano, phone interview with author, January 19, 2021.

23. Christine Runyan, "What's Happening in Our Nervous Systems?" interview by Krista Tippett, *On Being*, March 18, 2021. https://onbeing.org/programs/christine-runyan-whats-happening-in-our-nervous-systems/.

24. SOTANGO.WORLD, "Earth Virtual Milonga," *YouTube*, April 5, 2020, www.youtube.com/watch?v=EXwEd9lNokA.

25. Ross Alexander, Zoom interview with author, May 24, 2021.

26. Melissa Febos, "Getting to No," *New York Times Magazine* (April 4, 2021): 40.

27. Movimiento Feminista de Tango, "Protocolo de Actuación para situaciones de Violencias en espacios milongueros," https://docs.google .com/document/d/151RGzL0HehSbrpFVr7j52OiIOtvVnb_raYFavZS5kCI/ edit#heading=h.y6yscmfnhkok.
28. Philadelphia Argentine Tango School, "Safer Spaces," accessed October 19, 2023, www.philadelphiatangoschool.com/safer-spaces.
29. Mitra Martin, phone interview with author, May 8, 2021.
30. Kristina McFadden and guests, "Racism, Inclusivity & Tango," *Tango Roundtable*, June 7, 2020, www.facebook.com/kristina.mcfadden.73/videos/10159118443709 316.
31. Nicole Hill in McFadden and guests, "Racism, Inclusivity & Tango," Tango Roundtable, June 7, 2020. www.facebook.com/kristina.mcfadden.73/videos/10159 118443709316.
32. Nicole Hill, phone interview with author, September 19, 2021.
33. Misha Agunos, "Are You Actually Dancing Tango if You Aren't Dismantling Systems of Oppression?" *Oxygen Tango*, June 10, 2021, www.oxygentango.com/ blog/tangoandoppression.
34. German Kral, *Un tango más* (Culver City: Strand Releasing Home Video, 2016).
35. Ibid.
36. For further information about La Empoderada Orquesta Atípica, see https:// laempoderadaoa.bandcamp.com.
37. Ibid, 74.
38. Mariano Del Mazo and Adrián D'Amore, *Quien Me Quita Lo Bailado* (Buenos Aires: Ediciones Corregidor, 2001).
39. https://trabajadorestangodanza.com.
40. Anonymous, phone interview with author, May 31, 2020.
41. Phi Lee Lam, Zoom interview with author, May 25, 2021.
42. Ibid.

Further Reading

Agunos, Misha. "Are You Actually Dancing Tango If You Aren't Dismantling Systems of Oppression?" *Oxygen Tango*, June 10, 2021. www.oxygentango .com/blog/tangoandoppression.

Biss, Eula. *On Immunity: An Inoculation*. Minneapolis: Graywolf Press, 2014.

Del Mazo, Mariano, and Adrián D'Amore. *Quien Me Quita Lo Bailado*. Buenos Aires: Ediciones Corregidor, 2001.

Fabiano, Sharna. *Lead and Follow: The Dance of Inspired Teamwork*. Virginia Beach: Koehler Books, 2021.

Kral, German. *Un tango más*. Culver City: Strand Releasing Home Video, 2016.

Londoño, Ernesto. "'A Caricature of the Patriarchy': Argentine Feminists Remake Tango." *New York Times*, October 5, 2019. www.nytimes.com/2019/10/05/world/americas/argentina-tango-gender.html.

McGowan, Charis. "All-Women Argentina Tango Festival Calls for End to Machismo," *Al Jazeera*, March 12, 2019. www.aljazeera.com/news/2019/3/12/all-women-argentina-tango-festival-calls-for-end-to-machismo.

Merritt, Carolyn. *Tango Nuevo*. Gainesville: University Press of Florida, 2012.

McMains, Juliet. "Rebellious Wallflowers and Queer *Tangueras*: The Rise of Female Leaders in Buenos Aires' Tango Scene," *Dance Research* 36, no. 2 (2018): 173–197.

Runyan, Christine. "What's Happening in Our Nervous Systems?" Interview by Krista Tippett, *On Being*, March 18, 2021. https://onbeing.org/programs/christine-runyan-whats-happening-in-our-nervous-systems/.

PART IV

Interdisciplinary Tango Studies

14 | Nineteenth-Century Afro-Argentine Origins of Tango

PAULINA L. ALBERTO

The history of the Argentine tango is entwined with and indebted to the history of the Afro-Argentine community of Buenos Aires, or *Afro-porteños* (*porteños* are residents of that port city). Tango's imbrication with the Black community was hardly news to late nineteenth- and early twentieth-century observers. Yet a century later, scholars, practitioners, and activists struggle to make tango's African and Afro-Argentine components audible and visible. When UNESCO inscribed the tango on its "List of the Intangible Cultural Heritage of Humanity" in 2009, declaring it the special patrimony of Argentina and Uruguay, its Afro-Argentine origins and ongoing influences were barely discernible.

In the first decades of the twentieth century, as tango became the national dance of an Argentina imagined as white and European, it too was whitened, stripped of musical and choreographic components considered African and of once-copious references to Black Argentines and their cultures. In the following decades, most narrators of tango's history increasingly minimized, forgot, or disavowed its Black roots in favor of European ones.[1] Dissenting scholars and practitioners have pointed to the importance of Afro-Argentine musical and dance traditions, especially early nineteenth-century *candombe*, in the rhythms and dance innovations behind *milonga* (a word likely of African origin), the immediate precursor to the Argentine tango in the late 1800s. Others credited *milonga*'s syncopated rhythms and hip-forward choreographies to the Afro-Cuban *danza* or *habanera* (also known as a Cuban tango). A few highlighted the presence of Afro-Argentines – as composers, musicians, and dancers – in the early days of tango's formation, as it emerged from the *milonga* and moved from margins to mainstream.[2]

Yet even these accounts of tango's Black roots often reiterated elements of Argentina's dominant racial narratives. The entrenched myth of Afro-Argentines' "disappearance" over the nineteenth century (supposedly due to wars, disease, and displacement by European immigrants) makes it difficult to tell a continuous story of Afro-Argentine influences in the tango from the nineteenth century onward.[3] In particular, the idea that *candombe*, as a distinctly Afro-Argentine dance and music form, faded after the mid-1800s has at worst precluded close examination of its connections to tango; at best, it has cast *candombe* as a minor tributary in tango's development. The conviction that Afro-Argentines and their cultures "disappeared" from modern Argentina, moreover, has made it difficult to narrate Black influences on tango past 1900, when the genre's history began to be documented. When authors do record the presence of Afro-Argentines in the twentieth-century tango as dancers, composers, singers, and musicians, they tend to imagine them as isolated individuals rather than part of a centuries-old community that never stopped playing and dancing.[4] Finally, several early studies that challenged tango's whitened history nonetheless internalized ideas about the unrecoverability of Argentina's Black past. Their reconstructions of Black music are frequently shrouded in myth, short on documentation, riddled with stereotypes, and populated by undifferentiated masses.[5] These challenges to narrating tango's Afro-Argentine roots mirror those of writing about Blackness in that supposedly white nation. To the extent that tango crystallized as Argentina's national rhythm as part of the same processes that stamped Argentina as homogeneously white, these challenges are perhaps especially acute. The paucity of sheet music or recordings from the 1800s that pinpoint Afro-Argentine contributions exacerbates these difficulties.

Recent work helps paint a more fine-grained, evidence-based history of Black contributions to the tango. This newer history draws from historical archives, personal collections, the *Afro-porteño* press, and oral histories with the *Afro-porteño* community to locate the tango's rise not just in the better-known *academias* (dance halls offering lessons for pay), *peringundines* (dives), theaters, and brothels, but also in the social clubs, basements, tenement quarters, or living rooms of *Afro-porteños*. And it helps close the stubborn conceptual chasm between the nineteenth and twentieth centuries.

This chapter introduces readers to that rich history through a multigenerational case study of one family of *Afro-porteño* musicians, the Grigeras. Their story is remarkable but not unique: many Afro-Argentine families produced generations of renowned musicians, and contemporary accounts acknowledged their musical talents. The Grigeras' story spans the long nineteenth century: from an African-born man's founding of a storied gathering site for *candombe* music and dance in the 1820s, to the musical experimentation of his son and grandson at the helm of that establishment as it evolved through the 1880s, to his great-grandson's rise to stardom as a Black tango icon in the 1910s.[6] This case study is not a definitive history of tango's

Afro-Argentine influences. Rather, it illustrates the potential of grounding tango's past in the documented social history of *Afro-porteños*, in the hope that future investigations will yield a fuller picture of the cultural exchanges behind Argentina's world-famous dance form.

Tango, *Tambo, Nación, Candombe*: Early Nineteenth-Century Afro-Argentine Dance, Music, and Associational Life

Before coming to denote Argentina's national dance at the turn of the twentieth century, "tango" had various meanings, all involving the music and dance of Africans and their descendants. The earliest documented use of "tango" in the early 1800s described the meeting grounds of African ethnic associations on the city's margins. There, newly arrived African captives and their local-born descendants gathered to play music for ritual and secular festivities. Some scholars have suggested that the word is of African origin, while others hypothesize that it evolved from an Afro-Argentine pronunciation of the Spanish word for "drum" (*tambor* rendered as *tambó*). More important is that in the first decades of the 1800s, "tango" became synonymous with *nación*, *tambo*, and *candombe* – all terms describing both the meeting grounds of African ethnic associations and the music and dance performed therein.[7]

The first protagonist of our multigenerational history, a man known in Buenos Aires as Antonio, was born in Africa in the early 1780s. He was taken to the Río de la Plata during the peak in human traffic that transported an estimated 70,000 enslaved individuals to Montevideo and Buenos Aires between 1776 and 1810, the last decades of Spanish rule. In 1818, an appraiser listed him as being thirty-five years old and "of the Mina nation," suggesting he was among the minority embarked to the region from present-day Ghana and parts of the Bight of Benin. At this time, people of African origin accounted for at least 30 percent of Buenos Aires's inhabitants, about 11,837 individuals. Most were enslaved, including Antonio, who labored in the orchards of José Mariano Grigera in Flores, just outside the city limits.

Antonio appears to have gained his freedom following the deaths of the couple who held him in bondage, and, once free, to have taken their surname (a common practice). In 1823, he founded a *nación* or African ethnic association in Montserrat, one of the city's heavily African neighborhoods on the south-side of Buenos Aires. These *naciones* – also known as *tangos*, *tambos*, or (later) candombes – had existed since the late colonial period, providing spaces for Africans and their descendants, enslaved and free, to pursue the shared goals of survival and solidarity, community-building, and the maintenance of spiritual ties with ancestors and with Africa. Members regularly gathered on the *naciones'* grounds to celebrate feasts, stage Carnival parades, elect ceremonial kings and queens, bury the dead and honor ancestors, and raise money to buy members out of slavery or assist them during illness. Although they typically took the name of an ethnic group ("Congo," "Benguela," "Mina"), in practice these associations amalgamated people of various ethnic or linguistic backgrounds.

But the African associations were best known for weekly dances that drew hundreds or thousands and involved call-and-response chanting, drumming, and dancing in rounds or occasionally in pairs. The music, according to contemporaneous accounts, featured polyrhythmic percussion – drums of different shapes and timbres accompanied by marimbas, bones, gourds, and *masacallas* (shakers). These dances earned the area of Montserrat and Concepción, where most of the *naciones* were located, the nickname *el barrio del tambor* – the neighborhood of the drum.

The *naciones* and their dances were extremely visible, audible, concentrated Black urban territories, and spaces of relative freedom, not unlike maroon communities elsewhere in Latin America. Colonial authorities cracked down on the dances repeatedly, characterizing them as indecent and politically dangerous (contemporary reports suggest authorities encountered runaways and fugitives, plots for uprisings, and armed resistance). After independence from Spain in 1816, republican authorities permitted the *naciones* to operate provided they registered with the police, adopted charters modeled after the mutual-aid societies of European immigrants, controlled their members, and submitted to police supervision. This was the context in which Antonio Grigera founded his *nación*.

By 1829, the *naciones'* status improved with the rise to power of Juan Manuel de Rosas, who permitted them to hold dances unobstructed – including, at least once, in the city's posh central square. Rosas also famously received the leaders of *naciones* in his residence and visited their grounds with his wife Encarnación and his daughter Manuelita, whom he allowed to dance with Black men and women (scandalizing his white enemies and endearing him to many Afro-Argentines). During his rule (1829–1832, 1835–1852), the term *candombe* was increasingly used to denote both a *nación* and the kind of dance and music performed therein.

Antonio's candombe became famous in its time – reportedly a favorite of Manuelita Rosas. The Candombe de Grigera (as it was known) was, in the words of one influential ethnomusicologist, one of "legendary" proportions: "a candombe that had its history and that made history."[8] It stands out not least for its longevity: it functioned until 1901. In its early years, it appears to have been located at what is today México 1265 (Fig. 14.1). The building survived at least until 1970, and so did memories of its historic function as the Candombe de Grigera.

Little is known about this candombe in the first decades after Argentine independence. But Antonio Grigera appears to have created a candombe whose members "acted according to the most pristine traditions of the [African] continent," observing them with "discipline and diligence." Indeed, the Candombe de Grigera's unorthodox name – a surname, rather than the usual ethnonym (as in *nación Benguela*) – suggests just how much respect Antonio commanded as a community leader.

Candombe, Milonga, Tango: A Nonlinear History

Tango's history did not proceed in neat, linear stages from *candombe* to *milonga* to modern tango, shedding ever more African components along the way. But the presumption that *candombe*, along with Afro-Argentines, vanished in Argentina after the mid-nineteenth century has become

Figure 14.1 "México 1265, con Candombe de Grigera," n/d (ca. 1900).

a lasting obstacle to tracing Black contributions to the tango. The narrative of *candombe*'s demise emerged in the nineteenth century, in the writings of hostile witnesses who saw it as the essence of a "barbaric" African population – foreign, animalistic, and politically dangerous – which they hoped would rapidly disappear after Rosas' fall (1852). These writers bequeathed a static picture of Argentine *candombe* defined by what struck them as most troublingly salient: its loud drumming, absence of melody, and open-air setting. To the extent that *candombe* evolved outside these stereotypes, it ceased to be perceived as a *candombe*, allowing detractors to declare it disappeared.[9]

The Candombe de Grigera's nineteenth-century evolution helps illuminate how *candombe* persisted by shifting shape and becoming less readily legible through racial stereotype. It shows that *candombe* was not a time-bound stage deep in tango's prehistory, but a living musical and dance genre, embedded in a vibrant *Afro-porteño* community, that continued to feed into and from tango into the early twentieth century.

By the mid-1800s, Antonio's freeborn son Domingo (ca. 1828–1886) led the Candombe de Grigera. Its membership would have been increasingly Argentine-born and free. Slavery was not abolished in Buenos Aires until 1861, but by then most Afro-Argentines had achieved freedom through gradual emancipation laws, service in wars, or manumissions granted or purchased. Domingo Grigera was a well-respected member of the *Afro-porteño* community, a former soldier wounded in battle, and a pianist by profession. For observers steeped in the stereotypical definition of *candombe* bequeathed by the Rosas era, Domingo's instrument might make him unthinkable as a *candombe* leader. But the Candombe de Grigera was a memorable association precisely for being a "candombe with a piano."[10]

This detail sheds crucial light on the history of *candombe* and its relationship to the Argentine tango. *Candombe* music and dance (with drumming still a central feature), and the African ethnic associations that originally hosted it, continued to exist in the middle to late decades of the nineteenth century, as scores of articles in the *Afro-porteño* press of the 1870s and 1880s attest.[11] But *candombe* as a music and dance practice was gradually shifting shape, sounds, and sites.[12] The disapproval of *Afro-porteño* community leaders who stressed respectability led many to abandon, conceal, or transform its practice, driving it metaphorically underground. Yet the shift also reflected musical evolution, including experimentation with new instrumentation and melody. *Candombe*, it turned out, was difficult to eradicate, even among the community's self-appointed elite, and it was highly adaptable. Alongside more traditional *candombe* danced primarily by community elders at the meeting grounds of surviving *naciones*, at least three new, hybrid, and overlapping variants were taking shape: camouflaged *candombe*, orchestral *candombe*, and Carnival *candombe*.

In the first variant, the maligned drums were supplemented with, or supplanted by, other forms of percussion and performed less publicly, yielding a camouflaged *candombe* blended with rhythms considered more socially acceptable. This was the case in private parties hosted in *Afro-porteño* homes or tenement quarters. These soirées might begin with popular musical styles like Afro-Cuban *habaneras* (written for piano), *tangos* (a term used to describe festive satires of "Black" music, written for piano or strings, discussed later in this chapter), and *milongas* (a combination of *habanera* with the rural music of the hinterlands, usually for piano or guitar). But they often ended with full-blown *candombe*. Not only did the camouflaged *candombe* go "underground," then; by adopting new melodies and instrumentations built around Domingo's instrument, we might say that it became "*candombe* with a piano."

Similar dynamics likely played out in more public establishments, like *academias* or *peringundines*, in which Afrodescendants played key roles as musicians and *maestros de baile* or dance instructors. These establishments brought together people from the city's *orillas* (margins) – knife-toting *compadritos* (street toughs), soldiers, sailors, cart drivers, workers, and others – with slumming *niños bien*, the children of the elite. Extensive multi-racial and cross-class exchanges in these spaces have been credited with birthing *milonga*, tango's most direct predecessor, in which the rhythmic and choreographic elements of *candombe*, along with the Afro-Cuban influences of the *habanera*, were palpable.

The second (orchestral) variant of *candombe* appears to have flourished in elegant dance salons, in parties organized by upwardly aspiring *Afro-porteños*. These featured orchestras with respected *Afro-porteño* musicians and playlists with European styles like the waltz, polka, can-can, and mazurka, as well as the wildly popular *habanera*. Domingo's two sons, Estanislao and Pedro, would play the piano at such events. Yet even these soirées, for all their sophistication and aspiration to respectability, were sometimes criticized by disapproving *Afro-porteño* commentators as nothing but "*candombe* with orchestras" rather than drums.

The third and most public-facing variant of *candombe* emerged through the performances of Carnival *comparsas* (parade troupes) made up of *Afro-porteños*. Some *comparsas* played *habaneras* or other Europeanized styles on string and wind instruments as they marched through city streets. Others joined a new trend that swept Buenos Aires in the 1860s and

1870s: performing mockeries of "Black" or Africanized music during Carnival. Some of these musical styles were generically referred to as "tango," in an updated use of the colonial-era term for African dances and dance sites, and in confluence with a new use in contemporary Spanish and Cuban theater (which reached *porteño* stages) to refer to Black dances in a broader Atlantic context. As part of these trends, white *porteños* created *comparsas* with names like *Los negros*, in which elite young men blackened their faces and imitated *Afro-porteños'* perceived speech patterns, songs, and dances. Authors of Carnival hits played with metaphors of slavery and Blackness, using the figure of the *"negro"* who desperately pursued the untouchable white *amita* (master's daughter) as a metaphor for white men's own frustrated romantic longings. These *comparsas* of "false" or "cork-blackened" *negros* both belittled *Afro-porteños* and *candombe* and acknowledged their importance in the city's popular culture. In this context, some younger *Afro-porteños* also put on blackface and dressed up in ostensible "African" style while drumming and dancing a caricatured version of *candombe* and singing in exaggerated dialect, performing their own distance from that maligned custom, but also updating it.

The pianists in the Grigera family, acknowledged by musicologists as important figures in *candombe* and by contemporaries as respectable musicians, operated at these intersections. If the Candombe de Grigera provided a space where the music and dance of earlier generations of *Afro-porteños* intermingled with newer forms of popular dance music, it would have done so just as commentators began to declare *candombe* "disappeared." Yet the Candombe de Grigera, with Domingo's piano-based *candombe*, along with other establishments like it, may have been key to the musical innovations that emerged before the birth of the Argentine tango and fed into it. Some music scholars have argued that the drumbeat of the early *candombe* echoed in the percussive bass-clef piano chords of a *habanera*, the bass lines of a Carnival tango, and the strumming of the guitar in a *milonga*.[13] In this way, the underlying rhythmic "grammar" of *candombe*, with its syncopations and off-beat accents, made its way into contemporary popular music even as the once-defining drums dropped away.[14] As one account explains, "The rhythms of tango, which stem from Black influences, are characterized by a special polyrhythm arising from all the melodic and harmonic instruments together, due to the disappearance of the drums."[15] A pianist at the head of a candombe in these critical middle decades of the nineteenth century helps us understand these musical innovations happening in spaces continuously known as candombes, and not just in *academias*, *peringundines*, *comparsas*, or salon dances envisioned as separate or posterior.

Domingo passed away in 1886. If the Candombe de Grigera continued to operate for another fifteen years, it must have done so under his eldest son Estanislao Grigera (1856–1935) – a classically trained pianist, composer, piano instructor, and church organist (WP 14.1). Estanislao had received formal musical training at one of the nation's most prestigious conservatories. He was part of the group of elite-trained *Afro-porteño* musicians who disdained the open-air *candombe* dances and musical performances still held at the *naciones* in the late 1800s; his close friend, the famous *Afro-porteño* pianist and composer Casildo G. Thompson, derided these as "the semi-barbaric practices of our ancestors." But that does not mean that Estanislao and his generation did not experiment with the new forms of *candombe* that involved more "refined" melody and instrumentation and shifted percussion to the piano.

What might this Candombe de Grigera, now two generations removed from African leadership, have looked and sounded like? No recordings from this era survive, nor any sheet music explicitly labeled "*candombe.*" Yet Afro-Argentine musicians often interpreted or improvised upon popular music forms by playing them in a 2/4 time signature, in line with *candombe* meter. The *Afro-porteño* press published Carnival song lyrics in the 1870s and early 1880s, offering some insight into rhythmic phrasing, but not scores. Using oral history, musicologist Norberto Pablo Cirio has reconstructed the music for one such song, "Bum que bum" (ca. 1871–1873). As the title suggests with its onomatopoeic invocation of drumming, the song was understood as *candombe* – tellingly, the bassline resembles that of the early tango.[16]

The *Afro-porteño* press offers other important social and sonic clues. On December 10, 1881, according to the newspaper *La Broma*, Estanislao Grigera and his wife Alejandra hosted a private party at which Estanislao's pianist friends supplied the music: Casildo G. Thompson, Cayetano Olivera, Juan Espinosa, Lorenzo Espinosa, and Prudencio Denis. We have already heard one *Afro-porteño* reporter dismiss as "*candombe* with orchestras" precisely these sorts of aspirationally refined performances. So it is possible that outsiders to the *Afro-porteño* community, or younger *Afro-porteños* who later acted as informants for early twentieth-century ethnomusicologists, interpreted the percussive piano sounds coming from Estanislao's house in the 1880s and 1890s as "*candombe,*" explaining how the Candombe de Grigera was seen to last until 1901.

But if the family's links to previous forms of *Afro-porteño* music and dance are suggestive, those to new musical forms are even more so. One historian, identifying little-known Afro-Argentine pioneers of the tango, highlights most of the pianists who played the party at the Grigera home: "the brothers Espinosa, Casildo [G.] Thompson, [Cayetano] Olivera." He singles out Juan Espinosa – godfather to one of Estanislao's children – as "the first composer of a tango" ("La Broma," 1876, dedicated to the eponymous newspaper) to sound like what the genre would become: a melodic style with an orchestra including violins, flutes, clarinets, cello, and bass.[17] With this in mind, *La Broma*'s description of the music and dance at Estanislao's party begins to sound familiar: a "harmonious" sound with a "pulsing" rhythm, to which people delighted in "swinging" in a close embrace. That these descriptions make it difficult to distinguish the outlines of the "orchestral" or "camou-flaged" forms of *candombe* from the rhythmic, melodic, and choreographic innovations that birthed the *milonga* and early tango is precisely the point.

Accounts that credit the influence of *Afro-porteño* music and musicians in the birth of the Argentine tango toward the end of the nineteenth century typically highlight Rosendo Mendizábal (1868–1913), whose tango "El Entrerriano" "The Man from Entre Ríos," a province northeast of Buenos Aires) (1896) inaugurated the genre's so-called *guardia vieja* (Old Guard). Mendizábal played piano in cafés, *academias*, and upscale brothels. But *La Broma*'s account of the party in Estanislao's home in 1881 suggests that everyday gatherings like that one, alongside the *comparsas*, *academias*, and brothels usually credited with the tango's emergence, provided spaces where classically trained *Afro-porteño* musicians could apply their talents and varied instrumentation (piano, strings, or winds) to popular dance music, some of which had itself absorbed *candombe*'s influences in earlier decades. The resulting music, known variously as *candombe criollo*, *milonga-candombe*, or *habanera con corte*, became increasingly channeled into denominations bearing the term "tango" by the turn of the century: *tango-milonga*, *tango canyengue*, and *tango arrabalero*.

Into the Twentieth Century: *Candombe* as Tango, Tango as *Candombe*

The Grigera family's musical traditions continued into the twentieth century, by then tightly connected with the emergent Argentine tango, through two of Estanislao's sons: Luis Estanislao Leandro (1879–?), a noted pianist, music teacher, and tango composer, and Raúl Grigera

(1886–1955), who, after a tumultuous youth, rose to fame as a dandy and icon of the city's nightlife.

"Tango," by the second decade of the century, came to denote something like what it means today: a sensual dance in a close embrace marked by *cortes* – stops, turns, and other embellishments, such as entangling of the dancers' legs – and *quebradas* – a "breaking" or swiveling of the line of the hips, performed with the upper bodies in full contact. In other words, the label *tango* was increasingly, after 1900, applied to the dance style that had been known as *milonga* in the 1880s and 1890s.

At the turn of the twentieth century, the associations among Blackness, *milonga*, and tango were strong. As the ability to execute those dances became a currency of a form of tough masculinity, *Afro-porteños* "commanded respect in the dance that had been created with their rhythmic and choreographic elements."[18] So close was the association between Black people and tango prowess that "outdoing oneself in daring, showy turns was called 'dancing Black' [*bailar a lo negro*]." Popular theater at the century's turn portrayed *Afro-porteños* as unsurpassable tango or *milonga* dancers. And, as we have seen, many *Afro-porteño* men were pioneer musicians and composers in the genre increasingly consolidated as the Argentine tango. This included Estanislao's son Luis Estanislao Leandro, who in 1914 composed a *tango criollo* called "Unión Comunal" ("Municipal Union"), named after a new political party. Even into the early decades of the twentieth century, tango's Black variants and practitioners – along with the nickname "*negro*" itself – acquired a "heretical charge," functioning as emblems of a populist, off-white pride among some *tangueros*.[19]

The world of the early tango thus provided a unique space, in a society committed to whitening, in which a Black man like Raúl Grigera could rise to fame as a popular icon. In 1912, Ángel Bassi composed a tango (without lyrics) titled "El Negro Raúl: Seventh Tango Criollo for Piano" (WS 14.1). This tango was, like others in the *guardia vieja* years, upbeat, festive, cheerful – nothing like later tangos famously described as "a sad thought that is danced."[20] Featuring Raúl as the subject of this composition was also in keeping with the times. Early tangos were peppered with references to Black culture and folkloric Afro-Argentine "types" and imaginary characters. But Raúl Grigera stands out as a living, modern Black person, and as the rare celebrity who was visibly Black. Unlike some of his *Afro-porteño* relatives or acquaintances, he gained renown not as a creator or interpreter of popular music, but as its acclaimed subject.

Raúl's Blackness, in these years when tango's Afro-Argentine roots were still widely acknowledged, appears to have bolstered his fame. Decades later, essayist Ezequiel Martínez Estrada looked back on Raúl's appeal in precisely these terms, albeit through a contemptuous lens: "El Negro Raúl," he claimed, was a "slave to the fad that took root among young lads who lacked any decorum, long before Josephine Baker became all the rage; idol of the adorers of tango [and] *candombe*[.]"[21] Though Martínez Estrada found this embrace of Black culture revolting, the "fad" he identified – the "adoration" of tango and *candombe* by some young white men – discloses a selective fascination with Blackness within Argentine popular culture in the early 1900s.

It's no coincidence that subsequent critics (and admirers) of Raúl Grigera linked him to tango and *candombe* alike. His seamless movement between these forms reveals them not to have been as distant as subsequent accounts have imagined; indeed, tango and the updated forms of *candombe* that fed into and from it were, for some time and in some spaces, contemporaneous and coexistent. During the Carnival season of 1915, one of Buenos Aires' leading newspapers, *Crítica*, reported that the famous theater El Nacional on Corrientes Street was hosting a series of "candombes" (for-pay parties featuring *candombe* music and dance) for the city's "people of color." The coverage that followed this announcement provides new information on how *candombe* spanned the birth of the new century not just hidden in basements or backyards, but at the center of Buenos Aires' downtown nightlife.

The "candombes" ran for several weekends in January and February of 1915. They were, according to *Crítica*, organized by the management of El Nacional in conjunction with Raúl Grigera and a man known simply as "el negro Andrade." Andrade was the chief doorman at El Nacional. As such, he had the power to control who attended and entered the dances, and appears to have used it to grant entry to *Afro-porteños* not usually welcome in large numbers in public establishments. Raúl was presented variously by *Crítica* as a guest of honor who gave the dances their "luster," and as the dances' "director," "leader," "*bastonero*" (in nineteenth-century candombes, *bastoneros* were masters of ceremony who used a large cane or stick [*bastón*] to conduct the music and dance), and "Menelik" (the late king and emperor of Ethiopia).

These references were partly *Crítica*'s sarcastic riff on old stereotypes of Africans and Afro-Argentines who gave themselves airs of royalty as "kings" or "queens" of the candombes of yore. Yet these statements held truth, beginning with Raúl as the *bastonero*. *Crítica*'s repeated portrayal of Raúl as a "leader" and "director" of the dances suggests he might have officiated as master of ceremony at El Nacional. We know very little about what Argentine *candombe* looked like in 1915, but in neighboring Uruguay, the *bastonero* became a stock character of Carnival *candombe* after the 1870s. This character embodies a particular kind of Black male power: youth, dancerly grace, and sex appeal. Raúl, who in his childhood would have learned to dance the era's favorites (*habanera, milonga*, and of course, *candombe*), may have been a *bastonero* in this sense as well. Perhaps his alluring performances as a Black dancer explained the "luster" he brought to these interracial spaces.

Likewise, the quip that Raúl was Black royalty, and thus well-situated to convene fellow Black *candomberos* to dance, may have been a fair description. As the descendant of generations of candombe leaders and part of a family of pianists, Raúl certainly would have known enough musicians who could play at these events. Though laden with derision, then, *Crítica's* claim that Raúl and Andrade worked together to organize these dances offers glimpses of how *Afro-porteños* mobilized familial and social networks to project their community's dances into the city's nightlife well into the twentieth century's second decade.

But perhaps the most interesting thing about the dances that *Crítica's* theater pages labeled "*candombes*" is that less-hostile sources, like the daily *La Nación*, announced these simply as dances featuring "tango." In fact, the city's major theaters advertised nothing but "tango" – the style was becoming all the rage – during Carnival. *Crítica* itself began to report on the city's Carnival dances as "*El mundo del tango*" ("The world of tango"), a rubric that, tellingly, included the "*candombes* at El Nacional." This suggests there may have been other dances attended or organized by "*gente de color*" ("people of color") in these years, with more Africanized variants of tango or even *candombe* as their musical fare, that still pass unnoticed among countless announcements for "tangos" in the city's theater pages. *Crítica's* coverage thus offers a priceless glimpse into how tango's "whitening" in the mid-1910s may have occurred alongside a palpable Afro-Argentine *collective* presence, with the community actively engaged in defining the sounds and silhouettes of the thing we now know as "tango."

The interchangeability of the labels "tango" and "*candombe*" to describe what people danced at El Nacional suggests how strong the association between tango and Afro-Argentines still was in 1915. If this association was controversial, it was not for lack of evidence; elite critics of tango complained precisely about its African origins. In one account, tango's "lubricious" mixture between "the contortions of *negros*" and the coarse music of immigrants made it an "immodest *mulata*" from the slums.[22] The same year that *Crítica* covered the "*candombes*" at El Nacional, another newspaper noted (disapprovingly) that tango was a dance "cultivated principally by the *gente de color*."[23] So the fact that the dance styles at El Nacional, advertised as "tangos," were dubbed "*candombes*" by *Crítica* probably means that the dancers were disproportionately Afro-descendant, or were lower-class *porteños* dancing in ways that appeared markedly "Black" – or both.

Perhaps revelers at El Nacional danced the style that observers and composers began, around 1915, to label *tango canyengue* (a word of African origin), also known as "*candombe* rhythm."[24] Musically, it was characterized by percussive slaps to the strings or body of a bass or guitar, or even kicks to a piano, to create deep, syncopated beats, an innovation credited to *Afro-porteño* bassist Leopoldo Thompson. Choreographically, *canyengue* featured pronounced pelvic movements, hunched torsos, protruding rear ends, and various accentuations of the downbeats. One present-day Afro-Argentine commentator recalls a similar style, *milonga-candombe*, in which her elders recreated "the beat of the [absent] drum by striking the floor with the heel of the shoe."[25] Contemporaries recognized these "Black" forms of tango (and *candombe* itself) as the gritty, authentic origin of what was becoming a stylized, upright, stiff-hipped dance considered more elegant by the Europeanized elite, the so-called "*tango de salón*" (salon tango) or the more stripped-down "*tango liso*" (smooth tango).[26]

Indeed, even as *Crítica*'s coverage of the dances at El Nacional reveals the depth of tango's imbrication with Afrodescendants in the mid-1910s, it simultaneously exposes the processes by which many white *porteños* tried to force the two apart to shore up tango's acceptability. These processes involved making Blackness hyper-visible or hyper-audible the better to segregate it, as in *Crítica*'s attempt to degrade the dances at El Nacional by calling them "*candombes*," or the contemporary relabeling of some tango variants as *canyengue*. Explicitly classifying these tango variants as "Black" excised them from what increasingly became the white, unmarked, "normal" Argentine tango. At other times, ensuring tango's acceptability involved downplaying Blackness, rather than casting it out. In contrast to its depiction of El Nacional's disqualifying "Blackness," *Crítica* reported benevolently on dances at nearby theaters, despite the band directors in charge at each – Carlos Posadas and Manuel L. Posadas – being *Afro-porteños*. These renowned masters of the tango were part of Estanislao Grigera's tight-knit group of *Afro-porteño* artists and intellectuals. Yet in *Crítica*'s eyes, their presence did not "Blacken" dances at those nearby theaters, perhaps due to their arrangements and instrumentation, their classical training, or their position within a respectable *Afro-porteño* elite.

As in Argentine society more broadly, in the world of tango the overt labeling of some subgenres and people as "Black" worked together with racial silence to minimize and marginalize Blackness and normalize whiteness.

Re-Blackening Tango's History

The alchemy that began to meld tango, Argentineness, and whiteness in the mid-1910s made Afro-Argentines both hyper-visible and invisible in the tango world. On one hand, ascendant narratives of Black "disappearance" cast visibly Black Argentines, like Raúl Grigera, as the "last" of their kind. In Raúl's case, falling fortunes in the 1920s and 1930s turned him into the subject of derisive tangos. Alfredo Gobbi's "Las aventuras del Negro Raúl" (ca. 1929, named after a 1916 comic strip in which Raúl Grigera was the main character; WA 14.1), for example, recreated the blackface mockery of nineteenth-century Carnival tangos, with Raúl's character speaking in exaggerated Afro-Argentine dialect and breaking into childish, deranged laughter; Sebastián Piana and León Benarós' "Ahí viene el negro Raúl" ("Here Comes El Negro Raúl," 1973) cast Raúl as a "*títere roto*" ("broken puppet") – the pathetic, witless plaything of rich *porteño* playboys. On the other hand, those narratives made it increasingly difficult to discern the presence of Afrodescendants in the world of tango, or the African origins of some of its foundational composers, interpreters, and dancers. Raúl's eldest brother, Luis Estanislao Leandro, offers a case in point. In 1994, a writer for the popular history magazine *Todo es historia* puzzled over the freshly unearthed sheet music for a "tango criollo" by one "E.L. Grigera."[27] This was Luis Estanislao's "Unión Comunal," recorded for Discos Odeón around 1914. The writer could find no information on the composition's publishing house, publication date, or "any other data that would enable me to situate it within the history of the tango." Turning to an encyclopedia, he found biographies of illustrious white agriculturalist and military man Don Tomás Grigera (1755–1829) and his descendants, and assumed that "E.L. Grigera" was one of them.

This mistake illustrates how attenuated the association between Blackness and tango became by the end of the twentieth century. Tango's taken-for-granted whiteness deprived this author of the framework necessary even to imagine that the composer, far from being a member of Tomás Grigera's elite landholding family, might be a descendant of one of the people they enslaved. No one attempting to situate an unknown musician within the history of US jazz music, Brazilian samba, or Cuban *danzón* could have gotten away with the same assumption.

To be sure, in the twentieth century, as tango became the national rhythm of a population comprised primarily of European immigrants and their descendants, its Afro-Argentine imprints may have waned. But accounts of Black absences in the last hundred years of tango's history are exacerbated by the myth of Afro-Argentines' "disappearance," the official invisibility to which they have been subjected, and the paucity of sources preserving Afro-Argentine voices. Ethnographic work, oral histories, and a newly unearthed twentieth-century *Afro-porteño* press are revealing dozens of tango musicians and composers who straddled the nineteenth and twentieth centuries, and shedding new light on the trajectories of famous *tangueros*, like Horacio Salgán or Enrique Maciel, who were deeply embedded in their community's musical traditions, especially *candombe*.[28] As twentieth-century Afro-Argentine collective presences continue to be documented, more individuals will surely come to light who occupied salient places in the overlapping worlds of tango and other forms of *Afro-porteño* music and dance. And as an increasingly visible and vocal Afro-Argentine community continues to reinterpret tango for a more diverse Argentina, researchers may soon have to shift from unearthing tango's deep Afro-Argentine roots to describing its living, evolving Afro-Argentine branches.

Notes

1. Many specialists denied tango's African roots, at best conceding them in the (African) realm of rhythm, not the (European) realm of melody. See Carlos Vega, *Danzas y canciones argentinas* (Buenos Aires: Ricordi, 1936); Jorge Novati and Inés Cuello, eds., *Antología del tango rioplatense*, vol. I (Buenos Aires: Instituto Nacional de Musicología Carlos Vega, 1980); and examples in Óscar Natale, *Buenos Aires, negros y tango* (Buenos Aires: Peña Lillo, 1984), 251–252, 257n6. For overviews of these debates, see Natale; Fernando Guibert, *Los argentinos y el tango* (Buenos Aires: Ediciones Culturales Argentinas, 1973); and Omar García Brunelli, "Bases para una aproximación razonable a la cuestión del componente afro del tango," *Revista Argentina de Musicología* 18 (2017): 91–124.
2. Early examples include Vicente Rossi, *Cosas de negros* (Buenos Aires: Taurus, 2001 [1926]); Héctor Bates and Luis J. Bates, *La historia del tango* (Buenos Aires: Taller Gráfico de la Compañía General Fabril Financiera, 1936); Vicente Gesualdo, *Historia de la música en la Argentina*, vols. II and III (Buenos

Aires: Beta, 1961); Néstor Ortiz Oderigo, *Calunga: croquis del candombe* (Buenos Aires: EUDEBA, 1969); Néstor Ortiz Oderigo, *Aspectos de la cultura africana en el Río de la Plata* (Buenos Aires: Plus Ultra, 1974). More recent works are cited throughout this chapter.

3. On this myth, see George Reid Andrews, *The Afro-Argentines of Buenos Aires, 1800–1900* (Madison: University of Wisconsin Press, 1980).

4. For example, Natale, *Buenos Aires, negros y tango*, ch. 11; Gustavo Varela, *Tango. Una pasión ilustrada* (Buenos Aires: LEA, 2010), ch. 8.

5. Especially Rossi, *Cosas de negros*; Bernardo Kordon, *Candombe: contribución al estudio de la raza negra en el Río de la Plata* (Buenos Aires: Continente, 1938); José Luis Lanuza, *Morenada* (Buenos Aires, Emecé, 1946).

6. This chapter draws from the author's book on the Grigeras; for further details and source references, see Paulina L. Alberto, *Black Legend: The Many Lives of Raúl Grigera and the Power of Racial Storytelling in Argentina* (New York and Cambridge: Cambridge University Press, 2022).

7. For clarity, I italicize *candombe* when referring to the music/dance, but leave it unitalicized to refer to the site or meeting grounds. *Milonga* retains the same double meaning today, as both a music/dance form and a place where people gather to dance tango. On the associations, music, and dances described in this section, see Ricardo Rodríguez Molas, *La música y la danza de los negros en el Buenos Aires de los siglos XVIII y XIX* (Buenos Aires: Clio, 1957); Hugo E. Ratier, "Candombes porteños," *VICUS Cuadernos* 1 (1977): 87–150; Andrews, *Afro-Argentines*; Oscar Chamosa, "'To Honor the Ashes of Their Forebears': The Rise and Crisis of African Nations in the Post-Independence State of Buenos Aires, 1820–1860," *The Americas* 59, no. 3 (2003): 347–378; Pilar González Bernaldo de Quirós, *Civilidad y política en los orígenes de la nación argentina: Las sociabilidades en Buenos Aires, 1829–1862* (Buenos Aires: Fondo de Cultura Económica, 2008); Alex Borucki, *From Shipmates to Soldiers: Emerging Black Identities in the Río de la Plata* (Albuquerque: University of New Mexico Press, 2015).

8. Néstor Ortiz Oderigo, "Las 'naciones' africanas," *Todo es historia*, November 1980, 34, cited here and below.

9. Alejandro Frigerio, *Cultura negra en el Cono Sur: representaciones en conflicto* (Buenos Aires: Facultad de Ciencias Sociales y Económicas de la Universidad Católica Argentina, 2000).

10. Estanislao Villanueva, "El candombe nació en África y se hizo rioplatense," *Todo es historia*, November 1980, 46. Although Uruguayan *candombe* has a bass *piano* drum, the term is not used in Buenos Aires.

11. For reconstructions of this "ancestral African" *candombe*'s sounds, see Norberto Pablo Cirio, "Ausente con aviso: ¿Qué es la música afroargentina?," in *Músicas populares: aproximaciones teóricas, metodológicas y analíticas en la musicología argentina*, ed. Federico Sammartino and Héctor Rubio (Córdoba: Universidad Nacional de Córdoba, 2008), 81–134.

12. Discussion of changing practices of *candombe* in the next paragraphs draws from Lea Geler, *Andares negros, caminos blancos: Afroporteños, estado y Nación Argentina a fines del siglo XIX* (Rosario: Prohistoria Ediciones/ TEIAA, 2010). See also Gustavo Goldman, *Lucamba: Herencia africana en el tango (1870–1890)* (Montevideo: Perro Andaluz, 2008); John Charles Chasteen, *National Rhythms, African Roots: The Deep History of Latin American Popular Dance* (Albuquerque: University of New Mexico Press, 2004); Andrews, *Afro-Argentines*; Gesualdo, *Historia de la música*, 1961; Natale, *Buenos Aires, negros y tango*; Ricardo Rodríguez Molas, "Los afroargentinos y el origen del tango (sociedad, danzas, salones de baile y folclore urbano)," *Desmemoria* 7, no. 27 (2000): 87–132.

13. For musicological analysis, see Goldman, *Lucamba*.

14. On the underlying "grammar," see Brunelli, "Bases."

15. Juan Carlos Cáceres, *Tango negro. La historia negada: orígenes, desarrollo y actualidad del tango* (Buenos Aires: Planeta, 2010), 98.

16. Norberto Pablo Cirio, *Tinta negra en el gris del ayer: los afroporteños a través de sus periódicos entre 1873 y 1882* (Buenos Aires: Teseo, 2009), 74. For a musical description of these "traditional *Afro-porteño*" candombes, notated in a habanera rhythm in 2/4 meter, see Cirio, "Ausente con aviso."

17. Rodríguez Molas, "Los afroargentinos," 105–109.

18. Kordon, *Candombe*, 60, cited here and later in this chapter.

19. Matthew B. Karush, "Blackness in Argentina: Jazz, Tango and Race Before Perón," *Past & Present* 216, no. 1 (2012): 227. For further reading on Afro-Argentines in tango in the early decades of the twentieth century, see Norberto Pablo Cirio, "La presencia del negro en grabaciones de tango y géneros afines," in *Buenos Aires negra: Identidad y cultura*, ed. Leticia Maronese (Buenos Aires: CPPHC, 2006), 25–59; Norberto Pablo Cirio, *La historia negra del tango* (Buenos Aires: Museo Casa Carlos Gardel, 2010); Robert Farris Thompson, *Tango: The Art History of Love* (New York: Pantheon, 2005).

20. Attributed to the tango poet Enrique Santos Discépolo.

21. Ezequiel Martínez Estrada, *La cabeza de Goliat: microscopía de Buenos Aires* (Buenos Aires: Nova, 1957), 154.

22. Leopoldo Lugones (1913), cited in Gustavo Varela, *Tango y política: sexo, moral burguesa y revolución en Argentina* (Buenos Aires, Argentina: Ariel, 2016), 56.

23. "Nuestra escuadra sirve para fiestas y bailes," *La Vanguardia*, 7 Dec. 1915.

24. On the word's origins in the Kimbundu "ka-llenge," a Congo funeral dance practiced in the Río de la Plata, see Néstor Ortiz Oderigo, *Esquema de la música afroargentina* (Buenos Aires: Universidad Nacional de Tres de Febrero, 2008), 176–178, 205–210, 231–232.

25. Quote by Carmen Yannone, interviewed by Lea Geler, August 3 2021.

26. See especially Viejo tanguero (pseud.), "El tango, su evolución y su historia," *Crítica*, September 22, 1913.
27. "'Unión Comunal': Un tango criollo de Estanislao L. Grigera." *Todo es historia*, no. 328, 1994, 63.
28. Cirio, *La historia negra del tango*; Alberto, Paulina L., Lea Geler, and Chisu Teresa Ko, "'In Defense of the People of Color of South America': A New Source for Twentieth-Century Afro-Argentine History and Thought." *Latin American and Caribbean Ethnic Studies*, 2023. doi: https://doi.org/10.1080/17442222.2023.2246898. Maciel was also one of several twentieth-century Argentines (with Sebastián Piana, Juan Carlos Cáceres, Facundo Posadas, and others) who highlighted tango's Black roots and connections to *candombe*, musically or choreographically.

Further Reading

Alberto, Paulina L. *Black Legend: The Many Lives of Raúl Grigera and the Power of Racial Storytelling in Argentina*. New York and Cambridge: Cambridge University Press, 2022.

Alberto, Paulina L., Lea Geler, and Chisu Teresa Ko. "'In Defense of the People of Color of South America': A New Source for Twentieth-Century Afro-Argentine History and Thought." *Latin American and Caribbean Ethnic Studies*, 2023. doi: https://doi.org/10.1080/17442222.2023.2246898.

Andrews, George Reid. *The Afro-Argentines of Buenos Aires, 1800–1900*. Madison: University of Wisconsin Press, 1980.

Chasteen, John Charles. *National Rhythms, African Roots: The Deep History of Latin American Popular Dance*. Albuquerque: University of New Mexico Press, 2004.

Frigerio, Alejandro. *Cultura negra en el Cono Sur: representaciones en conflicto*. Buenos Aires: Facultad de Ciencias Sociales y Económicas de la Universidad Católica Argentina, 2000.

Geler, Lea. *Andares negros, caminos blancos: Afroporteños, Estado y Nación Argentina a fines de siglo XIX*. Rosario: Prohistoria Ediciones/TEIAA, 2010.

Goldman, Gustavo. *Lucamba: Herencia africana en el tango, 1870–1890*. Montevideo: Perro Andaluz, 2008.

Karush, Matthew B. "Blackness in Argentina: Jazz, Tango and Race before Perón." *Past & Present* 216, no. 1 (2012): 215–245.

Natale, Óscar. *Buenos Aires, negros y tango*. Buenos Aires: Peña Lillo, 1984.

Ortiz Oderigo, Néstor. *Aspectos de la cultura africana en el Río de la Plata*. Buenos Aires: Plus Ultra, 1974.

Thompson, Robert Farris. *Tango: The Art History of Love*. New York: Pantheon, 2005.

15 | Synthesizing Analyses: A Choreomusical Study of "La cumparsita"

REBECCA SIMPSON-LITKE

Composed in 1917 by Uruguayan pianist Gerardo Matos Rodríguez and premiered in Montevideo by Roberto Firpo's Orquesta Típica Argentina, the music of "La cumparsita" ("The Little Parade") has spent just over a century making its way around the globe in the form of thousands of published and unpublished musical arrangements, performances, sound recordings, film scenes, YouTube videos, and more. Dance interpretations of the piece have also been numerous and varied, arising both as spontaneous improvisations on the social dance floors of tango clubs and as meticulous choreographies on the professional stage.[1] In this chapter, I provide an in-depth choreomusical analysis of an exceptionally engaging and iconic performance of "La cumparsita" by dancers Cecilia Narova (b. 1960) and Juan Carlos Copes (1931–2021) from the 1998 motion picture *Tango* by director Carlos Saura.[2] To provide the necessary stepping stones to my analytic discussion, I begin by defining the positional listening/viewing perspectives that I adopt in my transcription of the performance, identifying the elements I have chosen to include and exclude.[3] I then explore the intriguing interactions that occur between the dance and the music, showing how movement patterns play with and against musical patterns to create interest and complexity in each large-scale section of the piece. I ultimately reveal how this innovative dance choreography creates an organic union with the music and goes far beyond the "little parade" suggested by its unpresumptuous title.

Explanation of the Transcription and Dance Notation

Before proceeding to the transcription examples, I provide the chart in Figure 15.1 to help orient readers in the ABCA' formal organization and structural proportions of this musical arrangement of "La cumparsita." Stars are placed above measure numbers to indicate the beginning of small- and large-scale musical units in the song, revealing regular two-, four-, and

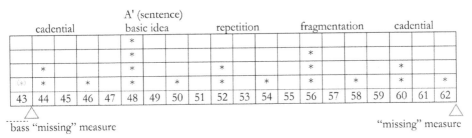

Figure 15.1 Form chart of "La cumparsita."

eight-measure subunits in each large section. The notable disruptions to this regularity are discussed later in this chapter.

Figure 15.2 provides the key to my transcription of music and dance elements in the following examples. First, the lower staves of each system provide the musical elements I consider to be of the most importance in this performance: the bass line (lowest staff, played by the double bass and piano), the (counter) melody (second-lowest staff, played at different times by the violin, piano, and bandoneón), and the melodic variations (third-lowest staff of the last section only, played by the bandoneón). Harmonies are identified with Roman-numeral analysis beneath the bass system. While many arrangements of this piece are notated in a 2/4 meter with durational units that are half the length of those in my transcription (i.e., replacing my quarter notes with eighth notes and so on), I have chosen

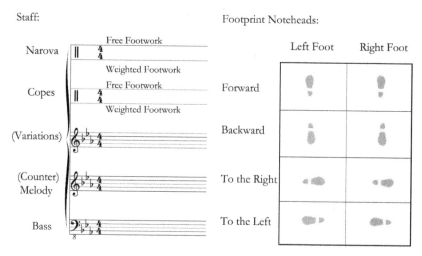

Figure 15.2 Transcription key. (Note: in the Web Examples, the footprint noteheads designate blue for the left foot and red for the right foot.)

to use 4/4 because it better matches the metric structure that is implied by the dancers in the majority of this performance and does not affect the placement of bar lines.[4]

Then, above the musical transcription are two staves dedicated to dance transcription. Readers will no doubt recognize the influence of Western music notation on the structure of my dance notational system, and I hope that, as a result, the dance transcription is simple enough to read and internalize after a minimal amount of study. Analogously, readers with prior knowledge of the footprint diagrams often used to represent ballroom and other partner dances will observe this influence as well; however, my analysis does not assume prior familiarity with the tango genre, and I do not attempt to provide a comprehensive account of tango, dance, or movement principles more broadly in this chapter.[5] My dance notation *is* designed to show the timing and directional elements of the dancers' footwork that I perceive to be most interesting in this specific performance of "La cumparsita." Indeed, there is plenty to discuss even within these rather limited parameters, which speaks to the richness and complexity of the performance. For the most part, other physical elements, like the movements of the dancers' upper bodies, the couple's navigation through space on the dance floor, and so on, are not represented, although I often refer to such elements in my discussion. Finally, it should be noted that the transcription is not intended to substitute for visual engagement with the performance itself; the video remains essential in understanding the analysis (WL 15.1, WL 15.2).[6]

As a partner dance, tango involves two distinct roles: leader and follower.[7] As shown in Figure 15.2, the follower's footwork (danced by Narova) is recorded on the top staff in each transcribed example, while the leader's footwork (danced by Copes) is on the staff immediately below. Within each dancer's two-line staff, the lower line records footwork involving changes of weight (usually marked by steps), while the upper line records embellishments with the free leg (kicks, taps, and toe touches). The placement of a footprint notehead along the dance staff's horizontal timeline indicates that I perceive this timepoint to be marked by a physical accent of some kind. For example, the footprint could represent the landing of a step, toe tap/touch, or stamp; alternatively, it could represent the farthest point in the trajectory of a kick (*patada*), leg hook (*gancho*), or swivel (as in moves like *ocho* or *boleo*).[8]

Vertical ticks (bar lines) divide the timeline into functionally equivalent durational units (measures). The metric location of each physical accent, then, can be identified by examining its proximity to each bar line, and the duration of time that passes from one accent to the next can be identified by examining the proportional space between them. In addition, the vertical alignment of the footprints with the musical timeline in each of the four transcribed examples later in this chapter provides more specific information about metric placement and duration. It should be noted that, to a certain degree, these measurements are still only approximate. Due to the fluid nature of movement, it is often difficult to say with absolute precision where a physical event begins and ends. While one might consider a sharp gesture like a kick, for example, to mark a particular moment in time, this moment is inextricably connected to a prior preparation that propels the foot to its climactic point and a subsequent rebound that carries it back to a more relaxed position afterward. In short, a physical gesture is not executed in a single instant but unfolds over time and space.[9] Despite this fluidity, there are passages in this dance performance that are executed with a high degree of rhythmic precision, and these will be my primary analytic focus.

Next, I often provide text in the space immediately above or below the footprints to identify more specifically the type of footwork executed in that moment. Rather than adopting the external perspective of an observer viewing the dancers on the stage from the audience, my notation encourages readers to put themselves in each of the dancers' shoes and to imagine what it would be like to execute these steps with their own feet. The orientation of footprints (up, down, or sideways) indicates the direction of foot movement (forward, backward, right, or left) for each individual dancer, while the shape (and in the Web Examples, color) of footprints indicates which foot (left or right) is engaged.[10] To internalize each dance perspective, readers will need to focus on one staff (Narova or Copes) at a time. However, the colors provided online (red for the right foot, blue for the left foot) enable simultaneous comparison of the two dancers' movements, allowing readers to see at a glance where Narova and Copes are walking in "parallel feet" (the dancers' simultaneous steps have the opposite-colored footprints) or "crossed feet" (the dancers' simultaneous steps have the same-colored footprints).

Finally, at the bottom of Figure 15.2, three other types of symbols add further directional/spatial information to the footwork. An X indicates a cross (*cruzada*) of a dancer's active foot in front (white X) or behind (black X) their other foot. A white straight vertical arrow indicates that the step incorporates or facilitates an upward movement of the body, while a black straight vertical arrow indicates a downward movement. A white curved horizontal arrow indicates that the step incorporates or facilitates a clockwise rotation of the body, while a black curved horizontal arrow indicates a counterclockwise rotation.

In the analysis that follows, I discuss each section of "La cumparsita," first describing its musical features and then examining how the dance interacts with those features. While this "music-first" approach seems appropriate, given that the music was composed long before the choreography, it is not meant to imply that the physical-visual components of the art form are of secondary importance.[11] Indeed, the main goal of my analysis is to highlight how the choreography is just as engaging and remarkable as the music and a true partner in the performance. At times, dance gestures align closely with musical gestures, while at other times, they seem to work deliberately against musical patterns, providing examples of what dance scholar Juliet McMains and composer Ben Thomas call dance-music "conformance" and "opposition" respectively.[12]

Perhaps most interesting, though, are passages in which the dance "reorchestrates" the music; that is, "the actions of the dancers cause the audience to hear the music differently than they would without seeing the dance, bringing certain instruments that would otherwise be experienced as background to the forefront of aural experience."[13] With these types of dance-music relations in mind, the following analysis moves through this performance of "La cumparsita" one section at a time.

The A Section

As shown on the lowest staff of Web Example 15.1, the bass line of the opening A section of "La cumparsita" features consistent *marcato* (marked) quarter notes, which arpeggiate the underlying harmony. The famous melody aligns with the bass line's quarter notes in odd-numbered measures, while offbeat eighth notes springboard away from an empty melodic downbeat in even-numbered measures. Although these initial observations seem to imply a general rhythmic principle of "straight" measures alternating with "syncopated" measures,[14] the metric place-ment of the contour accents (i.e., the high and low points of the melodic line, circled in WE 15.1) produces a complementary effect. In each odd-numbered measure, the melodic gesture leaps up to its high point on the metrically weak second beat, pulling the listener's attention off balance despite the evenness of the quarter notes. Then, in each even-numbered measure, the melody's low contour accent on the (relatively) metrically stable third beat counters the empty downbeat, providing an anchor for the motive and restoring the listener's sense of metric balance in the second half of the measure.[15] And so, these very small-scale seeds that form the organic building blocks of the entire opening section set up an intriguing interplay between accent, weight, tension, and balance – a feeling of different musical elements pushing and pulling against each other – that draws the listener into immediate bodily engagement with the music.[16]

This alternation between tension and stability also plays out in other musical aspects of the A section and on multiple structural levels. The regular harmonic changes (indicated by Roman numerals in WE 15.1) clearly articulate the two-measure motivic subunits, reinforcing the repetitive rhythm of the melody. Longer patterns of harmonic tension and release combine with larger-scale pitch repetition to define four- and eight-measure subunits. For instance, the opening two measures of

tension-filled dominant harmony (D Mm^7) lead to two measures of stable
tonic harmony (G minor), defining a four-measure melodic/harmonic
unit that is reproduced immediately in the next four measures and so
forming the "basic idea" (mm. 1–4) and "exact repetition" (mm. 5–8)
components of an emerging sentential phrase structure.[17] Throughout
this "presentation" half of the A section, the melody leaps dramatically up
from, and continually returns to, the dominant scale degree $\hat{5}$; the eighth-
note neighbor figures, then, provide accented elaborations that revolve
around this fundamental melodic pitch. Of particular interest is the E♭
that falls on the second beat of mm. 2, 4, 6, and 8 because it completes the
linear $\hat{5}$-$\hat{6}$-$\hat{5}$ figure that is a distinctive feature of many tango melodies.[18]

The dance choreography plays with similar ideas of tension and relax-
ation, but on its own terms. Sometimes it aligns closely with the music
(conformance), and sometimes it provides an intriguing counterpoint
(opposition) that adds to the richness of the sonic-visual experience. As
shown in the upper staves of Web Example 15.1, the dancers begin with an
opening flourish that literally kicks off the performance dramatically, then
reinforce the stability of the metric grid by stepping evenly on every
quarter-note beat in mm. 2–4. In m. 3, their change of direction in physical
space corresponds to the change from dominant to tonic in harmonic
space. Then, instead of simply mimicking the music's internal phrase
organization by repeating this same choreography alongside the repetition
of the basic idea in mm. 5–8, the dancers rechoreograph (or "reorche-
strate," to use McMains/Thomas's term) the passage by providing new
footwork that turns attention away from the metric grid and toward the
specific pitch patterns of the repeated melody.[19] In particular, note how
both Copes and Narova emphasize the high contour accent with a toe tap/
kick on beat 2 of m. 5 and the low contour accent with a toe point on beat 3
of m. 6. In contrast to the straight on-beat stepping of mm. 1–4, the
choreography of mm. 5–8 is characterized by syncopated kicks on weak
beats or offbeats and an absent downbeat articulation in m. 7. The harmonic change in the middle of the basic idea is represented physically once
again, but this time by a change in dance texture, moving from partner
work to Copes's brief passage of solo footwork in m. 7.

While patterns of tension and release subtly oscillate through different
musical and dance parameters in this eight-measure opening, the overall
effect of the first half of the A section is one of regularity and stability. In
the second half of the A section, however, the main melodic line begins to
move through an accented stepwise descent – leaving the opening stasis on

D ($\hat{5}$) for C ($\hat{4}$) in m. 9, B ($\hat{3}$) in m. 11, and A ($\hat{2}$) in m. 13 – to create the increased activity and destabilization expected of the "continuation" portion of the augmented sentence form. While Copes lends some physical emphasis to the downbeats of mm. 8 and 9, this metric stability in the dance is quickly undermined by the dramatic downward lunge (in opposition to the melody's upward leap) and kicks from both dancers on the weak beats of m. 9. The absent downbeat articulation in m. 10 contributes to the destabilization occurring simultaneously in this part of the musical sentence form. This second half of the musical sentence is also marked by a change in the dancers' relationship to each other, as they step on the same feet ("cross-system") in mm. 9–11, rather than on opposite feet ("parallel-system") as in mm. 1–8.

With beat 3 of m. 11, the dancers move briefly into a half-time pattern, where Narova provides clear strong-beat accentuation with her kicks on beats 1 and 3 of m. 12 before the couple comes together face-to-face in m. 13. As the music drives to the cadence in the last three measures of the A section, the melodic line features greater rhythmic syncopation and a faster harmonic rhythm. In the end, the concluding effect of the G-minor tonic arrival in m. 15 is undermined by the melody's leap back to the upper octave and the dominant-supported ascending triplet run that immediately follows the downbeat arrival.[20] In addition to these momentum-gathering surface elements, the form chart of Figure 15.1 reveals that this section is one measure shorter than expected of a complete sixteen-measure sentence structure. Indeed, rather than providing real stability, an opportunity for rest, and a distinct cadential break between formal sections, these final measures propel us immediately into the B section.[21] The camera's cutaway to the audience prevents us from clearly observing how the couple handles the "missing" measure in the music's cadential material, further heightening a sense of anticipation in the performance as we wait expectantly for the dancers' return.

The B Section

From a large-scale perspective, the B section's musical period structure shown in Web Example 15.2 is more "tightly knit" than the A section's sentence.[22] Two parallel eight-measure antecedent-consequent phrases combine to make a complete sixteen-measure section. However, each B-section phrase is less clearly segmented by internal motivic repetition than the two- and four-measure subphrase units of the A section; indeed, each eight-measure B-section phrase drives forward without any clear internal stopping points until it reaches its cadence. In achieving this effect, the bass line abandons its quarter-note harmonic arpeggiations for slinky, chromatic, stepwise descents – moving slowly at first, then faster, and with more syncopation as the phrase proceeds. The melody often joins these syncopated chromatic descents, moving from G ($\hat{1}$) down to C ($\hat{4}$) in mm. 16–19, then leaping up to A ($\hat{2}$) to begin another descent, this time sliding in irregular off-beat rhythms down to the lower G ($\hat{1}$) in mm. 20–23.

While the music has continued uninterrupted from the A section through this first phrase of the B section, the camera does not provide a view of the dancers' footwork again until m. 24. At this point, Narova and Copes engage with the second phrase of the music's parallel period struc-ture in an interesting and unexpected way. As the music restates its previ-ous material in mm. 24–25, both dancers execute a repeated three-step pattern that ends each time in a toe tap, alternately crossing in front or behind. The gray boxes in Web Example 15.2 highlight this brief hemiola, where the three quarter-note units of the dance create a grouping disson-ance with the two quarter-note units of the music.[23] The dance three-units also correspond roughly with the melodic patterning in m. 24, which provides a repeated three-note G-A-B♭ gesture, albeit in faster, irregular rhythms. The dancers then complete m. 25 with two quarter-note steps in response to the quarter notes of the melody on beats 1 and 2 and in sync with the quarter notes of the bass line on beats 3 and 4. In addition to the grouping dissonance and melodic-motivic translation that occurs in the dance here, this pattern of 3+3+2 is also significant because it references (in augmentation) the *habanera* rhythm common in tango and Latin music more broadly.[24]

In mm. 26–27, the dancers align their footwork once again to the metric grid, providing stability in opposition to the syncopated and chromatically slippery musical descent. However, in mm. 28–30, the dancers embody the slow, soaring violin line, while simultaneously marking the half-measure *síncopa* rhythm and durational accents of the bass line with their rotating half-time steps.[25] As in the A section, the B section does not rest long on its G-minor tonic arrival, moving quickly into the same dominant-supported triplets in the second half of m. 31 as were heard in m. 15. Interestingly, the dancers reprise their step-step-tap motivic pattern from mm. 24–25 in this final measure of the B section, but they speed up the second and third steps in order to land right on the strong beat 3 of m. 31. They then suspend their movement over the second half of the measure to allow the music's ascending triplet run to carry us into the C section.

The C Section

As shown in Web Example 15.3, the C section, beginning in m. 32, is also organized as a sixteen-measure sentence and forms the conventional Trio portion of the tango. Rather than being set in the typical contrasting parallel-major key, this section maintains the G-minor key of the A and B sections. Measures 32–35 form the basic idea, and mm. 36–39 provide its varied repetition; each of these four-measure units emphasizes D ($\hat{5}$) just as in the A section. In mm. 40–45, a new two-measure motivic unit is repeated sequentially (with slight variations) three times, gradually bringing the fundamental melodic line down via stepwise motion from D ($\hat{5}$) to A ($\hat{2}$). The cadential arrival on the downbeat of m. 47 and the leisurely quarter-note descent into the last section provide the most significant opportunity for rest thus far in the piece.

While the C section parallels the A section structurally, its surface elements provide an interesting reversal of the "straight-to-syncopated" rhythmic principle heard in the motivic material of the A section. In the C section's presentation half, the seeds of this reversal are planted but not yet fully in bloom. The melody's faster-moving, often *síncopa* rhythms in the first of every two-measure unit (i.e., mm. 32, 34, 36, 38) lead to durationally accented downbeats in every second measure (i.e., mm. 33, 35, 37, 39), and the bass line effectively contains each of these four-measure units by beginning and ending squarely on the tonic G.

As in the A section, the dancers take a different approach to each of these musically analogous four-measure units. For the first statement of the basic idea, their dance gestures complement musical gestures: in mm. 32–33, the dancers' footwork often fills in the on-beat spaces created by the melodic line's rhythmic syncopations, and in m. 34, the dancers' downward lunge in physical space provides a subtle but effective counterbalance to the music's upward contour peak in pitch space. For the varied repetition of the basic idea, then, dance gestures move in conformance with musical gestures: the rhythms of the dancers' rotating turns in mm. 35–36, and Narova's kicks and swivels in mm. 37–38 align closely with the melodic line's durational and contour accents.

The new "syncopated-to-straight" alternation comes to full musical fruition in the continuation half of the sentence. The two-measure sequential model features missing downbeat articulations and anacrustic gestures in every first measure (i.e., mm. 40, 42, 44, 46), leading to strong durational accents emphasizing beats 1 and 3 in every second measure (i.e., mm. 41, 43, 45). In retrospect, it is the unexpected $\hat{5}$-$\hat{1}$ bass gesture in mm. 39–40 that seems to motivate this feature of the continuation half of the C section. It pushes the beginning of the bass's next four-measure unit forward in time by one measure, creating an "orphan" measure that does not fit neatly into the section's otherwise regular two-measure subunits (refer back to Figure 15.1).[26]

After the camera cuts away again briefly to film audience reactions in m. 39, Copes slowly sweeps his left leg behind his right, presenting his shoe to Narova in an extended cross position; this dramatic move both fills the extra "orphan" measure in the musical form and initiates a solo passage for Narova. In mm. 41–44, the bass brings back the A section's arpeggiated quarter notes, establishing two-measure units that are offset from the two-measure units occurring in the melody above. Initially, the walking steps Narova takes in m. 41 and her step onto Copes's shoe in m. 42 appear to be executed in a rather leisurely manner, but upon closer examination, this footwork is precisely timed to the weak-beat contour accents heard in the returning A-section bass line. In this way, Narova adds a brief displacement dissonance between music and dance at the level of the beat to the displacement dissonance occurring within the music itself at the level of the measure.[27]

To resolve this metric dissonance and to keep the section from bursting its projected sixteen-measure musical container, the bass forgoes an expected repetition of the G-minor arpeggiation in m. 43 for an economical, chromatically inflected, stepwise descent (reminiscent of the B section) from the upper to the lower tonic in mm. 44–47. Following a series of high kicks, Narova descends from Copes's shoe in m. 45. The slow slide up from a lunge in mm. 46–47 provides a dance cadence that coincides with the musical cadence and prepares for the climactic final section.

The A' Section

As shown in Web Example 15.4, the piece's final section returns to the basic structure and musical content of the A section, but with some important additions and omissions. The bass line is essentially the same as in the opening section but incorporates the *síncopa* rhythm from the B section in mm. 56–59. In place of the original melody, the violins provide a slower-moving countermelody, above which the bandoneón plays faster-moving melodic variations (*variaciones*).[28] While these new instrumental parts conform to the original A section's fifteen-measure sentence structure, the bandoneón also introduces a new and unexpected element of motivic circularity into this final section, repeating the first two measures of basic-idea material in its approach to the final cadence (compare mm. 60–61 with mm. 48–49 and mm. 52–53).

Matching the flurry of undulating notes in the newly added bandoneón variations throughout the A' section, the increased dance activity features tight rotations and frequent energetic leg flourishes. While the music mainly summarizes previous material, the dancers introduce a new motivic pattern that creates another engaging grouping dissonance with the music. In mm. 57–59, a three-event dance motive is repeated four times, where Narova's high kick marks the end of the motive each time. In the first two statements of this dance motive, Narova steps on the quarter-note beats, creating the same kind of grouping dissonance of dance threes against musical twos observed previously in the B section. As shown in the hypothetical footwork in the transcription (WE 15.4), if Narova had continued this onbeat rhythm for the last two iterations of the motive, her final kick would have landed squarely on beat 4 of m. 59. Instead, she varies the rhythm of the three steps slightly, resulting in a half-beat reduction in the length of each of the third and fourth motivic statements. By completing her final kick on beat 3 – one beat earlier than anticipated – Narova can squeeze in a preparatory step on beat 4 of m. 59 that allows the couple to move into cadential material on the downbeat of m. 60.

Conclusion

In the liner notes to the soundtrack of *Tango*, director Carlos Saura writes:

TANGO is a film in which the dramatic action is based on the musical content, a review (though not in historical or chronological order) embracing creole waltzes, milongas and tangos. Perhaps for that reason I have trouble disentangling the music from the picture's other basic components, such as choreography, scenery, photography, and – indeed – the performances and even the camera movement ... Working together, the choreographer, dancer and tango master

Juan Carlos Copes, the choreographer Ana Maria Steckelman, Carlos Rivarola and the extraordinary dancer Julio Bocca gave rhythmic and danceable shape to the music we had chosen. This was often exhausting work. As I've already said, in a musical film like TANGO the music, photography, scenery, choreography and performances should come together to produce a unified whole. That was my job, to blend elements that at times seemed incompatible . . . I fervently hope that our film will stimulate an even greater appreciation of this exceptional music!

In this spirit of integration and collaboration between the arts, my close choreomusical analysis of "La cumparsita" from *Tango* has endeavored to show both how this famous music has inspired dancers to move for over a century and, in turn, how dancers can "give shape" to the tango classic in fresh and sometimes unexpected ways. Dance scholar Juliet McMains notes that the power of music to propel people into motion is created through an interplay of rhythms generated by different orchestra members, and dancers integrate themselves into this push and pull almost like another orchestra member, pushing and pulling on the rhythm too.[29] Rather than attempting to disentangle this beautiful intertwinement of sonic and physical patterns, then, I have focused on exploring the rich and complex dialogue that unfolds between music and dance in this piece, using choreomusical analysis to provide evidence that "La cumparsita" is far from just a "little parade" but a true masterpiece of the tango genre.

Notes

1. In addition to being officially recognized as the Cultural and Popular Anthem of Uruguay in 1997, the song's status as the quintessential representative of the tango genre is also reflected in the milongas (tango social dance events), many of which have developed a tradition of reserving it for the last song of an evening. For more information, see www.wfmt.com/2017/11/25/100-years-la-cumparsita/ and www.so-tango.com/blog/miscellanea/lacumparsitafirstdancelastsong.

2. The soundtrack to the film features a combination of arrangements of classic tangos like "La cumparsita," more recently composed pieces by prominent composers such as Astor Piazzolla, and music composed specifically for the film by Lalo Schifrin. Musicians include Néstor Marconi (bandoneón), Adolfo Gómez (bandoneón), Juanjo Domínguez (guitar), Norberto Ramos (piano), *El Nuevo Quinteto Real* – Horacio A. Salgán (piano), Ubaldo Aquiles De Lío (guitar), Oscar Giunta (bass), Antonio Agri (violin) – and the Orchestra Ensemble Lalo Schifrin conducted by Schifrin with assistance from Óscar Cardozo Ocampo. The film's many dance scenes were choreographed by Juan Carlos Copes, Ana Maria Steckelman, and Carlos Rivarola, with assistance from

Ángel Coria. For a discussion of the film's plot and cultural issues, see Navitski's Chapter 17 in this volume.

3. In this discussion, only basic music-theoretical and dance knowledge is assumed, with definitions of concepts that may not be familiar provided in footnotes or parentheses, to be accessible to readers with a variety of music and dance backgrounds.

4. That is, the basic stepping patterns of the dancers are oriented most often around four distinct beats per measure, rather than two as in 2/4. While early tango pieces (like this one) are commonly notated in 2/4, later tangos are also notated in 4/4. For more on this metric transition, see Kacey Link and Kristin Wendland, *Tracing Tangueros: Argentine Tango Instrumental Music* (New York: Oxford University Press, 2016): 91–92.

5. See Ann Hutchinson Guest, *Choreo-Graphics: A Comparison of Dance Notation Systems from the Fifteenth Century to the Present* (New York: Gordon and Breach, 1998) for a comprehensive history of dance and movement notation systems, and *Journal of Music Theory* 65, no. 1 (2021) for examples of more recent choreomusical notation systems. Readers of my contribution to this JMT issue will note that the notational approach and analytic techniques I have honed as a music theorist and social salsa dancer are applied here to my analysis of "La cumparsita."

6. The timestamps included in my transcription examples correspond to WL 15.1. For the complete film, see WL 15.2. The "La cumparsita" scene takes place near the end of the film and depicts the arrival of immigrants to Argentina at the turn of the twentieth century.

7. For a discussion of the physical/spatial mechanics and power dynamics in tango and other social partner dances, see David Kaminsky, *Social Partner Dance: Body, Sound, and Space* (New York: Routledge, 2020). While this performance is choreographed, and thus, neither dancer is leading or following as they would in a social context, many of the same movement patterns and physical principles are still at play.

8. Special thanks to Carolyn Merritt for help with the tango dance terms. For a helpful glossary of tango terms, see www.tejastango.com/terminology.html#G.

9. In our analysis of salsa, Chris Stover and I discuss why it is sometimes appropriate to make phenomenological equivalences in dance analysis – to suggest that a particular physical gesture is understood to occur at a particular moment in time – even while acknowledging the temporal fluidity of these physical gestures ("Theorizing Fundamental Music/Dance Interactions in Salsa," *Music Theory Spectrum* 41, no. 1 (2019): 7). See also works by Bosse, Pietrobruno, and Browning.

10. While I have attempted to represent some information about directions of travel, my notation does not attempt to capture the full bird's-eye perspective that would a ballroom footprint diagram or track-drawing system for court dances. In particular, those dance-notation systems use right to left on the page

to correspond to spatial locations on the floor, whereas I use the horizontal dimension of the staff (from left to right) to represent the flow of time.

11. At milongas that feature live bands, the dialogue is much less one-sided – a conversation, rather than a lecture – as musicians can interact spontaneously and in response to dancers.

12. Juliet McMains and Ben Thomas, "Translating from Pitch to Plié: Music Theory for Dance Scholars and Close Movement Analysis for Music Scholars," *Dance Chronicle* 36, no. 2 (2013): 210–211. Kaminsky discusses similar relations between music and dance, using the term "line matching" to refer to the practice of "moving tightly with the music," and "line weaving" to refer to "dancing a new line not present in the musical texture" (*Social Partner Dance*, 99).

13. McMains/Thomas, "Translating from Pitch to Plié," 210–211.

14. This alternation is also a feature of the clave and other Latin rhythmic patterns, as discussed by Gerard, Mauleón, Peñalosa, and Washburne.

15. As a chromatic secondary leading tone, the C♯ melodic low point of the A section's first eight measures also strongly directs the listener's attention back up to D. When this secondary tonic resolution enters on beat 4 of every even-numbered measure, it might seem to emphasize a weak metric event, throwing the listener off balance again. However, it soon becomes apparent that this beat-4 D is also strongly anticipatory, directing attention to, and thus serving to reinforce, the strong-beat metric emphasis of every odd-measured downbeat.

16. Physical and spatial metaphors are common in the descriptions and conceptions of musical experience. See also Cox, Godøy and Leman, Gritten and King, Hatten, Larson, and Macedo.

17. This formal terminology is from William Caplin, *Classical Form: A Theory of Formal Functions for the Instrumental Music of Haydn, Mozart, and Beethoven* (New York: Oxford University Press, 1998), Chapter 3. The prototypical sentence is an eight-measure phrase unit divided into the proportions 2+2+1+1+2: two measures of basic (motivic) idea and two measures of its (varied) repetition form the presentation first half, then two one-measure fragmentary subunits and two measures of cadential material form the continuation second half. Sentence structures in "La cumparsita" follow these proportions but in augmentation, with measure counts doubled to 4+4+2+2+4, and comprise entire sections rather than individual phrases within sections. For more information about large-scale form and phrase structures in tango, see Link and Wendland, *Tracing* Tangueros, 35–36.

18. See Kristin Wendland, "The Allure of Tango: Grafting Traditional Performance Practice and Style onto Art-Tangos," *College Music Symposium* 47 (2007): 2; and Link and Wendland, *Tracing* Tangueros, 33.

19. Kaminsky notes that tango and blues dancers will "sometimes discuss making a choice between 'dancing the rhythm' and 'dancing the melody.'" Regarding improvised social tango dance, he states that the music's metronomic *marcato*

pattern by itself does not compel motion; instead, its rhythmic austerity allows dancers to focus more on the lyrical elements of the music. *Social Partner Dance*, 98–99.

20. Wendland cites triplet figures as another common tango melodic characteristic, although usually in combination with the $\hat{5}$-$\hat{6}$-$\hat{5}$ melodic figure, "Allure of Tango," 2.

21. In many kinds of dance traditions, the eight-measure/count unit is prevalent and disruptions to this regularity can create very interesting effects. For example, see work by Mahinka and Simpson-Litke on hypermetric disruptions in salsa music and their effects on dancers.

22. See Caplin, *Classical Form* for definitions and examples of tight-versus loose-knit formal organization. While sentences and periods are both commonly used to structure themes in common-practice Western art music, sentences are looser in organization than periods due to their internal processes of fragmentation and destabilization.

23. In *Fantasy Pieces: Metrical Dissonance in the Music of Robert Schumann* (New York: Oxford University Press, 1999), Harald Kreb calls this type of situation a G3/2 grouping dissonance, where 1 = quarter note. Several dance-music scholars have observed these kinds of interactions between music and dance in various artforms, including ballet (Jordan, Leaman, and Bell), tap (Bilidas, Gain), musical theatre (Short), and salsa (Simpson-Litke).

24. Wendland notes that in 2/4, this "*tango-milonga*" rhythm would be notated as dotted-eighth, sixteenth, eighth, eighth, but is often syncopated with the sixteenth note tied to the following eighth note. The resulting rhythm – dotted eighth, dotted eighth, eighth (a durational pattern called "3-3-2" by *tangueros* in Argentina) – is common in many musical traditions, "Allure of Tango," 2. The rhythm is perhaps most strongly associated with Cuban music, in which it goes by the name *tresillo*. See Richard Cohn, "A Platonic Model of Funky Rhythms," *Music Theory Online* 22, no. 2 (2016) for an account of this rhythm in various styles of music.

25. In a 2/4 meter with durational values halved, this *síncopa* figure would be notated as sixteenth-eighth-sixteenth, but in my transcription, it is eighth-quarter-eighth. Wendland notes that this figure is used frequently in tango, both in melody and accompaniment, "Allure of Tango," 2.

26. For a discussion on "extra" measures in salsa and other Cuban music, see works by Mahinka, McMains, Gerard, Simpson-Litke/Stover, and Simpson-Litke.

27. Using the terminology in Krebs, *Fantasy Pieces*, both displacement dissonances would be described as D (2+1), but between melody and bass, 1 = the notated measure, while between music and dance, 1 = the quarter-note beat.

28. For more information about *variaciones*, see Link and Wendland, *Tracing Tangueros*, 33–34.

29. McMains, *Spinning Mambo*, 69. Link and Wendland include a similar statement from *milonguero* Julián Altabe, saying "the dance couple forms part of the tango texture as the partners respond in movement to the violins, bandoneones, and words of the singer." *Tracing* Tangueros, 17.

Further Reading

Bell, Matthew. "*Danses Fantastiques*: Metrical Dissonance in the Ballet Music of P. I. Tchaikovsky." *Journal of Music Theory* 65, no. 1 (2021): 107–137.

Bosse, Joanna. "Salsa Dance and the Transformation of Style: An Ethnographic Study of Movement and Meaning in a Cross-Cultural Context." *Dance Research Journal* 41, no. 1 (2008): 45–64.

Browning, Barbara. *Samba: Resistance in Motion*. Bloomington: Indiana University Press, 1995.

Guest, Ann Hutchinson. *Choreo-Graphics: A Comparison of Dance Notation Systems from the Fifteenth Century to the Present*. New York: Gordon and Breach, 1998.

Jordan, Stephanie. *Moving Music: Dialogues with Music in 20th Century Ballet*. London: Dance Books, 2000.

Kaminsky, David. *Social Partner Dance: Body, Sound, and Space*. New York: Routledge, 2020.

Leaman, Kara Yoo. "Musical Techniques in Balanchine's Jazzy Bach Ballet." *Journal of Music Theory* 65, no. 1 (2021): 139–169.

McMains, Juliet and Ben Thomas. "Translating from Pitch to Plié: Music Theory for Dance Scholars and Close Movement Analysis for Music Scholars." *Dance Chronicle* 36, no. 2 (2013): 196–217.

Simpson-Litke, Rebecca. "Flipped, Broken, and Paused Clave: Dancing Through Metric Ambiguities in Salsa Music." *Journal of Music Theory* 65, no. 1 (2021): 39–80.

Simpson-Litke, Rebecca and Chris Stover. "Theorizing Fundamental Music/Dance Interactions in Salsa." *Music Theory Spectrum* 41, no. 1 (2019): 74–103.

16 | Mixed Messages: Tango and Argentine Politics

MATTHEW B. KARUSH

As a commercial product intended to provide pleasure to a paying audience, tango has never been partisan. Tangos that pay homage to political figures, though rare, do exist, and certainly political parties have used tango bands to attract voters to their rallies. Occasionally, political opponents have taken sides within the tango: in the 1920s, for example, followers of the Radical party leader Hipólito Yrigoyen were said to be fans of the tango bandleader Francisco Canaro (1888–1964), while the more conservative Radical faction led by Marcelo Torcuato Alvear enjoyed the music of Julio De Caro (1899–1980).[1] Nevertheless, tango music, lyrics, and dance steps have not generally expressed a position with respect to the political movements or conflicts of the moment. The genre has had fans, as well as occasional detractors, from all points on the political spectrum.

Still, like other mass cultural commodities, tango is deeply political. From its emergence at the very beginning of the twentieth century, the tango has been implicated in, and shaped by, debates about national identity, modernization, class conflict, morality, and gender roles, among other inherently political issues. At a certain level of abstraction, the politics of tango in Argentina are similar to the politics of jazz in the United States, *samba* in Brazil, *son* in Cuba, or any of the musical genres that exploded in popularity with the invention of the phonograph, the radio, and the cinema.[2] These genres or their immediate precursors were associated with lower-class, marginalized, and racially or ethnically defined communities. They were attacked by elite commentators who saw them as disreputable, salacious, and immoral, and at times they became the object of regulation by the state. Yet partly due to the transgressive thrill they afforded, they also attracted fans from all social classes. Over time, all of them were transformed in ways that made them less scandalous, more appropriate for consumption by middle-class families. And eventually, all these genres, to one extent or another, became national symbols.[3] Tango, a genre that had been disdained by some as lowbrow and even immoral, became the musical icon of Buenos Aires and a source of national pride.

Along the way, tango came to embody a broad, often contradictory range of meanings. Tango was associated with urban modernity, but it retained a connection to rural tradition as well. It was clearly associated with Afro-Argentine roots at first, but later was transformed into a symbol of cosmopolitanism and immigration. It was deeply moralistic and conformist, yet it also expressed working-class pride, a stance that could have progressive implications. It evoked the desire for upward mobility, even as it warned of the dangers of social climbing. It tended toward misogyny, but it also empowered women in certain ways. In short, tango was deeply ambivalent; its profoundly mixed messages meant it was available for competing and contradictory forms of political appropriation. When the rise of Juan Perón's populist political movement in 1945 split the country into two enduring political factions, tango was inevitably implicated. In fact, competing versions of tango made vital contributions to both Peronism and anti-Peronism.

Origin Myth

Tango music and dance were a product of transnational cultural exchange made possible by the position of Buenos Aires and Montevideo, the twin port cities of the Río de la Plata, in Atlantic commercial networks. It was a cosmopolitan genre enjoyed by Argentines and Uruguayans from all walks of life. Nevertheless, almost from its inception, tango expressed an affiliation with local, popular culture. Within a couple of decades, this association hardened into a populist origin myth that depicted the genre as a product of a seedy yet colorful urban underworld. This myth has informed tango's politics ever since.

In the late nineteenth century, the word "tango" could sometimes signify dancing like a Black person. During the colonial period, Buenos Aires and Montevideo had substantial enslaved and free Black populations with their own musical cultures. Among these were the drumming and dance traditions known as *candombe*, which featured prominently in the annual pre-Lenten celebration of Carnival in Buenos Aires. Beginning in the 1860s, white Carnival troupes embraced the world-turned-upside-down ethos of the holiday by wearing blackface and performing a mocking version of Afro-Argentine music and dance. In the 1880s, Black *candomberos* began imitating their imitators, blackening their own faces to perform for Carnival. At roughly the same time, a new couple dance known as the *milonga* emerged in the outskirts of the city. A fully transnational innovation, the *milonga* appears to have been an Afro-Argentine adaptation of European dance styles performed to the Cuban *habanera* rhythm and informed by *candombe* choreography. In 1889, the Podestá theatre troupe included a *milonga* in *Juan Moreira*, their hugely popular play about a *gaucho* (cowboy) outlaw. From 1900 on, *porteños* (residents of the city of Buenos Aires) referred to this dance, still performed to the *habanera* rhythm, as tango. At this point, tango retained its association with the Afro-Argentine community, but it was already being performed and enjoyed by whites of all social classes.[4]

According to one very common narrative, tango was invented in the brothels and seedy clubs of the *arrabales*, the slums on the outskirts of the city, and was adopted by polite society only after it had become a fad in Paris and New York. As historian Ema Cibotti has shown, this story is a radical simplification that depends on a depiction of turn-of-the-century Buenos Aires as a "dual society" composed of rich and poor.[5] In fact, tango emerged in a rapidly modernizing city experiencing massive levels of immigration and an increasingly complex social structure. In this context, tango was certainly danced in brothels and working-class venues, but from the beginning it was also performed in nightclubs and theatres with a more respectable clientele. In fact, as its appearance in the plays of the Podestá family suggests, early tango is best understood as an offshoot of *criollismo*, a literary and theatrical tradition that delivered stories of brave and violent *gaucho* rebels to an audience comprised of both "natives" and immigrants. The tropes of *criollismo* are evident in the lyrics of such early tango songs as "El Porteñito" ("The Little Guy from Buenos Aires," Villoldo, 1903), in which a violent tough guy brags of his tango dancing ability and refers to his girlfriend with the *gaucho* term, *china*. As literary critic Adolfo Prieto famously argued, *criollista* celebrations of *gaucho* heroes were embraced by immigrants seeking to assimilate into their new nation. Tango was a part of this new popular culture, an anchor of cultural unity in a time of rapid and profound social change.[6]

Though it was enjoyed by the rich, poor, and in between, tango was understood as a product of the streets. An international tango fad and the advent of the global recording industry helped cement that association. In 1913 and 1914, the tango thrilled Parisians and New Yorkers with its allegedly primitive lasciviousness. Argentine musicians and dancers satisfied their European and American audiences by performing in stereotypical *gaucho* attire, depicting themselves as the bearers of an exotic tradition rather than a modern, cosmopolitan musical form.[7] The idea that tango was a local vernacular, fundamentally distinct from European and

American music, was reinforced by the commercial strategies of the multi-national record companies. As they entered foreign markets like Argentina, these companies divided their catalogues between North American and European genres, ostensibly of universal interest, and "local music," which invariably referred to popular rather than erudite forms.[8] Since American and European music provided Argentine consumers with a sophisticated, elitist product, the companies used a populist strategy to market tango records, depicting the genre as the authentic music of the people.

This populism was ironically reinforced by a new form of nationalist criticism leveled against tango in the 1910s. Argentina experienced massive waves of immigration in the decades after 1880, especially from Italy and Spain. By the early twentieth century, nearly half of the population of Buenos Aires and other major cities was foreign born. In this context, the emergence of a militant labor movement led by anarchists and syndicalists caused many elites to worry that immigration was undermining national identity. Intellectuals like Manuel Gálvez and Leopoldo Lugones now argued that tango was emblematic of Argentina's rootless, "cosmopolitan" society. Scandalized that Parisians and New Yorkers associated Argentina with a lowbrow cultural form, they attacked the tango as a repulsive dance created by lower-class foreigners.[9] Thus, whether celebrated or condemned, tango was linked to the lower classes.

By the 1910s, tango's origin myth was largely in place: the music was believed to have emerged in the brothels and nightclubs of the lower-class *arrabales* of Buenos Aires. The Afro-Argentine and semirural roots of the genre were gradually forgotten as the ideological whitening of the nation proceeded. For well-to-do Argentines, the transgressive thrill of dancing tango remained intact but was displaced from race to class. The origin myth implied a political gesture: to enjoy tango was to express pride in Argentine popular culture.

The Melodramatic Politics of the New *Tango Canción*

In 1917, Carlos Gardel's (1890–1935) recording of Pascual Contursi's (1888–1932) "Mi noche triste" ("My Sad Night") launched the genre of the new *tango canción* (tango song). Although there had been tangos with lyrics before, these new songs made stars out of tango singers and transformed the genre into a music well suited to listening on records and on the radios that became ubiquitous in Argentine homes during the 1920s and 1930s.[10] Pursuing an audience with disposable income, lyricists abandoned the glorification of violence in favor of melodramatic depictions of love and romantic betrayal.[11] Often, these changes are understood as a process of sanitization, a cleaning up of tango to remove any dangerous or subversive messages.[12] In that familiar story, massification depoliticized tango as producers sought to avoid offense in order to build the largest audience possible. Yet even if the new tango songs were more suitable for respectable, domestic consumption, they retained, or even deepened the genre's class politics. In this sense, the *tango canción* was well suited to the political moment. After an electoral reform established universal male suffrage in 1912, the Unión Cívica Radical, or Radical Party, dominated Argentine politics until 1930, winning elections both by distributing patronage jobs to its followers and by occasionally deploying pro-worker policies and rhetoric. Similarly, tango in this period expressed both the desire for upward mobility and pride in working-class identity.

The popularization of the phonograph and the radio made it possible for consumers to listen to music in the privacy of their own homes. In this new context of reception, lyrics became increasingly important, and record companies and radio advertisers hoped to harness the star power of singers. In terms of their lyrical content, the new tango songs reflected a growing partnership between composers and playwrights who produced one-act *sainetes* for popular audiences. In 1918, the enormously popular play *Los dientes del perro* (*The Teeth of the Dog*), which told the story of a doomed love affair between a cabaret singer and a young, upper-class man, included a performance of "Mi noche triste." The formula inspired imitation. New plays were written to showcase new tango songs, which were then recorded by Gardel and other stars. What emerged from this creative process was an archetypical tango plot: a *compadrito*, or urban tough guy, bemoans his abandonment by a girl from his neighborhood. Most frequently, the girl is a *milonguita*, a dancing girl for hire. Her fall from innocence and purity is most often a result of her seduction by an upper-class *niño bien* (rich kid) or simply by the bright lights of the downtown cabarets.[13]

The misogyny of so many tango songs reinforced the genre's working-class affiliation. Tangos, in Donna Guy's phrase, "berated women for the desire for conspicuous consumption that allowed men to lead them into lives of degradation."[14] As the narrator in Celedonio Flores's "Margot" (1919, WL 16.1) puts it, "it was your fault that you rolled over, and not innocently / The impulses of a rich girl you had in mind / since the day a millionaire dandy flirted with you!"[15] Tangos like this one expressed the anxiety of working-class men faced with the loss of their patriarchal power as increasing numbers of women entered the workforce. Tango melodramas dispensed poetic justice by punishing working-class women for abandoning the men of their class. In the downfall of the *milonguita*, working-class men could experience a reassuring feeling of moral superiority.

Tango, like melodrama more broadly, is often seen as escapist and, as a result, politically conservative. By displacing real-world conflicts and concerns into the arena of romantic love, these stories distract audiences from collective organizing or political activism. Furthermore, melodrama is fatalistic, its outcomes preordained. The *compadrito* will inevitably lose his woman to a *niño bien*; the *milonguita* will end up ruined and abandoned once she gets older and loses her looks. In such a universe, no change is possible. Tango lyrics were also deeply conformist: they counselled listeners to behave themselves according to a strict moral code, to be content with their lot in life, and to avoid social striving.[16]

Nevertheless, the meanings of these tango songs were multiple, their politics ambivalent. Fatalism could easily veer into cynicism and social critique, as in Enrique Santos Discépolo's (1901–1951) "Cambalache" ("Hodgepodge" or "Junk Shop," WL 16.2) written in 1934, when many Argentines were suffering from the effects of the global depression: "He who works / day and night like an ox / is the same as he who lives off of others / or kills, or cures the sick / or is an outlaw."[17] Moreover, the marketing of tango stars often undercut the genre's critique of social striving. Both male and female tango stars were celebrated for their rags-to-riches biographies. Gardel's most common nickname, "el Morocho del Abasto" ("The Dark Guy from Abasto") was an explicit reminder of his humble roots in a working-class, Buenos Aires neighborhood, while his aristocratic smoking jacket symbolized his rapid social ascent. Not only did this image constitute an endorsement of poor people's desire for upward mobility, but it also cemented the notion that tango authenticity required working-class origins.[18]

Finally, the conservatism of tango was counterbalanced by the genre's insistent critique of the rich. The most malevolent force in the tango universe was the *bacán*, a frivolous aristocrat who lured working-class women away from the men of their neighborhoods, introduced them to the immoral world of the cabaret, and then abandoned them. Though tango melodrama was a product of a complex, modernizing society, it depicted a Manichean world composed of hateful, selfish rich people and the noble, long-suffering poor. In the 1930s and 1940s, this depiction would generate more explicitly populist messages within tango.

Peronism's Tango Roots

Beginning in the 1920s, at the same moment when lyricists were developing the conventions of the new tango song and singers were emerging as stars, a new generation of composers and bandleaders – the *guardia nueva* (New Guard) – was revolutionizing the music. Musicians like Juan Carlos Cobián (1896–1953) and De Caro aimed to improve the tango, to turn a lowbrow form into sophisticated, modern music, such as De Caro's recording of "Gallo ciego" ("Blind Rooster," WL 16.3). Most of the *guardia nueva* bandleaders came from more prosperous families than the first generation of tango musicians. They brought more extensive musical educations to bear on their music, applying innovative harmonies and more elaborate orchestrations.[19] Spurred on by the marketing strategies of the record companies, the tango audience tended to split into fans of the *guardia nueva* "evolutionists," whose records typically came out on Victor, and supporters of "traditionalist" bandleaders like Canaro, under contract to Discos Nacional, the local Odeon affiliate.[20]

The dispute between evolutionists and traditionalists was ideological as well as aesthetic. Evolutionists embraced a modernizing ethos and a cosmopolitan outlook; by improving the tango and associating it with progress, they hoped to compete for listeners who might be attracted to more sophisticated genres and were embarrassed by tango's lowbrow associations. The leading proponent of this project was De Caro, who, by the 1930s, was promising to create a "symphonic tango." Depicting himself as the savior of the genre, he argued that "the tango needs to develop in another way, so that it acquires quality and establishes itself as an elevated musical expression."[21] Fans of De Caro and other evolutionists praised these bandleaders for injecting harmonic and melodic complexity and raising the musical standards of the *orquesta típica*, or tango band. Meanwhile, defenders of tango tradition argued that the evolutionists had gone too far, that by copying elements from foreign musical genres, they had lost tango's essence.

The enormous commercial success of tango bandleader Juan D'Arienzo (1900–1976) in the late 1930s swung the pendulum decisively in the direction of the traditionalists. Known as "el Rey del Compás" ("The King of the Beat"), D'Arienzo developed a style based on a rigid rhythm that appealed especially to dancers, such as "Pensalo bien" ("Think It Over," WL 16.4) Fans heard his music as a return to the tango of the *guardia vieja* (Old Guard), and they especially appreciated the bandleader's emphasis on rhythm. Though some critics attacked D'Arienzo's music as a step backward, others praised him for having returned the tango to its simple origins. As one put it, D'Arienzo "accentuated its rhythm, which had been getting lost among the very musical but not very 'tangoesque' harmonies of cornets and saxes, and he achieved the old novelty of playing a true tango."[22] Even though the debates over D'Arienzo did not map onto partisan conflicts, they were political. Given tango's symbolic status, what was at stake in these debates was Argentine national identity. Was this a nation that aspired to the cultural standard set by the modern nations of Europe and the United States, or was it a nation rooted in the authentic, distinctive culture of the people? In D'Arienzo's popularity, we can discern the outlines of a populist nationalism.[23]

These outlines would come more sharply into focus with the emergence of the tango singer Alberto Castillo (1914–2002). Although he was from a middle-class family and trained as a physician, Castillo became the most popular tango singer of the 1940s and 1950s by drawing out the working-class consciousness that had long been implicit in the genre. During the 1930s, tango lyricists had begun to abandon this orientation. Under pressure from government regulators who sought to sanitize the music played on the radio and in pursuit of a middle-class audience, lyricists like Gardel's writing partner, Alfredo Le Pera (1900–1935), abandoned *Lunfardo*, the working-class slang that had been a tango mainstay since Contursi's "Mi noche triste." Instead, Le Pera and others wrote with a more highbrow vocabulary, telling universal stories that were less clearly situated in the *arrabales* of Buenos Aires. Castillo sharply reversed course. The lyrics to his 1942 hit "Así se baila el tango" ("This Is How the Tango Is Danced," WL 16.5) were peppered with *Lunfardo* and proudly insisted that the tango was a working-class genre: "What do rich boys and fops know, what do they know about tango, what do they know about rhythm?"[24] And Castillo's class affiliations went beyond his lyrics; through his fashion choices – gaudy ties and wide lapels – and his aggressively masculine stage persona, he cultivated a style that audiences associated with the working class.[25]

Castillo's populist self-presentation was perfectly suited to the new Argentina that began to emerge on October 17, 1945, when thousands of workers filled the Plaza de Mayo in downtown Buenos Aires to demand Perón's release from prison. After playing a leadership role in the nationalist military coup of 1943, Perón had used his position as Secretary of Labor to provide tangible benefits to labor unions and thereby build a working-class following. As Perón's poor and often darker-skinned supporters rallied to his cause, middle-class Argentines were scandalized by the way he empowered those they considered culturally beneath them. The extent of the threat to middle-class status and prestige only deepened after Perón won the 1946 presidential election. For anti-Peronist intellectuals like Julio Cortázar, the tango singer Castillo represented everything that was wrong with Peronist Argentina. As Cortázar put it, "The simple delight in bad taste and in resentful meanness explains the triumph of Alberto Castillo."[26]

Needless to say, the populist tango styles of D'Arienzo and Castillo did not cause the rise of Peronism. Historians rightly look for such causes among patterns of economic development, the global rise of statist ideologies, years of organizing work by labor activists, the shifting geopolitical context at the end of World War II, as well as the conjuncture opened by the military coup of 1943. Nevertheless, the fact that populism emerged within tango before the rise of Perón is suggestive. Insofar as Peronism was a cultural revolution, a reshuffling of hierarchies that empowered some and threatened others, developments within tango helped make it possible. D'Arienzo's emphasis on rhythm and Castillo's working-class style tapped into a current that had been present in tango since the elaboration of the genre's origin myth early in the twentieth century. They sharpened the genre's association with working-class culture and, in so doing, they divided the tango audience along class lines. This division both anticipated and facilitated the emergence of the political rupture between working-class Peronists and middle-class anti-Peronists.

And yet, there were never any explicitly Peronist tangos. Some tango musicians, such as Osvaldo Pugliese (1905–1995), whose Communist sympathies were well-known, ran afoul of the Perón regime and experienced blacklisting and even arrests. By contrast, some tango musicians and singers enthusiastically embraced the regime as did several influential tango composers and lyricists, including Homero Manzi (1907–1951) and Discépolo. Yet the tangos composed in this period bore no traces of Peronist ideology. Manzi's most famous songs from the Perón years, including "Sur" ("South," referencing a neighborhood in the south side of Buenos Aires, 1948), avoided explicit political statements in favor of a poetic nostalgia for the Buenos Aires neighborhoods of the past. For his part, Discépolo expressed his fervent support for Peronism not in his tango lyrics but in a regular monologue on the radio. Tango's melancholy poetics, its depiction of downtrodden slums, made it ill-suited to convey Perón's promise to build a socially just future.[27] Nevertheless, even if the genre could not express a Peronist perspective, it thrived during Perón's first term (1946–1952). Peronism produced a dramatic improvement in working-class living standards, facilitating an expansion in popular dance, which took place in cabarets and social clubs throughout the city and across the social spectrum.[28] Tango experienced its Golden Age as many of the genre's most famous bandleaders thrived, including Aníbal Troilo (1914–1975), Carlos Di Sarli (1903–1960), Pugliese, D'Arienzo, and many others. Tango had helped deepen the class divisions that enabled Perón's populist strategy, but paradoxically, once Peronism came to power, the genre thrived as apolitical entertainment.

Piazzolla's Anti-Peronist Tango

Perón's second term (1952–1955) was cut short by a military coup in September 1955. The military regime that took power dubbed itself the *Revolución Libertadora* and went about "de-Peronizing" society by removing his loyalists from power and dislodging Peronist ideology from its hegemonic position. This process was traumatic for working-class Peronists, who not only stood to lose all the benefits they had gained under Perón, but also felt that their vision of the nation had come under direct attack. However, for many white-collar workers, intellectuals, and professionals, these were truly liberating years. These groups had forged a middle-class identity in opposition to the impoverished masses that Peronism had sought to lift up. They had felt stifled by Peronism's endorsement of "bad taste," its anti-intellectualism, nativism, and anti-modernism. For them, the fall of Perón represented an opportunity for the country to re-engage with cosmopolitan, intellectual, and artistic currents. With Perón gone, middle-class anti-Peronists were busy imagining a new way to be in the world as Argentines, and inevitably, tango would be implicated in this project.

The bandoneonist, composer, and bandleader Astor Piazzolla (1921–1992) quickly emerged as the standard-bearer for a new, cosmopolitan, and anti-Peronist approach to tango. Born in Mar del Plata, Piazzolla spent his youth in New York City before returning to Argentina as a young man and joining Troilo's orchestra. Piazzolla led his own tango band in the late 1940s, but he aspired to a career as a composer of serious concert music. He had earlier studied with the Argentine composer Alberto Ginastera, and in 1954, he moved to Paris to study with the legendary teacher Nadia Boulanger. Over the course of a six-month stay, he recommitted to tango, convinced that by applying lessons from both classical music and jazz, he could transform the genre into serious music for listening. He returned to Argentina during the final months of the Perón regime and launched the Octeto Buenos Aires, an avant-garde group through which he aimed to revolutionize the genre. In a published manifesto, Piazzolla promised not only to "raise the quality of the tango," but also to attract both foreign audiences and Argentine fans of foreign music.[29] Although Piazzolla did not express an opinion on the country's political situation, his years in New York and Paris as well as his extensive musical education made him well-suited to the anti-Peronist project of reimagining Argentine culture in a cosmopolitan and modernist vein.[30]

Piazzolla also hoped that the Octeto Buenos Aires could address the commercial decline of tango. Though the early years of Peronism had been a boon for tango bands, economic contraction in the 1950s had taken a toll. Moreover, tango seemed increasingly old-fashioned, unable to compete with new foreign genres and with Argentine folk music. However, while the sophisticated harmonies, complex counterpoint, and sudden tempo shifts of the Octeto Buenos Aires struck a chord with critics, the music was a bit too challenging for a mass audience, and Piazzolla abandoned the project. In 1960, after a brief, unsuccessful attempt to forge a tango-jazz synthesis in New York, Piazzolla created the Quinteto Nuevo Tango, the vehicle through which he would create his most enduring and influential musical innovations.

Though his new music proved a bit more accessible, the so-called nuevo tango (New Tango) remained a vanguardist project aimed at reconciling traditional elements with a cosmopolitan, modernist sensibility. Piazzolla's extensive use of the 3-3-2 rhythm and the percussive violin and bass sound effects known as *yeites* are examples of the way he took musical elements from tango's past and pushed them in new directions. Though his own instrument, the bandoneón, sounded unmistakably like tango, the Quinteto was in some ways more reminiscent of a jazz quintet than a traditional *orquesta típica*. Most obviously, like the Octeto Buenos Aires, the group included an electric guitar rather than the acoustic guitar often used to accompany tango singers. And even though Piazzolla's music avoided improvisation, the very notion of a small group of virtuosos playing a sophisticated version of what had been a popular dance genre was a jazz concept. Piazzolla was an avid fan of cool jazz musicians like Gerry Mulligan and the Modern Jazz Quintet; their example helped him reinvent tango as a modern music-for-listening performed in smoky nightclubs by a small group playing intricate arrangements.[31]

Because his version of tango seemed so modern, Piazzolla acquired substantial symbolic power in the Argentina of the early and mid-1960s. Middle-class men staking their claim to be the intellectual and cultural leaders of the nation needed models, and Piazzolla fit the bill. He was a frequent guest on Bernardo Neustadt's influential news program, which eventually adopted his "Fuga y misterio" ("Fugue and Mystery," WL 16.6) as its theme music. Likewise, he appeared on the cover of *Primera Plana*, the magazine that best expressed the cosmopolitan, modernizing world-view of the anti-Peronist middle class (Fig. 16.1). Though Piazzolla came under attack from defenders of traditional tango who thought his music represented a bastardization of the genre, he was also celebrated as a revolutionary capable of dragging the nation's stagnant traditions into the twentieth century.[32]

Though Piazzolla's *nuevo tango* was an important musical expression of middle-class anti-Peronism, we should be careful not to define its politics too narrowly. Fernando "Pino" Solanas, the radical filmmaker of the Peronist left, relied heavily on Piazzolla's music for the soundtrack to two films he made in the 1980s: *Tangos, el exilio de Gardel* (*Tangos: The Exile of Gardel*) and *Sur* (*South*, referring to the south side of Buenos Aires). By this point, Piazzolla's music sounded less revolutionary, and Solanas used it to express the nostalgia of Argentines thrown into exile by the violent military dictatorship of 1976–1983. However, it is also true that Solanas had been

Figure 16.1 Astor Piazzolla on the cover of *Primera Plana*, May 25, 1965.

a fervent admirer of Piazzolla as a young man in the early 1960s.[33] The modernizing, revolutionary sentiments evoked by Piazzolla's ground-breaking tango could be reconciled with both leftist and rightist political orientations.

Concluding Thoughts

Since its emergence at the beginning of the twentieth century, tango has expressed multiple and competing political messages. It has been associated with conservative sentiments including conformism, fatalism, and misogyny, but it has also been a vehicle for working-class consciousness and a moral critique of the rich. Whereas Gardel's smoking jacket sanctioned his audience's desire for upward mobility, Castillo's gaudy suits announced his proud affiliation with the poor. D'Arienzo created music his fans embraced as traditional and authentic, but both De Caro in the 1930s and Piazzolla in the 1960s attracted followers by elevating the tango, raising it up from its humble origins as the music of the *arrabales*. Tango provided populist cultural elements that Perón drew on in building his largely working-class movement, but it also proved amenable to anti-Peronist culture-building.

Tango's capacity to express opposing political ideologies has persisted in recent decades. In the 1990s, as President Carlos Menem presided over Argentina's neoliberal experiment, the tango, which had seemed on the point of disappearing as anything other than a tourist attraction, experienced a new boom. Leading the way were middle-class youth, but perhaps surprisingly these young people were not interested in Piazzolla's brand of modernism. On the contrary, this tango boom was first and foremost a revival of tango dance, and the preferred soundtrack at milongas (tango dance events) throughout Buenos Aires was the tango of the Golden Age: the 1930s, 1940s, and 1950s. As tango historian María Mercedes Liska has argued, this nostalgic turn to domestic popular culture was an apt response to the way neoliberalism had undermined the certainties of middle-class life. As the path of university education no longer seemed to promise upward mobility, young people's faith in the modernizing, cosmopolitan values of their class was shaken. For them, Golden Age tango – tango for dancing rather than intellectualizing – had appeal.[34]

But the political pendulum swung yet again after the economic crisis of 2001. As Presidents Néstor Kirchner and Cristina Fernández de Kirchner moved Peronism and the whole country to the left, young tango *aficionados* opened space within the genre for novel musical approaches informed by rock or punk aesthetics.[35] They created feminist and queer versions of tango, linking an old, nostalgic nationalism with an up-to-date set of political and ideological commitments. Once again, tango had proven flexible enough to speak to the pressing political questions of the day.

Notes

1. Blas Matamoro, *La cuidad del tango: Tango histórico y sociedad* (Buenos Aires: Editorial Galerna, 1969), 95.
2. Michael Denning, *Noise Uprising: The Audiopolitics of a World Musical Revolution* (London: Verso, 2015).
3. John Charles Chasteen, *National Rhythms, African Roots: The Deep History of Latin American Popular Dance* (Albuquerque: University of New Mexico Press, 2004).
4. Chasteen, *National Rhythms*, 51–70; Oscar Chamosa, "Lúbolos, Tenorios y Moreiras: reforma liberal y cultura popular en el carnaval de Buenos Aires de la segunda mitad del siglo XIX," in Hilda Sabato and Alberto Lettieri, eds., *La vida política en la Argentina del siglo XIX: Armas, votos y voces* (Buenos Aires: Fondo de Cultura Económica de Argentina, 2003), 115–35.
5. Ema Cibotti, "El tango argentino como genuina expresión de las clases medias," in Teresita Lencina, ed., *Escritos sobre tango* 2 (Buenos Aires: Centro 'feca, 2011), 91–107.
6. Adolfo Prieto, *El discurso criollista en la formación de la Argentina moderna* (Buenos Aires: Sudamericana, 1988); Julia Chindemi and Pablo Vila, "La música popular argentina entre el campo y la ciudad: música campera, criolla, nativa, folklórica, canción federal y tango," *ArtCultura* 19, no. 34 (2017), 9–26.
7. Marta Savigliano, *Tango and the Political Economy of Passion* (Boulder: Westview, 1995); Andrea Matallana, *El Tango entre dos Américas. Representaciones en Estados Unidos durante las primeras décadas del siglo XX* (Buenos Aires: Eudeba, 2016).
8. Karl Hagstrom Miller, *Segregating Sound: Inventing Folk and Pop Music in the Age of Jim Crow* (Durham: Duke University Press, 2010).
9. Gustavo Varela, *Tango y política: sexo, moral burguesa y revolución en Argentina* (Buenos Aires: Ariel, 2016), 61–67.
10. Andrea Matallana, *Locos por la radio: Una historia social de la radiofonía en la Argentina, 1923–1947* (Buenos Aires: Prometeo, 2006).
11. On the musical changes that accompanied this lyrical evolution, see María Mercedes Liska, "El arte de adecentar los sonidos: Huellas de las operaciones de normalización del tango argentino," *Latin American Music Review* 35, no. 1 (2014): 25–49.

12. Eduardo Romano, "Prólogo," in *Las letras del tango: Antología cronológica 1900-1980* (Rosario, Argentina: Fundación Ross, 1998); Donald Castro, "The Massification of the Tango: The Electronic Media, the Popular Theatre and the Cabaret from Contursi to Perón, 1917–1955," *Studies in Latin American Popular Culture* 18 (1999): 93–115.

13. Noemí Ulla, *Tango, rebelión y nostalgia* (Buenos Aires: Jorge Alvarez, 1967), 33–44; Eduardo Archetti, *Masculinities: Football, Polo and the Tango in Argentina* (Oxford: Berg, 1999), 152–155; Diego Armus, "Tango, Gender, and Tuberculosis in Buenos Aires," *Disease in the History of Modern Latin America* (Durham, NC: Duke University Press, 2003), 101–129.

14. Donna Guy, *Sex and Danger in Buenos Aires: Prostitution, Family, and Nation in Argentina* (Lincoln: University of Nebraska Press, 1990), 152.

15. "Vos rodaste por tu culpa, y no fue inocentemente. / Berretines de bacana que tenías en la mente / Desde el día en que un magnate cajetilla te afiló." All English translations are my own.

16. Matamoro, *La cuidad del tango*, 116–146.

17. "Es lo mismo el que labura / Noche y día como un buey / Que el que vive de los otros / Que el que mata, que el que cura / O está fuera de la ley."

18. Pablo Vila, "Tango to Folk: Hegemony Construction and Popular Identities in Argentina," *Studies in Latin American Popular Culture* 10 (1991): 113–121; Matthew B. Karush, *Culture of Class: Radio and Cinema in the Making of a Divided Argentina* (Durham, NC: Duke University Press, 2012), 87–105.

19. Kacey Link and Kristin Wendland, *Tracing Tangueros: Argentine Tango Instrumental Music* (New York: Oxford University Press, 2016), 46–49.

20. Marina Cañardo, *Fábricas de músicas: Comienzos de la industria discográfica en la Argentina (1919-1930)* (Buenos Aires: Gourmet Musical, 2017), 65.

21. *Canción Moderna* 297 (November 27, 1933).

22. *Sintonía* 270 (June 23, 1938).

23. Karush, *Culture of Class*, 148–150.

24. "¿Qué saben los pitucos, lamidos y shushetas / qué saben lo que es tango / qué saben de compás?"

25. Karush, *Culture of Class*, 197–198.

26. Horacio Salas, *El Tango* (Buenos Aires: Planeta, 1995), 297.

27. Varela, *Tango y política*, 148–154; Karush, *Culture of Class*, 198–200.

28. Gálvez, Eduardo, "El tango en su época de gloria: ni prostibulario, ni orillero. Los bailes en los clubes sociales y deportivos de Buenos Aires 1938-1959," *Nuevo Mundo, Mundos Nuevos* (February 6, 2009) https://journals .openedition.org/nuevomundo/55183.

29. The manifesto appeared under the title "Decalogue" and was published in the magazine *De Frente* in October 1955. See María Susana Azzi and Simon Collier, *Le Grand Tango: The Life and Music of Astor Piazzolla* (New York: Oxford University Press, 2000), 58–59.

30. Diego Fischerman and Abel Gilbert, *Piazzolla el mal entendido* (Buenos Aires: Edhasa, 2009), 107–162; Karush, *Musicians in Transit: Argentina and the Globalization of Popular Music* (Durham, NC: Duke University Press, 2017), 72–81.

31. Karush, *Musicians in Transit*, 81–89; Fischerman and Gilbert, *Piazzolla el mal entendido*, 178–181.

32. Karush, *Musicians in Transit*, 90–94.

33. Karush, *Musicians in Transit*, 105–106.

34. María Mercedes Liska, "La revitalización del baile social del tango en Buenos Aires: Neoliberalismo y cultura popular durante la década de 1990," *Ethnomusicology Review* 18 (2013) https://ethnomusicologyreview.ucla.edu/journal/volume/18/piece/702.

35. Morgan James Luker, *The Tango Machine: Musical Culture in the Age of Expediency* (Chicago: University of Chicago Press, 2016).

Further Reading

Archetti, Eduardo. *Masculinities: Football, Polo, and the Tango in Argentina.* Oxford: Berg, 1999.

Armus, Diego. "Tango, Gender, and Tuberculosis in Buenos Aires." In *Disease in the History of Modern Latin America*, 101–129. Durham, NC: Duke University Press, 2003.

Cibotti, Ema. "El tango argentino como genuina expresión de las clases medias." In *Escritos sobre tango 2*, edited by Teresita Lencina, 91–107. Buenos Aires: Centro 'feca, 2011.

Fischerman, Diego, and Abel Gilbert. *Piazzolla el mal entendido.* Buenos Aires: Edhasa, 2009.

Gálvez, Eduardo. "El tango en su época de gloria: ni prostibulario, ni orillero: Los bailes en los clubes sociales y deportivos de Buenos Aires 1938–1959." *Nuevo Mundo, Mundos Nuevos* (February 6, 2009). https://journals.openedition.org/nuevomundo/55183.

Karush, Matthew B. *Culture of Class: Radio and Cinema in the Making of a Divided Argentina.* Durham, NC: Duke University Press, 2012.

Liska, María Mercedes. "El arte de adecentar los sonidos: Huellas de las operaciones de normalización del tango argentino." *Latin American Music Review* 35:1 (2014): 25–49.

"La revitalización del baile social del tango en Buenos Aires: Neoliberalismo y cultura popular durante la década de 1990." *Ethnomusicology Review* 18 (2013). https://ethnomusicologyreview.ucla.edu/journal/volume/18/piece/702.

Matamoro, Blas. *La cuidad del tango: Tango histórico y Sociedad*. Buenos Aires: Editorial Galerna, 1969.

Savigliano, Marta. *Tango and the Political Economy of Passion*. Boulder, CO: Westview, 1995.

Varela, Gustavo. *Tango y política: sexo, moral burguesa y revolución en Argentina*. Buenos Aires: Ariel, 2016.

17 | (Trans)national Visions: Tango Onscreen

RIELLE NAVITSKI

The tango's affective qualities and transnational wanderings have shaped a long and productive *pas de deux* with the cinema. Marked by passionate intensity in its instrumental and danced version, and typically expressing longing for a lost love, a distant homeland, or a vanished past in the lyrical *tango canción* (tango song), the genre resonates with enduring cinematic themes like romance, betrayal, and loss. In its embodiment of a "sensationalized heterosexuality,"[1] tango is ripe for appropriation in a mass medium that has long fixated on male-female romance – at least in the fiction feature, its most popular and dominant form. In US and European film, tango often works to exoticize and eroticize a cultural Other, imagined as possessing an unbridled, "primitive" sensuality that offers liberation from the social constraints of capitalist modernity.[2]

Yet tango's presence in world cinema also represents a powerful countercurrent to the homogenizing force of cultural globalization so often associated with Hollywood. From the tango craze that swept Europe and the United States in the 1910s to the rise of tango as a major tourist attraction in twenty-first-century Buenos Aires, the genre has proven to be a profitable export. Its circulation complicates oversimplified notions of a one-way flow of cultural goods from "centers" to "peripheries." Featured in numerous US, European, and Latin American productions throughout the decades,[3] tango also embodies musical cosmopolitanism in East Asian and Middle Eastern films like Mizoguchi Kenji's *Naniwa ereji* (*Osaka Elegy*, Japan, 1936) and *Intisār al-Shabāb* (*Victory of Youth*, Aḥmad Badrakhān, Egypt, 1941).[4] The ways in which tango "epitomizes desire and difference, sensuality and antagonism, connection and loss [and] promises togetherness, [albeit] always a togetherness that requires a bridging of differences,"[5] lends it powerful resonance for the quintessentially global medium of film.

Tango and Film in the Silent Era (1900s–1920s)

Though it may seem counterintuitive, the cross-pollination between tango and cinema began over a decade before the transition to sound consistently synchronized music and dialogue with moving images. In the 1910s, tango and cinema roused a public fervor that inspired medical and psychiatric metaphors like "tango craze," "tango mania," and "tangoitis,"[6] and contemporary references to "movie mad" audiences.[7] As this language suggests, tango and cinema alike were viewed as disruptive forces that threatened to upend traditional relations between the sexes and social classes. Just as darkened movie theaters allowed for chance encounters and new intimacies in public space, tango involved close proximity between male and female dancers' bodies. It incorporated elements of spontaneity, breaking with highly regimented Victorian-era dances that sought to sublimate the sensuality inherent in partner dancing. Like other dance fads that drew on the music and dance of the African diaspora, such as ragtime, the tango's appeal in the United States was rooted in a racial and cultural otherness that was domesticated by figures like Vernon and Irene Castle, prominent white exhibition dancers who offered lessons to New York's elites.[8]

Beyond early nonfiction films depicting the dance like *Tango criollo* (1906), which was shot by French camera operator Eugène Py and is believed lost,[9] tango and cinema first intersected in US and European productions. These films capitalized on the tango craze that swept US and European cities – especially Paris, which would become "the second capital of tango"[10] – in 1913–1914. As Kristina Köhler observes, instructional films made in the United States, United Kingdom, and Germany to teach viewers tango and other dances were premised on a belief in cinema's unique capability to physically move the spectator's body. "Dancing mania comedies" of the period from the United States, France, and Italy similarly use the medium to produce a dizzying sense of corporeal motion.[11] Rudolph Valentino's famous dance number in the World War I drama *The Four Horsemen of the Apocalypse* (Rex Ingram, 1921, Figure 17.1) also traces its roots to early twentieth-century dance crazes. Before becoming an actor, Valentino had danced professionally. For unsympathetic commentators, he embodied the "tango pirate" – a social climber, often an immigrant, who seduced wealthy women with his dancing ability.[12] If Valentino's star persona linked tango with threatening new forms of social mobility, *The Four Horsemen of the Apocalypse* highlighted the dance's

Figure 17.1 Press for *The Four Horsemen of the Apocalypse*, highlighting Valentino's past career as a professional dancer.

geographic dispersion. Valentino plays the spoiled grandson of an Argentine landowner whose mastery of aggressive, sensuous tango steps makes him equally at home in the bars of La Boca and Parisian cabarets.

Early encounters between tango and cinema in Argentina were mediated less by dance than by orchestral accompaniment for films, the emerging *tango canción*, and the *sainete criollo* (a local form of one-act comedy). By the mid-twenties, *orquestas típicas* (tango orchestras) led by well-known bandleaders like Julio De Caro (1899–1980), Juan D'Arienzo (1900–1976), and Carlos Di Sarli (1903–1960) played in movie palaces,[13] and the lyrics and plotlines of the *tango canción* inspired a series of narrative films centered on fallen women or those who narrowly avoided this fate. Whether located in a seedy bar, an elegant cabaret, or an upper-class home, the silent era tango is predominantly depicted as a menace to female chastity, reflecting its marginal origins and association with sex work. In *Nobleza gaucha* (*Gaucho Nobility*, Humberto Cairo, Ernesto Gunche, and Eduardo Martínez de la Pera, 1915), an innocent country girl is kidnapped and brought to Buenos Aires by a wealthy villain, then rescued by the noble *gaucho* (the Argentine equivalent of a cowboy) referenced in the title. In a lost scene from the film, the antagonist's indulgence in the tango is presented as a sign of his debauchery.

The films of pioneering Afro-Argentine director José Agustín Ferreyra (1889–1943) take a similar path, as suggested by titles like *El tango de la muerte* (*The Tango of Death*, 1917) and *Melenita de oro* (*Golden Locks*, 1923), which shared its name with a popular song.[14] (Both films are considered lost.) In Ferreyra's *Perdón, viejita* (*Forgive Me, Mother*, 1927), a reformed prostitute's reluctant return to the realm of vice is signaled by her appearance singing tango. She had covered for her sister-in-law when the police came looking for a stolen ring she was given by a disreputable suitor, only to be derided by the family matriarch for her trouble. Other films, however, complicate tango's narrative function as a marker of the fallen woman's perdition. For instance, in Ferreyra's *La vuelta al bulín* (*Return to the Love Nest*, 1926, WL 17.1), the tough-talking character Pulguita ("little flea," actor not identified) leaves her husband, a petty gangster played by comedian Álvaro Escobar, for a rival who promises her an elegant lifestyle. Yet Pulguita quickly bores of elegant cabarets and decides to reunite with her husband. Edmo Cominetti's *La borrachera del tango* (*Tango Intoxication*, 1928), based on a *sainete* of the same title,[15] presents tango largely as a threat to male moral rectitude. The film contrasts two sons of an affluent family: the hard-working engineer Luis (Felipe Farah), and the wastrel Fernando (Eduardo Morera). The latter ends up expelled not only from the family home but also, once he is broke, from spaces of leisure where he indulged in tango and commodified sexual encounters.[16]

As these examples suggest, tango is heavily freighted with moral meanings in Argentine silent cinema. These meanings are largely absent from US and European films inspired by the tango craze, which invokes the seductive power of the dance without adopting the black-and-white moral logic encoded in the *tango canción*. During the 1930s, both Hollywood and Argentina's incipient industry took advantage of tango's growing cross-class and cross-border popularity in musical melodramas that would give Spanish-language cinema some of its most popular and enduring stars.

From the Golden Age of Argentine Cinema to the Decline of Tango (1930s–1960s)

The most popular tango musicals from the early years of the transition to sound were a series of seven Spanish-language features starring legendary singer Carlos Gardel (1890–1935). Produced by Paramount, these films were actually shot outside Paris and in New York as part of Hollywood's strategy to maintain hold of its foreign markets, which were threatened by the introduction of English-language dialogue.[17] Dubbing did not become technically feasible until the early 1930s, and subtitles were impractical in areas with low literacy rates, including much of Latin America. Thus, Hollywood studios initially opted to produce multiple-language versions of their films, translating scripts and remaking their films with Spanish-, French- and German-speaking casts for their key markets. The resulting Spanish-language versions usually lacked culturally specific reference points and included a disorienting mishmash of accents, since actors often hailed from different countries.[18]

Paramount's Gardel vehicles took a different approach, as they were based on original scripts. Yet they reflected Hollywood's efforts to appeal to a heterogeneous Spanish-language market in multinational plots that evoked Gardel's own globetrotting career. An immigrant to Argentina,[19] Gardel spent significant time in Paris and New York and toured Spain and Latin America widely. His characters travel from Buenos Aires to Hollywood in *El día que me quieras* (*The Day You Love Me*, John Reinhardt, 1935), to New York in *El tango en Broadway* (*The Tango on Broadway*, Louis Gasnier, 1934), and to Barcelona in *Tango Bar* (John Reinhardt, 1935, Figure 17.2).

Gardel's earlier features shot in Joinville, France, had drawn more heavily on tango's associations with criminality and threats to female morality. In *Melodía de arrabal* (*Melody of the Outskirts*, Louis Gasnier, 1934), he plays a gangster turned tango singer. The plot of *Las luces de Buenos Aires* (*The Lights of Buenos Aires*, Adelqui Millar, 1931) recalls *Nobleza gaucha*, as its heroine, Elvira (Sofía Bozán), leaves behind the humble *gaucho* Anselmo (Gardel) and travels to the capital to become a singer. Following Elvira to the city, Anselmo becomes disillusioned by her drunken behavior at a party, motivating a soulful rendition of the tango

Figure 17.2 Advertisement for *Tango Bar*, illustrating the transnational character and marketing of Gardel's films for Paramount.

"Tomo y obligo" ("I drink and oblige [you to drink]"). In the end, the two are reunited after a series of melodramatic complications, including a narrowly avoided kidnapping.

Like Paramount's Gardel vehicles, Argentina's earliest sound features shifted from plots that associated tango with urban marginality and female perdition to narratives that linked it with cosmopolitan mobility. *Muñequita porteña* (*Buenos Aires Doll*, José Agustín Ferreyra, 1931) parallels *Perdón, viejita* in linking tango with the female protagonist's moral downfall. Two years later, *¡Tango!* (Luis Moglia Barth, 1933), the debut feature from the major studio Argentina Sono Film, instead focuses on the Gardel-like trajectory of a male singer (Alberto Gómez) who travels to Paris to seek fame. He becomes involved with a successful tango singer (Libertad Lamarque), but pines for the sweetheart he left behind (Tita Merello) in the *barrio* (neighborhood). The first film from the rival Lumiton studio, *Los tres berretines* (*The Three Pastimes*, Equipo Lumiton, 1933), depicted tango, along with cinema and soccer, as an addictive but morally inoffensive passion.

In 1935, Gardel's premature death in a plane crash outside Medellín, Colombia, dashed hopes that he would lend his massive popularity to Argentina's industry. Still, Gardel's features continued to rake in huge profits after his passing, accounting for nearly a third of Paramount's box office takings in 1935.[20] The production of Spanish-language Hollywood films proved short-lived, though it continued in some capacity into the late 1930s. Even at the height of the Good Neighbor policy of the 1930s and 1940s, when the United States sought cordial relationships with Latin American nations for strategic reasons, Hollywood proved unable to render the region's musical rhythms convincingly. For instance, the musical numbers of *Down Argentine Way* (Irving Cummings, 1940) feature not tango but Cuban rumba.[21]

With US studios ill-equipped to capitalize on tango's popularity, Argentina's industry cultivated stars that rivaled Gardel in their popularity with Spanish-speaking audiences. The onscreen persona of Libertad Lamarque (1908–2000) challenged the genre's strong associations with the figure of the fallen woman, building on the growing middle-class acceptance of the tango. This shift is attributed to the rise of the sentimental *tango canción* in the late 1910s and the expansion of radio in the 1920s, which brought tango into domestic spaces. Lamarque felt little kinship with the femmes fatales and streetwise women of tango's traditional imaginary.[22] She played a virtuous love interest, wife, and (adoptive) mother in *El alma del bandoneón* (*The Soul of the Bandoneón*, Mario Soffici, 1935), as well as a trio of hugely successful melodramas directed by Ferreyra, including *Ayúdame a vivir* (*Help Me to Live*, 1936, WL 17.2), *Besos brujos* (*Bewitching Kisses*, 1937), and *La ley que olvidaron* (*The Law They Forgot*, 1937).[23] These films take melodrama's meaning of *melos* (music) plus drama literally; tangos sung by Lamarque underscore moments of intense emotion. Their narratives also draw heavily on the stock plots of radio drama and serial literature, forging a "more universally accessible brand of melodrama that did not rely on viewers' familiarity with the world of *porteño barrios*."[24] Matthew Karush observes how, despite the growing acceptance of tango, singers played by Lamarque often face condemnation from affluent characters, thus aligning her with the working classes.[25] He argues that Argentine tango and cinema exalted the moral righteousness of the downtrodden, nurturing the populist ideologies that helped propel General Juan Domingo Perón to power in 1946.[26] Yet Lamarque herself was essentially exiled from Argentina due to a dispute with María Eva Duarte de Perón (Evita) and enjoyed a long career in Mexican cinema. Known for playing self-sacrificing but independent mothers – often immigrants and single women who support themselves as singers[27] – Lamarque appeared in over forty Mexican features, though none screened in Argentina until after the fall of Perón in 1955.[28]

Tango's close, if ambivalent, links with Peronism are epitomized by the figure of Hugo del Carril (1912–1989). A staunch advocate of the general, the actor nevertheless ran afoul of the regime's repressive hold on the media, suffering a two-year blacklist after he offended the secretary of Perón's press bureau.[29] Del Carril appeared in several films that equated him with the essence of tango by chronicling its history.[30] Early examples include *La vida de Carlos Gardel* (*The Life of Carlos Gardel*, Alberto de Zavalía, 1939), a semi-biographical narrative that returns to the theme of the well-traveled singer pining for the girl next door, and *La vida es un tango* (*Life Is a Tango*, Manuel Romero, 1939, WL 17.3). In the latter film, del Carril's character is credited with key milestones in tango's development – the rise of the *tango canción*, the European tango craze – all portrayed with ample artistic license and interwoven with a melodramatic narrative of true love lost and regained. In the mid-forties, del Carril also spent time in Mexico, sidestepping difficult production conditions. Due to Argentina's neutrality in World War II, the United States sharply reduced the export of raw film negative on which its industry relied. Upon his return, del Carril embarked on a directing career that explored themes beyond tango at a moment when the genre's popular appeal had begun to wane.

In the 1940s and 1950s, folk music began to surpass tango in its ability to speak to new forms of working-class experience, shaped by waves of migration from the countryside to major cities.[31] Following Perón's overthrow in a 1955 military coup, Argentina's turn away from nationalist populism and toward a model of development backed by foreign investment was reflected in tango's increasing displacement by jazz and rock and roll. At the same time, the emergence of *nuevo tango* (New Tango), embodied by the classical- and jazz-influenced work of Astor Piazzolla (1921–1992) – who was also a prolific composer of film scores[32] – became "a potent symbol of a bourgeois project to build a modernized, cosmopolitan Argentina."[33] For the most part, tango was conspicuously absent from the soundtracks of Argentina's *nuevo cine* (new wave), though one notable exception was Piazzolla's music for *Prisioneros de una noche* (*Prisoners of the Night*, David José Kohon, 1962). Nevertheless, the genre persisted onscreen in Argentina. In the hugely successful *Buenas noches, Buenos Aires* (*Goodnight, Buenos Aires*, Hugo del Carril, 1964), a series of musical vignettes based on a stage show of the same name, del Carril's heartfelt rendition of the tango "Por qué la quise tango" (Why Did I Love Her So Much," Mariano Mores/Rodolfo Taboada) is immediately followed by a Latin-pop number featuring Ramón "Palito" Ortega, who would soon become a screen personality in his own right. As Matt Losada shows, despite capitalizing on his pop stardom, Ortega's early films mobilized an explicitly Peronist imaginary of tango-infused nostalgia against the rise of an international youth culture epitomized by rock.[34] This nostalgia was soon complicated by Perón's return to Argentina as president in 1973, which failed to stem the growing polarization between right and left. His death in 1974 triggered the rapid deterioration of the country's political situation, leading to the rise of a repressive military dictatorship (1976–1983), whose Dirty War against so-called subversives involved kidnapping, torture, and the deaths and disappearances of an estimated 30,000 citizens. In the decades that followed, tango would become a powerful source of nostalgia for a lost homeland and a national community torn asunder.

Exile and Nostalgia, Exoticism, and Eroticism (1980s–1990s)

The exodus of Argentines escaping the military dictatorship reshaped the cultural landscapes of their destinations in the 1970s and 1980s. While exiles were fleeing for their lives, their diaspora nevertheless overlapped with the growing mobility of individuals, commodities, and cultural goods in an age of globalization. As notions of national identity were increasingly destabilized, poststructuralism and postmodernism placed established cultural hierarchies and epistemologies into question, privileging ambiguity and openness over narrative clarity and closure. In this context, as Laura Podalsky argues, a trio of critically acclaimed films of the late 1980s and 1990s deconstruct the conventions of the Hollywood musical, placing the tango at the heart of their self-conscious exploration of artistic creation in a context of cosmopolitan rootlessness.[35]

Perhaps the most emblematic onscreen depiction of the Argentine exile experience, the Franco-Argentine co-production *Tangos, el exilio de Gardel*

Figure 17.3 Video still of a rehearsal scene from the *tanguedia* in *Tangos: The Exile of Gardel*.

(*Tangos: The Exile of Gardel*, Fernando Solanas, 1985, Figure 17.3) follows a group of political refugees grappling with their experiences of displacement through activism and the creation of a *tanguedia*. This fusion of tango, tragedy, and comedy takes shape through a collaboration between the writer Juan Uno (who never appears onscreen) and the composer Juan Dos (Miguel Ángel Solá). Living in Buenos Aires in internal exile, Juan Uno communicates with his collaborators through cryptic notes, refusing to send an ending to the show. This move constitutes a challenge to Eurocentric ideals of linearity and certainty, as Juan Dos tells the show's French director Pierre (Philippe Léotard), while also speaking to the political impasse faced by the exiles. "The show must end, but not the play – just as exile continues here and there," Juan Dos insists. Like Solanas's following film *Sur* (*South*, 1988), which depicts a political prisoner's homecoming, *Tangos* is suffused with the music of Piazzolla. His compositions embodied the modernization of tango in the 1950s and 1960s but were deeply nostalgic for Solanas by the 1980s,[36] evoking the desire to recover a national collectivity shattered by state-sponsored violence.

   These sentiments helped fuel a broader tango revival beginning in the 1980s, aided by the international tour of the stage show *Tango Argentino* (1983). In the 1990s, the dance appeared in Hollywood features like *Scent of a Woman* (Martin Brest, 1992), *Schindler's List* (Steven Spielberg, 1993), and *True Lies* (James Cameron, 1994). Tango also took center stage in a series of arthouse films in the 1990s.

In the Oscar-nominated *Tango* (Carlos Saura, 1998), a coproduction between Argentina and Saura's native Spain, Miguel Ángel Solá reprises his role at the helm of a troubled tango musical, though it's unclear if he is directing a show, a movie, or both. Virtuosic tango numbers performed to a score by Lalo Schifrin – some led by the famous dancer Juan Carlos Copes,[37] who plays a choreographer in the film – threaten to overwhelm *Tango*'s plot: bereft after his partner and leading lady Laura (Cecilia Narova) ends their relationship, Mario becomes involved with a younger dancer, Elena (Mía Maestro). He had cast Elena at the behest of her lover Angelo Larocco (Juan Luis Galiardo), a gangster and the show's major investor. This love triangle seems to culminate with Elena's stabbing onstage, yet we quickly learn that it is a stage illusion and Larocco's murderous jealousy only a performance. Despite fleeting moments of queer sensuality, such as a male-male tango number and a scene (marked as Mario's fantasy) where Laura and Elena kiss, *Tango* devotes scant screen time to questioning toxic masculinity or the rigid gender roles that govern heterosexual romance. In addition, the film privileges Mario's reflections on his romantic and creative fulfillment over a reckoning with Argentina's recent past. Despite a chilling number where dancers in military garb mime acts of torture and toss limp bodies into an onstage pit, state violence goes unmentioned in the first three-quarters of the film. Mario confesses that he has experienced the dictatorship at a geographic remove, leaving for Europe as a young man and returning to find his friends had disappeared. This disconnect mirrors Saura's own biographical distance from the material, suggesting how images of the dictatorship became disembedded from sites of political struggle and circulated as cultural commodities.[38]

Released the year before Saura's *Tango*, Sally Potter's *The Tango Lesson* (1997) inverts gendered narratives about creative production that assume a male artist and a female muse. At the same time, it participates in the neocolonial dynamics at play when individuals from the Global North develop an eroticized fascination with tango. The film fictionalizes the real-life professional and romantic partnership between the British filmmaker and renowned Argentine tango dancer Pablo Verón. *The Tango Lesson* opens as Sally (played by Potter herself) happens on a Paris stage show featuring Pablo (Verón) as she is struggling to complete a film script. Captivated with his performance, she secures an offer of a tango lesson after mentioning she works in cinema, suggesting Pablo has acting ambitions. After a false start, Pablo invites Sally to train to be his dance partner, while she decides to pursue a new film project on tango. The film's narrative tension is rooted in the clash between the protocols of tango dance that demand that she follow, and her career as a director, which requires that she lead. As critics have noted, the film lingers on Sally's acts of impassioned looking, rooted both in sexual attraction and an impulse toward cinematic creation.[39] Ultimately, the film offers no clear alternative to the impasse that casts Sally either as the passive recipient of Pablo's choreography or as holder of a gaze that threatens to objectify him, suggesting tango's enduring capacity to embody unresolved tensions.

The Contemporary Tango Revival Onscreen (2000s–2010s)

In the twenty-first century, tango's presence in fiction film has diminished even as documentaries celebrate its resilience in the face of changing musical fashions and the profound economic crisis that struck Argentina in 2001, triggering a new wave of emigration as its citizens sought economic opportunities abroad. This exodus is traced on an intimate level in Arne Birkenstock's *12 Tangos: Adiós Buenos Aires* (2005), which interweaves the stories of emigrants, including a young tango dancer/instructor, with evocative live performances of the *tango canción*. As neoliberal economic policies decimated the Argentine middle class, hopes for progress through privatization and economic globalization were dashed and with them, a vision of Argentina's promising future. As Fernando Rosenberg argues, these circumstances prompted a (re)turn to the tango in search of a usable past,[40] paralleling recent moves to treat tango as a valuable cultural resource, bolstered by a 2009 UNESCO declaration deeming it part of the "intangible cultural heritage of humanity."[41]

Rosenberg identifies two interrelated themes in post-2001 tango documentaries. *Orquesta típica* (Nicolás Entel, 2005), *El último bandoneón* (*The Last Bandoneón*, Alejandro Saderman, 2005), and *Si sos brujo* (*If You're a Sorcerer*, Caroline Neal, 2005) portray efforts to revive the *orquesta típica*. Other documentaries depict quests to track down aging tango musicians, whether to pass on their knowledge to a new generation (*Si sos brujo*); reunite for a last recording session (*Café de los maestros*, Miguel Kohan, 2008); or help make sense of a vanished past, as in *No sé qué me han hecho tus ojos* (named for the tango "I Don't Know What Your Eyes Have Done to Me," Sergio Wolf and Lorena Muñoz, 2003), which investigates singer Ada Falcón's abrupt withdrawal from public life in the forties.[42]

More recent documentaries pay tribute to giants of tango while registering the cultural labor involved in keeping its legacy alive. *Pichuco* (nickname for Aníbal Troilo, Martín Turnes, 2014, WL 17.4) a largely conventional portrait of storied bandoneón player, bandleader, and composer Aníbal Troilo (1914–1975), uses the commemorations of Troilo's centenary as its narrative frame. Similarly, in *Piazzolla, los años del tiburón* (*Piazzolla: The Years of the Shark*, Daniel Rosenfeld, 2019), the mounting of a museum exhibit on Piazzolla's life motivates his son Daniel's dive into the cache of home movies and intimate interviews that comprise the film. In *Un tango más* (*Our Last Tango*, Germán Kral, 2015), which explores the tumultuous on- and offstage relationship between renowned dancers Juan Carlos Copes and María Nieves Rego, stock documentary elements like interviews coexist with historical reenactments that resemble a fiction film in their production values. In a self-reflexive move, the viewer sees these scenes being supervised by Nieves herself.

The nostalgia manifest in these documentaries marks the contemporary spectator's historical distance from tango's heyday even as it embodies the sentiments of longing and loss that have informed the genre from its beginnings. If evocations of tango are necessarily untimely, being out of step with the present lends it timelessness. As tango's relationship with cinema enters its second century, the paradoxes and tensions that have marked its international reverberations persist.

Notes

1. Emily J. McManus, "The Tango in Translation: Intertextuality, Filmic Representation, and Performing Argentine Tango in the United States," *TranscUlturAl* 5, no. 1–2 (2013): 194.
2. For further reading about these general claims, see Marta Savigliano, *Tango and the Political Economy of Passion* (New York: Routledge, 1995); and Florencia Garramuño, *Primitive Modernities: Tango, Samba, and Nation*, trans. by Anna Kazumi Stahl (Stanford, CA: Stanford University Press, 2011).
3. For an exhaustive treatment, see Pedro Ochoa, *Tango y cine mundial* (Buenos Aires: Ediciones del Jilguero, 2003).
4. Margaret Jean Farrell, "Aspects of Adaptation in the Egyptian Singing Film" (Ph.D. diss., City University of New York Graduate Center, 2012), 193–199.
5. Kathy Davis, *Dancing Tango: Passionate Encounters in a Globalizing World* (New York: NYU Press, 2015), 1–2.
6. Kristina Köhler, "Tango Mad and Affected by Cinematographitis: Rhythmic 'Contagions' between Screens and Audiences in the 1910s," in *Performing New Media: 1890–1915*, ed. by Kaveh Askari et al. (Eastleigh: John Libbey Publishing, 2015), 204.

7. In the year 1921, the term "movie-mad" appeared over a hundred times in English-language film magazines according to the Arclight data analysis tool, which measures the frequency of words and phrases in the digitized collections of the Media History Digital Library.

8. For further reading, see Lewis A. Erenberg, "Everybody's Doin' It: The Pre-World War I Dance Craze, the Castles, and the Modern American Girl," *Feminist Studies* 3, no. 1–2 (1975): 155–170; and Mark Knowles, *The Wicked Waltz and Other Scandalous Dances: Outrage at Couple Dancing in the 19th and Early 20th Centuries* (Jefferson, NC: McFarland, 2009).

9. Guillermo Caneto, *Historia de los primeros años del cine en la Argentina, 1895–1910* (Buenos Aires: Fundación Cinemateca Argentina, 1996), 84–85.

10. Antonio Gómez, "Tango, Politics, and the Musical of Exile," in *Tango Lessons: Movement, Sound, Image, and Text in Contemporary Practice*, ed. by Marilyn G. Miller (Durham, NC: Duke University Press, 2014), 118.

11. Köhler, "Tango Mad and Affected by Cinematographitis," 208–210. See also Ochoa, *Tango y cine mundial*, 13–16.

12. Gaylyn Studlar, *This Mad Masquerade: Stardom and Masculinity in the Jazz Age* (New York: Columbia University Press, 1996), 151–152.

13. Jorge Finkielman, *The Film Industry in Argentina: An Illustrated Cultural History* (Jefferson, NC: McFarland, 2014), 95–100.

14. Jorge Miguel Couselo, *El negro Ferreyra, un cine por instinto* (Buenos Aires: Editorial Freeland, 1969), 35, 53.

15. Juan Sebastián Ospina León, *Struggles for Recognition: Melodrama and Visibility in Latin American Silent Film* (Oakland: University of California Press, 2021), 75–76.

16. Ibid.

17. On Gardel's Paramount musicals, see Marvin D'Lugo, "Early Cinematic Tangos: Audiovisual Culture and Transnational Film Aesthetics," *Studies in Hispanic Cinemas* 5, no. 1–2 (2009): 9–23; Rielle Navitski, "The Tango on Broadway: Carlos Gardel's International Stardom and the Transition to Sound in Argentina," *Cinema Journal* 51, no. 1 (2011): 26–49; and Nicolas Poppe, "Made in Joinville: Transnational Identitary Aesthetics in Carlos Gardel's Early Paramount Films," *Journal of Latin American Cultural Studies* 21, no. 4 (2012): 481–495.

18. Lisa Jarvinen, *The Rise of Spanish-Language Filmmaking: Out from Hollywood's Shadow, 1929–1939* (New Brunswick, NJ: Rutgers University Press, 2012), 3, 8.

19. Most historians believe that Gardel was born in Toulouse, France, though a minority maintain he was born in Uruguay.

20. Gaizka S. de Usabel, *The High Noon of American Films in Latin America* (Ann Arbor: UMI Research Press, 1982), 96.

21. Phillip Swanson, "Going Down on Good Neighbours: Imagining América in Hollywood Movies of the 1930s and 1940s (*Flying Down to Rio* and *Down Argentine Way*)," *Bulletin of Latin American Research* 29, no. 1 (2010): 82.

22. Dana Zylberman, "Entre la tierra argentina y el cielo mexicano: La transnacionalidad de Libertad Lamarque," in *Pantallas transnacionales: El cine argentino y mexicano del período clásico*, ed. by Ana Laura Lusnich, Alicia Aisemberg, and Andrea Cuarterolo (Buenos Aires: Imago Mundi, 2017), 133.

23. D'Lugo, "Early Cinematic Tangos," 17–19; Matthew Karush, *Culture of Class: Radio and Cinema in the Making of a Divided Argentina, 1920–1946* (Durham, NC: Duke University Press, 2012), 109.

24. Karush, *Culture of Class*, 111.

25. Ibid., 112.

26. Ibid., 16.

27. Valentina Velázquez-Zvierkova, "The Canonization of Libertad Lamarque in Mexican (Trans) National Cinema," *Hispania* 102, no. 4 (2019): 606.

28. Zylberman, "Entre la tierra argentina y el cielo mexicano," 132, 144.

29. César Maranghello, *Hugo del Carril* (Buenos Aires: Centro Editor de América Latina, 1993), 10–11.

30. Víctor Manuel Lafuente, "Hugo del Carril: historia del tango y política en el cine argentino," in *TangoMedia: Multimodality Matters*, ed. by Rolf Kailuweit and Vanessa Tölke (Baden-Baden: Rombach Wissenschaft, 2020), 168–170.

31. Pablo Vila, "Tango to Folk: Hegemony Construction and Popular Identities in Argentina," *Studies in Latin American Popular Culture* 10 (1991): 107–139.

32. Joaquín López González, "La música cinematográfica de Astor Piazzolla," *Imafronte* 18 (2006): 29–44; and Ochoa, *Tango y cine mundial*, 147–161.

33. Matthew Karush, *Musicians in Transit: Argentina and the Globalization of Popular Music* (Durham, NC: Duke University Press, 2016), 71.

34. Matt Losada, "*Muchacho que vas militando*: Stardom, Youth Culture, and Politics in Palito Ortega Films (1970–1975)," *Journal of Latin American Cultural Studies* 29, no. 1 (2020): 109–131.

35. Laura Podalsky, "'Tango, Like Scotch, Is Best Taken Straight': Cosmopolitan Tastes and Bodies Out of Place," *Studies in Latin American Popular Culture* 21 (2002): 131–133.

36. Karush, *Musicians in Transit*, 106.

37. For a choreomusical analysis of Copes's performance to "La cumparsita" with Cecilia Narova see Simpson-Litke's Chapter 15.

38. Ksenija Bilbija and Leigh A. Payne, "Time Is Money: The Memory Market in Latin America" in *Accounting for Violence: Marketing Memory in Latin America*, ed. by Ksenija Bilbija and Leigh A. Payne (Durham, NC: Duke University Press, 2011), 1–40.

39. Lucy Fischer, "'Dancing through the Minefield': Passion, Pedagogy, Politics, and Production in *The Tango Lesson*," *Cinema Journal* 43, no. 3 (2004): 50, 54;

Emanuela Guano, "She Looks at Him with the Eyes of a Camera: Female Visual Pleasures and the Polemic with Fetishism in Sally Potter's *Tango Lesson*," *Third Text* 18, no. 5 (2004): 461–474; and Catherine Fowler, *Sally Potter* (Champaign: University of Illinois Press, 2009), 77–80.

40. Fernando Rosenberg, "The Return of the Tango in Documentary Film," in *Tango Lessons: Movement, Sound, Image, and Text in Contemporary Practice,* ed. by Marilyn G. Miller (Durham, NC: Duke University Press, 2014), 145.

41. Quoted in Morgan James Luker, *The Tango Machine: Musical Culture in the Age of Expediency* (Chicago: University of Chicago Press, 2016).

42. Rosenberg, "The Return of the Tango in Documentary Film," 148, 153.

Further Reading

D'Lugo, Marvin. "Early Cinematic Tangos: Audiovisual Culture and Transnational Film Aesthetics." *Studies in Hispanic Cinemas* 5, no. 1–2 (2009): 9–23.

Kailuweit, Rolf and Vanessa Tölk, eds. *TangoMedia: Multimodality Matters.* Baden-Baden: Rombach Wissenschaft, 2020.

Karush, Matthew. *Culture of Class: Radio and Cinema in the Making of a Divided Argentina, 1920–1946.* Durham, NC: Duke University Press, 2012.

Ochoa, Pedro. *Tango y cine mundial.* Buenos Aires: Ediciones del Jilguero, 2003.

Miller, Marilyn G., ed. *Tango Lessons: Movement, Sound, Image, and Text in Contemporary Practice.* Durham, NC: Duke University Press, 2014.

18 | Tango, Emotion, and Transculturality in the Twentieth and Twenty-First Centuries[1]

YUIKO ASABA

> *Its accent is the song of a sentimental voice,*
> *its rhythm is the beat that lives in my city,*
> *it does not pretend,*
> *it does not disrespect,*
> *it is called tango and nothing more.*[2]
>
> "Una emoción" ("An Emotion")
> Lyrics by José María Suñé

Many contemporary Japanese tango musicians believe the ability to convey emotions is key to a "good" Argentine tango music performance.[3] They frequently draw upon their life experiences to convey Argentine tango's powerful, and sometimes painful emotions, fabricating discourses surrounding tango's authenticity in Japan. In my recent fieldwork in Japan and Argentina, many musicians and singers emphasized to me how life experience and feelings are interwoven. They believe that life feeds into such powerful feelings, and that empathy, meaning sympathy for all-encompassing human conditions, constitutes a key characteristic of a good tango musician. Empathy is often translated into Japanese as *kyōkan* (共感), literally "to feel" (感) "together" (共). Here, empathy becomes not only about a shared understanding (*kyōkan*) of all human conditions, but one that transcends the boundaries of the self and the other, embracing the past, present, and future, as well as the public and private. Such discourse around how one performs emotions through Argentine tango has become rooted in Japanese tango musicians through the channeling of cultural, moral, and historical symbols familiar in Japanese contexts.[4]

The construction of Argentina's national identity through tango and references to emotion date back to Argentina's modernization at the turn of the twentieth century.[5] A sense of nostalgia for the "pre-modern" past and a bygone era, as well as issues of suffering and joy of everyday life, became the central topics in shaping one key facet of Argentina's identity through tango. In creating a distinctive identity of the Argentine population, tango powerfully evoked and aestheticized another key emotional dimension – Argentina's sense of longing as a land of immigrants for a distant homeland between the late nineteenth and early twenty century.[6] Kacey Link and Kristin Wendland highlight tango's "musical lament" in their discussion of how the twentieth-century *tango canción* (tango song) captured the essence of tango's *tristeza* (sadness).[7] Through the *tango canción*, the words and one's ability to convey the feeling of the lyrics – imbued with life's suffering, happiness, or what is understood as life's reality – became considered crucial in a good tango performance by Argentine musicians as well as fans, and central to tango's vocal performance practice.[8]

Against this historical backdrop of the 1920s and 1930s, Matthew Karush points to Buenos Aires' popular cultural trends that embraced melodrama and emotions in tango music that invoked the "aesthetic of emotional excess."[9] Furthermore, Julie Taylor discusses tango's melodrama and the idea that emotions conveyed in tango reflect people's "everyday" feelings.[10] In this discussion about the performances of the "everyday," it is crucial to note that what is "framed as 'reality' or 'the everyday'" needs to be understood under the realist discourse, and what is described as "everyday" is "itself an aesthetic construction."[11] Similarly, psychologist Gerald C. Cupchik referred to the ways in which "everyday" feelings are imparted in the arts and performance as "the aesthetics of lived experiences."[12] Indeed, when we tell our life stories, we do not necessarily tell everything that happens to us every day, but instead choose *what* and *how* to tell our stories, and in *what* contexts. Thus, in certain respects, how we feel, remember, and tell what we think we remember and feel are already aestheticized.[13] To unpack how this entangled dynamic of performance and emotion is central to the aesthetics of tango, I turn to the notion of the "aesthetics of emotion,"[14] or "how emotion is ordered, given meaning, performed and ascribed beauty and value."[15] The concept concerns how people relate to the expressions of a particular genre's aesthetics and the "aesthetics of lived experiences"[16] – the *idea* that what is being expressed represents and resonates with our everyday feelings.

In this chapter, I build on these discourses and narrow my focus to the specific concern of the aesthetics of tango, showing how musicians and scholars relate themselves to the aesthetics of emotion through performance and narratives. I examine how they discuss tango performance in relation to emotion, regardless of their background, socio-economic status, and personal circumstances.[17] I further examine how this discourse around aesthetics, in turn, aids in one's understanding of the way tango performance imparts emotion. To clarify the obvious, I do not claim that tango intrinsically has feelings, nor do I examine each listener's emotional responses to a particular tango performance. This study is about how the discourse surrounding emotion and tango performance has been historically and culturally cultivated to refer to a "good" tango performance.[18]

Through historical and ethnographic approaches applied to my research and fieldwork in Argentina and Japan, I examine the cultivation of narratives surrounding the portrayal of emotion through tango performance in the transcultural contexts of modernity.[19] In this chapter, I use the adjectives "transcultural" and "transnational" to refer to the cultural and national crossings and transformations involved with Japanese musicians performing Argentine tango music.[20] I also discuss how contemporary tango music pedagogy incorporates the same aesthetics. I do not argue for the unique emotionality evoked through tango performance, nor do I essentialize Argentine and Japanese discourses of emotions and tango. On the contrary, how such narratives were historically cultivated reveals a Japan-Argentina connection through the aesthetics of emotion that has been influenced significantly by – and equally greatly impacted by – wider, global loops of mobilizing self-transformations through music.[21]

The chapter begins by illuminating the ways in which tango has been associated with nostalgia and, often, with painful emotions in Japan. Tango's renewed uses in Japanese popular song genres after World War II evoked an immense sense of nostalgia for the years before the war, revealing the devastating destructions caused by the war. In this context, and in the restored embrace of modernity in postwar Japan, the narratives surrounding associating Argentine tango and emotion were established in Japan. The chapter then moves on to its final investigation on the contemporary approaches to imparting emotions in tango performance in transcultural contexts by looking at the pedagogical language for conveying emotion through tango performance in Argentina and Japan.

Argentine Tango, Emotion, and Transculturality

From the Early to Mid-Twentieth Century

> When I was in the first year of junior high school, I found out that I was an adopted child, and that my birthmother had recently passed away. I felt so incredibly sad ... absolutely devasted ... Then, the sounds of Argentine tango poured out of the radio. The tone of the violin felt so melancholic, and the bandoneón's rhythm resonated like a heartbeat.[22]

Sugawara Youichi (b. 1933), a hugely successful Japanese popular singer, began his career as a tango singer in 1958 with the Orquesta Típica Tokio, led by the bandoneonist Hayakawa Shimpei (1914–1984). During our telephone interview, he described how the sounds of Argentine tango resonated with the pain he felt as a child, illuminating the depth of his sorrow through the medium of tango. Sugawara then told me how these powerful emotions mobilized his ambition to enter the music industry.

Argentine tango has been internationally popular since the start of the twentieth century. Finland's love affair with the art form since the 1930s has affectionately propelled tango to be Finland's "National Music."[23] Many pioneering developments in tango, such as jazz-tango fusions and tango in film, took place in the United States even though many tango devotees have considered that only tango from Argentina holds authentic value.[24] Argentine composers who immigrated to France have found artistic freedom to explore new forms of tango, making Paris one of the most vibrant *tanguero* cities in the world today.[25]

In Japan, tango was introduced from the Euro-American social dance circles as a modern practice during the country's modernization in the 1910s, attracting curiosity and interest from Japanese society. Despite tango's initial introduction via Europe and North America, Japanese musicians and dance aficionados turned to Argentina in search of tango's "authenticity" in the late 1920s.[26] In Japan today, Argentine tango is widely performed in Western art concert venues, milongas (social dance events), and expensive bars and restaurants dedicated only to offering tango music played by live bands every night (Figure 18.1). In fact, live Argentine tango shows are featured in a recently opened restaurant named Pampa Mía in Tokyo, established in 2021. Tango is popular among the younger generations of Japanese people; for instance, the thriving student-led professional tango orchestra, Orquesta de Tango Waseda at Waseda University in Tokyo, performs in major concert venues and at dinner shows.

Throughout the history of Argentine tango in Japan, Japanese tango music aficionados and musicians have cultivated a discourse surrounding tango's associated aesthetics of emotion. These narratives of tango and emotion became further established in Japan immediately after World War II, when embracing the idea of modernity again became the crucial ethos to rebuild the shattered country after its defeat. Various Argentine tango music associations founded across Japan at this time nurtured the narratives surrounding tango and emotion through discussions in the widespread, popular publications on Argentine tango and Argentine tango music radio programs.[27] In this popular discourse, conveying a powerful

Figure 18.1 Japanese tango musicians. Japanese tango orchestra, Orquesta Astrorico, performing at the Nagoya Shimin Hall, Japan, December 4, 2005. The author is pictured in the back row, third from the right.

emotion was considered a key factor in a good tango performance. These narratives surrounding tango and emotion in post-war Japan also nostalgically looked back to before World War II when tango was popular in Japan. In the 1930s, the well-known Argentine tangos "La cumparsita" ("The Little Parade") and "Poema" ("Poem") became huge hits among the Japanese public. The two tango songs were to be recorded as part of a popular Japanese tango song after the war,[28] reminiscing on the pre-war era that had not yet experienced the utter destruction of World War II.

The outbreak of World War II led to the closure of dance halls and the prohibition of popular entertainment, including ballroom dancing and other genres imported from the United States, such as jazz. However, tango, considered distinct from "the music of the enemy countries" by the Japanese military, continued to "warm Japanese people's hearts" in private settings even during the war.[29] This familiarity with tango, rooted in Japanese people's everyday lives before and during the war, became a key incentive for the tango boom – the "Golden Era of tango" in Japan – that followed the war from the late 1940s to early 1970s. Even members of the next generation that did not directly experience the war became tango fans due to the familiarity they acquired with the genre when their parents and siblings listened to it as children. Indeed, as this generation moved to adulthood, tango created a deep nostalgia, bringing back memories of their families. Accordingly, Japan's "Golden Era" of tango not only refers to its boom after the war, but also the era when tango represented comfort and hope during a time of political turbulence and tremendous threat to Japanese lives.

Following the war in 1952, a hugely popular Japanese singer, Kasaki Shizuko (1914–1985), recorded the song "Tango Monogatari" ("Tango Story," WL 18.1),[30] with the lyrics and music written by Hattori Ryōichi (1907–1993), one of the most influential *kayōkyoku* composers. In "Tango Monogatari," the melodies echo the much-loved "La cumparsita" and "Poema," and the words reminisce nostalgically about "Poema," the same song that had been recorded in Japanese by the acclaimed Japanese singer Awaya Noriko (1907–1999) before the war broke out. This potent sense of nostalgia was undoubtedly motivated by the immense destruction caused by the intervening war, but it also reflected how Argentine tango had become a deeply familiar sound for Japanese people.

Amidst this postwar renewed "tango boom," Japanese tango music aficionados and musicians continued cultivating a discourse around tango's associated aesthetics of emotion. Significantly, these ideas about tango's aesthetics of emotion were nurtured against the historical background of embracing tango as a "middlebrow culture," or a "middle culture" (中間文化) by the influential Japanese sociologist Katō Hidetoshi. In his 1957 essay "Chūkan Bunkaron" (中間文化論, or "A Study of the Middle Culture"),[31] Katō contributes *chūkan bunka* (middle culture) to the idea of "an infinite vertical scale" of comparing the arts between the "highbrow," "middlebrow," "lowbrow" – terms coined in the United States and Britain in relation to modernism.[32] Building on these notions of measuring the arts, Hidetoshi's *chūkan bunka* identified post-war Japan to be socially divided between the "highbrow dominant," "lowbrow dominant," and "middlebrow dominant" cultures.[33] According to him, *chūkan bunka* referred specifically to the postwar mid-1950s cultural trends in Japan that entailed a type of culture that was "not particularly high-class, while also not vulgar" – a type of culture that "satisfie[d] certain intellectual pride."[34] From this perspective, he argued, the middle culture was a "compromising culture that is intermediary, going in between the high culture (*kōkyū bunka*) and the popular culture (*taishū bunka*)."[35] In this "middle culture" hierarchical space, he listed such music genres as musicals and what he called "semi-classical music" such as tango, jazz, and "mood music." He argued that, although these genres were not as "refined" as Western art music, the possibility of playing them in a more "refined" Western art-music formation at a classical music venue afforded them the status of becoming closer to the "high-art" status.[36]

In this scale of measuring cultures, Western art music represented the "high culture," which people without a university education in postwar Japan may approach to gain cultural refinement. The "low culture sphere" was occupied by Japanese popular songs, which often reflected Japanese lives on the street, including the struggles of postwar prostitutes and people's poverty. From this perspective of evaluating tango as the "middle culture," the genre came to be both embraced and rejected, precisely due to it being outside the "high culture";[37] Western art-music listeners and Western art musicians in Japan, for instance, often described emotion conveyed in tango as "overly melodramatic." In many respects, thus, while associated with Euro-American modernity, tango's aesthetics of emotion that expresses melancholy, together with tango's hint of risqué exoticism,[38] and the fact that tango represented a popular culture, embodied a certain feel of the "middle culture" in postwar Japan. It attracted and simultaneously alienated listeners who aspired to belong to the "high culture" – a dynamic of embracing and rejecting that continues even to this day.

The demarcation of cultures in postwar Japan gave rise to a debate about tango and emotion among Japanese tango musicians and Japanese tango music aficionados. In this discourse, each musician's emotion came to be considered key to a good tango performance. In certain respects, portraying powerful emotion through tango became a musical protest against the cultural hierarchies and "refined," "high art." Indeed, the Japanese embrace of Argentine tango's aesthetics of emotion was also undoubtedly influenced by the deep-rooted tango's aesthetics of emotion in Argentina. As demonstrated, the importance of conveying everyday joy and suffering shaped a key ethos surrounding the aesthetics of emotion concerning tango performance in twentieth-century Argentina. Through Japanese tango musicians' and aficionados' search for the authenticity of Argentine tango music in the postwar years, discourses of performing emotion through tango became widely disseminated via teaching, reflecting such trends in Argentina's tango worlds as examined in the following discussion.

Conveying Emotion through Tango in Contemporary Argentina and Japan: Discourses and Pedagogy

In the worlds of tango music in contemporary Argentina, the deep-seated aesthetics of performing powerful emotion through tango continues to be transmitted through discourses and pedagogical approaches. As discussed earlier in the chapter, the aesthetics of emotion surrounding tango music performance in Argentina is believed to be created in part via its expression of "everyday life"[39] and, in some, a shared sense of "bad luck [in life]" is perceived to have "universal implications."[40] Furthermore, in my interview with acclaimed Argentine tango critic Nélida Rouchetto, she emphasized life's uncertainty and suffering as a crucial part of contemporary tango's aesthetic:

[T]ango musicians [in Buenos Aires] started to use the word *barro* (mud) around the 1960s to describe the quality of tango performance, metaphorically ... The mud here refers to that of *conventillo* [tenement houses] of Buenos Aires, where many immigrants and lower-class workers lived in the early twentieth century. *Barro* symbolized the unpaved roads of *conventillos* ... you know? These roads of *conventillos* that were covered with thick mud, mixed with the hardworking people's sweat and blood of suffering ...[41]

Here, the idea of "mud" fabricates the narrative surrounding tango's authenticity in contemporary contexts. Describing tango's aesthetics of suffering, Julie Taylor writes of Buenos Aires and tango after the *guerra sucia* (Dirty War) – the war in Argentina initiated by the military dictatorship from 1976 to 1983 – as having come to "express ... the particular forms of disorientation, loss and uncertainty of the nation's fate inculcated by years of terror."[42] Indeed, the immense devastation experienced by many in Argentina after the 2001 financial catastrophe continues to shape the narratives surrounding the nation's suffering, and so, in turn, tango's aesthetics of emotion in contemporary Argentina.[43]

Such narratives of suffering from recent Argentine history have simultaneously characterized the diverse approaches to imparting "lived emotions" through tango performance today.[44] The contested notion of *mugre* (dirt or grit), a noun mentioned to me several times during my fieldwork in Argentina and Japan in relation to conveying "lived emotions,"[45] illuminates one significant example of the way through which tango performers approach performing emotion via tango in contemporary contexts. *Mugre* also refers to life's hardships and reality.[46] The Spanish word *suciedad* has been suggested as its synonym,[47] and filth as its English equivalent.[48] In reference to the "wider cultural context" of tango's *mugre*, Jessica Quiñones writes:

[M]etaphors for *mugre* are shaped by the landscape of the tango experience, and are used to tell stories of everyday *porteño* [a person from the port city of Buenos Aires] life in a collective and shared manner. The images portrayed in various descriptions of *mugre* were contextualized through wider tango themes, such as destitution, social marginalization, class-struggles, the lover, disillusionment . . .[49]

Such historical and personal narratives surrounding people's suffering in Argentina's recent history have been superimposed on tango's aesthetics of emotion, further deepening how performers convey "lived emotions" through tango. For instance, violinist Fernando Suárez Paz (1941–2020, Figure 18.2), a former member of Astor Piazzolla's Quinteto Tango Nuevo, described *mugre* to me as the essence that is not written in music and how it draws upon each musician's emotions and life-experience.[50] In this interview, Suárez Paz seemed to argue against the idea that *mugre* can *just* be created, and how, though there is something ineffable and unpredictable about it, one knows when they hear it. He seemed to oppose the idea that there is a kind of recipe for producing it.[51] Instead of claiming it as something that can be learned through technique, he seemed to imply that it is about the "sentiment of each musician" and is built on experience and knowledge.[52] Rather than thinking of *mugre* as the immediate cause of the tango aesthetic, Suárez Paz stressed each musician's "feeling" imparted in a tango interpretation as the essence of a good performance.[53] Moreover, according to many Argentine and Japanese tango musicians the *mugre* rhythmic feel – or the "swing" – is believed to be honed through performing on stage: as such, experience gained from performing with other tango

Figure 18.2 Fernando Suárez Paz and the author in Buenos Aires, Argentina, July 4, 2004.

musicians constitutes an important part of learning to convey emotion through tango.

Nonetheless, the use of the word *mugre* in reference to tango performance is relatively new, as Rouchetto described to me:

[In the 1960s] when talking about tango performance, *barro* was used instead of *mugre* you see ... but from around the 1980s onwards some musicians began to use *mugre*.[54]

Rouchetto's comments regarding the recent introduction of the *mugre* concept are supported by Argentine bandoneonist Carlos Pazo, who, while expressing his dislike for the word *mugre* in relation to tango, explained that it only began to be used from the late twentieth century by musicians.[55]

Similarly, in Japan, the word *mugre* began to be used in the late 2000s, when more and more Japanese performers began traveling to Buenos Aires to study tango or polish their existing skills as tango musicians. By then, some Argentine musicians had started to use the word *mugre* when teaching tango performance to foreigners – even though the term was not favored by many Argentine musicians when associated with tango – as a pedagogical reference to transmit the knowledge of tango aesthetics. In this pedagogical context, *mugre*'s metaphorical meanings that refer to life's hard work and life experiences became superimposed on the urban aesthetics of tango.

In Japan's tango worlds today, this aesthetic contrasts with modern technology that enables achieving goals too easily, also made possible by the moderate wealth of today's middle-class Japanese society. As such, for many tango musicians in the older generation in Japan, the metropolitan context of contemporary Japan lacks the hardships they endured in the era of postwar destruction, which they view as key to tango's aesthetics of emotion. Here, *mugre* is indeed used in reference to economic hardship, suggesting a sense of moral value necessary to achieve a good tango performance. According to several Japanese tango musicians who I interviewed, the *mugre* of tango is achieved by learning on stage at dance hall venues as a way of undergoing *tataki age* (forging) training – a term derived from the Japanese word *tataku* (to strike) and originally referred to how a blacksmith forges iron into a shape in Japan. Accordingly, *tataki age* is a phrase used for disciplining and training in craftsmanship as well as in the worlds of the arts.[56] For the musician, it refers to how one trains their skills into shape, and it is generally understood that with drilling and hard work, they gain not only music's technical knowledge but the emotional depths surrounding hard work, thus feeding into the artistic outputs.

In Japan today, where dance halls are no longer the venues for experiencing tango, the ways of imparting life experience through tango are acquired through such pedagogical means. Through narratives and pedagogies, tango's emotions continue to take shape in performance in transcultural and transnational contexts, transcending the beauty of musical structure to powerfully convey "each musician's feelings" that resonate with each listener's life experiences.[57]

Conclusion

This essay has argued that Argentine tango's aesthetics of emotion were nurtured in the transnational contexts of modernization, modernity, and the histories of national catastrophes and their devastating aftermaths. Tango's emotionality reveals the transnational histories of celebrating and denying emotion against the backdrop of measuring cultures. In Argentina, it was propelled by the need to establish a national music genre that powerfully drew from the sentiments of the "pre-modern" past, and in postwar Japan it resonated with the wider, global circulations of debates surrounding musical "middlebrow." Through such transcultural connections, tango established particular aesthetics and ways of performing emotion in the two contemporary worlds.

Notes

1. This project has received funding from the European Union's Horizon 2020 research and innovation program under the Marie Skłodowska-Curie grant agreement no. 846143.
2. "Su acento es la canción de voz sentimental, su ritmo es el compás que vive en mi ciudad, no tiene pretensión, no quiere ser procaz, se llama tango y nada más." All translations in this chapter from Spanish and Japanese are by the author or otherwise stated.
3. I use the term "Argentine tango" to refer to repertory performed by Argentine and Japanese tango musicians and singers.
4. Yuiko Asaba, "'Folds of the Heart': Performing Life Experience, Emotion, and Empathy in Japanese Tango Music Culture," *Ethnomusicology Forum* 28, no. 1 (2019): 45–65.

5. This complicated construction of national identity involved "the Buenos Aires-centered nationalists" who celebrated and manipulated "the tango of the brothels and tenements." Marta E. Savigliano, *Tango and the Political Economy of Passion* (Boulder, CO: Westview Press, 1995), 165.

6. Savigliano, *Tango and the Political Economy of Passion.*

7. Kacey Link and Kristin Wendland, *Tracing* Tangueros: *Argentine Tango Instrumental Music* (New York: Oxford University Press, 2016), 11–14 and 33.

8. This concern for conveying emotion through tango's vocal performance was cultivated during the post-war years in Japan. On the study of tango performance and the importance of lyrics through the examination of the celebrated Japanese tango singer Abo Ikuo (1937–2021), see Asaba, "Folds of the Heart," which also discusses Argentina-Japan intimacy through tango performance.

9. Matthew B. Karush, *Culture of Class: Radio and Cinema in the Making of a Divided Argentina, 1920–1946* (Durham, NC: Duke University Press, 2012), 85–132.

10. Julie M. Taylor, *Paper Tangos* (Durham, NC: Duke University Press, 1998), 19.

11. James Butterworth, "Andean Divas: Emotion, Ethics and Intimate Spectacle in Peruvian Huayno Music" (Ph.D. diss., Royal Holloway, University of London, 2014), 131.

12. Gerald C. Cupchik, *The Aesthetics of Emotion: Up the Down Staircase of the Mind-Body* (Cambridge: Cambridge University Press, 2016), 9–11.

13. On emotion as aesthetics in studying the relationship between mind and body, see Cupchik, *The Aesthetics of Emotion.*

14. Butterworth, "Andean Divas." Cupchik, *The Aesthetics of Emotion.*

15. Butterworth, "Andean Divas," 36.

16. Cupchik, *The Aesthetics of Emotion*, 1–15.

17. On the cultural history of class and tango in Japan, see Yuiko Asaba, "Demarcating Status: Tango Music and Dance in Japan, 1913–1940," in *Worlds of Social Dancing: Dance Floor Encounters and the Global Rise of Couple Dancing, c. 1910–40*, eds., Klaus Nathaus and James Nott (Manchester: Manchester University Press, 2022), 154–176.

18. Considering realist aesthetics and an ability to convey powerful emotion as keys to a good performance are not limited to tango. See also Butterworth, "Andean Divas"; Lila Ellen Gray, *Fado Resounding: Affective Politics and Urban Life* (Durham: NC: Duke University Press, 2013); Aaron A. Fox, "The Jukebox of History: Narratives of Loss and Desire in the Discourse of Country Music," *Popular Music* 11, no.1 (1992): 53–72; Heather Willoughby, "The Sound of Han: P'ansori, Timbre and a Korean Ethos of Pain and Suffering," *Yearbook for Traditional Music* 32 (2000): 17–30.

19. I use "modernity" to refer to specific historical periods in which becoming modern was the ethos during pre-war and post-war years in Japan, including 1910s–1930s and 1945–1950. See Harry D. Harootunian, *Overcome by*

Modernity: History, Culture, and Community in Interwar Japan (Princeton, NJ: Princeton University Press, 2000).

20. Aihwa Ong argues, "Trans denotes moving through space or across lines, as well as the changing nature of something." Aihwa Ong, *Flexible Citizenship: The Cultural Logics of Transnationality* (Durham, NC: Duke University Press, 1999), 4.

21. For further discussion, see Asaba, "Folds of the Heart."

22. Sugawara Youichi, telephone interview by author, Oxford, United Kingdom–Tokyo, Japan, April 19, 2021. All Japanese names in this chapter take the conventional Japanese order of surname first, unless their publications appear in the English order of names.

23. Yrjö Heinonen, "Globalisation, Hybridisation, and the Finnishness of the Finnish Tango," *Etnomusikologian vuosikirja* 28 (2016):1–36.

24. Dorcinda Celiena Knauth, "Discourses of Authenticity in the Argentine Tango Community of Pittsburgh" (Master's thesis, University of Pittsburgh, 2005).

25. Caroline Pearsall, "Tango in Diaspora – An Argentine Abroad: An Examination of the Parisian Tango Music Community" (Master's thesis, Royal Holloway University of London, 2011).

26. Yuiko Asaba, "The Reception of Tango and the Creation of Its Authenticity in Twentieth Century Japan: A Study from the Perspective of 'Internalized Modernity'." (「20世紀日本におけるタンゴの受容と「本場」意識の形成 ― 内面化されたモダニティという視点からの一考察」) Popular Music Studies (『ポピュラー音楽研究』) 24 (2020): 3–15.

27. Asaba, "The Reception of Tango."

28. I use the term "Japanese tango" to refer to a repertory that was composed by Japanese popular music composers in the *ryūkōka* (popular song) genre in pre-war Japan, and in the broader Japanese popular music genre, *kayōkyoku*, through the latter half of the twentieth century. This repertory uses lyrics in Japanese, often evoking Japanese and Chinese "traditional" melodies, and utilizes melodies and rhythms that invoke genres such as jazz and tango. See Toshio Azami, *Tango and the Japanese (Tango to nihonjin)* (Tokyo: Shūeisha, 2018), 177–199.

29. Hayato Tajima, "Modern Japan's Melodramatic Imagination and 'Crossing of Borders': Discourse Analysis of Argentine Tango" ("Modan Nihon no merodrama teki sōzōryoku to 'ekkyō': Aruzenchin/tango wo meguru gensetsu bunseki"), *Bigaku Geijutsugaku Kenkyū* 27 (2009): 157–160.

30. "Tango Monogatari" is also in the audio collection of the National Diet Library of Japan, https://ndlonline.ndl.go.jp/#!/detail/R300000003-I8270279-00.

31. See Katō Hidetoshi, "Chūkan Bunkaron" ("A Study of the Middle Culture"), in *Katō Hidetoshi Chosakushū 6 (Collection of Essays by Katō Hidetoshi Vol. 6)*, ed. Katō Hidetoshi (Tokyo: Chūō Kōronsha, 1957/ 1980), 259–298; and Reo Nagasaki, *"Tsunagari" no sengo nihon-shi: Rō-on, soshite Takarazuka,*

Banpaku (*Cultural History of Post-War Japan, the "Cultural Connectivity":
From Rō-on, to Takarazuka, Banpaku*) (Tokyo: Kawade Shuppan, 2013).

32. Lawrence W. Levine, *Highbrow Lowbrow: The Emergence of Cultural
Hierarchy in America* (Cambridge, MA: Harvard University Press, 1988), 3.
Following film and literature studies, many musicologists have published
research on twentieth-century music and the middlebrow. See also
Christopher Chowrimootoo, *Middlebrow Modernism: Britten's Operas and the
Great Divide* (Oakland, CA: University of California Press, 2018);
Kate Guthrie, *Music and Middlebrow Culture in Modern Britain* (Oakland, CA:
University of California Press, 2019); John Howland, *Between the Muses and
the Masses: Symphonic Jazz, "Glorified" Entertainment, and the Rise of the
American Musical Middlebrow, 1920–1944* (Redwood City, CA: Stanford
University Press, 2002); Joan Shelley Rubin, *The Making of Middlebrow
Culture* (Chapel Hill, NC: University of North Carolina Press, 1992).

33. Katō Hidetohi wrote: "[i]n my opinion, post-war Japan has already passed the
two processes [of embracing both 'high' and 'low' cultures], and is now in its
third process. So what are the three processes? Hypothetically, I consider that
the three [socio-cultural processes] can be identified as one that is centered
around high culture (highbrow dominant), around popular culture (lowbrow
dominant), and around middle culture (middlebrow dominant). In other
words, it is now the era of middle culture." Katō, *Chūkan Bunkaron*, 259 ("私
の考えでは、戦後の日本文化はすでに二つの段階を経過して、いまや
第三期にはいってきている。その三つの段階とは何か。私はこれを仮
に高級文化中心の段階(highbrow dominant)、大衆文化中心の段階
(lowbrow dominant)および中間文化中心の段階(middlebrow dominant)
として区別ができるように思う。つまり、現代は中間文化の時代であ
る。" Katō [加藤).

34. Katō, *Chūkan Bunkaron*, 269.

35. Ibid.

36. Ibid.

37. Musicologist Christopher Chowrimootoo describes "middlebrow modernism"
as an aesthetic space in the twentieth-century Western art music. It has
"allow[ed] contemporary audiences to have their modernist cake and eat it: to
revel in the pleasures of tonality, melody, sentimentality, melodrama, and
spectacle, even while enjoying the prestige that comes from rejecting them."
Chowrimootoo, *Middlebrow Modernism*, 3. Tango's emotionality,
characterized as melodramatic while forming part of an important genre
aesthetic, contributes to this idea of tango's emotion as both "rejoiced and
rejected" in the vertical cultural hierarchy: rejoiced as an outward-looking
genre by Japanese tango performers and aficionados, while its emotional
expressions rejected by some Western art music listeners and musicians in
Japan due to its deep-seated characterization as being outside the "high art." In

many respects, the idea of the "middle culture" demonstrates the possibilities and, above all, limits of measuring cultures.

38. See Florencia Garramuño, *Primitive Modernities: Tango, Samba, and Nation*, translated by Anna Kazumi Stahl (Redwood City, CA: Stanford University Press, 2011).

39. Taylor, *Paper Tangos*, 19.

40. Ibid., 4.

41. Nélida Rouchetto, interview with author. Buenos Aires, Argentina, June 23, 2006.

42. Taylor, *Paper Tangos*, 19.

43. See, Morgan James Luker, *The Tango Machine: Musical Culture in the Age of Expediency* (Chicago: University of Chicago Press, 2016).

44. I use "lived emotion" from Christine Yano's study on Japanese *enka* performers. Their emotion in singing, considered key in a good *enka* performance, is portrayed by practicing what Yano has referred to as Japanese "*kata.*" *Kata* is a set of fixed movements in the Japanese traditional performing arts, and here it points to vocal techniques and body movements that carry particular emotional meanings. Christine R. Yano, *Tears of Longing: Nostalgia and the Nation in Japanese Popular Song* (Cambridge, MA: Harvard University Press, 2002), 24.

45. "Contested," because many Argentine tango musicians prefer not to use the term *mugre* to refer to a tango performance.

46. Yuiko Asaba, "The Notion of *Mugre* in Argentine Tango Violin Performance" (Conference paper, National Graduate Conference for Ethnomusicology, University of Cambridge, 2006), 1. In writing about concepts of uncleanness, Mary Douglas referred to "dirt" as "disorder" that "offends against order." See Mary Douglas, *Purity and Danger: An Analysis of Concepts of Pollution and Taboo* (New York: Routledge, 1966), 2. In many respects, Argentine tango's aesthetics of *mugre* (dirt) represents a critique of society and "ordered" Western art music.

47. Ramón Pelinski, "Astor Piazzolla: entre tango y fuga, en busca de una identidad estilística," in *Estudios sobre la obra de Astor Piazzolla*, ed. Omar García Brunelli (Buenos Aires: Gourmet Musical Ediciones, 2008), 50.

48. Maria Susana Azzi, "The Tango, Peronism, and Astor Piazzolla During the 1940s and '50s," in *From Tejano to Tango: Latin American Popular Music*, ed. Walter A. Clark (New York: Routledge, 2002), 38. The aesthetic of "dirt" as a positive quality in a good performance is not unique to tango. For example, David Hughes notes that in Japanese traditional folk song an "earthy (*tsuchikusai*) . . . [and] somewhat rough-edged voice quality" is considered a key quality in good folk song performance. See, David W. Hughes, *Traditional Folk Song in Modern Japan: Sources, Sentiment and Society* (Folkestone: Global Oriental, 2008), 197. Similarly, Frederick Moehn observes that the aesthetics of "dirtiness," "mess," and "swing" are important to

Brazilian carnival samba performance. See Frederick Moehn, *Contemporary Carioca: Technologies of Mixing in a Brazilian Music Scene* (Durham, NC: Duke University Press, 2012), 98–111.

49. Jessica Quiñones, "Constructing the Aesthetic: Approaching the '6 Tango-Etudes Pour Flûte Seule' by Astor Piazzolla (1921–1992) for Interpretation and Performance" (Ph.D. diss., University of Huddersfield, 2013), 87.

50. "In music, it [*mugre*] is the sound that is not necessarily considered beautiful . . . It is also not necessarily the correct sound or way of performing . . . It is the *rubato*, the *portato* . . . and the *glissando*. It is hard to describe and it is unclear (*algo que no está claro*) and not written (*algo que no está escrito*), and it is the *sentimiento* (feeling) of each musician." Fernando Suárez Paz, interview with author, Buenos Aires, Argentina, May 24, 2006.

51. "Well, it is better not to be tied to the word *mugre* when playing tango. It is the feeling of listening to a piece of music [tango] and thinking 'wow this passage [of music] is really nice.' Why, because it has '*mugre*,' rather than other way round . . . " Ibid.

52. For in-depth discussions on the ways in which "each musician's feelings" are perceived to become interwoven with Argentine tango's aesthetics of emotion, see Asaba, "Folds of the Heart."

53. Suárez Paz, interview. According to Suárez Paz, *mugre* also refers to the rhythmic feel as seen, for instance, in the double bass execution of *arrastre* (drag): "[A] classical [tango] double bassist plays the *marcato* like this [demonstrates on the violin playing in *détaché*], but really, it needs this [demonstrates on the violin with *arrastre*] . . . there are musicians who mistakenly say . . . 'that is not written on the score.' I would say, 'of course it is not written.' That is the trap, and the essence of tango." Suárez Paz, interview. *Mugre* is also used to refer to tango's swing, as well as to sound effects uniquely used in tango instrumental performance. See Asaba, "The Notion of *Mugre*."

54. Nélida Rouchetto, interview with author, Buenos Aires, Argentina, June 23, 2006.

55. Carlos Pazo, interview with author, Buenos Aires, Argentina, June 11, 2006. Pazo, however, insisted that *mugre* does not represent "true tango." Playing Aníbal Troilo's recording during my interview, he protested passionately, "how can the sounds of Troilo be *mugre* (dirty)? How can his sound be described as 'dirty'? It is beautiful!". Indeed, gatekeeping the "right" or "wrong" feelings in performance always needs to be understood in relation to a particular historical ethos. See Martin Stokes, *Republic of Love: Cultural Intimacy in Turkish Popular Music* (Chicago: University of Chicago Press, 2010), 188–193.

56. See Dorinne K. Kondo, *Crafting Selves: Power, Gender, and Discourses of Identity in a Japanese Workplace* (Chicago: University of Chicago Press, 1990).

57. It has been argued that evoking the sympathy of a listener in a performance is an important aesthetic quality to powerfully invoke "imaginations of the

sentimental subject." Stokes, *Republic of Love*, 63. A performer's "sincerity" is also seen to form an important part of popular music's aesthetics of emotion. Simon Frith, *Performing Rites: On the Value of Popular Music* (Cambridge, MA: Harvard University Press, 1998), 197.

Further Reading

Asaba, Yuiko. "'Folds of the Heart': Performing Life Experience, Emotion, and Empathy in Japanese Tango Music Culture." *Ethnomusicology Forum* 28, no. 1 (2019): 45–65.

Tango in Japan: Cosmopolitanism Beyond the West. Honolulu: University of Hawai'i Press, (forthcoming, 2025).

"The Reception of Tango and the Creation of Its Authenticity in Twentieth Century Japan: A Study from the Perspective of 'Internalized Modernity.'" (「20世紀日本におけるタンゴの受容と「本場」意識の形成 — 内面化されたモダニティという視点からの一考察」) *Popular Music Studies* (『ポピュラー音楽研究』) 24 (2020): 3–15.

Heinonen, Yrjö. "Globalisation, Hybridisation, and the Finnishness of the Finnish Tango." *Etnomusikologian vuosikirja* 28 (2016): 1–36.

Howland, John. *Between the Muses and the Masses: Symphonic Jazz, "Glorified" Entertainment, and the Rise of the American Musical Middlebrow, 1920–1944*. Redwood City, CA: Stanford University Press, 2002.

Levine, Lawrence W. *Highbrow Lowbrow: The Emergence of Cultural Hierarchy in America*. Cambridge, MA: Harvard University Press, 1988.

Moehn, Frederick. *Contemporary Carioca: Technologies of Mixing in a Brazilian Music Scene*. Durham, NC: Duke University Press, 2012.

Pearsall, Caroline. "Tango in Diaspora – An Argentine Abroad: An Examination of the Parisian Tango Music Community." Master's thesis, Royal Holloway, University of London, 2011.

Stokes, Martin. *Republic of Love: Cultural Intimacy in Turkish Popular Music*. Chicago: University of Chicago Press, 2010.

Willoughby, Heather. "The Sound of Han: P'ansori, Timbre and a Korean Ethos of Pain and Suffering." *Yearbook for Traditional Music* 32 (2000): 17–30.

19 | Tango Studies Abroad: Gustavo Beytelmann and Codarts University

BÁRBARA VARASSI PEGA

Tango music has become one of the most widespread popular music genres since its birth over one hundred years ago. Recently, it has aroused a huge international interest among musicians, resulting in tango concerts, shows, events, videos, and recordings. In addition, music scholars have engaged in academic research, publications, and diverse educational tools, including online platforms and social media channels that explore tango history, analysis, and composing/arranging techniques. Nevertheless, besides a few offerings in the form of courses provided by private tango schools or academies and state or private universities in several countries, including Argentina, France, and the United States, only a few higher-education institutions offer opportunities for formal tango studies today. In this regard, the teaching activities of tango pianist, arranger, composer, and educator Gustavo Beytelmann (b. 1945, Figure 19.1) hold an exceptional place in tango studies. His endeavors as the artistic director of the Tango Department at Codarts University of the Arts in Rotterdam, the Netherlands have generated a unique artistic and pedagogic model for teaching and transmitting tango as a musical language within a vocational university. His work represents an unparalleled institutional-ization effort of tango studies from the 1990s to the present day.

This chapter first sheds light on Beytelmann's life as a tango artist and educator, and how he approached communicating the musical language of tango. I discuss how he formed his tango ensembles and shaped his distinct teaching philosophy outside of tango's birthplace, the Río de la Plata region in Argentina and Uruguay. Next, I consider the systematization of tango studies both inside Argentina through various key institutions and outside of Argentina at Codarts University of the Arts in the Netherlands. The following text results from my experience as a musician, researcher, and educator specializing in tango. My insight draws first from my time as a student and now as a teacher at Codarts. I also base this chapter on years of working with Gustavo Beytelmann and, most recently, on my interview with him on April 29, 2021. Beytelmann's quotes in this text come from this interview, and I translated them to English.

Figure 19.1 Concert-lecture by Gustavo Beytelmann at the World Music and Dance Centre, Codarts University of the Arts, Rotterdam, the Netherlands, February 14, 2022.

Tango Transmission: From Empirical Practice to Systematic Studies

Background of Gustavo Beytelmann

Gustavo Beytelmann was born in Venado Tuerto, Argentina, into a family of musicians and music lovers. As an adolescent and young adult, he became fully immersed in Argentine tango musical life through studies and work in his hometown and later in the cities of Rosario and Buenos Aires. In 1976, Beytelmann immigrated to Paris, and in 1977 he joined Astor Piazzolla's (1921–1992) Octeto Electrónico European tour. That same year Beytelmann also founded the ensemble Tiempo Argentino with other expat Argentine musicians. In the 1980s, he joined forces with bandoneonist Juan José Mosalini and bassist Patrice Caratini to create the Mosalini–Beytelmann–Caratini trio. This groundbreaking ensemble became internationally famous for some of Beytelmann's avant-garde compositions and arrangements as well as their great musical artistry. Throughout his career, Beytelmann has composed, arranged, and performed pieces of a diverse array of styles, including Argentine folk music, tango, rock, jazz, pop, film, and contemporary Western art music. Beytelmann's unique musical language integrates his varied musical experiences yet carries his own signature sound. His teaching activities at Codarts also reflect his distinctive musical language.

Learning Tango through Oral Transmission

Dating back to its origins, tango has been traditionally passed down orally through generations of musicians. Tango ensembles and orchestras in the Río de la Plata region were often the "schools" where fledgling musicians could gain knowledge and practice. These musicians, in turn, metaphorically learned to fly and continued the process of creating new ensembles and orchestras, and eventually training new musicians. As bassist Andrés Serafini points out, "musicians would learn the language and styles from their fellow orchestra members and conductors. The craft, the tradition, and its innovations were developed directly in the professional field."[1] Besides training with *orquestas típicas* (typical tango orchestras, with the usual formation of three or more violins, three or more bandoneones, piano, double bass, and sometimes cello or guitar), some students studied privately with tango musicians through individual lessons (although this was not a regular activity because of the artists' busy performance schedule), but there were no systematic studies of tango until recently.

According to Beytelmann, the systematic teaching of tango is something new. Over the last thirty years, tango studies have moved beyond oral transmission by practicing tango musicians to a more formalized approach. He remarks how even tango musicians who were skilled arrangers and composers never "thought of setting up a tango school," but rather transmitted information by working together in both rehearsal and performance. For example, Beytelmann recounts the musical relationship of guitarists Ciro Pérez and Roberto Grela. He states, "Ciro went to Grela's house almost every day, and they played for two or three hours before going to the club. That is to say, they spent the day playing, and they also spent the day transmitting and receiving knowledge and information."

During tango's Golden Age (1930s–1950s), *tangueros* (tango musicians) arranged standard tango compositions for various orchestras, and specific musicians – such as Pugliese and Troilo – had a very precise idea of their orchestral style. Apprentices learned these styles through practice as the masters would grab a pencil and an eraser to show them how to work, write, and orchestrate. Beytelmann mentions the very well-known example of the young Piazzolla playing with and arranging for Troilo and his orchestra: "It's the same thing that Piazzolla did when he learned to write for an *orquesta típica*. He learned to write for an *orquesta típica* by being part of an *orquesta típica*, Troilo's orchestra, and making his first steps in the orchestra." Beytelmann points out that this method entailed learning from mistakes and things that went well during daily rehearsals and performances. He further states that this method embraced empiricism, in which the art form was transmitted through experience. It combined oral transmission with written scores (both arrangements and compositions alike). In parallel, this tradition also demonstrated direct education from teacher to student. But in any case, the pedagogy was neither institutionalized nor coordinated.

Beytelmann's Formative Ideas for Teaching Tango Outside Argentina

Beytelmann recalls how his professional activities in Paris pushed him for the first time to find answers about conceptualizing how tango is played and conceived. When he first arrived in Paris in the 1970s, he realized that many European musicians were unfamiliar with playing tango in an Argentine style. He recognized that he needed to explicitly identify many aspects of tango practice that, until then, had only been implicit knowledge for him. He explains:

In Argentina, I didn't have much of an idea of this [the features of tango music]. Because my father was also a musician and I was born in that very home, so that was the violin, and this is the piano, and I had a good ear and so I listened to tangos and played them . . . The first important shock was in Paris when I began to interact with different professional musicians, and that's when I realized . . . they had no idea about tango and what sounded were the notes, but it didn't sound like tango. Then, I discovered that the tango component was not in the notes or in the harmony but in the "how." So that was the eureka moment for me.

For Beytelmann, this eureka moment was the beginning of developing a vocabulary to explain the musical components of tango music and how to approach and integrate this vocabulary into practice. He defined the "how" of tango music to non-tango musicians. Beytelmann reflects on the work done not only by him, but also by Mosalini, César Stroscio, the Gennevilliers conservatory, and others that created the basis to access this "how": "I say why the 'how'? Because the students who play the bandoneón, with the ideas that Mosalini had, learn by playing Bach's inventions, that's why I say that it [tango] is [a] language, it's not [an] idiom." This experience was also the case for other professional tango musicians who started creating ensembles and playing tango outside of Argentina with musicians who did not have previous experience with tango music. Like musicians learning in the *orquestas típicas* in Argentina, some of these newly trained tango musicians outside Argentina would, in turn, continue establishing new ensembles and training non-tango musicians, only within a different context. One may consider such transfer of knowledge a tango training school in its own right. This ultimately brought new experiences and expertise in tango outside the Río de la Plata region.

Despite growing up listening to, playing, and being surrounded by tango, disseminating the mechanisms of what tango music entails to non-tango musicians was not an easy task for many *tangueros*. It took much effort for many of them to make explicit the implicit knowledge they owned, which is a crucial aspect in transmitting knowledge. When remembering a recording session for a film score with the concertmaster of the Paris Opera orchestra, Beytelmann states:

I wasn't able to tell him [the concertmaster] why I didn't like the solo he was playing. I couldn't tell him, because I wasn't aware of it myself. I knew like the tango musicians who tell you, "That's not tango," but I didn't know how to explain it. I felt very stupid. And I tried to find not words but the reasons, why the violin, the four strings, it's the same technique but it doesn't sound the same . . . And Bajour is there to tell you, which is what I like so much about that quintet with Bajour [Piazzolla's], that you hear a classical violinist, a Russian violinist, who plays tango. But you hear both, you don't hear one. Well, that's me. I [then] came to an enriching idea by deconstructing [tango].

Beytelmann first approached teaching the "how" of tango performance by forming ensembles and playing with musicians who did not have tango knowledge. Coming from a tango background, he understood tango's unique musical characteristics and the *códigos* (codes) that define the art form. He then established a vocabulary to make this information explicit to others. To understand the *códigos*, conventions, and practices of tango music, or in other words, the "how," Beytelmann has come to stress the importance of analyzing and understanding what is played, the structure, and the musical idea that governs not only the interpretation but also the arrangement. To him, this all makes a particular tango sound world.

Beytelmann identifies another crucial factor in teaching tango – what he calls "music with geography included." In other words, students must understand and integrate tango's history and culture. He thinks that "geography" – meaning to him the culture and relationships of people relating to a place – is a main aspect to consider. He describes how Piazzolla was less influenced by the American jazz musician Gerry Mulligan than by the Argentine master Julio De Caro:

Contrary to the official story, Piazzolla's Octeto Buenos Aires owes much less to Gerry Mulligan than to Julio De Caro and his sextet. Not only because the octet is the sextet plus a cello and an electric guitar, but also because of the way it is written.

You need to have an ear with a historical perspective and understand that the opposite for a *tanguero* is still tango, but another tango. And saying: "No . . . he [Piazzolla] listened to Mulligan's octet at the Salle Pleyel." Come on! Above all, what Piazzolla knew was De Caro and what is there is a De Caro from the middle of the twentieth century, not from the beginning of the twentieth century but from the middle.

Beytelmann further explains his approach to tango music studies outside Argentina:

You need to have one foot outside to be able to look [inside] with more objectivity, and to look with more objectivity for me means language. To create a language that allows you and anyone else with those study tools to analyze Beethoven, Chopin, Stockhausen and Villoldo. That has been the path for me, the hope, my task has been more linked to this: to provide tools that are universal and that can be applied like any sound organization to language.

First Formal Tango Studies in Argentina

The study of tango in formal academic settings is a recent reality. Tango historians generally agree that the decade of the 1980s marks the beginning of a period of global artistic expression for tango. One could characterize this multifaceted phenomenon by the touring of "stage tango" shows, the teaching of tango as a ballroom dance worldwide, and the international success of Astor Piazzolla's oeuvre. Additionally, the globalization of tango music has resulted in a growing interest in researching, preserving, and developing the practice of historical tango styles in Argentina and abroad.

In Argentina, Osvaldo Pugliese's creation of La Casa del Tango in 1985 represents one of the first efforts to institutionalize tango studies. Pugliese's idea was to create a place to learn, practice, and experiment with tango music. He sought to create a type of music center – notably, still open today under the guidance of Nélida Rochetto – where lectures could be given and research carried out in a first-class library.

More broadly, Beytelmann describes the new tango environment in Argentina in the 1980s: "[A] market was created with the accumulation of experience of popular music, which was fabricated by the phonograph, radios, television, among others." Beytelmann cites two factors that resulted in the creation of tango schools. First, the accumulation of knowledge from within Argentina created the necessity to systematize it into an academic curriculum. Second, from outside Argentina, the international success of the school systems in the United States boosted tango studies.

The first factor leading to the creation of tango schools in Argentina was the most important to Beytelmann: "From the inside, a case like [Horacio] Salgán for example, is to be aware that we have reached an amount of knowledge and experience that we should systematize and try to transmit."

One of the first schools created in Argentina to systematically teach tango was the Escuela de Música Popular de Avellaneda (EMPA, School of Popular Music of Avellaneda) in 1987.[2] Created by the government of the Province of Buenos Aires, it aimed to institutionalize the training of musicians in popular music genres including Argentine folklore, tango, and jazz. The creation of the curriculum content for the tango program was commissioned to maestro and pianist Horacio Salgán, who gave lessons along with other acclaimed tango musicians such as pianist Dante Amicarelli. Beytelmann recalls the EMPA milestone: "There, many people with an interest and awareness of the development of *popular music* . . . could study and learn." To the present day, the EMPA is one of the very few institutions where students can formally study tango music with a complete curriculum and earn a diploma.

After the founding of EMPA, several state-run and private institutions and organizations began to offer tango performance training for tango-related instruments, including the bandoneón. These institutions include the Orquesta Escuela de Tango Emilio Balcarce and the municipal conservatories "Manuel de Falla" and "Astor Piazzolla." In addition, some departments include tango in their Argentine music studies, such as the Universidad Nacional de San Martín, Universidad Nacional de las Artes, Universidad Nacional de Villa María, and Universidad Católica Argentina. In my hometown Rosario, students may study tango with an *orquesta escuela* (teaching orchestra) and participate in a bandoneón class at the Universidad Nacional de Rosario, next to a municipal and a provincial conservatory.

From the 1990s onwards, tango began to attract musicians again, especially younger generations. As a result, ensembles proliferated, and more tango teaching institutions emerged, creating the need for more instructional materials to transmit tango. Salgán's 2001 self-published book *Curso de tango* (Tango Course) signals this renewed interest in tango studies. The groundbreaking work is the first published technical source on arranging and performing tango music. More recently, a growing list of published articles, books, and manuals transmit a wealth of information on tango, covering its idiomatic features, including instrumentation, specific terminology, compositional/arrangement practices, and performance techniques. One example is my book *The Art of Tango* (2021) on arranging, composing, and performing tango elements and techniques. In addition, several freelance musicians share and distribute tango-related scores and material and offer in-person and online options for informal tango meetings and tutorials, such as private lessons, courses, and workshops. The online EPSA publisher and the non-profit tango collective Tango sin fin are contributing a great wealth of scores and study materials, and the latter also organizes intensive workshops called "Tango para músicos" ("Tango for Musicians") internationally.

In the mid-1990s, the tango pianist/composer, educator, and cultural promoter Julián Peralta founded a school specifically devoted to tango in Buenos Aires called Escuela de Tango Orlando Goñi. Peralta manages the school jointly with other young tango musicians, and together they have been an invaluable group in terms of building and disseminating theoretical and practical knowledge of the tango language, focusing on *orquestas típicas*. The school's founders studied with some of the last-living tango musicians and have since transcribed several pieces themselves. They sought to pass on their acquired knowledge to pave the way for new musicians in tango. Peralta channeled such knowledge into his book *La orquesta típica*,[3] which provides unique and comprehensive information about tango music, including orchestration, composition, arranging, and performing features. In an interview, he recalls the impetus to write his tango book: "The institutional offer[ings] at that time did not include anything other than the European tradition crystallized in the conservatory formats, focused on classical and jazz musical languages, while everything else seemed *not serious*."[4]

Peralta's concerns about the "serious" study of tango highlight a major obstacle in the *how* of teaching tango music. This is still the case in most institutions for music studies in Argentina. Even when these institutions allow or welcome certain popular music repertory in some instrumental or ensemble lessons, they rarely offer a specific popular music degree track in the style. Therefore, if students want to formally study and receive a diploma, they frequently must study Western Art music, even though it is not their primary interest as artists and aspiring professionals.

Tango Studies at the World Music Department at Codarts University of the Arts

Background of the World Music Department

Codarts University of the Arts bridges this educational gap between traditional Western art-music training and studying popular or world music for music students. It is a vocational university aimed at combining the "oldest tradition and latest trends in its professional arts education" and at passing on "the most divergent cultures, styles, and disciplines to new generations of performing artists who indeed see the world as their operational field."[5] Within this framework, Dr. Joep Bor,[6] the founder of the World Music Department at Codarts University, has always advocated for open-minded educational spaces where diverse musical languages can be explored and coexist, and even open up new possibilities for musical dialogues and cross-over experiences. Bor explains his concept behind the creation of the World Music Department:

Though it was obvious to me that the term "world music" was a Western construct, at the time, I did not think it was necessary to define it. In my opinion, it was a refreshing and pragmatic term that was quite self-explanatory: it represented all the genres and styles of the *musics* of the world, and all the crossovers that did not fit into the existing boxes.

Following Bor's vision, the World Music Department at Codarts opened new educational offerings in the 1980s. Even though many institutions are opening their doors to a more diverse musical curriculum nowadays, the mainstream continues to revolve around Western Art music. His educational concept is to embrace different sound and training worlds, which better represent our diverse society. In order to do this, Codarts established its core mission to gather the best experts in the diverse musical fields covered in the new program, and these experts were happy and proud to join. Bor invited great masters of the different music traditions to set up the curriculum, teach, and train other teachers to teach:

When I started [The World Music Department at Codarts], I told the director . . . that I would start it if it had the same status as classical, jazz or whatever, otherwise it made no sense . . . Paco Peña was already teaching [flamenco guitar] at Codarts, so when I brought Indian music and Hariprasad Chaurasia[7] this director was very much impressed . . . because he [Chaurasia] is one of the best musicians in the world. We had then Latin music already, Indian, flamenco guitar only, and then tango came in 1993. And at the end, when I was still the head of the department, we started the Turkish [department] in 2000, which currently has Kudsi Ergüner[8] as its artistic director . . . It is very important that you have an international network, that you listen to people, that you keep developing things according to your vision, and that you update the available knowledge and experts.

The Beginnings of the Tango Department

The Tango Department at Codarts was founded in 1993 by the Dutch bandoneonists Leo Vervelde and Carel Kraayenhof. Along with the Classical Indian, Flamenco, Turkish, and Latin Music departments, it makes up the overarching World Music Department at Codarts. This department runs parallel to the Classical (Western art music), Jazz, and Pop Departments at Codarts. When consulted about why tango was selected among the main musical languages the academic office wanted to cover at Codarts, Bor explained the idea behind the project was "to have music that was really international rather than music that, even being fantastic, never spread over the world." He pointed out that, while not all musics of the world can be taught at the conservatory as some are unteachable in such a setting, he was convinced that tango was one of those musics that would fit in. After the tango program opened, Bor highlighted how the newly established program received a lot of media attention because there was nothing comparable worldwide, and students came from all over the globe to study there.

The Artistic Direction: Origins and Present

The first artistic director of the Tango Department at Codarts was Osvaldo Pugliese, appointed in 1993. As one of the greatest tango pillars, the Argentine pianist, composer, arranger, and celebrity is famous for his unique style and revolutionary tango orchestra. Beytelmann succeeded Pugliese in 1996. Beytelmann recalls how, after more than ten years of professional life in Europe, he accepted the invitation to take part in the Tango Department at Codarts without thinking twice. It seemed to him "quite a challenge to be able to imagine a bridge between Europe and Argentina, and to be able to work on the problems of the 'how' [of playing, arranging, and composing tango] and the acquisition of a grammar, of a way of saying and doing that is exclusively tango."

Beytelmann's Tango Educational Philosophy at Codarts

Beytlemann's role within the Tango Department at Codarts, together with other teachers, resembles the earlier method of how tango was taught and learned, namely how the knowledge and interpretative secrets were passed on through oral transmission from masters to students and by imitating recordings. Today, however, these practices are further accompanied by the study of the existing literature and sources on tango, written scores, analysis of recordings, and student reflections on writing, arrangements, and the like. In line with Bor, Beytelmann stresses the need to have a good team of teachers and a good coordinator with a network in the field.

When asked what he considers to be the main characteristic in the transmission of tango knowledge, Beytelmann cites the concept of sound as the most important. He states that "what had to be taught was a way of conceiving sound, a way of organizing it, [and] accepting that this is the language [sound] and that tango is an idiom of that language. That's what it has been all my life; I've always believed in this." Furthermore, in developing his teaching abilities and how to communicate with students, Beytelmann – like the classical twentieth-century composer Arnold Schoenberg – learned from his students. He humbly observes: "I learned with time and mostly and above all, to paraphrase Schoenberg, I learned more from the students. I had some ideas, but the students taught me more than I taught them."

The Student Body

Broadly speaking, students can fulfill their tango studies at Codarts in a flexible way tailored to their interests and profile. They come from different parts of the world, with a keen interest in delving into tango's musical language. Beytelmann reflects on the international community of students enrolled in the Codarts tango program: "It is very clear that people don't come here looking for a diploma to try to get by in life, but rather they come to delve into tango because it appeals to them as a means of artistic expression." He further remarks on how these international students study and learn tango far away from its birthplace, and how they have learned the codes and conventions of tango music despite not being Argentine: "[T]hey overcame the geographical and cultural problem and took possession of a very important part of what would be the spirit of a part of that which is 15,000 kilometers away from these lands, and they play it as if it were their own."

How Tango Is Taught at Codarts

Applied Music Curriculum

In addition to offering individual lessons as a main subject, the tango program at Codarts devotes special attention to transcription, arrangement, composition, history, analysis of scores and recordings, and individual and ensemble playing. Both in main subject and ensemble lessons, the diverse elements and techniques of tango music are explored for a well-rounded education in traditional tango music that provides a foundation for future endeavors. Transcriptions of recordings of the great masters provide written scores when they are otherwise unavailable for understanding the main styles of tango and their possibilities for performance. When studying typical tango rhythms, accompanimental patterns, melodic phrasing, ornamentation, and special effects (extended techniques), students are encouraged to delve into the main features of tango music while becoming familiar with representative styles and even creating their own arrangements and compositions.

In addition, and thanks to the unique World Music Department running parallel to the Jazz and Classical departments at Codarts, students can collaborate on cross-over projects with other departments, and form or join ensembles with students of different backgrounds and fields of specialization. For example, the Orquesta Típica de Rotterdam Integrada por Alumnos (OTRA, the typical tango orchestra including alumni of the Tango Department) regularly welcomes students from other departments who wish to perform tango music and expand their musicianship with new expressive tools. Interdisciplinary projects are increasingly more common as well, with students from circus arts, dance, and music jointly creating new artistic works.

Artistic Research

Artistic research is a crucial part of the studies at Codarts, at both the bachelor's and master's trajectories, and the Codarts Research statement reflects the institution's mission and vision: "Codarts Research focuses on practice-oriented research in the domain of the performing arts, art education, dance therapy, and music therapy."[9] The Manual for Artistic Research describes the Codarts student-centered approach, "where their own perspectives, experiences, inspirations and ideas become vitally woven into the results of the research." Students answer their research questions by performing and/or creating work while reaching new knowledge and understanding. Their artistic research invites them "to enter a space of questioning and rethinking accepted or automatic ways of doing things." In this way, students explore and find their own ways of creating and performing music as they strive to shape their ideas into their unique artistic signature. In keeping with this educational philosophy, the Tango Department promotes artistic research throughout a student's academic career, supporting the need for the student to acquire validated knowledge independently. Bor further supports the study and systematization of tango and other musics of oral tradition through student research at Codarts "to create educational material and to modernize the teaching, as there is very little material in the field."

Networking and Educational Exchange with Scholars and Practitioners Worldwide

As part of its ongoing outreach activities and continuing education, the Tango Department at Codarts promotes and fosters international connections by regularly inviting renowned international tango artists to participate in both online and onsite activities. Prestigious musicians and scholars who have recently collaborated with the department include pianists Peralta, Hernán Possetti, Lisandro Baum, Pablo Estigarribia, and Diego Schissi; bandoneonists Víctor Villena (bandoneón instructor 2004–2014 and 2016–2017 parallel to Vervelde),[10] Alfredo Marcucci, Milagros Caliva, Roberto Álvarez, Martín Sued, Pablo Mainetti, and Eva Wolf (also an alumna of Codarts); violinist Ramiro Gallo; and double bass players Juan Pablo Navarro and Ignacio Varchausky. Bor highlights the importance of students having such an international network to promote learning from people directly involved in the genre. In this way, students may develop projects and skills according to their vision and update the available knowledge through experts promoted by the Codarts Tango Department. Bor also notes that, besides inviting the masters to teach in the Netherlands, Codarts must build international collaborations and partnerships with departments and conservatories in the countries of origin of the different musical languages. As some traditions, such as tango, are changing very quickly, studying abroad in those countries is crucial for students to stay up to date.

Performance Opportunities within the Curriculum

Codarts offers students in the tango program enriching opportunities for on-stage performances with their teachers and past students, including for their graduation recitals (as their final exams) and other events. Students may be organized in various formations ranging from small ensembles to full *orquestas típicas*. In addition to this wide array of tango ensembles formed by students, the Codarts Tango Department is proud to have the Orquesta Típica de Rotterdam integrada por alumnos (OTRA), a full tango *orquesta típica*, as its representative ensemble to give professional performances both at national and international concert venues. Such performances offer invaluable possibilities for professional international-level collaboration, which has enabled many alumni to collaborate with world-renowned artists and to establish themselves as respected artists in their own right.

Conclusion

The teaching of tango has recently gained ground within academic settings worldwide as institutions broaden their offerings beyond the mainstream Western art music curriculum. More and more tango musicians and scholars are connecting the actual practice of tango to the transmission of its musical language both inside and outside Argentina. Beytelmann's work and the Tango Department at Codarts serve as fine examples of possible approaches to teaching and transmitting tango, in this case, far from its origins. Its holistic approach ties together a unique curriculum that encompasses applied instruction by tango masters, practice-oriented artistic research, international networking with tango artists, and mentored performance opportunities.

It remains to be seen how these worldwide institutional efforts will continue to elevate tango and other popular genres as "serious" music in the future. More informed possibilities promise to emerge as our world becomes more interconnected through technologies that bridge regional and artistic walls, and as musicians search for new ways to express their art across borders, hierarchies, and classifications. Yet, there is still much to discover, experiment with, and discuss in the field of the pedagogy of tango and other popular music.

Notes

1. Andrés Serafini, "Yeites de tango," *SEDICI Repositorio Institucional de la Universidad Nacional de La Plata*, October 2016.
2. Editors' note: For more information on tango educational institutions in Argentina, see Michael Seamus O'Brien, "Contemporary Tango in Buenos Aires, Argentina: A Globalized Local Music in a Historicized Present," master's thesis, University of Texas, 2005; and "Disciplining the Popular: New Institutions for Argentine Music Education Systems," Ph.D. diss., University of Texas at Austin, 2010.

3. Julián Peralta, *La orquesta típica: mecánica y aplicación de los fundamentos técnicos del tango* (Buenos Aires: Departamento de Impresiones de la H. C. D. de la Provincia de Buenos Aires, 2008), and *The Tango Orchestra: Fundamental Concepts and Techniques*, trans. Morgan James Luker (Warwickshire, UK: Tanguero Publishing/Presto Music, 2016).

4. Natacha Scherbovsky, "Julián Peralta: Hacemos tango desde este lugar de resistencia," *La Tinta* (March 15, 2017), https://latinta.com.ar/2017/03/julian-peralta-hacemos-tango-desde-este-lugar-de-resistencia. Author's translation.

5. "Mission and vision," *Codarts University of the Arts*, www.codarts.nl/en/mission-and-vs.

6. Dr. Joep Bor was born in 1946 in Amsterdam, the Netherlands, into a family of musicians. He is a botanist, sarangi player, musicologist, and professor at the Academy of Creative and Performing Arts, Leiden University (ACPA). Bor is the founder of the World Music Department at Codarts, and as such interviewed by the author on May 14, 2021. All quotes in this text belong to that interview.

7. Hariprasad Chaurasia is an Indian flutist in the Hindustani classical tradition, and his performances and compositions have brought global recognition to the *bansuri*, a simple side-blown bamboo flute.

8. Kudsi Ergüner is considered a master of traditional Mevlevi Sufi music and is one of the best-known players of the Turkish ney flute.

9. "Codarts Research," *Codarts Rotterdam*, www.codarts.nl/en/codarts-research.

10. Víctor Villena currently teaches bandoneón at the International Institute of World Music in Aubagne, France.

Further Reading

Bor, Joep. "Studying World Music: The Next Phase." In *Teaching Musics of the World: The Second International Symposium*, Basel, October 14–17, 1993, edited by Margot Lieth-Philipp and Andreas Gutzwiller, 61–81. Affalterbach: Philipp, 1995.

"Manual Artistic Research Design: Methodology toolbox for research in-and-through artistic performance and creation." Rotterdam: Codarts University of the Arts, 2021.

García Brunelli, Omar. "Los estudios sobre tango observados desde la musicología. Historia, música, letra y baile." *El oído pensante* 3, no. 2 (2015): 68–99. http://revistascientificas.filo.uba.ar/index.php/oidopensante/article/view/7463.

Gonnet, Daniel H. "La construcción de conocimientos pluriversales en la escena del tango de principios de siglo XXI. La experiencia de la Escuela Orlando Goñi." *Revista Internacional de Educación Musical* 5 (2017): 111–118. www.revistaeducacionmusical.org/index.php/rem1/article/view/127.

Peralta, Julián. *La orquesta típica: mecánica y aplicación de los fundamentos técnicos del tango*. Buenos Aires: Departamento de Impresiones de la H. C. D. de la Provincia de Buenos Aires, 2008; and later *The Tango Orchestra: Fundamental Concepts and Techniques*, trans. Morgan James Luker. Warwickshire, UK: Tanguero Publishing/Presto Music, 2016.

Scherbovsky, Natacha. "Julián Peralta: Hacemos tango desde este lugar de resistencia." *La Tinta* (March 15, 2017). https://latinta.com.ar/2017/03/julian-peralta-hacemos-tango-desde-este-lugar-de-resistencia/.

Serafini, A. 2016. "Yeites de tango. Análisis de gestos musicales y técnicas extendidas en el tango para su utilización creativa y pedagógica." Paper presented at *I Congreso Internacional de Música Popular*, La Plata, October 2016. La Plata: SEDICI, Repositorio Institucional de la Universidad Nacional de La Plata, http://sedici.unlp.edu.ar/handle/10915/77184.

Varassi Pega, Bárbara. *The Art of Tango*. New York: Routledge, 2021.

20 | Tango and Healing: A Clinical Research Perspective

MADELEINE E. HACKNEY AND J. LUCAS MCKAY

Dance and Tango's Possibilities for Healing

Throughout history and across cultures, dance has played a role in promoting health and preventing or changing health conditions. The twenty-first century has had critical neurological problems to solve, such as spinal cord injury, Alzheimer's disease, Parkinson's disease, multiple sclerosis, chronic pain, cerebral palsy, and mental health, among others. Dance, including tango, is a pleasurable physical activity and provides access to unique learning strategies that can access neuroplasticity – the brain's ability to change because of experiences – to improve, perhaps even heal, these conditions.

Dance's therapeutic potential has been the subject of numerous studies over the last decade with observed benefits in the physical, cognitive, and emotional domains – particularly in neurodegenerative conditions. Although rehabilitation medicine used to be essentially synonymous with manual physical therapy, it is now commonly acknowledged that rehabilitation therapy, which combines physical and cognitive challenges, may be the most effective treatment in inducing beneficial, lasting effects on the brain's structure and function.[1] Dance may be an ideal medium for combining physical and cognitive training because it is substantially more engaging than other modalities, for example, stationary bicycling while completing computerized cognitive training.[2] For many, dance is a rewarding activity because of the combined experience of moving to music and socially interacting. The inclusion of sensory elements, such as aspects of touch, sound, and sight, may contribute to this enjoyment and enhance the potential to acquire new, flexible ways of moving in an environment. All of these positive factors increase the likelihood that dance participants will adhere to it as a regimen, which is critical for effective therapy.

Among the myriad of dances worldwide, partnered dance, which involves a leader and a follower, stands out as a potential therapy because it is a cognitively demanding, mentally stimulating *movement conversation*

347

that anyone can do. In tango, for example, the leader serves as the planner of movement, while the follower receives nonverbal cues to execute specific steps. The dancing pair maintain an embrace, also known as a "frame," which is a fixed arm position linking the two dancers. This physical connection enables a sophisticated, yet accessible tactile communication system that conveys motor intentions and goals between dancers. Both dancers must maintain internal focus while being also highly attuned to the environment and other individuals, including their partner. In tango, dancers do not memorize step patterns; instead, a follower moves by responding to the leader's tactile cues, which indicate where they go next. While tango dance draws on a core vocabulary of steps (such as *ochos* [figure eights] and *cruzadas* [crosses]), dancers improvise the order and execution of the steps in social dancing. Leading and following roles in tango offer the potential for effective healing. This chapter largely concerns a modified form of tango called "Adapted Tango," which was first created in 2006 and has since been refined.

Adapted Tango is an instructed form of physical activity that does not require prior knowledge or skill in any dance genre, or specifically tango. In Adapted Tango dance classes – which can be taught anywhere from formal dance studios to simple, open spaces – participants learn how to interpret motor goals through touch and perform activities to foster an understanding of the temporal relationship between movement and music. Many elements of Adapted Tango rehabilitation are very similar to traditional dance classes. In our approach to Adapted Tango, each class follows a structured syllabus with new steps, rhythms, and *adornos* (embellishments) added progressively at each class. Participants hear diverse tango music, including standards from the *guardia vieja* (Old Guard) of the early twentieth century and tango's Golden Age (1930s–1950s), as well as more modern *nuevo tango* (New Tango) pieces and ballroom tangos. Participants dance with new partners every fifteen to twenty minutes, which is a widely practiced dance teaching method to enhance learning and adaptability.

Clinical research makes some key adjustments for Adapted Tango to accommodate the movement needs of the participants who engage in the therapy. The dance frame and several steps of tango are modified in Adapted Tango to accommodate people with differing ability levels.[3] Someone with an impairment may partner with a healthy individual, such as a caregiver, spouse, friend, or volunteer from a local university, so that a participant who might be at risk of falling is always in contact with someone who can help them with balance. Finally, rather than leader and

follower roles being gender specific, as they often are in traditional partnered dance, all Adapted Tango participants practice both the leader and
follower roles for equal amounts of time.

The success of Adapted Tango has been promising. The first studies in
older adults repeatedly showed that Adapted Tango improved motor and
cognitive function.[4] Since then, in over fifteen years and hundreds of
sessions in diverse participant groups, Adapted Tango has consistently
been safe for participants with no adverse events or even reports of
soreness. Moreover, in multiple studies, participants have had better or
equal attrition rates to nondance training.

In this chapter, we explore how current research about Adapted Tango
has demonstrated improved motor and cognitive functions in individuals
with Parkinson's and Alzheimer's diseases after participating in the
training. This work is based on Hackney's training in dance and movement science and McKay's training in electrical and computer engineering and movement science. Both authors conduct research and teach at
Emory University in Atlanta, Georgia, and they study function in older
people with neurodegenerative disease and use different movement techniques as therapies. We first discuss the research to date, then illustrate
potential mechanisms for healing, then finally propose topics for future
studies.

Research to Date[5]

Benefits of Dance on Impairment

Studies since 2007 have shown that dance training improves mobility in
people with Parkinson's disease. Many studies have shown improvements
in behavioral measures of balance and functional mobility used by physical therapists. These measures usually require participants to complete
a series of movement tasks like standing on one foot for a length of time or
walking heel to toe. Amusingly, participants often joke that these measures remind them of a roadside sobriety test. Studies have also shown
improvements in "freezing of gait," a particularly debilitating symptom
experienced by many people with Parkinson's disease. In this case, they
paroxysmally, or suddenly, "freeze" during walking and feel that their feet
are glued to the floor. Other studies have shown that dance training can
improve cognition, mood, quality of life, self-efficacy, and social connect-
edness. After Adapted Tango, people with Parkinson's disease have

experienced significant gains in mobility, balance, and quality of life, endurance, cognition, and social participation. These improvements have been demonstrated to be maintained after both one month and up to three months later. Dance may have an immediate effect on mobility in those with Parkinson's disease, as improvements have been found in as little as two weeks of Adapted Tango or contact improvisation training. In addition to these broad benefits for individuals with Parkinson's disease, a series of studies has also investigated how Adapted Tango can improve motor-cognitive function in the general geriatric community with cognitive impairment, low vision, and motor-cognition in older adults in senior living.

Although the physical activity of Adapted Tango training is primarily composed of whole-body rhythmic movement and walking, studies have also shown that it can improve the overall motor symptoms, distinct from walking, of people with Parkinson's disease. For example, after participating in one year of Adapted Tango classes offered in a community in the midwestern United States, participants with Parkinson's disease demonstrated less overall parkinsonian symptoms, which can include problems as varied as speech, tremors, rigidity in the limbs, and a persistent masked face.[6]

The neuroanatomical basis for how Adapted Tango and other dance training could have such broad effects remains unknown. However, neuroimaging studies with expert dancers have shown that there are measurable biological changes associated with dance that may be both neuroprotective and neurorehabilitative. From studies of regions involved in learning choreography to looking at how long-term practice of dance may be reflected in structural and functional differences in diffuse brain areas, these investigations provide a potential explanatory framework for how dance may impact neurodegenerative disorders.

Multimodal Benefits of Adapted Tango

Although guided movement may not be the first type of therapy that comes to mind as a candidate for improving problems with thinking and memory, Adapted Tango has shown broad benefits in conditions like early Alzheimer's disease and mild cognitive impairment when compared to a cognitively engaging but nonmotor rehabilitation. In 2012 in Atlanta, forty-four older adults, aged fifty-nine to ninety-five years with mild cognitive impairment, were assigned to twenty ninety-minute sessions of Adapted Tango or a health education class (thirty-four participants in tango and ten in education) over twelve weeks (WF 20.1). To measure outcomes, the participants were evaluated with assessments to determine balance confidence, cognitive processing speed, complex motor function, motor cognitive integration, and simple motor function. As shown in Web Figure 20.1, there were marked improvements. Large Cohen's *d* (the statistical *standardized mean difference that* specifically measures the effect size between two averages) effects were noted in the Four Square Step Test (which assesses the ability of a person to step over one-inch diameter rods, such as shower rods, in a particular sequence), as well as challenging mobility tasks, such as backward gait speed, fast gait speed, and the Timed Up and Go Test. Medium effects were noted in balance confidence and other tests of motor-cognitive integration such as Timed Up and Go with a cognitive component (including counting backward by threes), and Body Position Spatial Task (a test of whole body spatial working memory, in which participants are asked to observe, recall, and reproduce a series of steps and turns in specific patterns). Small effects were noted in mental processing and visual scanning with the Trailmaking Test, as well as endurance with the Six-Minute Walk Test. Notably, gains were maintained three months postintervention.

Improvement in Automatic Balance Responses after Adapted Tango[7]

In patients with Parkinson's disease, muscle activity and body motion during automatic postural responses, that is, how one adjusts a step, hip, and/or ankle when their balance is disturbed, can serve as robust markers of balance impairment and falls, as well as balance improvement after Adapted Tango.[8] In one series of studies, researchers used a moving force plate to disturb the participants' balance, and they measured body motion with 3-D motion capture and muscle activity with electromyography to examine changes in balance responses after Adapted Tango. Figure 20.1 illustrates the results.

In this testing paradigm, the floor moves rapidly forward under participants' feet, similar to a subway car starting to move, causing them to sway backward over their heels. The researchers used electrodes placed on the lower legs, like those used in an electrocardiogram, to record the activity of the muscles used to correct the disturbance to balance. In a young, healthy subject (Fig. 20.1, left column), the nervous system automatically activates the tibialis anterior muscle (the shin muscle, shown in light gray above the divide) and deactivates the medial gastrocnemius muscle (the calf muscle,

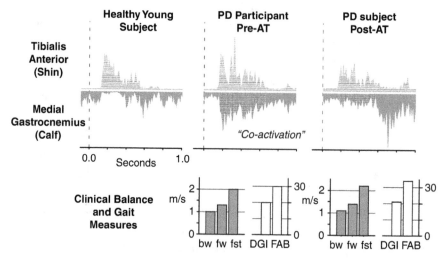

Figure 20.1 Improvement in balance muscle activity (top) and clinical balance and gait measures (bottom) after Adapted Tango in people with Parkinson's disease. 2022. Abbreviations in the lower panel signify bw (backward), fw (forward), and fst (fast).

shown in dark gray below the divide) to bring the body back to upright. Conversely, in a person with Parkinson's disease, the two muscles engage at the same time or "coactivate" (compare the middle vs. left columns in Fig. 20.1). This is comparable to stepping on the accelerator and brake at the same time in a car. For the individual with Parkinson's disease, this is an inefficient use of energy and causes the body to become more unstable. This coactivation has been documented previously and is known to be only modestly affected by levodopa treatment, the most effective pharmaceutical treatment for Parkinson's disease.[9] The researchers found that this debilitating coactivation could be substantially reduced after Adapted Tango (compare Fig. 20.1, right vs. middle columns). After twenty-two hours and thirty minutes of Adapted Tango over the three-week period, not only was coactivation significantly reduced, but participants improved in other gait speed and clinical outcome measures areas. Such areas included their dynamic gait index (DGI), in which a therapist observes a participant perform a series of tasks while walking, and their Fullerton Advanced Balance Scale (FAB), a balance scale including rated items of static and dynamic balance like standing on foam with eyes closed (Fig. 20.1, lower panel). As illustrated in Figure 20.1 (right column), the medial gastrocnemius (calf) muscle activated after the tibialis anterior (shin) muscle. This result was positive. The pair of muscles was not activating at the same time, reducing the cocontraction or coactivation described above, and the overall activation time of the calf muscle was less. Subsequent studies demonstrated that Adapted Tango was associated with improved integration of muscle activation across tasks like balance and walking.[10]

Adapted Tango as a Health-Promoting Behavioral Intervention

Older Black women caregivers at risk for cognitive impairment or dementia have shown benefits from Adapted Tango. We have found that this demographic, commonly underrepresented in research, is open to and accepting of a partnered dance intervention. In one of our studies in 2018 in Atlanta, twenty-four Black middle-aged women caregivers participated in fifteen to twenty Adapted Tango lessons. They all agreed (87% strongly agreed) that they enjoyed participating in this program. Most (82%) agreed that they would continue to participate if possible, and that they had been more physically active (83%). Participants self-reported other benefits from Adapted Tango, including improved endurance, enhanced body movement, meeting new people (including participants, instructors, and volunteers), and positive health effects because of training. Interestingly, when comparing the "Pre Mean" and "Post Mean" effects, participants showed improvements related to caregiver confidence; spatial cognition and whole body positioning; color word and naming, including visual scanning; and executive function. Web Figure 20.2 illustrates the data from our study.

Impacts of Adapted Tango on Cognitive Decline and Mood Disorders

Additionally, pilot studies of Black women with a family history of Alzheimer's disease showed Adapted Tango decreased expression of inflammatory biomarkers in blood samples in concert with improved cognition and psychosocial function. Sex and ethnicity-related genetic factors indicate that Black women with a parental history of Alzheimer's disease are at great risk for developing it themselves. An early phase pilot study with thirty-four participants assessed the impact of Adapted Tango intervention with experimental and control groups on measures of plasma inflammatory markers, cognition, and motor and psychosocial performance. After twelve weeks and twenty lessons, Adapted Tango participants had significantly decreased inflammatory cytokines, which are biomarkers that impact cognition and mood, compared to control group participants. Large effects were noted for the tango group on tests of executive functioning and inhibition. Participants in tango also improved in dynamic and static balance, and functional lower body strength. These data demonstrate substantial reductions in inflammatory biomarkers along with cognitive and motor improvements through a nonpharmacologic, affordable intervention among a small, well-characterized cohort of Black women with a parental history of Alzheimer's disease.

Potential Mechanisms

Several physiological mechanisms may explain Adapted Tango's beneficial effects on multiple aspects of function across populations. In this section, we propose how such mechanisms for Adapted Tango may facilitate improvements in symptoms associated with neurodegenerative disorders.

Adapted Tango and Motor-Cognitive Integration

We hypothesize that various cognitive processes are related to and engaged in dance, specifically within the sensory/motor and goal/communicative structure of partnered dances, and tango may target motor-cognitive integration and enhance aspects of cognitive function. These cognitive processes include attention, executive function, memory, and language, as well as musical beat detection and interpretation. Adapted Tango may rehabilitate motor-cognitive integration because it requires cognitive engagement from several domains. Participants divide their attention between maintaining postural control and the pattern and trajectory of the dance, both of which challenge balance and cognition. They exercise executive function, because of the planning and organizing involved with the dance, including the inhibition and switching needed to rhythmically leave one step and begin another.

Given that Adapted Tango offers an opportunity to learn coordinated relationships between people in space, participants expand their spatial cognition as they walk in step patterns with intricate and often changing spatial relationships. This, in turn, may enhance the encoding of spatial information to memory. They also exercise attention to their partner and to other paired individuals to coordinate the next step as they safely navigate the space.

Dance, and Adapted Tango in particular, has been shown to improve spatial cognition in people with Parkinson's disease. Such improvement likely results because dance requires participants to learn, memorize, recall, use, and be cognizant of spatial postures, relationships, patterns, and paths.[11] Adapted Tango also improves memory, as participants must store new steps and recall previously learned steps in a sequence or through improvisational patterns. As participants detect and interpret musical beats, they coordinate body movement with an external musical source and partner, even as they build their working memory via learning steps and practicing them immediately. Finally, they build new language skills via a new vocabulary for a dance context as they string together steps into phrases, holding "conversations" with partners via nonverbal communication.

Adapted Tango and Vascular Dysfunction

As a form of cardiovascular exercise, Adapted Tango may indirectly decrease Alzheimer's disease by reducing vascular burden. Cardiovascular exercise can address vascular dysfunction, which is common in and aggravates Alzheimer's disease neurodegeneration.[12] The antioxidant effect of long-term exercise may counteract oxidative stress in mild cognitive impairment, or even before onset.[13] Antioxidant effects of long-term exercise may counteract oxidative stress in mild cognitive impairment.[14] The Adapted Tango physical activity component may also impact vascular dysfunction by decreasing arterial stiffness. In people with mild cognitive impairment, cardiovascular fitness is associated with increased regional brain volumes in the medial temporal and parietal cortices. Thus, maintained or improved cardiovascular fitness may alter Alzheimer's disease–related brain atrophy.[15]

Adapted Tango and Movement Conversation

Tango dancers say "tango is a conversation without words," and Adapted Tango, which includes this key movement feature, aligns with overwhelming evidence demonstrating the benefits of visual and auditory cueing in behavioral studies for people with Parkinson's disease.[16] Tactile cues, like those conveyed from leader to follower in Adapted Tango, have been studied less than visual and auditory cues, yet they may be processed faster and more efficiently than visual and auditory cueing with less attentional demand. Other researchers have suggested evidence of how somatosensory cueing can supersede visual distractors; tactile cues can decrease timing errors during a dual task; and rhythmic somatosensory cues may increase turning speed, and may be more effective than visual cues. Interestingly, humans can abstract a pattern of beats from tactile rhythms as efficiently as from auditory patterns, which followers accomplish in Adapted Tango when receiving and responding to the step timing information conveyed with touch cues by the leader.

Scientists already know that constant human-to-human contact has therapeutic benefits. Therapeutic touch yields both emotional and behavioral benefits for those with Alzheimer's disease and dementia. It has reduced physical nonaggressive and agitated behaviors, such as vocalization, manual manipulation, and pacing. The information conveyed by tactile cues may also be why people with Parkinson's disease strongly prefer partnered to unpartnered Adapted Tango classes.

While researchers are a long way from understanding how people communicate through touch, they have begun to learn the "language" of the movement conversation in Adapted Tango using assistive robots. One of the earliest studies in this area demonstrated that older people were able to perform partner dance-based exercise with a robot partner based on touch information alone,[17] similar to what social dance teaches. While our earlier research was a proof-of-concept study, and not intended to represent how tactile communication could be realistically implemented in assistive technologies, it provided an important first step toward understanding how tactile cues are used to enable movement conversation. In follow-up studies, researchers gave pairs of dancers (novice and expert) robotic force sensors to record the forces provided by the tactile cues they used to communicate.[18]

In this study, pairs of dancers held on to opposite ends of robotic force sensors (Fig. 20.2, left) during a simple stepping task derived from Adapted Tango. Compared to expert-novice dancer pairs, expert-expert dancer

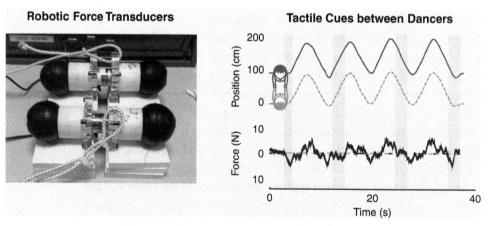

Figure 20.2 An experiment to learn the language of movement conversation.

pairs used significantly stronger interaction forces (tactile cues) to communicate movement intention. Characterizing the language of movement conversation may eventually allow us to interact more naturally with a wide range of technologies.

Rhythmic Movement in Rehabilitation

Dance and other rhythmic training likely provides a synergistic multi-sensory adjuvant to motor skills training in both aging and disease models. As one hallmark of Adapted Tango, such rhythmic movement may have a profound effect for rehabilitation. A meta-analysis recently demonstrated that music-based therapy, including dance, positively affects Parkinson's disease gait and gait-related activities.[19] Proprioceptive (joints and muscles) and kinesthetic (body motion) inputs based on tactile cues are crucial for motor adaptation and dance performance. Visual cues play a role in postural control, navigation, and emotional understanding. However, auditory cues such as performing musical rhythms with percussion instruments, play a strong role in guiding movement.

Therapy programs have used auditory cues with some type of consistent rhythmic auditory stimulation in the form of a metronome or music to facilitate movements to improve gait. Studies have shown the positive effects of rhythmic auditory stimulation on freezing and gait parameters in people with Parkinson's disease.[20] Leow et al. examined the impact of beat salience in effectively improving gait cadence and other parameters by comparing "high groove" to "low groove" music.[21] Because of the salience of the beat, high groove music helped those with a poorer perception of beat timing. Such musical support might help benefit those with impaired gait. This finding is highly relevant to dance- or music-based rehabilitation, including Adapted Tango, because poor or good beat perception affects gait performance when synchronized to music.

Leow et al. also showed that more familiar music elicited fewer variable strides, faster stride velocity, and better synchronization with the music.[22] Salience of a beat (as just mentioned), and familiarity with music are therefore considerations for rehabilitative purposes. Recently, a team of researchers trained people with Parkinson's disease on musically cued gait therapy, consisting of synchronizing movement to familiar folk music without lyrics (a bell cued participants' movement). Findings included increased gait speed and stride length, but also strong gains in motor synchronization (tapping) and perceptual awareness on just noticeably different tasks.[23]

Findings from stroke literature and the application of music-supported therapy also show beneficial effects of rhythmic movement with auditory support. Music-supported therapy uses musical instrument playing to treat paresis (slight paralysis, a weakness often observed in stroke patients) of the upper limb and adheres to four principles: massive repetition, audio-motor coupling, shaping, and emotion-motivation effects. After four weeks of music-supported therapy in combination with usual care, chronic stroke participants assigned to music-supported therapy showed improvements on an upper extremity motor function test (the Wolf motor test) in comparison to a control group.[24]

Future Studies

The anatomical mechanisms underlying improvement after Adapted Tango remain unclear. Despite the profound behavioral benefits of Adapted Tango, researchers are only beginning to understand which brain regions are affected by successful rehabilitation. Initial evidence shows that, after Adapted Tango, increased activation was noted in brain areas related to language and speech production, and visual object recognition frontal areas in older adults with neurodegenerative disease (WF 20.3). Data in people with Parkinson's disease show that three months of biweekly Adapted Tango improved visuospatial cognition,[25] and this trial also examined neural mechanisms of dance-like movements for improving mobility and cognition. Pre– and post–Adapted Tango participants lay in a scanner and performed a foot-tapping task with the more affected foot. They tapped their responses on their third ipsilateral metacarpal (the middle finger's knuckle) or self-guided themselves to tap a learned rhythm. Foot tapping amplitude variability and timing accuracy were correlated with balance and gait measures. Although the results are pending, they will illuminate neuromechanisms underlying tango approaches to enhancing mobility and cognitive function. More studies must examine neural changes in combination with observed clinical motor and cognitive changes, particularly with respect to motor training strategies, and how they may impact cardiovascular, inflammatory, and neural pathways.

Although the ideal amount of Adapted Tango therapy remains unknown, some results of the studies may help direct the process.

Assignment to the different leader or follower roles should be based upon responses to treatment so that future work may better identify which role is most appropriate for a patient. Prior studies of dance therapies have identified lasting effects following cessation of intervention;[26] future evaluations of Adapted Tango in Blacks at risk for Alzheimer's disease and/or caregivers should also implement testing postintervention to identify the length of effect. A further step in understanding the benefits of tactile cueing would be to know for whom it is better to give or receive these cues. At this point, it is unclear what role external musical auditory or visual (and tactile, in the case of any partnered/contact dance) cues play to elicit therapeutic effects versus the improvements gained by increased attention and cognitive engagement used to plan and enact movement. More studies are needed to answer these questions when considering research that has accumulated supporting beneficial effects of rehabilitative methods involving rhythmic training.

Timing of Adapted Tango Application

There is a critical need to identify early, *preventative*, motor-cognitive protective interventions for individuals with conditions like early Alzheimer's disease and Parkinson's disease. Conditions such as these have complex, multifactorial – but potentially mild – presentations. Deficiencies in any one domain, such as social withdrawal or impaired cognition, may not provide sufficient information to suggest that Adapted Tango could be beneficial.

Evidence suggests that in early disease stages, therapy should focus on executive function skills like selective/divided attention, and inhibition, and switching.[27] Such skills are required by Adapted Tango, which involves walking in complex patterns to varied rhythms with a partner. In fact, Adapted Tango trains motor-cognitive integration and affects cardiovascular, neural, and sociobehavioral areas, all of which are affected by conditions like early Alzheimer's disease. A clinical trial with an evidenced-based, socially, cognitively, and physically stimulating approach could address failures in prior drug development and non-pharmacological treatments by accounting for the multifactorial presentations of conditions like Alzheimer's disease and Parkinson's disease. Future studies will identify better markers – behavioral, cognitive, as well as traditional biomarkers – for when Adapted Tango could be beneficial.

Conclusion

Research has shown that partnered dance – particularly Adapted Tango – stands out as a potentially healing treatment for many conditions, because it is a cognitively demanding and mentally stimulating *movement conversation* that anyone can do. The creative environment of a dance intervention can produce novel strategies for movement; it cultivates an atmosphere of exploration, which is empowering. Dance programs challenge participants to attempt both unfamiliar and rehearsed movement combinations, hold multiple tasks in their memory, and attend to multisensory cues, all while aiming for an aesthetic output. Growing evidence suggests that participation in partnered dance can induce long-term neuroplasticity in human movement, enhance independence, and delay the deleterious effects of aging and neurodegenerative diseases; however, the precise neuroanatomical mechanisms underlying these benefits remain unknown. Studies should further investigate the precise amount and timing of mentally stimulating, cognitively engaging, and potentially neuroprotective properties of rehabilitation like Adapted Tango.

Notes

1. Gerd Kempermann, "The Neurogenic Reserve Hypothesis: What Is Adult Hippocampal Neurogenesis Good for?" *Trends Neuroscience* 31, no. 4 (2008): 163–169, doi: https://doi.org/10.1016/j.tins.2008.01.002.
2. Kirsten Hötting et al., "Effects of a Cognitive Training on Spatial Learning and Associated Functional Brain Activations," *BMC Neuroscience* 14 (2013): 73, doi: https://doi.org/10.1186/1471-2202-14-73.
3. Madeleine E. Hackney and Kathleen McKee, "Community-Based Adapted Tango Dancing for Individuals with Parkinson's Disease and Older Adults," *Journal of Visualized Experiments* 94, e52066 (2014a): 1–12, doi: https://doi.org/10.3791/52066.
4. Madeleine E. Hackney et al., "Adapted Tango Improves Mobility, Motor-Cognitive Function, and Gait but Not Cognition in Older Adults in Independent Living," *Journal of the American Geriatrics Society* 63, no. 10 (2015a): 2105–2113, doi: https://doi.org/10.1111/jgs.13650; Madeleine E. Hackney et al., "Multimodal Exercise Benefits Mobility in Older Adults with Visual Impairment: A Preliminary Study," *Journal of Aging and Physical Activity* 23, no. 4 (2015a): 630–639, doi: https://doi.org/10.1123/japa.2014-0008.
5. In this section, we summarize relevant research to our work. Please see the Bibliography online for complete references and further reading below.

6. Ryan P. Duncan and Gammon M. Earhart, "Randomized Controlled Trial of Community-Based Dancing to Modify Disease Progression in Parkinson Disease," *Neurorehabilitation and Neural Repair* 26, no. 2 (February 2012): 132–143, doi: https://doi.org/10.1177/1545968311421614.

7. J. Lucas McKay, Lena H. Ting, and Madeleine E. Hackney, "Balance, Body Motion, and Muscle Activity after High-Volume Short-Term Dance-Based Rehabilitation in Persons with Parkinson Disease: A Pilot Study," *Journal of Neurologic Physical Therapy* 40, no. 4 (October 2016): 257–268, doi: https://doi.org/10.1097/NPT.0000000000000150.

8. Ibid.

9. Fay B. Horak, John Frank, and John Nutt, "Effects of Dopamine on Postural Control in Parkinsonian Subjects: Scaling, Set, and Tone," *Journal of Neurophysiology* 75, no. 6 (June 1996): 2380–2396, doi: https://doi.org/10.1152/jn.1996.75.6.2380.

10. Jessica L. Allen et al., "Increased Neuromuscular Consistency in Gait and Balance after Partnered, Dance-Based Rehabilitation in Parkinson's Disease," *Journal of Neurophysiology* 118, no. 1 (July 2017): 363–373, doi: https://doi.org/10.1152/jn.00813.2016.

11. Léa A. S. Chauvigné, Michel Belyk, and Steven Brown, "Taking Two to Tango: fMRI Analysis of Improvised Joint Action with Physical Contact," *PLoS One* 13, no. 1 (January 2018): e0191098, doi: https://doi.org/10.1371/journal.pone.0191098.

12. Daniele M. Guizoni et al., "Aerobic Exercise Training Protects against Endothelial Dysfunction by Increasing Nitric Oxide and Hydrogen Peroxide Production in LDL Receptor-Deficient Mice," *Journal of Translational Medicine* 14, no. 1 (2016): 213, doi: https://doi.org/10.1186/s12967-016-0972-z.

13. Didem Sener Dede et al., "Assessment of Endothelial Function in Alzheimer's Disease: Is Alzheimer's Disease a Vascular Disease?" *Journal of the American Geriatrics Society* 55, no. 10 (October 2007): 1613–1617, doi: https://doi.org/10.1111/j.1532-5415.2007.01378.x.

14. Didem Sener Dede et al., "Assessment of Endothelial Function in Alzheimer's Disease," 1613–1617.

15. Robyn A. Honea et al., "Cardiorespiratory Fitness and Preserved Medial Temporal Lobe Volume in Alzheimer Disease," *Alzheimer Disease and Associated Disorders* 23, no. 3 (July–September 2009): 188–197, doi: https://doi.org/10.1097/WAD.0b013e31819cb8a2.

16. See the online Bibliography for studies that support this evidence.

17. Tiffany Chen et al., "Older Adults' Acceptance of a Robot for Partner Dance-Based Exercise," *PLoS One* 12, no. 10 (October 2017): e0182736, doi: https://doi.org/10.1371/journal.pone.0182736.

18. Andrew Sawers et al., "Small Forces That Differ with Prior Motor Experience Can Communicate Movement Goals during Human-Human Physical

Interaction," *Journal of NeuroEngineering and Rehabilitation* 14, no. 1 (January 2017): 8, doi: https://doi.org/10.1186/s12984-017-0217-2.

19. Miek Johanna de Dreu et al., "Rehabilitation, Exercise Therapy and Music in Patients with Parkinson's Disease: A Meta-analysis of the Effects of Music-Based Movement Therapy on Walking Ability, Balance and Quality of Life," *Parkinsonism & Related Disorders* 18, Suppl. 1 (2012): S114–119, doi: https://doi.org/10.1016/S1353-8020(11)70036-0.

20. Jinhui Song et al., "Rhythmic Auditory Stimulation with Visual Stimuli on Motor and Balance Function of Patients with Parkinson's Disease," *European Review for Medical Pharmacological Sciences* 19, no. 11 (2015): 2001–2007, www.ncbi.nlm.nih.gov/pubmed/26125261.

21. Li-Ann Leow, Taylor Parrott, and Jessica A. Grahn, "Individual Differences in Beat Perception Affect Gait Responses to Low- and High-Groove Music," *Frontiers in Human Neuroscience* 8 (October 2014): 811, doi: https://doi.org/10.3389/fnhum.2014.00811.

22. Li-Ann Leow, Cricia Rinchon, and Jessica Grahn, "Familiarity with Music Increases Walking Speed in Rhythmic Auditory Cuing," *Annals of the New York Academy of Sciences* 1337 (March 2015): 53–61, doi: https://doi.org/10.1111/nyas.12658.

23. Simone Dalla Bella et al., "Effects of Musically Cued Gait Training in Parkinson's Disease: Beyond a Motor Benefit," *Annals of the New York Academy of Sciences* 1337 (2015): 77–85, doi: https://doi.org/10.1111/nyas.12651.

24. Yanna Tong et al., "Music-Supported Therapy (MST) in Improving Post-Stroke Patients' Upper-Limb Motor Function: a Randomised Controlled Pilot Study," *Neurological Research* 37, no. 5 (2015): 434–440, doi:https://doi.org/10.1179/1743132815Y.0000000034.

25. Madeleine E. Hackney et al., "Rationale and Design of the PAIRED Trial: Partnered Dance Aerobic Exercise as a Neuroprotective, Motor, and Cognitive Intervention in Parkinson's Disease," *Frontiers in Neurology* 11 (October 2020): 943, doi: https://doi.org/10.3389/fneur.2020.00943.

26. Madeleine E. Hackney et al., "Adapted Tango Improves Mobility, Motor-Cognitive Function, and Gait but Not Cognition in Older Adults in Independent Living," *Journal of the American Geriatrics Society* 63, no. 10 (October 2015): 2105–2113, doi: 10.1111/jgs.13650. Madeleine E. Hackney et al., "Multimodal Exercise Benefits Mobility in Older Adults with Visual Impairment: A Preliminary Study," *Journal of Aging Physical Activity* 23, no. 4 (October 2015): 630–639, doi: https://doi.org/10.1123/japa.2014-0008.

27. Anna-Mariya Kirova, Rebecca B. Bays, and Sarita Lagalwar, "Working Memory and Executive Function Decline across Normal Aging, Mild Cognitive Impairment, and Alzheimer's Disease," *BioMed Research International* 2015 (October 2015): 1–5, doi: https://doi.org/10.1155/2015/748212.

Further Reading

Chauvigné, Léa A. S., Michel Belyk, and Steven Brown. "Taking Two to Tango: fMRI Analysis of Improvised Joint Action with Physical Contact." *PLoS One* 13, no. 1 (January 2018): e0191098. doi: https://doi.org/10.1371/journal.pone.0191098.

Hackney, Madeleine E., Colleen Byers, Gail Butler et al. "Adapted Tango Improves Mobility, Motor-Cognitive Function, and Gait but Not Cognition in Older Adults in Independent Living." *Journal of the American Geriatrics Society* 63, no. 10 (October 2015): 2105–2113. doi: https://doi.org/10.1111/jgs.13650.

Hackney, Madeleine E., and Gammon Earhart. "Effects of Dance on Movement Control in Parkinson's Disease: A Comparison of Argentine Tango and American Ballroom." *Journal of Rehabilitation Medicine* 41, no. 6 (May 2009): 475–481. doi: https://doi.org/10.2340/16501977-0362.

Hackney, Madeleine E., and Kathleen McKee. "Community-Based Adapted Tango Dancing for Individuals with Parkinson's Disease and Older Adults." *Journal of Visualized Experiments* 94 (December 2014): 52066. doi: https://doi.org/10.3791/52066.

Hackney, Madeleine E., Svetlana Kantorovich, Rebecca Levin, and Gammon M. Earhart. "Effects of Tango on Functional Mobility in Parkinson's Disease: A Preliminary Study." *Journal of Neurological Physical Therapy* 31, no. 4 (December 2007): 173–179. doi: https://doi.org/10.1097/NPT.0b013e31815ce78b.

Kreutz, Gunter. "Does Partnered Dance Promote Health? The Case of Tango Argentino." *The Journal of the Royal Society for the Promotion of Health* 128, no. 2 (March 2008): 79–84. doi: https://doi.org/10.1177/1466424007087805.

Low, Lee Fay, Sophie Lee Carroll, Dafna Lev Merom et al. "We Think You Can Dance! A Pilot Randomised Controlled Trial of Dance for Nursing Home Residents with Moderate to Severe Dementia." *Complementary Therapies in Medicine* 29 (December 2016): 42–44. doi: https://doi.org/10.1016/j.ctim.2016.09.005.

McKee, Kathleen E., and Madeleine E. Hackney. "The Effects of Adapted Tango on Spatial Cognition and Disease Severity in Parkinson's Disease." *Journal of Motor Behavior* 45, no. 6 (2013): 519–529. doi: https://doi.org/10.1080/00222895.2013.834288.

Sacco, Katiuscia, Franco Cauda, Leonardo Cerliani et al. "Motor Imagery of Walking Following Training in Locomotor Attention. The Effect of 'the Tango Lesson'." *Neuroimage* 32, no. 3 (September 2006): 1441–1449. doi: https://doi.org/10.1016/j.neuroimage.2006.05.018.

Zafar, Manal, Ariyana Bozzorg, and Madeleine E. Hackney. "Adapted Tango Improves Aspects of Participation in Older Adults versus Individuals with Parkinson's Disease." *Disability and Rehabilitation* 39, no. 22 (November 2017): 2294–2301. doi: https://doi.org/10.1080/09638288.2016.1226405.

Epilogue: Carrying Tango Studies into the Future

KRISTIN WENDLAND AND KACEY LINK

As we laid out the final chapter order of this book, we reflected on the research questions we initially posed when soliciting proposals from an array of tango scholars and scholar-artists. How do diverse humanistic fields of inquiry further shape our understanding of the tango art form? Inversely, how does the tango help us further understand culture and society? How do interdisciplinary perspectives on tango influence current scholarship? How do international perspectives on and research approaches to tango differ, and why are they important?

The answer to the final question is perhaps the simplest, yet as editors of this volume, the most challenging. International perspectives on tango vary greatly, depending on the scholar's country of origin, training, and research approach. Christophe Apprill's French and European approach to understanding tango is far different from Carolyn Merritt's North American, US perspective. To truly understand tango studies as a global phenomenon, it is imperative to account for such diverse international perspectives. As editors of this volume, we were faced with the task of uniting these varied approaches and methodologies under the umbrella of tango, while still retaining the essence and style of each scholar's background in their respective country and field. Additionally, we had to overcome translation challenges as many of the chapters were originally written in an author's native language, and we carefully edited the English to ensure its flow and syntax for our target audience. We hope the reader relishes the opportunity to engage with such diversity, and the wide range of international references and resources it presents. Notably, many of the authors publish primarily in their first language; thus, if you do not read Spanish, you would not be familiar with the works of Romina Dezillio or Omar García Brunelli. And this, we believe, is the first English publication of Christophe Apprill and Ortaç Aydınoğlu.

The answers to the initial research questions took more thought. Although we organized Chapters 1–13 around a traditional framework for studying tango as a three-spoked system of music, dance, and poetry, and grouped Chapters 14–20 as Interdisciplinary Tango Studies, we realized the collection as a whole reveals broader topics. We identified several themes that are threaded throughout the entire volume – even though they are viewed through various discipline-specific lenses – that resonate with tango studies today: Gender, Race, and Politics; Cultural Exchange and Globalization; Past, Present, and Future; and Embodied and Applied Research. We propose that the reader use these themes to step back and reflect on what they have learned in *The Cambridge Companion to Tango* in broader, humanistic contexts.

Gender, Race, and Politics: New perspectives in tango scholarship reflect how gender, race, and politics have impacted tango and how tango may now reflect on them. As one may have noticed, five chapters unpacked how such dynamics play out in the art form, particularly in the genre's history, music, and dance. Paulina L. Alberto wrote about race in Argentina as she explored how Black musicians shaped early tango in Chapter 14, "Nineteenth-Century Afro-Argentine Origins of Tango." Using the Grigera family as a case study, she challenged the entrenched myth of Afro-Argentine "disappearance" over the course of the nineteenth century. As Christophe Apprill examined stereotypes in relation to tango dance in Chapter 10, "Tango's Journey from a Río de la Plata Dance to a Globalized Milonga," he revealed new insights into traditional gender relations and roles. Kathy Davis, too, put gender relations under the microscope as she showed how they impact the lead/follow dynamic in the dance, and how dancers embody passion in Chapter 11, "Tango Lessons: What Research on Tango Dancing Can Teach Us." Through her study of three famous female tango singers during tango's Golden Age, Romina Dezillio shed new light on gender relationships in Argentine society in Chapter 8, "Audacious Women: Profiles of Early *Cancionistas*." Matthew B. Karush sought to understand how the tango is reflected in the political climate in Argentina through time and amid political upheaval, as he analyzed how race and class are reflected in tango music and dance in Chapter 16, "Mixed Messages: Tango and Argentine Politics."

Cultural Exchange and Globalization: Since its exportation abroad from Argentina over 100 years ago, tango has evolved into a transnational art form. Although some chapters touched on the theme of globalization, especially Davis and Apprill through the lens of tango dance, four chapters directly confronted issues related to tango's globalization. In Chapter 18, "Tango, Emotion, and Transculturality in the Twentieth and Twenty-First Centuries," Yuiko Asaba utilized ethnographic approaches to discuss affect and transculturality in Japan, showing how Argentine tango has adapted to and been influenced by the Asian culture. Julián Graciano brought together two musical genres typically associated with the United States and Argentina, jazz and tango respectively, to show how they have impacted each other in sound, style, and technique in Chapter 7, "Tango and Jazz: Cross-Genre Relations in History and Practice." In her study of tango and film in a historical context, Rielle Navitski raised crucial issues about how tango is a representation of cultural exchange and cultural hegemony in Chapter 17, "(Trans)national Visions: Tango Onscreen." Kendra Stepputat argued that the social dance of *tango argentino* has been adapted to a European translocal tango practice in Chapter 12, "*Encuentros Milongueros*: Europe's Twenty-First-Century Tango Dance Practice," and so challenged the reader to rethink what it means to call tango a transnational art form, and how this definition is evolving.

Past, Present, and Future: Tango's historical narrative has been changing as scholars discover new archival material; its present touches on new fields of research and inquiry, and its future poses exciting possibilities for study across disciplines. Seven chapters drew attention to all three of these time dimensions by exploring topics related to tango history, how it flourishes as an art form today, and new interdisciplinary approaches to understanding it for future studies. In his fresh overview of tango music, dance, and poetry from its origins to the present, Omar García Brunelli provided the reader with key figures and points of reference in Chapter 1, "A Brief History of Tango." Turkish bandoneonist and tango scholar Ortaç Aydınoğlu recounted the international travels and "adventures" of his instrument through time, enlightening the reader about how and why it came to symbolize tango in Chapter 2, "The Bandoneón: The Magical Sound and Soul of Tango." Ethnomusicologist Morgan James Luker, who works with archival recordings, showed the reader how to move from the narrative-driven mode of "causal listening" to the object-driven mode of "matrix listening," and so view individual recorded sound objects as things with agency. Luker illuminated our understanding of tango artist Ángel Villoldo as a case study in Chapter 3, "Ángel Villoldo and Early Sound Recordings." Guitarist and scholar Eric Johns in Chapter 5 recounted the historical and stylistic lineage of another iconic tango instrument by highlighting the two important schools of guitar playing established by Aníbal Arias and Roberto Grela. We moved tango into the post–Golden Age era by comparing the lives and musical styles of its two great pillars, Horacio Salgán and Piazzolla, and we offered insight into how these *tangueros* shaped the next generation into the twenty-first century in Chapter 6, "Post–Golden Age Pillars: Horacio Salgán and Astor Piazzolla." In chapter 9, cultural historian

Pablo Palomino analyzed Golden-age tango poetry in its historic context and around three central themes to show how tango lyrics became a sentimental, philosophical, and aesthetic lens for several generations of listeners in Argentina and beyond. Bárbara Varassi Pega presented the reader with a unique educational model for teaching and transmitting tango that could serve other institutions of higher education in the future in her Chapter 19, "Tango Studies Abroad: Gustavo Beytelmann and Codarts University."

Embodied and Applied Research: As interdisciplinary research across performative, humanistic, and even scientific fields provides new under-standings of tango, four authors showed various ways to embody and apply such knowledge. Madeleine E. Hackney and J. Lucas McCay's medical work applying "Adapted Tango" to people suffering from neurological diseases demonstrated the healing power of embodying the dance, and how broadly the art form reaches across research disciplines, in Chapter 20, "Tango and Healing: A Clinical Research Perspective." As anthropologist and social tango dancer Carolyn Merritt pursued dance lessons in leading, she applied the research of her embodied personal quest to larger questions about how tango impacted the total human experience during the COVID-19 restrictions. She especially focused on tango's political and gender issues as she proposed a better future by transforming tango's culture while preserving its essence in Chapter 13, "Re-Imagining the Future of Tango Dance." Rebecca Simpson-Litke's Chapter 15, "Synthesizing Analyses: A Choreomusical Study of 'La cumparsita'" showed the reader how the common embodied element of rhythm between music and dance connects sound and movement through her choreomusical analysis of Juan Carlos Copes's choreography of the famous "La cumparsita." Ignacio Varchausky's Chapter 4, "Orchestral Rhythmic Designs and Performance Practices: Juan D'Arienzo and Aníbal Troilo," illustrated musical tech-niques and practices that may provide a listener with sounds of tango's history, and how musically embodying the art form may advance our understanding of its culture.

As these themes have generated significant scholarly interest in the tango studies represented in this Cambridge volume, we hope they will inspire the reader to broaden their present conception of tango. This was our experience as we came to tango – Link initially as a performing pianist drawn to the powerful music of Piazzolla, and Wendland who fell in love with tango music by first embodying it as a social dancer. We have come to view the art form now through interdisciplinary lenses rather than narrowly only through its dimensions of music, dance, and poetry. We hope these themes and international perspectives will help direct the reader's understanding of tango and guide them in their own future tango studies.

The authors listed here, all of whom are contributors to this volume, have added other important publications to the growing field of tango studies. Some of them are established scholars in their research trajectory; some are practitioners who have channeled their creative tango work into instrumental guides; and others are emerging scholars. We offer the reader the following list of seventeen sources as guidance for further reading in their future exploration of this rich and complex art form.

Further Reading

Alberto, Paulina L. *Black Legend: The Many Lives of Raúl Grigera and the Power of the Racial Storytelling in Argentina*. Cambridge: University of Cambridge Press, 2022.

Apprill, Christophe. *Tango: le couple, le bal, la scène*. Paris: Autrement, 2008.

Asaba, Yuiko. "'Folds of the heart': performing life experience, emotion, and empathy in Japanese tango music culture." *Ethnomusicology Forum* 29, no. 1 (2019): 45–65.

Davis, Kathy. *Dancing Tango: Passionate Encounters in a Globalizing World*. New York: New York University Press, 2015.

Dezillio, Romina. "Historizar la experiencia. Hacia una historia de la creación musical de las mujeres en Buenos Aires (1930–1955): fundamentos, metodología y avances de una investigación." *Boletín de la Asociación Argentina de Musicología* 27/68 (2012): 18–27.

García Brunelli, Omar. *Discografía básica del tango, 1905–2010: su historia a través de las grabaciones*. Buenos Aires: Gourmet Musical Ediciones, 2010.

Graciano, Julián. *Método Guitarra Tango/Tango Guitar Method*. Buenos Aires: Melos, 2016.

Karush, Matthew. *Musicians in Transit: Argentina and the Globalization of Popular Music*. Durham, NC: Duke University Press, 2017.

Link, Kacey, and Kristin Wendland. *Tracing Tangueros: Argentine Tango Instrumental Music*. New York: Oxford University Press, 2016.

Luker, Morgan James. *The Tango Machine: Musical Culture in the Age of Expediency*. Chicago: Chicago University Press, 2016.

Merritt, Carolyn. *Tango Nuevo*. Gainesville, FL: University Press of Florida, 2012.

Navitski, Rielle. "The Tango on Broadway: Carlos Gardel's International Stardom and the Transition to Sound." *Cinema Journal* 51/1 (Fall 2011): 26–49.

Palomino, Pablo. *The Invention of Latin American Music: A Transnational History.* New York: Oxford University Press, 2020.

Stepputat, Kendra, Wolfgang Kienreich, and Christopher Dick. "Digital Methods in Intangible Cultural Heritage Research: A Case Study in Tango Argentino." *ACM Journal on Computing and Cultural Heritage* 12, no. 2 (2019): 1–23.

Varassi Pega, Bárbara. *The Art of Tango.* New York: Routledge, 2021.

Varchausky, Igancio. *El contrabajo en el tango/The Bass in Tango* (in Spanish and English). Buenos Aires: Tango Sin Fin, 2018.

Wendland, Kristin. "So You Think You Know Tango?" Coursera Mini-MOOC, with the Emory Center for Faculty Development and Excellence, July 2019.

Appendix: Tango Chronology

This general chronology outlines selected historical events with a specific focus on Argentina. Framed in a backdrop of political, social, and cultural events, it will aid the reader in understanding how the tango art form grew in the context of history.

15th–18th Century

1480 – Incan empire conquers present-day northwestern Argentina.
1516 – Spanish navigator Juan Días de Solís lands in present-day Argentina.
1587 – First slave ships arrive in the Río de la Plata region; slavery is the main commercial activity in Buenos Aires through the mid-1600s.
1776 – Spain establishes the Viceroyalty of Río de la Plata, consisting of present-day Argentina, Uruguay, Paraguay, and some of Bolivia; 1776–1810 marks the peak of the slave trade.

1800–1850	Political/Social/Cultural Events	Key Tango Events
	1810 – Viceroy of Río de la Plata is overthrown. 1816 – Argentina declares independence, followed by civil war and attempted foreign intervention. 1828 – Uruguay becomes an independent country. 1829 – Manuel de Rosas becomes governor of Buenos Aires.	1820s – *Naciones* form in Buenos Aires as a community space for Afro-Argentine ritual dance and music, including *candombe* and early roots of tango.

1850–1900	Political/Social/Cultural Events	Key Tango Events
	1853 – Slavery is abolished in all Argentine provinces except Buenos Aires. 1857–1890 – Population of Argentina increases by 2.2 million. 1861 – The province of Buenos Aires unites with Argentine Confederation. – Slavery is abolished in Buenos Aires. 1862 – Bartolomé Mitre is elected president of Argentina. Economic growth begins from foreign investment, foreign trade, and immigration. 1877 – Thomas Edison invents the phonograph, established the Edison Speaking Phonograph Company to sell the new machine in 1878. 1890 – Economic crisis in Argentina due to the inability to keep up with foreign debt. 1889 – Moulin Rouge opens in Paris, signifying a lively cabaret lifestyle.	1850 – Heinrich Band begins developing the bandoneón in Germany. – Beginning of the fusion of musical and dance elements of tango, combining *payada, milonga, candombe, zarzuela,* African rhythms and dance, and Italian bel canto song. 1858 – *Afro-porteño* and *payador* Gabino Ezeiza is born. 1870 – Bartolo ("El Brasilero," "The Brazilian") plays the bandoneón in Argentina. 1871–1873 – "Bum que bum" appears as an *Afro-porteño* Carnival song, resembling early tango rhythm. 1897 – *Afro-porteño* Rosendo Mendizábal writes early tango "El entrerriano." 1898 – *Payador* José Bettinotti sings with Ezeiza at a circus in Buenos Aires.

(cont.)

1900–1920	Political/Social/Cultural Events	Key Tango Events: *Guardia vieja* (Old Guard)
	1900 – Gramophone begins to appear in Buenos Aires.	1903 – Vicente Greco forms his first tango ensemble.
	1908 – Teatro Colón opens in Buenos Aires with Verdi's *Aïda*.	1908 – Flora Hortensia Rodríguez records "La Morocha."
	1909 – Ballet Russes is founded in Paris.	1910 – Mistinguett begins dancing tango in Paris.
	1912 – The Titanic sinks off the coast of Newfoundland.	1911 – Columbia Records signs Greco.
	1914 – Henry Ford starts the first automobile assembly line.	1912 – Ángel Bassi publishes tango "El Negro Raúl: Seventh Tango Criollo for Piano."
	–Panama Canal opens.	1913 – Eduardo Arolas records "El choclo."
	1914–1918 – World War I.	1914 – *Modern Dancing* by Vernon and Irene Castle is published as
	1916 – Hipólito Yrigoyen of the Unión Cívica Radical (UCR) becomes president of Argentina, begins Argentina's first wave of democracy, mobilizing the middle class politically, socially, and economically.	they brought tango to the United States.
		1915 – *Candombe* danced in El Nacional theater in downtown Buenos Aires.
	1919 – Max Glücksmann's Teatro Grand Splendid opens as a silent film theatre, films accompanied by tango orchestras.	1916 – Gerardo Matos Rodríguez writes "La cumparsita," first performed by Roberto Firpo and his orchestra.
		1917 – Carlos Gardel and José Ricardo perform and later record "Mi noche triste," the first *tango canción*.

1920–1930	Political/Social/Cultural Events	Key Tango Events: *Guardia nueva* (New Guard)
	1923 – Radio Splendid begins broadcasting tango music.	1920 – Enrique Delfino, Osvaldo Fresedo, and Tito Roccatagliata
	1924 – The elegant Chanteclair opens as a tango venue in Buenos Aires. Other popular theaters in Buenos Aires include the Teatro San Martín and the Teatro Opera.	record with Victor's Orquesta Típica Select in the United States.
		1921 – Rudolph Valentino dances the first Hollywood tango in the film *The Four Horsemen of the Apocalypse*.
	–George Gershwin composes *Rhapsody in Blue*.	1923 – De Caro forms his famous Sextet, which makes two sets of
	1927 – *The Jazz Singer* premieres as the first movie with synchronized dialogue.	historic recordings for Victor (1924–1926) and (1926–1928).
	1929 – Stock market crashes in the United States, sending many countries of the world into the Great Depression.	1925 – Francisco Canaro performs in Paris and other European countries.

1930–1950	Political/Social/Cultural Events	Key Tango Events (Golden Age)
	1930 – Military coup overthrows democratic government; General José Félix Uriburu assumes power and returns Argentina to an oligarchy; begins Argentina's "infamous decade," marked by high unemployment and government corruption. – First FIFA World Cup of Football (Soccer) is held in Uruguay. 1932 – Amelia Earhart completes the first solo transatlantic flight by a woman. 1939–1945 – World War II. 1943 – Military coup, known as Revolution '43, overthrows government of Ramón Castillo in Argentina. 1945 – Argentina enters World War II, siding with the Allies. 1946 – Juan Domingo Perón takes office (1946–1955), championing social justice, economic freedom, and political sovereignty. 1947 – Women's suffrage approved in Argentina.	1931 – De Caro and his ensemble tour Europe. 1932 – De Caro and Fresedo expand their orchestras. 1933 – Argentine film *¡Tango!* is released featuring dancers, "El Cachafaz" (Ovidio José Bianquet) and Carmencita Calderón as well as famous Argentine singers/actresses Libertad Lamarque, Tita Merello, and Azucena Maizani. 1935 – Juan D'Arienzo establishes his orchestra; records for RCA Victor 1935–1975 and releases 952 tango recordings. – Gardel and the young Astor Piazzolla are in the film, *El día que me quieres*. 1937 – Aníbal Troilo forms his orchestra. 1938 – Carlos Di Sarli forms his orchestra. 1939 – Osvaldo Pugliese forms his orchestra. 1943 – Argentine government bans *Lunfardo*, tango's dialect. 1944 – Horacio Salgán forms his orchestra. 1946 – Piazzolla forms his orchestra. –Pugliese records his famous "La yumba."

1950–1970	Political/Social/Cultural Events	Key Tango Events (Post–Golden Age)
	1952 – Death of Eva Perón. –Elizabeth II is crowned Queen of the United Kingdom. 1954 – First color television becomes available. 1955 – Military coup ousts Perón leading to a series of dictatorships and subsequent coups. 1963 – Rev. Dr. Martin Luther King, Jr. delivers "I Have a Dream" speech. 1969 – *Cordobazo* occurs, citizens held riots and burned buildings in response to government policies.	1950 – Editorial house Julio Korn publishes Argentino Galván's arrangement of Troilo's "La trampera." 1953 – Troilo begins partnership with guitarist Roberto Grela. 1954 – Juan Canaro's orchestra is the first to perform in Japan. 1955 – Piazzolla forms his Octeto Buenos Aires in pursuit of *nuevo tango*. 1955 – Celebrated Argentine author Jorge Luis Borges writes essay "History of Tango." 1959 – Pugliese's orchestra tours China and the USSR.

(cont.)

	Political/Social/Cultural Events	Key Tango Events
	–Neil Armstrong is the first man to set foot on the moon.	1962 – Dancer Juan Carlo Copes appears on the Ed Sullivan Show. 1964 – De Caro's memoir is published, *El tango en mis recuerdos.* – Celebrated club Caño 14 opens and features tango music. 1967 – Radio Belgrano Orchestra dissolves. 1969 – Piazzolla and Horacio Ferrer partner to create "Balada para un loco." –Tango singer Edumund Rivero opens club El Viejo Almacén.
1970–1990	**Political/Social/Cultural Events**	**Key Tango Events**
	1970 – Guerrilla organizations Ejército Revolucionario del Pueblo (ERP) and Montoneros begin holding wealthy executives for ransom and executing high-powered officials. 1973 – Ezeiza massacre, thirteen people die and hundreds are injured from riot with the return of Perón, who later begins third term as president. 1974 – Perón dies of heart attack, wife Isabel then assumes the presidency. 1974–1983 – Dirty War, military abducts, arrests, and executes any persons suspected of antigovernment activity. 1976 – Military coup overthrows Argentine government. – The first Apple computer is released. 1982 – War with Great Britain over the ownership of the Falkland Islands (Islas Malvinas in Argentina). 1983 – The Internet begins. 1984 – Canon demonstrates first electronic camera. –Sony introduces the first portable CD player. 1989 – Carlos Menem becomes president of Argentina; to overcome a bankrupt state and poverty, he privatizes all major utilities and pegs the Argentine peso to the US dollar.	1972 – Troilo and his orchestra perform at the Teatro Colón. 1976 – Leopoldo Federico's orchestra travels to Japan (first of seven trips). 1985 – *Tango Argentino* opens on Broadway featuring Sexteto Mayor. –First Finnish tango festival, Tangomarkkinat. 1986 – Escuela de Música Popular Avellaneda opens; cofounded by bandoneonist Rodolfo Mederos. 1988 – *Sur* premieres at Cannes Film Festival featuring Piazzolla's film score.

1990–2022	Political/Social/Cultural Events	Key Tango Events
	1990 – Demolition of the Berlin Wall begins.	1990 – Ferrer opens the Academia Nacional del Tango in Buenos Aires.
	1992 – IBM unveils the first smart phone.	1993 – Dutch bandoneonists Leo Vervelde and Carel Kraayenhof found Tango Department at Codarts University in the Netherlands.
	1999 – The euro becomes the major currency of Europe.	
	2001 – Argentina defaults on international debts spinning the country into an economic crisis.	1995 – Dancer Carlos Gavito tours with show *Forever Tango*.
	2003 – Peronist Nestor Kirchner becomes president of Argentina and restructures the defaulted debt.	1997 – Bandoneonist Néstor Marconi records Grammy Award-winning CD *Soul of the Tango* with cellist Yo-Yo Ma.
	2009 – UNESCO declares tango an "intangible cultural heritage of humanity" of Argentina and Uruguay.	1998 – *Tango* film by Carlos Saura featuring Copes and Salgán's Nuevo Quinteto Real.
	2015 – Mauricio Macri becomes president of Argentina.	2000 – Orquesta Escuela de Tango Emilio Balcarce begins its first season.
	2017 – International #metoo Movement against sexual harassment, sexual abuse, and rape.	2001 – Salgán publishes his *Curso de tango*.
	2020 – COVID-19 pandemic impacts global political, social, and cultural life, restricts in-person music and dance events.	2002 – Ignacio Varchausky founds TangoVia, dedicated to tango preservation.
		2003 – International Tango Festival and World Cup begin in Buenos Aires.
		2008 – Julián Peralta publishes his orchestration and performance practice manual *La orquesta típica: mecánica y aplicación de los fundamentos técnicos del Tango*.
		2009 – Café Vinilo opens in Buenos Aires, featuring live concert performances of contemporary tango musicians.
		2017 – Artistic Director Tomer Zvulun creates a new production of Piazzolla and Ferrer's *María de Buenos Aires*, mounted by Atlanta Opera and New York City Opera, again in Atlanta in 2019.
		2020 – Virtual milongas begin, for example, Earth Virtual Milonga.
		2022 – Tango Festival and World Cup returns following the pause of the COVID-19 pandemic.

Song Title Index

376

Index

Printed in the USA
CPSIA information can be obtained
at www.ICGtesting.com
CBHW082116270324
5983CB00006B/252

9 781108 971423